HEALTH POLICY AND ECONOMICS

In memory of Professor Mo Malek, 1949-2001

Professor Mo Malek – 1949–2001 – A Dedication

This text is dedicated to Professor Mo Malek, Professor of Health Care Policy, Planning and Management at the University of St Andrews, and founder of the *Strategic Issues in Health Care Management* (SIHCM) conferences. Sadly, Mo passed away on 12 March 2001 after a short illness. Our thoughts are with his family, especially his wife Linda, and children Rebecca, Ali, Miriam and Gemma. Mo went to school in Switzerland and obtained his first degree, in economics, at the University of Tehran. He taught in Iran for a couple of years before coming to Queen Mary College of London University, first as a postgraduate student, then research assistant, then temporary lecturer. Mo moved to St Andrews in 1981, as a Lecturer in Economics, being promoted to Reader in 1991, and being awarded a Chair in Health Policy, Planning and Management in 1995.

Mo contributed much, both internationally and across disciplines. However, it is perhaps for his work in pharmacoeconomics that he is best known, much of it conducted through the PharmacoEconomics Research Centre (PERC), which he founded and directed. For many people though, it is through the SIHCM conferences that Mo was first encountered.

Mo organised the first SIHCM conference in 1993. Further meetings followed in 1994 (on the theme of *Setting Priorities in Health Care*), 1998 (*Managing Quality, Controlling Costs*) and 2000 (*Efficiency, Quality and Access in Health Care*). Mo's work continues after him as the fifth meeting is planned for April 2002 (on *Policy, Finance and Performance in Health Care*).

Throughout these meetings many hundreds of people from dozens of countries encountered Mo's great hospitality and warmth. The SIHCM meetings were a source of some pride for Mo, and he delighted in the eclectic mix of disciplines and cultures in attendance. He was also concerned that as many as possible should be given a chance to share their work – and many a delegate gave their first ever conference presentation at an SIHCM meeting.

Mo was a tireless worker for his subject area, his institution, and his colleagues. He cared greatly about the development of health care and the appropriate use of health technologies, especially in developing nations. It is with great sadness that we record his death; and it is to his boundless energy, enthusiasm and generosity that this text, which explores some of these issues, is dedicated.

Huw Davies, Manouche Tavakoli, Rosemary Rushmer
SIHCM editors

Health Policy and Economics
Strategic issues in health care management

Edited by
MANOUCHE TAVAKOLI, HUW T.O. DAVIES AND MO MALEK

LONDON AND NEW YORK

First published 2001 by Ashgate Publishing

Reissued 2018 by Routledge
2 Park Square, Milton Park, Abingdon, Oxon OX14 4RN
711 Third Avenue, New York, NY 10017, USA

Routledge is an imprint of the Taylor & Francis Group, an informa business

Copyright © Manouche Tavakoli, Huw T.O. Davies and Mo Malek 2001

All rights reserved. No part of this book may be reprinted or reproduced or utilised in any form or by any electronic, mechanical, or other means, now known or hereafter invented, including photocopying and recording, or in any information storage or retrieval system, without permission in writing from the publishers.

Notice:
Product or corporate names may be trademarks or registered trademarks, and are used only for identification and explanation without intent to infringe.

Publisher's Note
The publisher has gone to great lengths to ensure the quality of this reprint but points out that some imperfections in the original copies may be apparent.

Disclaimer
The publisher has made every effort to trace copyright holders and welcomes correspondence from those they have been unable to contact.

A Library of Congress record exists under LC control number: 2001095879

ISBN 13: 978-1-138-70158-8 (hbk)
ISBN 13: 978-0-415-79305-6 (pbk)
ISBN 13: 978-1-315-20997-5 (ebk)

Contents

List of Figures	viii
List of Tables	ix
Acknowledgements	xi
Editors' Preface	xii

SECTION ONE: ECONOMICS AND CLINICAL GUIDELINES   1

1   Economics and Clinical Guidelines – Pointing in the Right Direction?   3
Anne Ludbrook and Luke Vale

2   From Guidelines to Good Practice: Improving the Quality of Economic Evaluations   20
Christopher Evans, Lisa Kennedy, Bruce Crawford and Mo Malek

3   The Use of Databases in Health Economics and Outcomes Research: An International Perspective   33
Christopher Evans, Lisa Kennedy and Bruce Crawford

4   Charging Ahead: The Policy and Practice of Health Charges in Britain   54
Allan Bruce

5   Staging Type 2 Diabetes: Future Challenges in Cost of Illness Modelling, Health Policy and Global Health   67
Marsha A. Dowell, Billie R. Rozell and Matthew Dowell

SECTION TWO: INEQUALITIES AND ACCESS   85

6   Tackling Health Inequalities: Explaining the Outcomes of the Policy Process   87
Mark Exworthy, Martin Powell and Lee Berney

7   Accessibility and Availability of Health Services: Has the Gap
    between the South and the Other Areas of Israel Diminished
    since Implementation of the National Health Insurance Law?   104
    *Nurit Nirel, Dina Pilpel, Bruce Rosen, Irit Zmora,
    Miriam Greenstein and Sima Zalcberg*

SECTION THREE: DEMAND   127

8   Demanding to Manage or Managing to Demand?   129
    Annabelle Mark, David Pencheon and Richard Elliott

9   Citizen, Consumer or Both? Re-conceptualising 'Demand' in
    Health Care   146
    Richard D. Smith and Brian Salter

10 Income, Income Distribution and Hospitalisation: an Ecologic
    Study in Rome, Italy   158
    *Laura Cacciani, Enrico Materia, Giulia Cesaroni, Giovanni Baglio,
    Marina Davoli, Massimo Arcà and Carlo A. Perucci*

11 Health Care Tax Relief and the Demand for Private Health
    Care for the Over-60s   172
    Manouche Tavakoli and John O.S. Wilson

SECTION FOUR: PERFORMANCE   183

12 Comparative Costs and Hospital Performance   185
    Diane Dawson, Maria Goddard and Andrew Street

13 Turkish Hospital Managers' Perceptions of their Job Satisfaction
    and Job Abandonment   203
    Yavuz Yıldırım and Gülsün Erigüç

SECTION FIVE: REFORMS   217

14 What Structures Health Care Reforms? A Comparative Analysis
    of British and Canadian Experiences   219
    Damien Contandriopoulos, Jean-Louis Denis and Ann Langley

15 Lessons from the Provincial Health Care Reforms in Canada:
   When the Same Objective of Cost Containment Leads to
   Heterogeneous Results   237
   Astrid Brousselle, Marc-André Fournier and François Champagne

16 The Process of Health Priority Setting in France: an Attempt at
   Critical Analysis   256
   *Pascal Jarno, Françoise Riou, Jean Pascal, Christophe Lerat,
   Christine Quelier, Jacques Chaperon and Pierre Le Beux*

17 Turkish Healthcare Reforms and Reasons for Failure   271
   Mehtap Tatar and Gülsün Erigüç

List of Contributors   287

List of Figures

Figure 1.1	Matrix linking evidence on effectiveness and cost	5
Figure 4.1	NHS income by source – expressed as a percentage of total income	55
Figure 4.2	Payments by patients 1951–98	61
Figure 4.3	Real income from charges (1952=100)	61
Figure 4.4	Prescription items dispensed per capital 1978–97	63
Figure 4.5	Percentage of net ingredient cost of prescribed medicines recovered from prescription charges	64
Figure 5.1	Global instances of diabetes	69
Figure 5.2	Relationship of total charges and diabetes diagnosis	79
Figure 5.3	Staging of diabetes by incremental costs	79
Figure 7.1	Market shares – 1993	120
Figure 7.2	Changes in market shares between 1993 and 1997	121
Figure 7.3	Market shares – 1997	122
Figure 8.1	A model of emotion-driven choice	136
Figure 8.2	The relationship between demand and need	138
Figure 10.1	Relationship between age-standardised hospitalisation rates (x 1,000) and mean per capita annual income (in millions of Italian lire) by district, males, Rome, 1997	163
Figure 10.2	Relationship between age-standardised hospitalisation rates (x 1,000) and mean per capita annual income (in millions of Italian lire) by district, females, Rome, 1997	164
Figure 12.1	Variations in ranks across NHS cost indices	193
Figure 15.1	Public health care expenditures (per capita)	243
Figure 17.1	Healthcare reforms: provision model	283
Figure 17.2	The Turkish internal market	284

List of Tables

Table 1.1	Hypothetical example of resource use and health effects of implementing a hospital at home scheme	10
Table 2.1	Elements found in national pharmacoeconomic guidelines	22
Table 3.1	Data elements common to most claims databases	36
Table 3.2	Data elements common to clinical and practice databases	38
Table 5.1	Global estimates of direct costs of diabetes	70
Table 5.2	Type 2 diabetes admissions and discharges (1994)	75
Table 5.3	Outcomes by client characteristics for Type 2 diabetes mellitus without complications (HCUP–3 1994)	76
Table 5.4	Outcomes by patient characteristics for Type 2 diabetes mellitus with complications (HCUP-3-1994)	77
Table 5.5	Number of discharges and mean LOS by age group and sex for clients with Type 2 diabetes mellitus without complications	78
Table 7.1	Physicians and registered nurses per 1,000 population, weekly physician and registered nurse work hours per 1,000 population and the average physician and registered nurse weekly work hours	111
Table 7.2	Primary care physicians: average weekly work hours, average length of patient list, and average number of patients seen per day, by region, in 1993 and 1997	112
Table 7.3	Primary care physicians: the ratio between the south and the centre of the country	113
Table 7.4	Ratio of acute hospital beds (number of beds per thousand population), by region, in 1994, 1996 and 1997	114
Table 7.5	Occupancy rates in selected wards, national average, Barzilai Hospital and Soroka Hospital, 1996	114
Table 7.6	Ratio of the south to the national average in beds per thousand population and in hospital occupancy rates	115
Table 7.7	Variables explaining the dependent variable, 'waited more than three months for hospital admission/surgery' (logistic regression)	116
Table 7.8	Variables explaining the dependent variable, 'involved in choice of hospital' (logistic regression)	117

Table 7.9	The ratio between the south and the centre of the country in perception of accessibility and availability of services and overall satisfaction with sick fund services	118
Table 7.10	Variables predicting waiting times of up to 30 minutes to see a family physician in 1997 (logistic regression)	119
Table 7.11	Comparison of proportions of respondents 'satisfied' and 'very satisfied' with sick fund services in 1995 and 1997, by region (in %)	120
Table 10.1	Number of discharges, mean length of hospital stay and mean age by income level and gender; Rome, 1997	165
Table 10.2	Exponential regression coefficients of the natural logarithm of length of hospital stay and their 95% confidence intervals by income level and gender; Rome, 1997	166
Table 11.1	Selective health statistics	175
Table 11.2	Tax relief on private medical insurance contracts for individuals aged 60 or over	178
Table 12.1	The NHS cost indices published in 1998/9	191
Table 12.2	Summary of experience outside the UK	198
Table 13.1	Discrepancy between desires from job satisfaction dimensions and their fulfilment level	209
Table 13.2	Hospital managers' satisfaction level in job satisfaction dimensions by managerial position	210
Table 13.3	Hospital managers' views about quitting their job by managerial position	210
Table 13.4	The difference between hospital managers' views about quitting their jobs and job satisfaction	211
Table 14.1	Structural regionalisation of the health care system in Canada	222
Table 15.1	Health care price index – public sector	241
Table 15.2	Health care price index – private sector	241
Table 15.3	Public health care expenditures over a two year period after reforms began	247
Table 17.1	Infant mortality rate and under-5 mortality rate by urban/rural residence and region (1998)	272

Acknowledgements

We wish to thank, first of all, participants in the Fourth International Conference on *Strategic Issues in Health Care Management* held at the University of St Andrews, Scotland in spring 2000. Over 20 countries were represented from many disciplines, and this eclectic mix ensured rich and varied debates on the problems facing health care as we enter the new millennium. Special thanks go to our plenary speakers, Professors Andrew Bindman and Thomas Rundall from the University of California (in San Francisco, and at Berkeley, respectively), and Sir David Carter, Chief Medical Officer at The Scottish Executive. Their contributions, which both opened and closed the conference, set the tone for some thoughtful discussions throughout. In addition, we are particularly grateful to the session chairs, manuscript reviewers and contributors for their efforts in shaping the material in this volume.

Appreciation is also due to our colleagues in the Department of Management, and the School of Social Sciences, at the University of St Andrews. We are likewise grateful for the excellent support provided by Reprographics, Printing, and Residential and Business Services at St Andrews. These capable and friendly people assisted in preparing conference materials and ensured the smooth running of the conference. Central to the conference planning and management was our conference secretary, Claire Topping. Claire performed wonders before, during and after the meeting, for which we are eternally grateful. In addition, Mehran Zabihollah, Eli Brock, Barbara Lessels and Liz Brodie also contributed to the conference management, and we thank them for their assistance.

Finally, Pat FitzGerald contributed great skill and considerable patience in the preparation of the text, and our publishers Ashgate greatly smoothed the production process: we thank them both.

Of course, none of the above can be held responsible for the final product. Responsibility for the presence of any errors or omissions lies solely with the editors and the contributing authors.

Huw Davies
Manouche Tavakoli
Mo Malek
Rosemary Rushmer

Editors' Preface:
Challenges and Choices in Health Care

Introduction

The *Fourth International Conference* on *Strategic Issues in Health Care Management* took place in St Andrews in spring 2000. Delegates from over 20 countries heard around 100 presentations on a diverse range of topics – from the big issues of national health systems reform, to the human problems of developing a patient-focused culture. The result of those three days intense activity was not only new friends and expanding professional networks, but also three eclectic collections of papers on key issues facing health services development: managing quality; developing organisations; and controlling costs. The papers in this volume, selected from nearly 100 original high quality submissions, reflect the upsurge of innovative work currently taking place in health economics. Papers in companion volumes examine health policy issues from a quality control perspective (*Quality in Health Care: Strategic Issues in Health Care Management*, Ashgate, 2001), and the challenges of organisational development in health care (*Organisation Development in Health Care: Strategic Issues in Health Care Management*, Ashgate, 2001).

Economics and Clinical Guidelines

The first five chapters in this collection examine the role of economics within clinical guidelines and suggest methods of improving the quality of economic evaluation which is now at the centre of decision making in the NHS. In the UK this is done through the National Institute for Clinical Excellence.

First, Anne Ludbrook and Luke Vale from the University of Aberdeen examine the way in which economics have influenced the development of clinical guidelines both at national and local levels. They argue that incorporation of economic analysis in guidelines is not just about cost containment *per se*, but aims to improve resource allocation within the health sector. More specifically they examine the impact of cost-effectiveness, taking into account the quality of data, on guideline recommendations and how they are interpreted both at the local and national decision-making levels. They argue that this will depend on whether budgets are fixed or varied and finally make some recommendations.

The following two papers by Christopher Evans and colleagues look more closely at the quality of economic and patient data using national and international databases as a way of improving the quality of economic evaluations and to make it possible to carry out international comparisons. Although they highlight the potential use of such databases, they also warn potential users of their shortcomings. The authors also highlight the fact that although standardisation of the content of guidelines in carrying out an economic evaluation will provide a common framework to report and compare such analyses, it could be argued that the issue of the appropriateness and the validity of any economic evaluation has been missing and they suggest a more rigorous approach to the conduct of economic evaluations.

The paper by Allan Bruce looks at the impact of prescription and dental treatment charges in raising revenues, and the argument that these could be used to limit demand. He argues that their use in both capacities is rather limited, especially in the latter case, because of prescription payment exemptions.

Finally, Marsha Dowell and colleagues use a secondary database aimed at describing how a decision support model is set up in order to predict chronic illnesses and to provide the costs at different stages over the lifetime of patients.

Inequalities and Access

This section of the book is comprised of two papers. The first, written by Mark Exworthy, Martin Powell and Lee Berney focuses specifically on the policy process surrounding inequalities, and the interaction between local and national bodies that attempt to reduce such inequalities. This paper presents some evidence from the current strategies to tackle health inequalities and the degrees to which such policies have been successful.

The second paper by Nurit Nirel and associates, examines the health inequalities between the central and southern areas of Israel since the implementation of the National Health Insurance Law. Their findings suggest that although the gap in availability and accessibility still persists, the introduction of the law has reduced inequalities in health care services between the regions. This in turn suggests that government intervention can make an impact and may be further required in order to achieve the desired goal.

Demand

This section contains four papers, two of which cover reviews and tackle some theoretical issues regarding demand, and two that are applied case studies. To manage demand, different countries adopted different systems of delivery, and with each system, a large volume of information has emerged explaining different strategies suggesting how to achieve this.

The paper by Annabelle Mark and colleagues is an attempt at a review of the new developments in demand management strategies in the UK and US health systems. The authors argue that demand management strategies (from both policy makers and patients' perspectives) in both countries, reflect to a large extent their cultural and health systems. They also believe that a wider based knowledge on organisational and consumer behaviour should provide a clearer understanding of the issues the two parties are facing and which need to be reconciled.

The paper by Richard Smith and Brian Salter is an interesting theoretical paper looking at a patient in two ways; as a consumer and a citizen. They argue that the way to manage demand is to move away from the 'neoclassical' conceptualisation of demand. They provide suggestions for an alternative approach towards conceptualisation of demand which would not only acknowledge, but integrate this dual role.

Laura Cacciani and colleagues examine the relationships between income distribution and hospitalisation, and also the length of hospital stay and income. The study was carried out in Rome, and they found a significant inverse relationship between hospitalisation rates and average per capita income. They also found that the length of hospital stay increased as socioeconomic status decreased for all types of hospitalisation. Their results suggest that those living in low-income areas are more likely to require hospitalisation with a longer staying time.

Finally, the paper by Manouche Tavakoli and John Wilson is an attempt to explain that although it may be reasonably argued that tax incentives can provide a method of limiting health care demand, in practice a large amount of detailed individual data is required which are not always available. However, given the limited data available, they suggest providing the incentives to the over-60s age group may not be an appropriate way of using scarce resources and may not have much impact on demand.

Performance

In the UK and elsewhere setting performance targets has become widespread and a primary tool for the management of public sector activities. The aim has been to eliminate the X-inefficiency characterised by wide differences in unit costs between various health providers and also to provide incentives for public sector organisations to seek out and adopt more productive management strategies and to bring about clinical change.

The paper by Diane Dawson and associates looks specifically at cost comparisons between various hospitals in different countries and suggests that it is rare to find performance targets based on comparative hospital cost data. This is partly because of wide differences in the efficiency ranking due to the various techniques employed and costs measured.

The other paper in this section is by Yavuz Yıldırım and Gülsün Erigüç and it assesses Turkish Hospital Managers' job satisfaction and the way in which it may affect their performance. Their results show that dissatisfaction was high for the payment dimension and that this might have a negative impact on their performance.

Reforms

The final four papers review current health reforms in a number of countries including the UK, Canada, France and Turkey. This is a much researched area and one that a large number of countries are finding difficult as they have to reconcile the needs of their people with their financial and human resources. The provisions of the health reforms range from taxation to a state of being almost completely financed from insurance and out of peoples' own pockets or, alternatively, to a hybrid system. In both developed and developing countries the pace of reform and restructuring of health care systems has been rapid.

Firstly, the paper by Damien Contandriopoulos and colleagues compares British and Canadian reforms. They show that while the British reforms favoured the purchaser-provider split, the approach taken by the Canadian reforms was purchaser-provider integration! This is rather interesting because the problems faced by the two countries that prompted the need for the reforms were very similar.

On the other hand, the study carried out by Astrid Brousselle and her colleagues looks at the Canadian Provincial health care reforms and tries to discover to what extent the reforms were successful. More specifically, it seeks to find out whether the objectives of health reforms in terms of containing cost, and their impact on private health care provision were achieved and if so, how. They have come up with some interesting findings.

Penultimately, the paper by Pascal Jarno and his colleagues looks at the French health care reform experience. The earlier French health care reforms were similar to health reforms in other countries that aimed at controlling costs while reducing inequalities was deemed less important. However, since 1996, the new health care reforms take into account health priorities and allocate resource based on needs assessments. The authors look at the process of setting priorities and matching resources and also the way in which public debates have influenced the priority setting process. They found a weak link between resource allocation and priority setting partly due to the fact that the priority setting process is more technocratic than political.

Finally, the paper by Mehtap Tatar and Gülsün Erigüç from Turkey examines the proposed Turkish reform focusing on provisions, which is heavily influenced by the British internal market NHS reforms, the purchaser-provider split and self-governing trusts. However, they report that reforming the financial side has been more challenging.

Concluding Remarks

Improving access, controlling costs, and maintaining health care quality remain at the top of the agenda in many developed nations, with developing nations now also paying greater attention to these issues. The rising costs of health care provision and the ever-increasing demand by citizens upon health care have brought about the reality that decision-makers now have to make hard choices. This has resulted in an ever-increasing rate of production of guidelines with economic evaluation being central to the design-making process. We hope that you enjoy these contributions to the debate, and we look forward to welcoming you to SIHCM 2002 – to be held in St Andrews in spring of 2002.

Manouche Tavakoli, Huw Davies, Mo Malek
Department of Management
University of St Andrews

* For further information on SIHCM 2002 please email SIHCM@st-and.ac.uk

SECTION ONE
ECONOMICS AND CLINICAL GUIDELINES

Chapter One

Economics and Clinical Guidelines – Pointing in the Right Direction?

Anne Ludbrook and Luke Vale

Introduction

Clinical guidelines aim to promote effectiveness and improve the quality of care. It is accepted that recommendations provided by guidelines should be evidence based if their implementation is to improve the quality of care (CRD, 1999).

Current practice on the inclusion of economic information in guidelines is variable. The Committee on Clinical Practice Guidelines in the US has recommended the inclusion of information on the cost implications of alternative strategies for the management of the clinical problem under consideration (Field and Lohr, 1992). The North of England Evidence Based Guideline Development Project has incorporated economics into its methodology (Eccles et al., 1998). Other guideline methodologies have not explicitly included economics (Mann, 1996) and some are currently exploring the best way to incorporate economics (SIGN, 1999). The National Institute for Clinical Excellence (NICE) has recognised that there has been a lack of cost-effectiveness information in clinical guidelines and has included cost-effectiveness as one of 10 key principles underpinning its guideline development process (NICE, 2000).

The introduction of an economic framework into clinical guidelines raises a number of issues. Whilst clinicians may find it difficult to resist the argument in favour of clinical guidelines that are designed to promote effective practice, the question of cost-effective practice appears to be more problematic. The difficulties lie in at least two areas; the first relates to the methods for incorporating economic information and the second is the interpretation of such information and the potential conflict between what is most effective and what is most cost-effective practice. In this chapter it is argued that

Health Policy and Economics: Strategic Issues in Health Care Management, M. Tavakoli, H.T.O. Davies and M. Malek (eds), Ashgate Publishing Ltd, 2001.

guidelines will be more useful for decision-makers if they are formulated to include economic information.

The first part of the chapter briefly describes why the economic perspective is important. The next section is primarily concerned with technical issues relating to the ways in which economics can be incorporated into guidelines and the type of information that should be included. The issues addressed in this section are the quality of economic evidence available and the importance of identifying both the volume and cost of resources involved. The final section deals with the decision-making context. It looks at how the same guideline information can be interpreted and implemented at a local decision-making level, where budgets may be fixed in the short term, and at a national priority setting level, where there may be more potential to vary funding. The chapter also discusses how the scale of the implementation influences the guideline development process and the problems inherent in unthinking use of cost-effectiveness ratios and cost-per-quality adjusted life year (QALY) thresholds in decision-making.

The Economic Perspective

The definition of the 'best' practice that guidelines are designed to promote depends upon many factors (effectiveness, cost, efficiency, etc.) all of which may be of relevance to decision-makers and should be included within the guideline. A decision-maker should be interested in efficiency because they have the task of maximising the benefits (health gain) obtained from the resources they have available. An intervention is efficient if the benefit provided is greater than that forgone had the limited resources been used for other desirable uses. This represents the economic concept of opportunity cost, where cost is defined in terms of the benefits that could have been obtained from the opportunities forgone. Opportunity cost is not always easy to measure but the principle that underlies it is important, as it emphasises benefits as the key factor in decision-making. Economic appraisal provides a means of providing information about efficiency as it involves the comparative analysis of alternative courses of action in terms of both their costs (resource use) and effectiveness (health effects) (Drummond et al., 1997).

This approach is not particularly contentious when one intervention can be shown to provide greater health benefits at the same or less cost. However, where an increase in health benefit is achieved at greater cost, judgements have to be exercised about the value of additional benefit and how it compares with other uses of health care resources. Figure 1.1 illustrates how data on costs and effectiveness can be brought together in an economic appraisal to aid the judgement about whether one intervention should be preferred to a comparator.

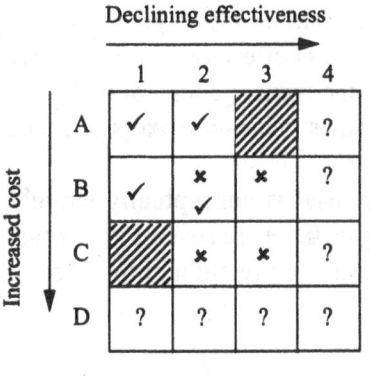

✓ = yes ✗✓ = indifferent

✗ = no ? = not enough evidence

▨ = judgement required as to whether a more effective intervention is worth the extra expense

Compared with the control intervention the experimental intervention has:

Cost
A evidence of cost savings;
B evidence of no difference in costs;
C evidence of greater costs;
D insufficient evidence to judge difference in costs;

Effectiveness
1 evidence of greater effectiveness;
2 evidence of no difference in effectiveness;
3 evidence of less effectiveness;
4 insufficient evidence to judge difference in effectiveness.

Figure 1.1 Matrix linking evidence on effectiveness and cost

In squares A1, A2 and B1, the intervention is more efficient than a comparator and is assigned a 'Yes' response to the question outlined in Figure 1.1. In squares B3, C2, and C3 the procedure is less efficient than the comparator and this receives a 'No' response to this question. In the shaded areas (A3 and C1), a judgement would need to be made as to whether the more (less) costly intervention is worthwhile in terms of the extra (lower) benefits to patients. Square B2 is neutral, as there is no difference in either costs or effectiveness.

In clinical guidelines, best practice is often defined in terms of effectiveness alone. In terms of Figure 1.1 clinical guidelines provide information on rows 1 to 4. However, recommendations based on effectiveness data alone could be modified if cost data were also considered. In most situations the inclusion of cost data clarifies the choice that should be made. This is most apparent in the second column of the matrix where the interventions under consideration have equal effectiveness. In this situation differences in cost provide the means of distinguishing between the interventions.

Only in two situations will there be any real tension between guidelines based on cost and effectiveness data and those based on effectiveness data alone (areas C1 and A3), as it is in these areas that the use of both cost and effectiveness data may potentially reverse recommendations. However, even in these situations the 'cost-effectiveness' data are open to interpretation and judgement has to be exercised as to whether a more effective and costly intervention should be recommended above a less effective and less costly one. The provision of information on cost-effectiveness does not make the decision for the decision-maker; rather, it allows decision-makers to make more informed judgements.

As Figure 1.1 illustrates, economic appraisal is conceptually straight forward but as the rest of this chapter highlights there are several issues that need to be addressed in both the production and interpretation of this type of data.

Technical Issues in Incorporating Economics into Guidelines

If economic criteria are to be used to aid decision-makers, economic evidence needs to be identified or derived and, once obtained, consideration is required on how to appraise and present it in a form useful to decision-makers.

Identifying the Evidence

Methods to identify economic studies are evolving (CRD, 1996; Mugford, 1996). Standard sources for references of published economic evaluations include bibliographic databases; in addition to MEDLINE and EMBASE there are a number of other potential sources economic appraisal references, such as CINHAL, ECONLIT, SIGLE, and Social Science Citations Index. The choice of which databases to interrogate is dependent upon the nature of the topic for which economic analyses are sought. The search strategies used also need to be adapted for each database, as they depend upon the indexing terms the database uses.

Other potentially useful sources of economic literature exist. The Office of Health Economics, together with the UK and International Federation of Pharmaceutical Manufacturers Associations, produce the Health Economic Evaluation Database (HEED). HEED contains approximately 19,000 articles of which about 9,000 are reviewed using a structured reporting format that provides a breakdown of the methodology and results of the study. The smaller

NHS Economic Evaluation Database also seeks to identify published economic appraisals. However, in addition to summarising their methodology, results and conclusions it also seeks to critically appraise them in a rigorous and systematic way. In addition to the electronic databases, there are a number of secondary journals such as Evidence Based Health Policy and Management and ACP Journal Club, which review and critically appraise published economic appraisals.

In some situations, the existing literature may be inadequate to address the issues raised by the guideline and in such cases primary research may be required. This may be obtained by extending the results of existing evaluations (see for example the Cochrane Economic Methods Group guidance for using the results of Cochrane reviews to provide evidence for subsequent economic evaluations (CEMG, 1999)).

Assessing the Quality of the Evidence

Guidelines for the practice and critical appraisal of economic appraisal of health interventions exist (Drummond and Jefferson, 1996; Gold et al., 1996; Association of British Pharmaceutical Industries, 1994; Canadian Co-ordinating Office for Health Technology Assessment, 1997; Commonwealth of Australia, 1995). Unfortunately, there is considerable variability in the quality of published economic appraisals (Udvarhelyi et al., 1992; Mugford, 1995; Jefferson and Demicheli, 1998; Gerard et al., 1999). This makes it difficult to compare studies and has implications for attempts to synthesise and transfer data to other settings (Jefferson et al., 1996; Rigby et al., 1996).

The object of synthesising data is to provide information that is relevant to the decision-making context. Numerous options exist for combining data, ranging from the simple narrative synthesis through to quantitative synthesis of economic evaluations (Jefferson et al., 1996) and modelling (CEMG, 1999). However, regardless of the approach taken and in common with evaluations limited to efficacy or effectiveness, economic appraisals frequently encounter uncertainty in both the method of application and the interpretation of their result (Briggs and Gray, 1999).

Role of Evidence in Economic Evaluation

It has been suggested that economic evidence need not be as strong an evidence base as data on clinical effectiveness (Johnstone et al., 1999). The strength of evidence required is dependent upon the extent of uncertainty and the nature of the decision-making context. In terms of economics in guidelines, the evidence provided must be robust enough for judgement to be exercised. For example, if plausible changes in estimates of efficiency do not change the judgement made (in Figure 1.1 the results always lie in an area marked with a Yes (or No)), then the fact that the economic data are less than perfect is irrelevant. Even in situations where the uncertainty is such that precise estimates on efficiency are not available, the nature of the decision-making context may help clarify the situation. For example, if the resource consequences (and the opportunity costs) of alternative courses of action are small (e.g. on row B of Figure 1.1) recommendations can be made on effectiveness alone. Results should be presented in a way that permits decision-makers to substitute local information or value judgements (Eccles et al., 1998).

An illustration of how these issues can be addressed in practice is provided by Mason et al. (1999), who considered a guideline recommending more appropriate use of ace inhibitors for heart failure in primary care. They showed that more appropriate use of ACE inhibitors may result in a gain in life expectancy of 0.203 years per patient and a reduction in cost of £206 per patient (area A1 in Figure 1.1). However, it was also possible that adopting the recommendation would result in an increase in costs of £1,578 per patient, which would result in an incremental cost per life year of £7,770 (area C1 in Figure 1.1). The difference in cost per patient was primarily caused by different estimates of the dosage of ace inhibitors required (British National Formulary, 1999) and of course dosage is an area where judgement is required. However, by quantifying both the extent and cause of the uncertainty around the estimates of cost-effectiveness, decision-makers can make an informed judgement.

A decision-maker needs to consider whether the economic evidence is sufficiently robust to be used in the context that it is required for, (i.e. are the data transferable?). This is of particular importance when economic appraisal is used to provide information as part of national guidelines. As with any study, the degree to which the results of an economic appraisal may be transferable from one location to another is crucial. This is influenced by the transferability of the clinical effectiveness and costs data. Clinical guidelines must already consider the transferability of effectiveness data, therefore, this chapter concentrates on the transferability of costs.

Transferability of Cost Data

Costs are a composite of the volume of resources used and the unit cost (or price) of those resources. The price of the resource should be a reflection of the opportunity cost of the resource. The problem that arises is that both resource use and opportunity cost may change between settings. Whether or not such data are transferable is a matter for judgement on the part of the decision-maker. However, judgements about transferability can be aided by transparency in the methods that have been used to perform an economic appraisal and clear and explicit detail of the quantities of resources consumed and the unit costs attached.

In particular, volumes or counts of individual items are more useful than cost information alone for decision-makers because they have to judge whether the level of resource utilisation and the opportunity cost ascribed are appropriate for their situation. For example, if an intervention was to be recommended which would reduced the length of hospitalisation and provided at least the same benefits to patients, the cost savings that would accrue would depend upon the scale of implementation. At low levels of implementation the average cost per patient would increase as many aspects of resource use are fixed (wards cannot be closed) and the only resources saved would be hotel services. At higher levels of implementation the number of beds could be reduced and wards closed which would release some resources for use elsewhere.

A practical example, similar to this is provided by early supported discharge schemes. Early supported discharge schemes involve the planned provision of additional support in the patients or carers home, which facilitates the transfer of selected patients to home early. Published studies investigating the use of early supported discharge scheme suggest that the reduction in hospitalisation, costed on the basis of average cost per bed day, more than compensates for the cost of the early supported discharge scheme (Cameron et al., 1994; O'Cathain, 1994; Farnworth et al., 1994; Hollingworth et al., 1993; Currie et al., 1994; Sikorski et al., 1993; Parker et al., 1991; Cameron et al., 2000). In practice, it is unlikely that these hypothetical cost savings could ever be realised as it would require that wards are closed and staff made redundant. However, any freed bed days could be made available for other beneficial uses.

To reflect the need of decision-makers to consider both the quality and transferability of economic information provided as part a guideline the results of economic appraisal can be presented in a disaggregated way using a balance sheet approach. This approach can be illustrated again using the example of a early supported discharge scheme (Table 1.1).

As is suggested above the results of those studies that have looked at early supported discharge schemes have mostly been based on hospital costs

Table 1.1 Hypothetical example of resource use and health effects of implementing a hospital at home scheme

Area of resource use	Description	Costs		Benefits
		Quantity per patient		
Secondary care	Hospital at home service	Physiotherapist Nurse Occupational therapist Service coordinator	1.75 hrs (at £13.90 per hour*) 9 hrs (at £14.00 per hour*) 2.4 hrs (at £13.90 per hour*)	Health outcome — No evidence of any difference
	Hospital stay	Reduction by 2 to 6.9 days		Other patient benefits — Care in own home Use of freed up beds — Benefits of earlier treatment of other patients or more appropriate discharge
	Treatment of extra patients	Cost of treating any extra patients		
Primary care	General practice contacts	Unclear		
Local authorities	Nursing home or other accommodation	16% fewer patients requiring long term care		
	Social work	Increase social work contacts		
Patient and their families	Informal care	Increased informal care required		

Note

* Based on salaries for occupational therapist and physiotherapist of £23,968 per annum and a mid point G grade nurse at £25,184 per annum. All costs include employer contributions to National Insurance and superannuation. Hourly rates are based on a 46 week year and standard working week of 37.5 hours.

and have assumed that a freed bed day results in cost savings. As Table 1.1 shows, the issue may be more complicated. There is uncertainty surrounding some of the implications of adopting such a scheme, such as the magnitude of any changes in the length of hospital stay. In addition, as existing studies have been focused on the hospital perspective little attention has been focused on the extent of cost shifting on to primary care, local authorities or patients/carers. Furthermore, although reductions in length of stay may not result in cost savings, the hospital bed space made available by discharging patients into an early supported discharge scheme could be used to provide treatment for extra patients (who would obtain health benefits but incur additional costs for their treatment).

Some data on cost can also be provided by the balance sheet approach. For example, taking the time estimates of resource use and using information on UK salary costs from Table 1.1 it is possible to estimate that it would cost at least £336 per patient to provide the staff required for an early supported discharge scheme. A decision-maker can use this data to assess whether the resource use and unit costs are transferable to their setting. The balance sheet can also provide information to a decision-maker on the effect of adopting the guideline on the distribution of costs and benefits either to other areas of the health service or to patients. For example, by using a balance sheet it can be highlighted that a early supported discharge scheme may shift costs onto general practice and patients and their families and even though the magnitude of such cost shifts may not be known there presence should be recognised by a decision-maker. This may be of particular importance if the decision-maker is also interested in how costs are distributed as well as effectiveness and efficiency.

Although methods such as the balance sheet can be used to provide information to decision-makers about the economic implications of adopting a guideline, how these decision-makers use these data is crucial and this is the subject of the next section.

The Decision-making Context

The previous section has dealt with the more technical issues of how to incorporate economics into guidelines and concerns about the quality of the economic information available. This is an important issue given that, in some circumstances, the final recommendations may be influenced by cost considerations. However, these concerns about the quality of cost data can be exaggerated if the way in which economic information is interpreted in different contexts is misunderstood. This section attempts to clarify the arguments surrounding this issue by considering the potential different uses of guidelines and the different types of decisions with which they are concerned. Attention is then given to the main use of guidelines in the UK, namely improving clinical practice, and the role that economics has in this context.

Guidelines

Part of the problem surrounding the incorporation of economic analysis into guidelines may be due to the different ways in which guidelines are used, particularly in an international context:

> guidelines can fulfil a range of different (implicit or explicit) functions, including improving clinicians' awareness of the effectiveness of health care interventions, containing health care costs, setting priorities for resource allocation and general regulatory purposes (Grilli et al., 1999).

Systems such as the British NHS do not have a global cost containment problem, in the sense that the total sum available is fixed through the budget setting process. In other insurance based systems, total spending is more open ended and a variety of regulatory mechanisms are employed to restrict the growth in costs. Thus there is more focus in the UK on problems of resource allocation or priority setting within this fixed sum whilst other countries may focus on cost containment. However, a further purpose of guidelines, not referred to above, is improving the quality or effectiveness of care. Systems of managed care based on guidelines are often promoted on the basis that they combine improvements in quality and cost control, although the evidence on this is mixed (Robinson and Steiner, 1998).

In the UK, carrying out appraisals of individual technologies and producing guidelines for the management of a disease are seen as separate but linked tasks. The National Institute for Clinical Excellence (NICE) has programmes of work relating to both areas. In Scotland, the tasks are currently the separate responsibilities of the Health Technology Board for Scotland (HTBS) and the Scottish Intercollegiate Guidelines Network (SIGN). This separation between appraisals and guidelines draws a distinction between decisions about whether or not a particular intervention provides value for money (appraisal) and how clinical practice should be organised to provide effective and efficient care (guidelines).

Types of Decision

Different approaches, appraisal or guidelines, may be needed depending upon the nature of the decision that is to be addressed. The introduction of the new class of drugs known as statins provides a useful example. Unlike other interventions that have been rejected on the grounds of a combination of high costs and low effectiveness, statins are very effective lipid lowering agents, which reduce morbidity and mortality from coronary heart disease (CHD). The problem that they pose for health services is the large number of people who could potentially benefit, given the high levels of cholesterol in the populations of western countries. In this case, the effectiveness of the intervention is directly related to the individual's risk of CHD and this has emerged as the determining factor in setting priorities for the use of statins (Ebrahim et al., 1999). The cost per QALY is lower for the high risk groups because the benefits obtainable are greater. The need to restrict the use of the drug is certainly driven by budget constraints but the priority setting is driven by differences in effectiveness. This type of decision is generally taken at the national funding level, although the way in which it is applied will depend upon the regulatory and funding framework of the national system.

However, the overall role of statins in the prevention and treatment of CHD is best considered within the framework of clinical guidelines and it is here that economic information has a more important role to play. Whilst statins may be cost-effective, in the sense that the extra health gain they can produce may be considered worthwhile and the costs are comparable to the costs of other funded interventions, this therapy is not the *most* cost-effective intervention for primary or secondary prevention of CHD. Although statins are more effective than most of the alternatives available, this ranking is altered significantly when economic information is introduced. Diet, smoking cessation and other drug interventions produce greater health gains per unit of cost (Ebrahim et al., 1999). Guidelines based on cost-effectiveness would therefore promote the optimal use of other interventions but not exclude the use of statins; guidelines based on effectiveness alone would give greater prominence to statins.

The process described above, by which the appraisal of a therapy considers relative cost-effectiveness and the results are translated into guidelines, can be contrasted with the so-called threshold approach. In the latter case, as well as demonstrating effectiveness, a therapy or intervention has to pass a threshold, usually based on a cost-per-QALY figure, in order to be recommended for use within the health service. The cost-per-QALY for the intervention of interest is compared with other already funded interventions or with some arbitrary threshold but is generally not compared directly with other interventions for the same condition. For example, the guideline on treatment and prevention of CHD produced for the Netherlands concentrated on the role of lipid lowering drugs and does not make comparisons with other drug based interventions (Simoons and Casparie, 1998). The recommendations are developed first and foremost on the basis of effectiveness and are then tested in terms of the cost-per-QALY implications. The figure of NLG 40,000 per life year is considered reasonable and is compared with other examples including heart transplants (NLG 60,000) and breast cancer screening (NLG 30,000). Not only does this approach fail to promote the use of more efficient therapies, but the threshold is fairly arbitrary. It is not clear that health systems could fund the aggregate cost of all therapies that pass the threshold.

National Guidelines/Local Context

It has been suggested that instead of basing guidelines on cost-effectiveness information, costs could be taken into account by local decision-makers when national guidelines are being implemented. However, this implies that cost-effectiveness is about calculating the cost implications of effectiveness recommendations. Cost-effectiveness is actually about comparing the costs *and* effectiveness of alternatives, in a way that allows decision-makers to consider potential trade offs in the event that recommendations that improve effectiveness lead to higher costs. Indeed, one of the perceived problems with some of the national guidelines that are currently produced is that they do not provide information on what is second best if the recommended action is not affordable or not feasible in certain contexts. Nor do they identify the consequences of not implementing each particular recommendation, although this would help to identify priorities for action.

Consideration of cost-effectiveness should not dominate the decision-making process. It is not the case that the most cost-effective treatment should always be adopted, particularly where additional gains can be achieved at additional cost. It is necessary for decision-makers to exercise judgement about the value of the additional health gains, in the context of competing claims for resources. In order to do this, information about the costs and consequences of alternatives should be collected at national level but should be presented in a format that allows local interpretation and the exercise of local value judgements and priorities. This would be recognised to be good practice in the presentation of economic information (Drummond and Jefferson, 1996).

In particular, the presentation of the cost-effectiveness information should:

1 show separately the costs of interventions and the savings that may arise from treatments that are avoided;
2 identify the time at which costs and savings arise, in order that decision-makers can see the impact on annual budgets;
3 recognise that cost savings from avoided hospital admissions, in particular, may be difficult to realise in financial terms. Unless beds are closed, very little saving is achieved but the opportunity to admit other patients may be an important benefit;
4 identify whether different budgets incur costs and savings.

Ideally a balance sheet of costs and consequences would be presented, identifying the parties to whom they accrue (McIntosh et al., 1999). This information can then be interpreted in specific decision-making contexts.

Conclusions

This chapter has explored issues relating to the inclusion of economic information in clinical guidelines. The discussion of technical problems has made it clear that the inclusion of such data is feasible. Whilst there may be concerns about the quality of the data, these should be lessened by the need to interpret any form of economic information according to the context in which it is to be used. It should be noted that whilst clinical guidelines seek to use the best available evidence on effectiveness, this information may also be of variable quality. Both the economic and clinical effectiveness data should be 'fit for purpose' but it should be recognised that improving the quality of such information is not a cost free exercise. The question that remains is to consider whether clinical guidelines should be used to promote efficiency or only effectiveness.

The argument can be put the other way; what happens if guidelines are not used to promote efficiency? If interventions are adopted on the basis of their effectiveness for a particular group of patients, this may divert resources from other activities that produce greater health gains. This presents clinicians with a conflict between what they see as the best interests of their own patients and the wider good of the health service as a whole. Nevertheless, even individual clinical decisions are taken in a context of resource availability. Clinical guidelines have been defined as 'systematically developed statements to assist practitioner and patient decisions about appropriate health care for specific clinical circumstances' (Field and Lohr, 1990). However, it must be recognised that a guideline is just that:

> The ultimate judgement regarding a particular clinical procedure or treatment plan must be made by the doctor in light of the clinical data presented by the patient *and the diagnostic and treatment options available* (Notes for the users of the Guideline, SIGN, 2000, emphasis added).

There are several factors that may affect whether or not a guideline is applied, some of which will relate to individual patient circumstances and some of which will relate to the setting in which care is being provided. The options that are available will be subject to local resource constraints.

Whether or not one is convinced of the economic argument for including cost-effectiveness information in guidelines, there is a very practical problem of implementing guidelines when faced by resource constraints.

> if a guideline does not incorporate cost-effectiveness, then there will be a conflict between what the guideline says physicians should do and what physicians *can* do (Eddy, 1999).

This situation is exacerbated by the fact that guideline recommendations frequently do not identify a second best alternative, if the recommended action cannot be implemented. Neither do they indicate the clinical importance of the action recommended but concentrate rather on the strength of the supporting evidence. The introduction of economics into the analysis ensures that the relative size of clinical effects is considered, as well as the costs of achieving them.

Clinical guidelines that incorporate cost-effectiveness should not produce treatment plans that are cost driven. Rather, they should ensure that decisions are taken on the basis of the best available information on both costs and effectiveness and in the light of local value judgements concerning the value to be attached to more effective interventions that are also more costly. By making such decisions more open and explicit, greater consistency may also be achieved. Resource constraints exist at all levels within health services. It is by recognising these constraints, rather than ignoring them, that better decisions can be made.

Acknowledgements

The Health Economics Research Unit is funded by the Chief Scientist Office of the Scottish Executive Health Department. The views expressed here are those of the authors not necessarily those of the funding body.

References

Association of British Pharmaceutical Industries (ABPI) (1994), 'Pharmaceutical Industry and Department of Health agree Guidelines for the Economic Analysis of Medicines', Press release, 20 May.

Briggs, A. and Gray, A. (1999), 'Handling Uncertainty when Performing Economic Evaluations of Healthcare Interventions', *Health Technology Assessment*, 3 (2).

British National Formulary (1999), Number 38 (September 1999), British Medical Association and The Pharmaceutical Press, Bath Press, Bath.

Cameron, I.D., Crotty, M., Currie, C. et al. (2000), 'Geriatric Rehabilitation fFollowing Fractures in Older People: A systematic review', *Health Technology Assessment*, 4 (2).

Cameron, I.D., Lyle, D.M. and Quine, S. (1994). 'Cost-effectiveness of Accelerated Rehabilitation after Proximal Femoral Fracture Neck of Femur', *Journal of Clinical Epidemiology*, 47, pp. 1307–13.

Canadian Co-ordinating Office for Health Technology Assessment (1997), *Guidelines for the Economic Evaluation of Pharmaceuticals: Canada*, 2nd edn, CCHOTA, Ottawa.

CRD (Centre for Reviews and Dissemination) (1996), *Making Cost-effectiveness Information Accessible: The NHS economic evaluation database project. CRD guidance for reporting critical summaries of economic evaluations*, (CRD report 6), NHS Centre for Reviews and Dissemination, University of York, York.

CRD (Centre for Reviews and Dissemination) (1999), 'Getting Evidence into Practice', *Effective Health Care*, 5(1), February, University of York, York.

Cochrane Economic Methods Group, Methods Group Module (1999), Cochrane Collaboration, The Cochrane Library, Issue 1, Update Software, Oxford.

Commonwealth of Australia, Department of Health, Housing and Community Services (1995), *Guidelines for the Pharmaceutical Industry on Preparation of Submissions to the Pharmaceutical Benefits Advisory Committee*, Australian Government Publishing Service, Canberra.

Currie, C.T., Christie, J., Phillips, J., Closs, J., Tennant, S., Campbell, G. and Daly, R. (1994), *Outcomes of Surgery and Rehabilitation after Fractured Neck of Femur: An interdisciplinary, interboard and international audit. Report on the first year's experience*, Directorate of Orthopaedic Surgery, Royal Infirmary of Edinburgh.

Drummond, M.F. and Jefferson, T.O., on behalf of the BMJ Economic Evaluation Working Party (1996), 'Guidelines for Authors and Peer-reviewers of Economic Submissions to the BMJ', *British Medical Journal*, 313, pp. 275–83.

Drummond, M.F., O'Brien, B., Stoddart, G.L. and Torrance, G.W. (1997) *Methods for the Economic Evaluation of Health Care Programmes*, Oxford University Press, Oxford.

Ebrahim, S., Davey Smith, G., McCabe, C., Payne, N., Pickin, M., Sheldon, T.A. et al. (1999), 'What Role for Statins? A review and economic model', *Health Technology Assessment*, 3, (19).

Eccles, M., Freeman, N. and Mason, J. (1998), 'North of England Evidence Based Guidelines Development Project: Methods of developing guidelines for efficient drug use in primary care', *British Medical Journal*, 316, pp. 1232–5.

Eddy, D.M. (1999), *Doctors, Economics and Clinical Practice Guidelines: Can they be brought together?*, Office of Health Economics, London.

Farnworth, M.G., Kenny, P. and Shiell, A. (1994), 'The Costs and Effects of Early Discharge in the Management of Fractured Neck of Femur Hip', *Age and Ageing*, 23, pp. 190–4.

Field, M.J. and Lohr, K.N. (eds) (1990), *Clinical Practice Guidelines: Directions for a new program*, Washington DC, National Academy Press.

Field, M.J. and Lohr, K.N. (eds) (1992), *Guidelines for Clinical Practice. From development to use*, Washington DC, National Academy Press.

Gerard, K., Smoker, I. and Seymour, J. (1999), 'Raising the Quality of Cost Utility Analyses: Lessons learnt and still to learn', *Health Policy*, 46, pp. 217–38.

Gold, M., Siegel, J., Russell, L. and Weinstein, M. (1996), *Cost-effectiveness in Health and Medicine*, Oxford University Press, New York.

Grilli, R., Trisolini, R., Labianca, R. and Zola, P. (1999), 'Evolution of Physicians' Attitudes towards Practice Guidelines', *Journal of Health Service Research Policy*, 4(4), pp. 215–19.

Hollingworth, W., Todd, C., Parker, M., Roberts, J.A. and Williams, R. (1993), 'Cost Analysis of Early Discharge after Fractured Neck of Femur', *British Medical Journal*, 307, pp. 903–6.

Jefferson, T. and Demicheli, V. (1998), 'Methodological Quality of Economic Modelling Studies: A case study with Hepatitis B vaccines' *Pharmacoeconomics*, 14, pp. 251–7.

Jefferson, T., Mugford, M., Gray, A. and Demicheli, V. (1996), 'An Exercise on the Feasibility of Carrying out Secondary Economic Analyses', *Health Economics*, 5, pp. 155–65.

Johnstone, K., Buxton, M., Jones, D. and Fitzpatrick, R. (1999), 'Assessing the Costs of Healthcare Technologies in Clinical Trials', *Health Technology Assessment*, 3(6).

McIntosh, E., Donaldson, C. and Ryan, M. (1999), 'Recent Advances in the Methods of Cost-benefit Analysis in Healthcare', *Pharmacoeconomics*, 15(4), pp. 357–67.

Mann, T. (1996), *Clinical Guidelines: Using clinical guidelines to improve patient care within the NHS*, Leeds, Health Care Directorate, NHS Executive.

Mason, J., Eccles, M., Freemantle, N. and. Drummond, M (1999), 'A Framework for Incorporating Cost-effectiveness in Evidence-based Clinical Practice Guidelines' *Health Policy*, 47(1), pp. 37–52.

Mugford, M. (1995). 'The Cost of Neonatal Care: Reviewing the evidence', *Social-und Preventivmedizin*, 40, pp. 361–8.

NICE (National Institute for Clinical Excellence) (2000), 'Clinical Guidelines Development Process', http://www.nice.org.uk/nice-web/article.asp?a=6834 (accessed on 14 September 2000).

O'Cathain, A. (1994), 'Evaluation of a Hospital at Home Method for the Early Discharge of Patients with Fractured Neck of Femur', *Journal of Public Health Medicine*, 16, pp. 205–10.

Parker, M., Pryor, G. and Myles, J. (1991), 'Early Discharge after Hip Fracture: Prospective 3 year study of 645 patients', *Acta Orthopoedica Scandinavica*, 62, pp. 563–6.

Rigby, K., Silagy, C. and Crockett, A. (1996), 'Health Economic Reviews. Are they Compiled Systematically?', *International Journal of Technology Assessment in Health Care*, 12(3), pp. 450–9.

Robinson, R. and Steiner, A. (1998), *Managed Health Care. US Evidence and Lessons for the National Health Service*, Open University Press, Buckingham.

Shepperd, S. and Iliffe, S. (1999), 'Hospital at Home versus In-patient Hospital Care', *Cochrane Library*, Issue 4.

SIGN (Scottish Intercollegiate Guidelines Network) (1999), *SIGN Guidelines. An introduction to SIGN methodology for the development of evidence-based clinical guidelines*, SIGN publication number 39, Edinburgh.

SIGN (Scottish Intercollegiate Guidelines Network) (2000), *Secondary Prevention of Coronary Heart Disease*, SIGN publication number 41, Edinburgh.

Sikorski, J. and Senior, J. (1993), 'The Domiciliary Rehabilitation and Support Program: Rationale, organisation and outcome' *Medical Journal of Australia*, 159, pp. 23–5.

Simoons, M.L. and Casparie, A.F. (1998), 'Behandeling en preventie van coronaire hartziekten door verlaging van de serumcholesterolconcentratie; derde consensus "Cholesterol"', *Nederlands Tijdschrift voor Geneeskunde*, 142, 38, pp. 2096–101.

Udvarhelyi, S., Colditz, G.A., Rai, A. and Epstein, A.M. (1992), 'Cost-effectiveness and Cost-benefit Analyses in the Medical Literature. Are the methods being used correctly?', *Annals of Internal Medicine*, 116, pp. 238–44.

Chapter Two

From Guidelines to Good Practice: Improving the Quality of Economic Evaluations

Christopher Evans, Lisa Kennedy, Bruce Crawford and Mo Malek

Introduction

In recent years there has been a proliferation of pharmacoeconomic studies. Concomitant to this rise in research has been an effort to set out a basic framework for economic evaluations in the form of national guidelines. Guidelines which were developed initially for Australia and Ontario, Canada, have been adapted or are under consideration in other health care settings as diverse as Finland, Norway, Portugal and the United States. The guidelines have been developed to create a set of core principles that should be followed in pharmacoeconomic studies. One goal of the guidelines is that they have prescriptive elements on study design so that a rigorous, valid and relevant pharmacoeconomic study may be used to inform decision-making about the allocation of health care resources.

However, owing to the dearth of research into methodological issues in some areas of pharmacoeconomics, and the relative newness of pharmacoeconomics as a discipline, the proposed and existing guidelines are not prescriptive concerning detailed methods (Brown and Schulpher, 1999). Further, the guidelines take a rather broad approach to economic evaluations in that they permit several different analytic strategies (different types of economic evaluations as well as prospective and retrospective assessments) and varied approaches to resource measurement and valuation.

It has been seven years since the guidelines for Australia were implemented, and since that time elements of these guidelines have been incorporated into other national guidelines. Although these other guidelines are not as prescriptive as the original Australian ones their importance in

Health Policy and Economics: Strategic Issues in Health Care Management, M. Tavakoli, H.T.O. Davies and M. Malek (eds), Ashgate Publishing Ltd, 2001.

providing a reference standard is evident. As both the number of guidelines and pharmacoeconomic research has increased in recent years it is worth examining whether or not guidelines encourage rigorous pharmacoeconomic studies. Further, does adherence to the principles set forth in the guidelines produce pharmacoeconomic studies that are relevant to decision-makers.

The first part of this chapter briefly reviews the content and state of guidelines. The chapter then examines areas where the guidelines fail to address important areas of pharmacoeconomic methodology. The relevance of endpoints encouraged by guideline developers is also reviewed in order to determine whether or not pharmacoeconomic studies are being adopted in practice. The chapter concludes with a discussion as to how best to ensure good practice in pharmacoeconomic studies in the context of guideline development and adaptation.

National Guidelines for Pharmacoeconomic Studies

Guidelines have been developed that set out a methodological framework for the conduct of pharmacoeconomic studies. Guidelines have been developed for several countries including the US (Gold et al., 1996), Ontario, Canada (Canadian Coordinating Office, 1994; Glennie et al., 1999), the UK (England and Wales Department of Health, 1994; Drummond and Jefferson, 1996), Australia (Australia Commonwealth Department of Health, 1995), New Zealand (PHARMAC, 1998), Italy (Garattini et al., 1995) and the Netherlands. In Ontario and British Columbia (Annis, Rahman and Schechter, 1998), Canada, Australia and the Netherlands the guidelines are formal in the sense that they must be followed in order to secure reimbursement for pharmaceutical agents and devices. In other countries, such as the United States and Italy, the guidelines provide recommendations as to study design; however, adherence to them is not required as there is no formal requirement for pharmacoeconomic information in drug listing decisions.

Guidelines for pharmacoeconomic studies all have several items in common. On the whole the guidelines offer recommendations as to the information that should be included in pharmacoeconomic studies. As such they offer an important reference for researchers who wish to ensure that they capture information that is relevant to decision-makers who must decide whether or not to reimburse for certain products. Table 2.1 outlines the elements commonly found in guidelines.

Table 2.1 Elements found in national pharmacoeconomic guidelines

Area	Information covered by guidelines
Comparator	Recommendations cover the use of the most relevant comparator (most commonly used and least expensive) as well as a do-nothing option.
Type of study	Cost minimisation, cost effectiveness and cost utility are the studies most commonly recommended.
Time horizon	Studies should include information on long run outcomes.
Perspective	The societal perspective with results disaggregated for other perspectives is recommended.
Outcome selection	Final outcomes are preferred over surrogate markers. Quality adjusted life years are typically encouraged as well as the measurement of quality of life through the use of a valid and reliable instrument.
Data collection strategy	Randomised controlled trials are generally preferred; however other studies are acceptable including modelling studies.
Costing	All relevant costs (particularly direct medical and indirect costs) should be included.
Discounting	Discounting of both costs and outcomes. The discount rate varies by country, but typically a five per cent discount rate is recommended as well as no discount rate.
Sensitivity analysis	Recommended to test the robustness of study results.

Source: adapted from Jacobs, Bachynsky and Baladi, 1995.

Shortcomings of Existing Guidelines

The weaknesses in existing guidelines can be traced to two areas: methodological problems and the relevance to decision-makers. Existing guidelines are relatively silent as to the appropriate measurement techniques to take in pharmacoeconomic evaluations. For instance, guidelines encourage the use of the societal perspective; however, they are mute as to which method of data collection should be used (or preferred) in order to derive accurate information for the chosen perspective. As shown below, the lack of guidance can lead to serious miscalculation. The relevance of the guidelines is also questionable. Several commentators (Towse, 1997; Langley, 1997; Duthie et al., 1999) have suggested the information collected in pharmacoeconomic studies that is consistent with the recommendations of guidelines may be of little value to decision-makers. For instance, Langley (1997) has noted that direct medical costs are most relevant to US insurers and the societal perspective recommended by the guidelines may be of little relevance to them.

Methodological Issues

Methodological issues in the design and conduct of pharmacoeconomic studies do not receive adequate consideration in existing guidelines. Guidelines overwhelmingly concentrate on the information that should be included in pharmacoeconomic studies, with little consideration as to the impact on study validity. At their best, and only in certain instances, the guidelines seek to limit the use of methodologically suspect techniques. For instance, expert opinion is relegated to a tertiary source of data in pharmacoeconomic studies in the US, Australia and Canada. However, in many cases, there are no recommendations at to the appropriate use of alternative sources of data.

For instance, US guidelines (Gold et al., 1996) recommend that information on effectiveness is derived from the least biased source of information and resource use should include all relevant items. Of course, this is important; and, the recommendations advance the argument that the validity of the estimates varies depending on the study design chosen. Thus, the familiar refrain that RCTs have higher internal validity is made, while other study designs chosen will lead to less accurate estimates. The guidelines and many researchers recognise that the high level of internal validity found in RCTs comes at the expense of a low level of external validity. O'Brien (1996) has suggested that there are seven 'threats' to the validity of pharmacoeconomic study results based on RCT data. These threats are: 1) the inappropriate choice of comparison therapy; 2) gold standard measurement of outcomes; 3) the use of intermediate rather than final outcomes; 4) inadequate patient follow-up or sample size; 5) the presence of protocol driven costs and outcomes; 6) geographic transferability of trial evidence; and 7) selected patient and provider populations.

These threats are directed primarily at the external validity of RCT data. However, consideration must be made of other possible problems. Guidelines do not address the situation where the internal validity of a pharmacoeconomic study based on an RCT may be quite low. An eighth threat can be added to O'Brien's typology: the source of data and data collection strategies may influence the results of pharmacoeconomic studies. Three areas which the guidelines ignore and are of concern are: the reliance of patient self-reported data; the use of proxy respondents for estimates of resource use; and the costing techniques employed.

Evans and Crawford (1999) reviewed the impact that the use of patient self-reported data has on the validity of estimates in pharmacoeconomic studies. This review noted that compared to estimates of resource use that could be verified in a patient's chart, the reliance on patients to provide estimates of resource use could be problematic. It was noted that the salience of an event impacted in the accuracy of the recall of an episode of resource use. For instance, hospitalisations are recalled more accurately than GP visits, which in turn are recalled with more accuracy than drug consumption. In addition, the time elapsed between the episode and the recall of the estimate impacts the internal validity of the reported data. Episodes that occur further away from the point of recall are recalled with less precision. Even in the case of highly salient events such as inpatient hospitalisations, lengthy gaps between the episode and the report may lead to substantial errors in resource utilisation estimates.

The social desirability of the event was also found to be an important factor in determining the precision of estimates. Resource utilisation associated with socially undesirable events was reported less. Demographic and the social characteristics of self-reporters were also found to influence the ability or willingness of patients to recall events. Educational status, age, marital status and mental condition were all factors associated with the ability to recall health care resource use. If taken as a whole, the various factors would lead to an underestimate of resource utilisation data (Evans and Crawford, 1999).

The net underreporting of resource use may be further worsened by using proxies to provide estimates in pharmacoeconomic studies. In general, proxies suffer the same problems of patient reporters in terms of demographic and social characteristics; however, for the other areas, proxies may be less reliable sources of resource use. For instance, the salience of an episode of heath care resource, for some proxies, will be lower than that of the patient. This will tend to lead to a further net underreporting of resource use by the proxy when compared to the patient (and a gold standard such as the medical record).

The method of valuing resource use is often ignored in guidelines and the method employed may impact the validity of estimates in pharmacoeconomic studies. In the United States this may be a larger problem than in Europe. In the US there are several different methods measuring and costing resource use: measurement based on CRFs, codable CRFs, hospital bills, and cost prediction models. The different methods yield different levels of internal and external validity (Evans and Crawford, 2000). For instance, the accuracy of cost estimates derived from hospital bills is questionable due to the presence of an incentive to 'upcode' in order to maximise reimbursement. A higher level of internal validity of cost estimates may be obtained by measuring resource use through the use of a CRF or a codable CRF; however, the external validity of these estimates fall compared to the bill data. Even if the bill data has some inaccuracies it is potentially more generalisable as it reflects the amount that is charged (eventually stepped down to a cost) and must be paid for by some entity. Prediction models fall somewhere between the two in terms of validity. As prediction models are necessarily based on a sample of patients, the model will not reflect the actual resource use and costs as accurately as if they were measured on all of the trial participants.

The absence of guidance in the areas of self-reported data, proxy estimates and costing may lead researchers to develop studies with different degrees of validity. This implies that pharmacoeconomic studies that adequately consider these issues will have a higher level of precision than those that do not and decision-makers may be reasonably confident that the results of the studies are an accurate reflection of the impact of a therapy on costs and effect. However, unfortunately, the existing guidelines by remaining silent on these matters implicitly endorse some methodological suspect procedures.

Relevance to Decision-makers

The technical merits of the study designs and the endpoints recommended in national guidelines are easily recognised. Most of the guidelines permit different endpoints and all encourage the use of the cost-utility studies and the use of the composite endpoint of a quality adjusted life year (QALY) (Jacobs, Bachynsky and Baladi, 1995). In a QALY improvements in quantity of life are weighted with an expression of the quality of life (utilities). In several cases the use of utility measures and QALYs are strongly recommended (Canadian Coordinating Office, 1994; Australian Commonwealth Department of Health, 1995).

The advantage of cost utility studies that use this endpoint is that different therapies may be compared across disease states. That is a cost per QALY can be calculated in one disease area and compared to a cost per quality adjusted life year in another disease state. The general idea is that the results of these studies can then be ranked from the lowest cost per QALY to the highest cost per QALY on a league table. The subsequent rankings can then be reviewed by policy makers to determine which therapies and diseases should receive (priority) funding and which areas should only receive some or no funding. Thus, the use of a QALY as an endpoint allows decision-makers to consider the adoption of therapies based on a rational approach to health care delivery: scarce health care resources can be directed where they will provide the most benefit in terms of both cost and effect.

However, is the guideline recommendation (and sometimes preferential use) of the QALY justifiable? In other words, do decision-makers use quality of adjusted life years in making decisions about the allocation of resources? In the United States one might expect that the use of quality adjusted life years would be limited. The health care delivery system is characterised by a multiplicity of providers and payers (local and national public payers, indemnity insurers and managed care) and thus there is no overall central allocation mechanism. However, even within managed care organisations and state funded health care it would be possible to allocate each health care budget based on cost per QALY (on the assumption that studies that presented these results were applicable to each institution's population). Although there have been many cost utility studies conducted in the US the actual impact on decision-making has been minimal. Two recent surveys conducted in the US have concluded that studies that incorporate QALYs are not well understood by decision-makers. Motheral and others (2000) found that only 58 per cent of decision-makers were familiar with cost utility studies compared to 97 per cent for cost effectiveness studies. In addition, Evans, Dukes and Crawford (2000) found that fewer than 5 per cent of decision-makers understood the term league table, thus the rankings of therapies by cost per QALYs has not occurred in the US by non-governmental insurers. This limited use of QALYs can be traced to three areas: practical problems with creating a policy around a QALY, a lack of understanding of what a QALY is and the belief that a QALY does not make any sense as a composite endpoint.

The Oregon experiment is a case where it was difficult to implement cost effectiveness arguments into practice. In the US, the state of Oregon wanted to provide extended publicly financed medical care to the Medicaid population. Faced with constrained budgets, the state government decided that the rationing of health care services through prioritisation would allow for the expansion of services while still being able to cover the existing Medicaid population. The original plan incorporated societal based utilities to generate QALYs. However, when the commission reviewed the cost per QALY results and did not find them logical, they used their own judgement and moved selected treatments up or down the list (Blumstein, 1997). The results, from the commission's lack of understanding the underlying economic concepts, were unexpected and challenged by residents and legal entities. The Office of Technology Assessment (OTA) concluded that net benefit had surprisingly little effect on the final ranking. According to the OTA, what was more important was the 'exercise of subjective judgement by the Commissioners in determining the category rankings and, particularly, in making the final line-by-line ranking adjustments' (Blumstein, 1997, p. 547). Thus the lack of understanding of a QALY led to the manual adjustment of the league table.

Counsel representing the Americans with Disabilities Act (ADA) raised a simultaneous challenge to the rankings developed through public weighting of health states. The counsel felt the Oregon rankings would perpetuate, rather than eliminate, societal and individual prejudices about the value of life when living with disabilities. It was felt that the ADA was being compromised in two respects:

> First, it incorporates arbitrary and discriminatory assessments of disabilities into the ranking process. Second, the plan conflates appropriate assessments of a treatment's necessity, effectiveness, and burdensomeness with inappropriate assessments of the quality of a patient's overall, post-treatment condition in order to rate a treatment's net benefit (Anonymous, 1997).

It was noted that people without disabilities are more likely to place lower preferences, and thus associated quality of life, to conditions they have not experienced (Peters, 1995). Thus from a legal perspective, the use of QALYs in government policy has been challenged, and this will likely pose a threat to the future use of utility analysis for policy making.

Others objected to these rankings because they felt it was more important to produce a life saving interventions than 'comforting' treatments. This has been referred to as the severity argument (Nord, 1999) or Rule of Rescue (Hadorn, 1991), which states that 'people cannot stand idly by when an identified person's life is visibly threatened if effective rescue measures are available' (ibid., p. 2219). This conflict will often arise when what is best for a person at one point in time, is not necessarily best for them when they are at a different point in time. This struggle between the individual and society represents a classic paradox in health care rationalisation.

Philosophical objections such as these were raised with Oregon's plan. Thus the use of any measure of effectiveness, regardless of how neutral or objective it may appear, will raise issues between distributive justice and allocative efficiencies (Peters, 1995). Researchers and policy makers ignore the issues of allocation and focus primarily on the distribution of health care resources. These individuals have little use for QALYs. Policy making may therefore be limited by the beliefs of those forming the policy and their constituents.

In the private insurance arena considerable questions can be raised as to the usefulness of a quality adjusted life year. Although cost-effectiveness studies are reported to be of some use in reimbursement decisions (Grabowski, 1998), an exploratory survey of managed care decision-makers' attitudes found that results of utility assessments may not be adopted in practice (Crawford et al., 1999). This survey found that out of the 41 medical and pharmacy directors (who sat on their institution's formulary committees) only a minority of respondents were familiar with common, direct utility elicitation techniques. Only 12 per cent and 9 per cent of respondents were familiar with the Health Utilities Index (HUI) and the EuroQoL, respectively. This in itself is not an indictment against utility elicitation as it is not necessary for decision-makers, or for that matter outcomes researchers, to be familiar with every measure of utility or quality of life. However, one would reasonably expect that if techniques of utility assessment were to be adopted in practice members of formulary committees would have a good understanding of key concepts. Unfortunately, this may not be the case. In the same survey fewer that 30 per cent of respondents reported that they understood the term QALY.

In the European context, QALYs are generally recognised as a relevant endpoint in economic evaluations. However, consistent with the US situation, decision-makers may be wary of QALYs. Koening et al. (1999) conducted a survey of 41 German physicians on their attitudes to health related quality of life (HRQL) assessment. Ninety per cent of the respondents felt that health related quality of life assessments were a relevant measure of clinical effectiveness, but only 54 per cent of the physicians had a clear notion of the concept of HRQL. Moreover, only 43 per cent of the physicians accepted the multiplicative way of calculating QALYs.

In the United Kingdom, Duthie and others (1999) conducted interviews with 34 GPs, fund managers, pharmacists and health authority directors and advisors to determine the relevance and the appeal of a number of health economic measures to decision-makers. The interviews consisted of the sample's reactions to several health economic statements. Two statements were included that were applicable to utility assessment: 'research amongst patients has shown that they would prefer near perfect health for five years on treatment A than 10 years of life with significant impairment on treatment B'; and 'treatment A costs less per quality adjusted life year than renal dialysis but more than kidney transplantation'. In the former case the interviewees did not accept the premise. In the latter case, the statement was not understood by the sample, indicating that the use of QALY was viewed more as technical jargon rather than a meaningful endpoint.

Further qualitative evidence of the suspicion of health economic measures can be found in the literature. Lemkin (1996) has taken issue with the adjustment that health economists make to endpoints found in clinical trials. He noted that in cancer trials small improvements in survival (measures in months rather than years) may be transformed to years of life saved. He states:

> I believe it to be a statistical fallacy to describe a value for a year of life saved, when in fact, very few patients have a full year of life improvement as their individual benefit (Lemkin, 1996, p. 688).

A resistance to endpoint transformations and the use of health economics jargon was also found in Duthie's (1999) study. One clinician remarked: '… per quality adjusted life year, I'd reach for my revolver I think … it should belong in *Private Eye* that one' (Duthie, 1999, p. 154).

This is not to say that information recommended in guidelines will not have an impact on decision-makers. For instance, even if clinicians and payers do not easily understand some endpoints other information may be more readily accepted. Guidelines universally recommend the use of the societal perspective in the measurement and costing of resource use. Duthie's study (1999) found that the societal perspective had merit to decision-makers. In the UK comparative statements relating to lost work time were viewed as relevant by decision-makers.

From Guidelines to Good Practice

Our objection to current guidelines is that they do not go far enough in terms of making recommendations as to the appropriate study design or in highlighting weaknesses in pharmacoeconomic studies. In addition, it can be argued that the use of a composite endpoint (such as a cost per QALY or cost per life year saved) may have little value to decision-makers in some countries.

Guidelines should encourage and include information on the best methodological practices and encourage the use of sound procedures in study design and analysis. In addition they should be relevant to decision-makers so that information that is derived from pharmacoeconomic studies is adopted into practice. This article has noted that there are several serious methodological issues not addressed by guidelines. In addition, it is questionable whether or not the guidelines encourage the use of economic analyses in drug purchasing and prescribing decisions. Langley (1997) has suggested that the traditional approach covered in existing guidelines which is focused on generating incremental cost/outcomes ratios is of little relevance to decision-makers. He also notes that although the societal perspective recommended by all national guidelines has intuitive appeal, it is of little relevance to the majority of health care purchasers in the United States. Under Langley's framework guidelines that encourage 'traditional' pharmacoeconomic evaluations should be replaced with guidelines that take a systems approach as these will meet the needs of drug purchasers (Langley, 1999). A systems assessment provides the impact of introducing a novel agent on costs and outcomes while taking explicit account of the constraints imposed by available budgets.

This is not to imply that what is appropriate for the United States should be transported to other countries. This is particularly true of countries or provinces that have mandatory requirements for pharmacoeconomic assessments. A recent review of 32 pharmacoeconomic submissions in British Columbia (Anis, Rahman and Schechter, 1998) found mixed adherence to Canadian guidelines. Those studies that only adopted the third party perspective over the more comprehensive societal perspective were rejected by the Drug Benefit Committee. However, it was also noted that several submissions that did not adhere to the guidelines were approved which suggests that decision-makers view some aspects of the guidelines as more relevant than others. In other countries the usefulness of guidelines probably varies. Guidelines for these countries will be weak in the sense that they do not adequately address the methodological problems highlighted above. Whether the guidelines are relevant will be partially dependent on the health care delivery system found in those countries. Where there is comprehensive public financing and provision of health care guidelines may be of more relevance. A rational health care delivery system, based on rankings of interventions in terms of costs and effect, are more likely to be present. However, even where this condition is present, such as the UK, this chapter has noted resistance to some elements commonly found in guidelines.

There is no reason to expect, or even desire, for guidelines to remain immutable. For instance, the Dutch guidelines are in a trial period where adjustments are anticipated as policy makers, researchers and pharmaceutical companies become more familiar with the process. The importance of good practice as opposed to guidelines will become more important as more countries incorporate pharmacoeconomic arguments formally into reimbursement decisions. The presence of existing guidelines is not sufficient to ensure that sound studies are conducted or that the results of the studies are easily understood by decision-makers. Good practice implies that valid research is carried out that has a meaningful impact on decision-making. Existing guidelines should be updated to reflect advancements in the field. The lack of gold standard data and validation studies will prevent firm recommendations from being made concerning some aspects of data collection such as proxy reports. However, existing and new guidelines can incorporate information on the use of patient self-reported data and the impact of different data collection modes as these areas have been well researched in the fields of epidemiology and survey methods. In addition, pharmacoeconomic researchers should give careful consideration to altering the type of study design recommended and endpoints used in order to ensure that this information is presented in a manner that addresses the needs of insurers and reimbursement authorities.

References

Anis, A.H., Rahman, T. and Schechter, M. (1998), 'Using Pharmacoeconomic Analysis to Make Drug Insurance Coverage Decisions', *PharmacoEconomics*, 13, pp. 119–26.

Anonymous (1994), 'ADA Analyses of the Oregon Health Care Plan', *Issues in Law and Medicine*, 9(4), pp. 397–424.

Australia Commonwealth Department of Health, Housing and Community Services (1995), 'Guidelines for the Pharmaceutical Industry on Preparations of Submissions to the Pharmaceutical Benefits Advisory Committee', Australian Government Publishing Service, Canberra.

Blumstein J. (1997), 'The Oregon Experiment: The Role of Cost-Benefit Analysis in the Allocation of Medicaid Funds', *Social Science and Medicine*, 45(4), pp. 545–54.

Brown, J. and Schulpher, M. (1999), 'Benefit Valuation in Economic Evaluation of Cancer Therapies: A Systematic Review of the Published Literature', *PharmacoEconomics*, 16(1), pp. 17–31.

Canadian Coordinating Office for Health Technology Assessment (1994), 'Guidelines for the Economic Evaluation of Pharmaceuticals', CCOHTA, Ottawa.

Crawford, B., Dukes, E., Bailey, L. and Evans, C. (1999), 'The Role of Quality of Life Information in Managed Care Decision Making', *Value in Health*, 2(3), p. 212.

Duthie, T., Trueman, P., Chancellor, J. and Diez, L. (1999), 'Research into the Use of Health Economics in Decision Making in the United Kingdom – Phase II: Is Health Economics 'for Good or Evil?', *Health Policy*, 46, pp. 143–57.

Drummond, M. and Jefferson, T. (1996), 'Guidelines for Authors and Peer Reviewers of Economic Submissions to the BMJ, The BMJ Economic Evaluation Working Party', *BMJ*, pp. 275–83.

England and Wales Department of Health (1994), 'Guidelines on Good Practice in the Economic Evaluation of Medicines', Department of Health, London.

Evans, C. and Crawford, B. (1999), 'Patient Self Reports in Pharmacoeconomic Studies: Their Use and Impact on Study Validity', *Pharmacoeconomics*, 15(3), pp. 241–56.

Evans, C. and Crawford, B. (2000), 'Direct Medical Costing for Economic Evaluations: Methodologies and Impact on Study Validity', *Drug Information Journal*, 34, pp. 173–84.

Evans, C., Dukes, E. and Crawford, B. (2000), 'The Role of Pharmacoeconomic Information in the Formulary Decision Making Process', *Journal of Managed Care Pharmacy*, 6(2), pp. 108–21.

Garattini, L., Grilli, R., Scopelliti, D. and Mantovani, L. (1995), 'A Proposal for Italian Guidelines in Pharmacoeconomics', *PharmacoEconomics*, 7(1), pp. 1–6.

Glennie, J., Torrance, G., Baladi, J.F. et al. (1999), 'The Revised Canadian Guidelines for the Economic Evaluation of Pharmaceuticals', *PharmacoEconomics*, 15(5), pp. 459–68.

Gold, M., Siegel, J., Russel, L. and Weinstein, M. (eds) (1996), *Cost Effectiveness in Health and Medicine*, Oxford University Press, New York.

Grabowski, H. (1998), 'The Role of Cost-effectiveness Analysis in Managed Care Decisions', *PharmacoEconomics*, 14(Suppl 1), pp. 15–24.

Hadorn, D. (1991), 'Setting Health Care Priorities in Oregon: Cost-Effectiveness Meets the Rule of Rescue', *Journal of the American Medical Association*, 265(17), pp. 2218–25.

Jacobs, P., Bachynsky, J. and Baladi, J.F. (1995), 'A Comparative Review of Pharmacoeconomic Guidelines', *PharmacoEconomics*, 8(3), pp. 182–9.

Koening, H.H., Hoffman, C., Schulenburg, J.M. and Leidl, R. (1999), 'Do Physicians Consider Quality Adjusted Life Years Relevant for Clinical Decision Making', *Medical Decision Making*, 19(4), p. 528.

Langley, P. (1999), 'Formulary Submission Guidelines for Blue Cross and Blue Shield of Colorado and Nevada: Structure, Application and Manufacturer Responsibilities', *PharmacoEconomics*, 16(3), pp. 211–24.

Langley, P. (1997), 'Pharmacoeconomics-achieving Gold Standards', FT Healthcare, London.

Lemkin, S.R. (1996), 'Cost-effectiveness: Let's Get 'Real'?, *Journal of Clinical Oncology*, 14(2), pp. 687–8.

Motheral, B., Grizzle, A., Armstrong, E., Cox, E. and Fairman, K. (2000), 'Role of Pharmacoeconomics on Drug Benefit Decision Making: Results of a Survey', *Formulary*, 35, pp. 412–21.

Nord, E. (1999), *Cost-Value Analysis in Health Care: Making Sense out of QALYs*, Cambridge University Press, Cambridge.

O'Brien, B. (1996), 'Economic Evaluation of Pharmaceuticals: Frankenstein's Monster or Vampire of Trials', *Medical Care*, 34, DS99–108.

Peters, P. (1995), 'Health Care Rationing and Disability Rights', *Indiana Law Journal*, 70, pp. 491–547.

PHARMAC (1998), 'A Prescription for Pharmacoeconomic Analysis (Draft 4 March 1998)', PHARMAC, Wellington.

Towse, A. (1997), *Guidelines for the Economic Evaluation of Pharmaceuticals: Can the UK Learn From Australia and Canada*, Office of Health Economics, London.

Chapter Three

The Use of Databases in Health Economics and Outcomes Research: An International Perspective

Christopher Evans, Lisa Kennedy and Bruce Crawford

Introduction

The use of databases in health economics and outcomes research has become more prominent in the last two decades as researchers have sought out a wider range of methods for assessing health care delivery. Researchers who were stymied by a lack of information, sponsors who were wary of substantial financial commitments to large randomised clinical trials (RCTs) or constrained by time, turned to a variety of public and private clinical and claims databases in an effort to gain information relevant to their particular studies. The creation of the Agency for Health Care Policy and Research in 1989 in the US, and the subsequent development of patient outcome research teams (PORTs) with their emphasis on identifying the most effective treatment, greatly increased interest in claims databases (Paul and Tilson, 1995). It was clear from the outset that the use of databases necessitated an eclectic and methodologically untested approach to health services research. To date, databases have been used in pharmacoeconomic studies, outcomes research, epidemiology, drug utilisation reviews and overall cost control.

Databases have been used for research purposes in two ways: comprehensively and selectively. Under a comprehensive approach, the database becomes the primary source of all data used in a study. For example, a cost of care study may be performed through a database. The identification of patients may be made via diagnoses, procedures, and pharmaceutical use. Once patients have been identified, their resource utilisation may be collected to determine the cost of care for the disorder. The selective use of a database only permits that a database be mined for specific data. For instance, as part

Health Policy and Economics: Strategic Issues in Health Care Management, M. Tavakoli, H.T.O. Davies and M. Malek (eds), Ashgate Publishing Ltd, 2001.

of an economic model that compares standard therapy to an innovative treatment, the extraction of statistics may be limited to length of stay (LOS) data. Estimates of the probabilities programmed into the same model may be derived from the published literature and the resource utilisation figures acquired from a Delphi panel. Thus, the use of information derived from clinical and claims databases provide a component to research that may supplement information from randomised trials, expert opinion, models and literature surveys.

All types of health care databases are used *partially* to describe and measure the production function for health care: the relationship between inputs of resources and the underlying condition of a patient and his environment with his outcome as measured by a change in health status, mortality, morbidity and functional status. The use of databases in health care research can identify some of the underlying factors that influence health status such as risk factors and co-morbidities. Databases can also be used to identify the process of care: how health care resources such as medical procedures, diagnostic testing, drug therapy and other care activities are combined to produce a health status output.

This review examines the recent use of health care related databases and is presented in four main components. The first part provides a general description of the different types of databases currently used in research: administrative, registry, clinical and practice. The second part reviews how these databases have been used in the areas of cost analyses, cost-effectiveness, epidemiology, and predictive modelling. The third part weighs the benefits and the risks of using databases in health care research, while the fourth part offers some recommendations for improving the use of databases in health services research.

Types of Databases

Claims or Administrative

Claims databases contain claims (or bills) from providers to the patient's insurer for reimbursement. Specifically, they contain patient, provider and service information for a given population of insured individuals. Table 3.1 lists the main elements commonly found in claims databases. Of the various types of databases in the US the Medicare databases are the most frequently used due to the ease of accessibility and its relevance (approximately 30 per cent of health care expenditures in the US is Medicare related). In the UK, the Department of Health (DoH) database is very close to a claims database in the information that it carries and it is representative of activity within England. It contains diagnoses, length of stay, waiting times and the number of episodes occurring for different operating procedures and has approximately six years of validated inpatient data, encompassing 60 million hospital episodes.

Entry to a claims database is usually in the form of an ICD-9 diagnostic code for a particular condition. Once the code has been selected, an episode of care or illness can be constructed for all or some of the individuals who have that code (Hornbrook, 1995). The cohort of patients can then be examined, at various intervals, for changes in outcomes and/or resource utilisation. Typically mortality is the most common outcome used in claims analysis. It is also possible to use proxies or intermediate outcomes in administrative studies, such as readmission to the hospital or admission to nursing home as a proxy for physical disability (Roos et al., 1988). In pharmacoeconomic studies where resource utilisation estimates are an important component, the procedures listed in the database and LOS form the basis for the cost estimates.

Registries

There does not exist a strict definition as to what constitutes a registry (Antczak-Bouckoms et al., 1991). A registry has been loosely defined as a list of patients with some clinical and demographic descriptors (ibid.). For our purposes we define a registry as a list of patients who are participating in a research-based study who have a common condition and who are followed up for an extended period of time. Most registries have an epidemiological and institutional focus: they concentrate on the incidence of disease and mortality and the care that is received. In addition, they contain detailed patient level and demographic information. Registries differ from claims databases as it is often possible to examine co-morbidities and a patient's history in detail as well as several outcome measures. The Surveillance, Epidemiology and End Results (SEER) cancer registry (Klawansky et al., 1991), the Connecticut Tumor Registry (Wyshak et al., 1991), the Framingham Heart Study (Roberts et al., 1991) and the International Bone Marrow Transplant registry (Rimm et al., 1991) are examples of registries that have been used recently in health services research in the US. For Europe, disease-specific patient registries on a large scale are a relatively unexplored concept. There are specific projects that will cover the care of patients on an individual hospital basis and additionally, there are larger patient registries from projects meant to research the specific care of

Table 3.1 Data elements common to most claims databases

Claim information	Data elements
Patient specific	Patient name, address and identifier[1]
	Insurance type (HMO, PPO, IPA, etc.)
	Employer/group number
	PCP number
	Date of birth
	Gender
	Zip code
Provider specific	Provider identifier
	Provider speciality
	Provider county
Delivery information	Date of admission and discharge from hospital
	Date of service
	Diagnoses (ICD-9-CM) Location of service
	Procedure codes and dates of procedures
	Charge by procedure
	Total charge or amount submitted
	Total amount reimbursed to the provider or submitter
	National drug code[2]
	Days supply[2]
	Quantity of the drug[2]

Notes

1. For the purpose of accessing a database this information is deleted and is replaced with a scrambled or encrypted identifier.
2. Not included in the Medicare database.

patients for various CNS (central nervous system) diseases, however, access to this data is limited or nonexistent, owing to the incentives behind this research and those funding it.

Practice and Clinical

Practice and clinical databases fall between the comprehensiveness and breadth of claims databases and the specificity of disease registries. A clinical database is institution specific: it contains information on the process of care for a particular facility (Safran, 1991). Typically, clinical databases focus on predicting patients' outcomes, however they may also be used for improved outpatient management, superior diagnostic ability (Pryor and Lee, 1991) and to measure the quality of care (Hannan et al., 1997). In many instances clinical information is merged with administrative information held by the same facility. Unlike administrative databases, clinical databases only capture the treatment services rendered at the specific site. A practice database is usually a component of a larger medical information system: one hospital (Garber et al., 1984), a consortium of hospitals or a combination of hospitals, outpatient facilities, clinics and pharmacies (Tierney and McDonald, 1991). Unlike claims databases they are developed by a health care institution and the information contained in the database consists of routine items of health care delivery. Also, in contrast to claims databases the information comes from a variety of sources: laboratory and diagnostic test results, pharmacy reports and medical records. As such, specific patient information in the areas of history, diagnoses, clinical activity, diagnostic and laboratory tests and therapies is recorded. Table 3.2 provides a list of data elements that are likely to be found in practice databases. Practice databases often contain specific information on a range of diseases, whereas registries contain specific data on one disease or condition and claims databases contain relatively general information on many diseases. Previously, practice databases have been used in the areas of epidemiology, risk assessment, post marketing surveillance of pharmaceutical products, practice variation, resource utilisation, quality assurance and decision analysis (Tierney and McDonald, 1991).

Practice databases like the RMRS (Regenstrief Medical Record System) (McDonald et al., 1992) or the Indianapolis Network for Patient Care and Research) (Overhage et al., 1995) may be accessed, for a range of conditions, at the patient level or an aggregate level via diagnostic codes, procedures or prescriptions written. In the case of the RMRS, database information on billed charges are included in the information available thus allowing for economic evaluations.

In Europe, there are a few specific practice databases, such as Medicines Monitoring Unit (MEMO) in the UK (MacDonald and McDevitt, 1994; Evans, McDevitt and MacDonald, 1995), the General Practitioner's Research Database in the UK and IMS, Mediplus databases in the UK, France, Germany and The Netherlands. The MEMO database is an inpatient database. Based in Scotland, MEMO is a university organisation which operates a database which covers 400,000 patients in Scotland's Tayside Region. This database contains detailed outpatient prescription data as well as detailed inpatient data such as procedures, patient demographic region, diagnosis and length of stay for various conditions coded by ICD-9. The General Practitioner's Research

Table 3.2 Data elements common to clinical and practice databases

Practice information[1]	Data elements[2]
Administrative	See Table 3.1
Baseline information	History and vital signs
Laboratory	Resources and results tests
Diagnostic	Resources and results for x-ray, ultrasound, echocardiograms, etc.
Procedures[3]	Surgical and outpatient procedures Surgical reports
Medications	Prescriptions written, dosage and duration
Delivery	Date of admission and discharge Date of service Diagnoses (ICD-CM) Charges (may have to be linked)

Notes

1 Information may only be available in the hospital portion of the database.
2 Data elements may not be available in all practice databases.
3 Data on outpatient procedures that occur outside of a hospital will usually only be available in practice databases (not in clinical databases).

Database (GPRD) (formerly the VAMP database), an outpatient database, is a primary care patient practice database in the UK (Office of National Health Statistics, 1996; Hall et al., 1988; Lockwood, 1996; Van Staa and Abenhaim, 1995; Jick et al., 1992a, 1992b; Mann et al., 1992). The GPRD contains over 4 million anonymous UK patient records collected from 1990. IMS, Mediplus also offer a similar primary care database for the UK, France, The Netherlands and Germany. Through Mediplus and the GPRD, it is possible to assess the co-morbidity of patients in primary care, all primary care drugs, consultations plus most tests and procedures for the countries they cover. Additionally, records of a patient's entry into a hospital are recorded. The contents of the Mediplus databases are partially driven by the health care system in each country. For example, in Germany, where there is no 'gatekeeper' and continuity in a patient's treatment is not assured, the database may not have the capacity to pick up all co-morbidities of patients because of the variation in who they may see for treatment. The French Mediplus database only goes back to 1996 and so it is difficult to receive a historical picture of what has happened to the patient. In the UK and The Netherlands, there is a 'gatekeeper system' and therefore it is easier to maintain continuity of treatment and co-morbidities. Also, there are differences in how information is recorded on these databases. For instance, in the UK, Mediplus and the GPRD are very similar in that these capture GP data, except that whereas the GPRD uses

ICD-9 codes, Mediplus uses Read (Smith et al., 1995) codes which are more symptomatically oriented clinical classification codes which can be cross-referenced to ICD-9 and OPCS-4. Coverage is large for many of these databases, for example, in the UK, the Mediplus database covers 1.5 million patient records with 976,000 active patient files.

Use of Databases

Cost Analysis

Although database research is moving more toward examining the efficiency of health care interventions, initially database research was applied to one aspect of economic efficiency: the cost of care. One of the most notable uses of cost control was the development of the prospective payment system (PPS) which produced a financial incentive for hospitals to care for patients in the least costly manner as they received a predetermined sum for each hospitalisation. Other important works include Rogerson et al. (1985) and Schumacher (1979) who used practice databases to extend the PPS to an ambulatory setting and to identify the factors that account for hospital costs in different settings. In the United Kingdom, the NHS has relied on the Chartered Institute of Public Finance and Accountancy (CIPFA) Health Database to benchmark expenditure across both purchasers and providers (CIPFA, 1995).

More recently, databases have been used to detail the costs associated with treatments (cost accounting and cost-minimisation) and the effects of interventions on costs (pre-test/post-test). These interventions may be a change in reimbursement structure, practice guidelines, practice patterns, and even the introduction of a new treatment (much like a budgetary impact analysis). In cost studies, databases may provide information on the substitutability of inputs to provide a given health output. That is, they may be used to compare an established therapy to a novel agent for the purpose of showing that the new drug permits fewer medical resources than the usual therapy with no sacrifice in health outcome.

In the US, Medicaid and Medicare claims data have been examined extensively (Simmons et al., 1995; McCombs et al., 1990; Mitchell et al., 1996). McCombs et al. (1990) used a pre-test, post-test study design to examine the cost of treatment failure in depressed patients. From prescription profiles, treatment success was compared to treatment failures in terms of resource utilisation and Medicaid expenditures.

Hillman and others (1990 and 1992) retrospectively examined the frequency of diagnostic imaging tests for self-referring physicians compared to physicians who referred to radiologists. Their studies identified patients for inclusion based on an index ICD-9 classification from an insurance database provided by the United Mine Workers of America Health Retirement Funds and Medstat. Subsequently, they examined the charges between the two provider groups and found that physicians who owned their own equipment had a higher imaging frequency than those that did not. Thompson et al. (1996) examined patterns of antidepressant use in terms of switching, therapy augmentation, upward titration and compliance and found that costs varied according to the pattern of use. Mitchell et al. (1996) randomly selected patients over the age of 65 with a diagnosis of ischemic stroke to examine the impact the attending physician speciality has on costs and outcomes.

Fitzgerald, Moore and Dittus (1988) examined the impact that a change in reimbursement practice had on health status in the US. Their study used a practice database in a pre-test, post-test design to assess the influence the PPS has had on outcomes following hip fracture care. Nazareth et al. (1993) used the GPRD database to assess the treatment approach of care of schizophrenia in general practice to patients with chronic physical disease and patients randomly selected from the practice register for 16 London general practices (ibid.). From this, they were able to assess the management of schizophrenia and concluded that a more structured approach to the care of these patients was necessary.

Since 1992 the Agency for Health Care Policy and Research has developed several guidelines to improve, measure and evaluate the quality of care. As part of this process, potential sources of data were identified and later used in the development of guidelines. Primarily, the focus has been on administrative claims data in an effort to draw out information on the acute phase of treating a condition. Such database driven research to inform guideline development has occurred in the areas of billiary tract, childbirth, cataracts in adults, hip replacement, pneumonia and stroke (Lee and Bergman., 1994).

Lee, Huber and Stason (1996) have recently expanded on the efforts of the Stroke PORT and examined the non-acute phase of stroke care. Their study, which was intended to supplement the guideline effort, examined the post stroke rehabilitation experience of Medicare patients. They extracted six months of Medicare claims to examine the post stroke rehabilitation patterns that are reimbursable by Medicare. Their analysis noted that non-acute hospital treatment made up nearly 40 per cent of the cost of treating stroke survivors and demonstrated that there is a significant variation in post stroke rehabilitation.

Interest in drug utilisation studies has increased due to the wide variations in prescribing and consumption patterns, concerns over long term adverse consequences (Jick et al., 1992), and the increasing costs of pharmaceutical treatments (Lee and Bergman, 1994). Drug utilisation review can qualitatively assess the appropriateness of drug use and quantitatively identify and describe problems. Once these problems have been detected, a drug utilisation program may be instated to intervene in the prescribing patterns to ensure appropriate use: this will ensure a minimisation of both the costs and consequences of misprescribing.

Cost-Effectiveness

In cost-effectiveness studies, the focus of database research is on the identification and measurement of input and process indicators and health related outcomes. These studies use databases to support prospective, retrospective (Simmons et al., 1995; Oster et al., 1987; Rendell et al., 1993; McCombs et al., 1990; Thompson et al., 1996) and modelling studies (Bentkover and Feighner, 1995; Safran and Philips, 1989). In prospective, naturalistic clinical economic trials, data on outcomes and resource utilisation are collected on a case report form (CRF) for every patient enrolled in the trial. This data can then be linked to published information or a database to fulfil the specified perspective of the study. A database may also be mined for relevant resources to be collected in a clinical trial.

Information contained in databases may also be used to support retrospective evaluations. A cohort of patients may be specified by a variety of parameters, including: age, gender, (sometimes) race, CPT-4 or ICD-9. The database is then searched for patients with the specified inclusion criteria over a particular period of time. Resource utilisation can be examined in terms of HCPCS/CPT codes and outcomes can be compared by breaking the cohort into two different therapies. This application represents a naturalistic setting, in as much as there are no protocols for the doctors to follow, thus allowing an examination of 'usual care' practice.

Roos et al. (1989) examined three large administrative databases in Denmark (n=36,703), Oxfordshire (n=5,284) and Manitoba (n=12,090) to compare the outcomes of two surgical procedures: transurethal resection of the prostate (TURP) to open prostatectomy. An unusual approach to database supported pharmacoeconomic research is provided by Safran and Philips (1989). In contrast to the normal technique of comparing two competing therapies, these researchers created a simulation, based on data from a hospital computing and billing system, that tried to determine the cost and level of success an intervention programme needed in order to effectively reduce readmissions to the hospital. Their novel use of a database led the researchers to conclude that an intervention programme that cost around $250 and with a 9 per cent success rate would demonstrate an economic benefit.

In addition, in Europe, 'therapeutic auditing' has been performed to assess the clinical, social and economic consequences of pharmaceuticals (Westerholm, 1986) These 'audits' have been performed at several levels affecting consumption – patients, physicians prescribing, hospitals, countries. Results have been used to increase compliance and change prescribing patterns (Westerholm, 1986; Bergman et al., 1979).

Epidemiology

Hospital admissions and length of stay due to drug adverse reactions and misuse have been examined in several countries, documenting the importance of appropriate used (Steel et al., 1981; Bergman and Wiholm, 1981; Davidsen et al., 1988). A number of studies have used the GPRD database to analyse risks associated with drugs (Jick et al., 1992b, 1995 and 1996). In the UK the MEMO database has also been used to assess associated risks (MacDonald et al., 1996; Evans et al., 1995a, 1995b and 1996). Studies of patients taking nonsteroidal anti-inflammatory drugs have found that the risk of upper gastrointestinal complications associated with oral NSAIDS is constant with continuous exposure (MacDonald, 1995). Davidsen et al. (1988) in a study of cardiac admissions in Denmark, found 15.8 per cent of hospital admissions were drug related. They found there was an increased risk of admission for adverse drug reactions with an increased number of drugs prescribed. They also found that most admissions for noncompliance could have been avoided by further patient education. Kaiser Permanente of Northern California, in a pharmacoepidemiologic study, used an all-inclusive approach to examine the carcinogenic effects of drugs by linking their clinical and pharmaceutical databases (Friedman, 1994).

Insurance and claims databases have been used successfully in numerous studies (Oster et al., 1987; Rendell et al., 1993; Hillman et al., 1990 and 1992). In an epidemiologic study that used a state-wide managed care database, differences in health care utilisation between benzodiazepine users and controls that occurred as a result of accident or injury were studied. Procedure and ICD-9 codes were linked to determine the resource utilisation.

Wennberg et al. (1987) used claims data from the Medicare programme in Maine and the Manitoba Health Services Commission (Canada) to evaluate variations in outcomes among alternative treatments and regions. Their research demonstrated how mortality differed among institutions in terms of size and the operations performed. This insurance claim oriented research demonstrated that databases may provide alerts as to the appropriateness and quality of care.

Predictive Modelling

Although some databases are often limited to mortality or intermediate outcome measures, they have been used successfully in the field of outcomes research. Roos et al. (1988) examined claims data for Manitoba, Canada, and the Survey of Ageing in Manitoba separately and merged them in order to predict health outcomes for an elderly population as measured by the final outcome of mortality and two proxies: admission to nursing home and admission to hospital. The results of their model demonstrated that administrative data provided a better predictor of death and hospital entry than survey data, and that the two data sets combined, provided some improvement over analysing just claims data.

Strengths and Limitations

There are five main areas of weakness in database research: the limited information on settings contained on claims; the dearth of outcome data in claims databases; the absence of true cost data; the inability to construct comprehensive inclusion/exclusion criteria in claims databases; and the lack of generalisability of clinical and practice databases and registries. These drawbacks, however, need to be weighed against the advantages of database driven research: the relative inexpensiveness, the potential for external validity, savings in investigation time and the potential to provide a snapshot of current care.

The chief limitation of claims databases is that they only include information that is included on the claim form. For instance, Medicare does not reimburse for outpatient drugs or nursing home care, thus it is impossible to describe the full process of health care for Medicare patients who are admitted to a nursing home. Some insurers in the US only partially cover or do not cover substance abuse (Garnick et al., 1996). Often databases only cover a certain geographic area and specific patient population. This limitation also applies to practice databases and registries which often have a specific population.

Claims databases only provide limited information that can be used as inclusion criteria and on health related outcomes. Claims databases do not include information on the indirect costs associated with a disease, intangible costs or direct measures of disability. As far as outcomes are concerned, the main focus is on mortality. Only a relatively small amount of information can be obtained in other areas. For example in order to examine treatment failure it is necessary to look, within a specified period of time, for a repeat of the original diagnosis or procedure(s) or for the occurrence of a specified procedure (say a CABG after a PTCA). For private claims databases in the US, the information collected is improving. With the increasing pressure insurers are receiving to improve quality of care from employer groups, the National Committee on Quality Assurance (NCQA), and the Health plan Employer Data and Information Set (HEDIS), many are starting to collect additional patient data, including risk factors such as smoking and alcohol and drug use. This data has been employed to identify potentially high risk pregnancies, such that women may be closely monitored for signs of problems. The data in practice databases is much richer in detail as it is used in the day-to-day care of patients. For instance, patients may be identified for a study based on a diagnostic code, lab results and medication use which is often not possible with claims databases.

The reasons data are recorded on a database may not coincide with the objectives of outcomes research and disease management. Only now in very limited areas is there consideration for the integration of this information into the data collection process. For instance, in a study for disease management in asthma, FEV1 may not have been recorded for every patient, as is the case of the Mediplus or the GPRD databases in the UK and in claims databases and some practice databases in the US. Similarly, in a study for the management of COPD, smoking status of the patient may not be present on the database. In large databases such as Medicare most outpatient drugs are not recorded. From this, it becomes difficult to measure the impact of these drugs, which is fundamental to any disease management approach. Similarly in the UK, the MEMO database does not cover those procedures during follow-up after patients leave the hospital. For disease management, even if a database records all the necessary treatment information for a specific cohort, it still may not be applicable for analysis because of the sample size of those patients. Suppose a disease management study in ovarian cancer patients would like to assess all patients over 70 with stage IIIb/IV disease who have experienced neutropenia and have had tumour progression three months after treatment. Although a database may contain some of these patients, the sample it contains will not be representative enough to make any substantial conclusions for a disease management programme.

Finding databases that cover outpatient care can be relatively easy in the UK and those that cover secondary care may be only slightly more difficult, but finding those that have both inpatient and outpatient care for each patient can be extremely difficult. This may be fine for those diseases confined to inpatient care, or those diseases confined to outpatient care; however, the progression of disease rarely takes on such a definitive pattern. What is likely to happen is that those trying to assess various diseases through databases will be given a poor option of having to do a retrospective patient chart analysis: marrying claims data with a patient chart, or assessing an outpatient database such as the GPRD in the UK. The latter involving an extraordinary amount of time and associated payments to hospital consultants to receive in-hospital information for each patient.

Clinical and practice databases frequently have no information on costs or charges and claims databases often only include information on charges and the reimbursed amount. For pharmacoeconomic research the use of charges may be inappropriate. In the Medicare database, charges can be easily converted to the Medicare allowed charge or can be converted to cost figures by applying standard cost-to-charge ratios; however, this is not possible in other databases.

The use of ICD-9 codes is both an advantage and disadvantage in database research. It is a strength in the sense that it offers a fairly specific common reference for identifying patients for a study. It is currently weak in that the ICD-9 classifications do not always allow for the severity of the illness to be captured. For example, the ICD-9 code for acute myocardial infarction does not differentiate as to when a heart attack occurred: a significant risk factor (Hannan et al., 1997). In addition, identifying co-morbidities may be difficult as it is unclear as to whether the secondary diagnosis reflects a co-morbidity or a complication of an illness (Mitchell et al., 1994). Although several diagnoses may be recorded on a claim form, often only one is documented as that is all that is necessary to get reimbursed. The lack of information has important implications for creating baseline groups who have been stratified based on all important variables and discriminating factors that influence patient outcomes from those that do not.

Claims databases offer several advantages over other sources of data. Compared to RCTs, retrospective studies that use claims data can demonstrate the effectiveness of a treatment in a real world situation. As RCTs are used to demonstrate safety and efficacy of a new compound and are constrained by numerous protocol inclusion and exclusion criteria, their potential for addressing what will occur in actual practice is limited. Clinical and practice databases are also able to do this but to a lesser extent than claims databases: they represent the current treatment (no protocol resource utilisation) but are limited to the institution(s) that collects the data. Hence, they may not be used as successfully to generalise to a larger population.

Second, practice and claims databases and registries offer the promise of a longer follow-up period compared to most RCTs. The use of a database for longitudinal purposes depends upon the stability of the patient population. This is not a major concern for the Medicare databases, where virtually everyone over the age of 65 in the US receives care until their death, and some European databases. In these databases it is possible to construct episodes of care over one year or more with little potential for loss to follow-up. In other claims databases, such as those provided by MCOs, and in practice databases and registries the stability of the patient population is questionable. Individuals may loose their current coverage if they become unemployed, their employer changes plans, they change employers, relocate with the same employer, and, for dependants, if their guardians divorce or they reach the age of majority. The various Medicaid databases suffer from the same problem, transient participation. Individuals may 'float' in and out of Medicaid for a variety of reasons: pregnancy, they become employed, become eligible for Medicare or their asset situation improves. Therefore, care must be taken when using these databases to avoid loss to follow up. Selection bias is also possible in private administrative databases. This is a particular problem with substance abusers who may not seek treatment due to their problem, or the stigma and fear of (employer) retribution, or may deny the need for treatment (Garnick et al., 1996).

This is not to suggest that databases do not suffer from problems of accuracy. Two issues are of concern: reliability and validity. The reliability of information refers to the consistency or reproducibility of a measure over time. That is, for example, would a person who records information on charts, discharge summaries or claim forms record the same information exactly the same way at a later date or would someone else who examined the same information abstract the same way as the original coder. The reliability of databases need to be assessed individually. Demlo and Campbell (1981) in an early study noted that the reliability of medical information based on discharge data contained in the National Hospital Discharge Survey was rather poor, while Roos et al. (1982) found that the data held by the Manitoba Health

Services Commission to be of generally good quality when tested with several reliability studies. Tierney and McDonald (1991) report that reliability may be a more significant problem in practice databases where different facilities in the system may measure and record data dissimilarly.

The validity of a claim form refers to whether or not the claim lists accurately all of the appropriate procedures and diagnoses. On claim forms, three issues directly related to the above may arise. First, the codes (e.g. ICD-9 or CPT-4) may be misspecified. This implies that the physician or coder listed an inaccurate or poorly supported diagnosis or procedure. The physician may list an ICD-9 diagnosis code that does not denote the underlying disorder, thereby protecting the patient from potential targeting by the insurer. Second, miscoding may occur where a coder may make an error when translating physician notes into codes on the claim form. For example, he may fail to record a diagnosis that was specified or enter the data erroneously as a keypunch error. Third, a diagnostic code may be missequenced. That is, a secondary diagnosis may be substituted for a primary diagnosis. Safran (1991) has noted coding error rates in excess of 40 per cent on hospital discharge abstracts. These problems are less likely to occur with clinical data, which is less subjective and is often based on a primary source. Quam et al. (1993) used medical records and a patient survey as a validation source for three claim records. They found that in terms of identifying patients, the medical and pharmacy claims had a high level of agreement with the patient record and the survey. Roos et al. (1982), however, note that these problems pale in comparison to deriving accurate information from patients. Related to the above is the fact that there are few edit checks for data that is entered into databases. It has been reported (Paul and Tilson, 1996) that this problem may be overcome through the cumbersome process of selectively accessing primary records. In the case of practice databases the information is considered more accurate than other sources of data as the data is frequently reviewed by physicians (Tierney and MacDonald, 1991).

Conclusion

Database driven research has proved to be a useful tool in the past. We have noted that there is a trade-off between the breadth of administrative databases and the specificity of disease specific registries and the high level of internal validity found in registries and clinical databases weighed against their low level of generalisability. The medium and long-term future of database research will need to address how patient outcomes are influenced by various factors. We have noted that databases, with varying degrees of accuracy, can control for some demographic factors (gender and age), the severity of a patient's condition as well as comorbidities. In the future it may prove possible to record and evaluate other factors that impact a patient's outcome such as other demographic factors (socioeconomic level, education and employment category), clinical parameters (lab results, blood pressure), risk factors (smoker, obesity), the level of education of treating physicians, the presence or absence of special procedures (e.g. disease specific guidelines) within an organisation and the composition of health care delivery (e.g. emphasis on preventative care versus curative/specialised care or the use of disease specific arrangements such as the presence of stroke nurses).

The expansion of the contents of health care related databases will allow researchers to determine more appropriately the process of care and the impact of interventions on patient outcomes. In pharmacoeconomics the current state of research is limited in that improvement in patient outcomes are attributed to the difference in treatment regimes, even though the inclusion/exclusion criteria are much less rigorous than the favoured vehicle for clinical research – RCTs. Improvements in the scope of existing databases and the creation of new databases which collect additional and relevant information will allow pharmacoeconomic and outcomes research to more accurately measure the health care production function and the outcomes that occur as a result of continuing technological change.

The retrospective or current treatment pattern nature of database analysis is much less expensive than a clinical trial. A database may act as a complement to an existing trial or may actually provide better results than a clinical trial in that a database analysis can give a picture of current (or recent) use of a drug under non-protocol conditions. Moreover, the inclusion/exclusion criteria for database searches is more general than found in clinical trials with their homogeneous populations. As such, practice and claims databases may be used for the post marketing surveillance of drugs to uncover adverse events not shown in RCTs and allow for an expanded patient population.

In pharmacoeconomic models there has been a tradition of using a variety of data sources in order to estimate the costs and effect of various interventions. Future research in the field of clinical economics may allow for database research to be integrated with other study design types: piggyback studies and naturalistic trials. The incorporation of database research with prospective economic evaluations may help to balance the trade-off that occurs between internal validity and external validity. First, preliminary database research may guide the design of a naturalistic trial. In contrast to using the information gained from a phase III trial as the basis for designing a naturalistic trial it is possible to examine relevant databases to identify settings of care, current therapies and procedures. Indeed it may be possible to use a combination of registries and administrative databases to inform the design of trials: claims databases can focus on resource utilisation and registries can focus on confounding factors, disease progression and outcomes.

Second, databases can be used in earlier phase pharmaceutical research to adjust the data that is derived from RCTs. One obvious application would be to eliminate the protocol driven costs from the RCT data output based on the findings of a database research. This, in essence, would increase the external validity of the pharmacoeconomic portion of the trial without compromising the internal validity. Third, database research can be extended within decision analytic and Markov models. Previously, some researchers have only used a database to gather information on charge or cost data. Administrative databases may be used to derive estimates of resource utilisation and registries may be used to derive some probability estimates. This would allow the researcher to discard his reliance on the questionable technique of expert panels and Delphi panels. In this way, both the external and internal validity of models would be improved: externally in the sense that results become more generalisable when compared to results based on expert estimates; and internally, in that claims records or registry information would constitute a more accurate estimate than the opinion of only a few experts.

In relation to guideline development, databases are likely to have a profound impact on disease management. Because databases can be used to assess outcomes in local care settings with a substantial representativity and high external validity, they have the potential to be an invaluable tool in disease management. Initially, various treatment approaches may be assessed through a database and treatment algorithms may be built from databases that assess the safety, effectiveness and cost-effectiveness of various treatments. The result of this research would represent disease maps from which different treatment approaches could be tested. From this information and in conjunction with panels of clinicians, one appropriate, well defined disease management strategy for a given disease could be developed. Such a strategy may then be disseminated to all clinicians currently treating the disease in a given locality.

Selection of the appropriate database for research purposes is important and should be approached with care. Given that databases provide a generally accurate description of care, and with the limitations noted, they represent a cost-effective way of conducting health services research.

References

Antczak-Bouckoms, A., Burdick, E., Klawansky, S. and Mosteller, F. (1991), 'Using Medical Registries and Datasets for Technology Assessment', *International Journal of Technology Assessment in Health Care*, 7(2), pp. 123–8.

Bentkover, J. and Feighner, J. (1995), 'Cost Analysis of Paroxetine versus Imipramine in Major Depression', *PharmacoEconomics*, 8(3), pp. 223–32.

Bergman, U., Norlin, A. and Wiholm, B. (1979), 'Inadequacies in Hospital Drug Handling', *Acta Medica Scandinavia*, 205, pp. 79–85.

Bergman, U. and Wiholm, B. (1981), 'Drug-related Problems Causing Admission to a Medical Clinic', *European Journal of Clinical Pharmacology*, 20, pp. 193–200.

CIPFA (incorporating the Healthcare Financial Management Association), London, 1995.

Davidsen, F., Haghfelt, T., Gram, L. and Brrsen, K. (1988), 'Adverse Drug Reactions and Drug Non-compliance as Primary Causes of Admission to a Cardiology Department', *European Journal of Clinical Pharmacology*, 34, pp. 83–6.

Demlo, K., Campbell, P. (1981), 'Improving Hospital Discharge Data: Lessons From the National Hospital Discharge Survey', *Medical Care*, 19(1), pp. 1030–40.

Evans, J., Hayes, H., Lipworth, B. and MacDonald, T. (1996), 'Potentially Hazardous Co-prescribing of ß-adrenoceptor Antagonists and Agonists in the Community', *British Journal of General Practice*, 46, pp. 423–25.

Evans, J., McDevitt, D. and MacDonald, T. (1995), 'The Tayside Medicines Monitoring Unit (MEMO): A Record-linkage System for Pharmacovigilance', *Pharmaceutical Medicine*, 9, pp. 177–84.

Evans, J., McGregor, E., McMahon, A., McGilchrist, M., Jones, M., White, G., McDevitt, D. and MacDonald, T. (1995a), 'Non-steroidal Anti-inflammatory Drugs and Hospitalization for Acute Renal Failure', *Quarterly Journal of Medicine*, 88, pp. 551–7.

Evans, J., McMahon, A., McGilchrist, M., White, G., Murray, F., McDevitt, D. and MacDonald, T. (1995b), 'Topical Non-steroidal Anti-inflammatory Drugs and Admission to Hospital for Upper Gastrointestinal Bleeding and Perforation: A Record Linkage Case-control Study', *BMJ*, 311, pp. 22–6.

Fitzgerald, J., Moore, P. and Dittus, R. (1988), 'The Care of Elderly Patients with Hip Fracture: Changes Since the Implementation of the Prospective Payment System', *New England Journal of Medicine*, 319, pp. 1392–97.

Friedman, G. (1994), 'Kaiser Permanente Medical Care Program: Northern California and Other Regions', in B. Strom (ed.), *Pharmacoepidemiology* (2nd edn), John Wiley & Sons, New York.

Garber, A., Fuchs, V. and Silverman, J. (1984), 'Case Mix, Costs and Outcomes: Differences Between Faculty and Community Services in a University Hospital', *New England Journal of Medicine*, 310, pp. 1231–7.

Garnick, D., Horgan, C., Hendricks et al. (1996), 'Using Health Insurance Claims Data to Analyze Substance Abuse Charges and Utilization', *Medical Care Research and Review*, 53(3), pp. 350–68.

Hall, G., Luscombe, D. and Walker, S. (1988), 'Post-marketing Surveillance Using a Computerised General Practice Data Base', *Pharmaceutical Medicine*, 2, pp. 345–51.

Hannan, E., Racz, M., Jollis, J. et al. (1997), 'Using Medicare Claims Data to Assess Provider Quality for CABG Surgery: Does it Work Well Enough?', *HSR: Health Services Research*, 31(6), pp. 659–78.

Hillman, B., Joseph, C., Mabry, M., Sunshine, J., Kennedy, S. and Noether, M. (1990), 'Frequency and Costs of Diagnostic Imaging in Office Practice – A Comparison of Self-referring and Radiologist-referring Physicians', *New England Journal of Medicine*, 323, pp. 1604–8.

Hillman, B., Olson, G., Griffith, P., Sunshine, J., Joseph, C., Kennedy, S., Nelson, W. and Bernhardt, L. (1992), 'Physicians' Utilization and Charges for Outpatient Diagnostic Imaging in a Medicare Population', *Journal of the American Medical Association*, 268(15), pp. 2050–4.

Hornbrook, M. (1995), 'Definition and Measurement of Episodes of Care in Clinical and Economic Studies', in M. Grady and K. Weis (eds), *Cost Analysis Methodology for Clinical Practice Guidelines*, AHCPR Publication No. 95-0001, Rockville.

Jick, H., Jick, S., Gurewich, V., Myers, M. and Visilakis, C. (1995), 'Risk of Idiopathic Cardiovascular Death and Nonfatal Venous Thromboembolism in Women Using Oral Contraceptives with Differing Progestagen Components', *The Lancet*, 346, pp. 1589–93.

Jick, H., Jick, S., Myers, M. and Vasilakis, C. (1996), 'Risk of Acute Myocardial Infarction and Low-dose Combined Oral Contraceptives', *The Lancet*, 347, pp. 627–8.

Jick, H., Terris, B., Derby, L. and Jick, S. (1992a), 'Further Validation of Information Recorded on a General Practitioner Based Computerised Data Resource in the United Kingdom', *Pharmacoepidemiology and Drug Safety*, 1, pp. 347–9.

Jick, S., Jick, H., Knauss, T. and Dean, A. (1992b), 'Antidepressants and Convulsions', *Journal of Clinical Psychopharmacology*, 12(4), pp. 241–5.

Klawansky, S., Burdick, E., Adams, M., Bollini, P., Orza, M. and Falotico-Taylor, J. (1991), 'Use of the SEER Cancer Registry for Technology Assessment', *International Journal of Technology Assessment in Health Care*, 7(2), pp. 134–42.

Lave, J. et al. (1994), 'Costing Medical Care: Using Medicare Administrative Data', *Medical Care*, 32(7), JS77–89.

Lee, A.J., Huber, J. and Stason, W. (1996), 'Poststroke Rehabilitation in Older Americans: The Medicare Experience', *Medical Care*, 34(8), pp. 811–23.

Lee, D. and Bergman, U. (1994), 'Studies of Drug Utilization', in B. Strom (ed.), *Pharmacoepidemiology* (2nd edn), John Wiley & Sons, New York.

Lockwood, M. (1996), 'General Practice Research Database Provides Detailed Anonymised Data', *British Medical Journal*, 313, p. 757.

MacDonald, T. (1995), 'Side-effects of Non-steroidal Anti-inflammatory Drugs: Studies From the Tayside Medicines Monitoring Unit', *Inflammopharmacology*, 3, pp. 321–6.

MacDonald, T. and McDevitt, D. (1994), 'The Tayside Medicines Monitoring Unit (MEMO)', in B. Strom (ed.), *Pharmacoepidemiology* (2nd edn), John Wiley & Sons Ltd, London.

Macdonald, T., McMahon, A., Reid, I., Fenton, G. and McDevitt, D. (1996), 'Antidepressant Drug Use in Primary Care: A Record Linkage Study in Tayside, Scotland', *British Medical Journal*, 313, pp. 860–61.

Mann, R., Hall, G. and Chukwujindu, J. (1992), 'Research Implications of Computerised Primary Care', *Post Marketing Surveillance*, 5, pp. 259–68.

McCombs, J., Nichol, M., Stimmel, G., Sclar, D., Beasley, C. and Gross, L. (1990), 'The Cost of Antidepressant Drug Therapy Failure: A Study of Antidepressant Use Patterns in a Medicaid Population', *Journal of Clinical Psychiatry*, 51(6 suppl), pp. 60–69.

McDonald, C., Tierney, W., Overhage, M., Martin, D. and Wilson, G. (1992), 'The Regenstrief Medical Record System: 20 Years of Experience in Hospitals, Clinics and Neighborhood Health Centers', *Clinical Computing*, 9(4), pp. 206–17.

Mitchell, J., Ballard, D., Whisnant, J., Ammering, C., Samsa, G. and Matchar, D. (1996), 'What Role do Neurologists Play in Determining the Costs and Outcomes of Stroke Patients?', *Stroke*, 27, pp. 1937–43.

Mitchell, J., Bubolz, T., Paul, J., Pasos, C., Escarce, J., Muhlbaier, L., Weisman, J., Young, W., Epstein, R. and Javitt, J. (1994), 'Using Medicare Claims for Outcomes Research', *Medical Care*, 32(7), pp. JS38–51.

Nazareth, I., King, M., Haines, A., Tai, S. and Hall, G. (1993), 'Care of Schizophrenia in General Practice', *British Medical Journal*, 307, p. 910.

Office for National Statistics (1996), 'The General Practice Research Database', Office for National Statistics, London.

Oster, G., Russell, M., Huse, D., Adams, S. and Imbimbo, J. (1987), 'Accident- and Injury-related Health-care Utilization Among Benzodiazepine Users and Nonusers', *Journal of Clinical Psychiatry*, 48(12), pp. 17–21.

Overhage, J.M., Tierney, W. and McDonald, C. (1995), 'Design and Implementation of the Indianapolis Network for Patient Care and Research', *Bulletin of the Medical Library Association*, 83(1), pp. 48–56.

Paul, J. and Tilson, H. (1996), 'Use and Opportunities for Administrative Databases in Pharmacoeconomic Research', in B. Spilker (ed.), *Quality of Life and Pharmacoeconomics in Clinical Trials* (2nd edn), Lippincott-Raven, New York.

Pryor, D. and Lee, K. (1991), 'Methods for the Analysis and Assessment of Clinical Databases: The Clinician's Perspective', *Statistics in Medicine*, 10, pp. 617–28.

Quam, L., Ellis, L., Venus, P., Cloue, J., Taylor, C. and Leatherman, S. (1993), 'Using Claims Data for Epidemiological Research: The Concordance of Claims-based Criteria with the Medical Record and Patient Survey for Identifying Hypertensive Patients', *Medical Care*, 31(6), pp. 498–507.

Rendell, M., Kimmel, D., Bamisedun, O., O'Donnell, T. and Fulmer. J. (1993), 'The Health Care Status of a Diabetic Population as Reflected by Physician Claims to a Major Insurer', *Archives of Internal Medicine*, 153(June 14), pp. 1360–66.

Rimm, A., Barr, J., Horowitz, M. and Bortin, M. (1991), 'Use of Clinical Data Registry to Evaluate Medical Technologies; Experience from the International Bone Marrow Transplant Registry', *International Journal of Technology Assessment in Health Care*, 7(2), pp. 182–93.

Roberts, M., D'Agostino, R., Dillon, M. and Odell, P. (1991), 'Technology Assessment in the Framingham Heart Study', *International Journal of Technology Assessment in Health Care*, 7(2), pp. 156–70.

Rogerson, C., Stimson, D., Simborg, D. and Charles, G. (1985), 'Classification of Ambulatory Care Using Patient-based, Time-oriented Indexes', *Medical Care*, 23(6), pp. 780–88.

Roos, L., Roos, N., Cagegeorge, S. and Nicol, J.P. (1982), 'How Good Are the Data? Reliability of One Health Care Databank', *Medical Care*, 20(3), pp. 266–76.

Roos, N., Roos, L., Mossey, J. and Havens, B. (1988), 'Using Administrative Data to Predict Important Health Outcomes: Entry to Hospital, Nursing Home and Death', *Medical Care*, 26(3), pp. 221–39.

Roos, N., Wennberg, J., Malenka, D., Fisher, E., McPherson, K., Andersen, T., Cohen, M. and Ramsey, E. (1989), 'Mortality and Reoperation After Open and Transurethtral Resection of the Prostrate for Benign Prostatic Hyperplasia', *New England Journal of Medicine*, 320(17), pp. 1120–24.

Safran, C. (1991), 'Using Routinely Collected Data for Clinical Research', *Statistics in Medicine*, 10, pp. 559–62.

Safran, C. and Phillips, R. (1989), 'Interventions to Prevent Readmission: The Constraints of Cost and Efficacy', *Medical Care*, 27(2), pp. 204–11.

Schumacher, D., Horn, S., Solnick, M., Atkinson, G. and Cook, J. (1979), 'Hospital Cost per Case: Analyses Using a Statewide Data System', *Medical Care*, 17(10), pp. 1037–46.

Simmons, W., Rizzo J., Stoddard, M. and Sith, E.S. (1995), 'The Costs and Effects of Switching Calcium Channel Blockers: Evidence From Medicaid Claims Data', *Clinical Therapeutics*, 17(1), pp. 154–73.

Smith, N., Wilson, A. and Weekes, T. (1995), 'Use of Read Codes in the Development of a Standard Data Set', *British Medical Journal*, p. 311.

Steel, K., Gertman, P., Crescenzi, C. and Anderson, J. (1981), 'Iatrogenic Illness on a General Medical Service at a University Hospital', *New England Journal of Medicine*, 304, pp. 638–42.

Thompson, D., Buesching, D., Gregor, K. and Oster, G. (1996), 'Patterns of Antidepressant Use and Their Relation to Costs of Care', *American Journal of Managed Care*, 2, pp. 1239–46.

Tierney, W. and McDonald, C. (1991), 'Practice Databases and Their Use in Clinical Research', *Statistics in Medicine*, 10, pp. 541–57.

Van Staa, T. and Abenhaim, L. (1995), 'The Quality of Information Recorded on a UK Database of Primary Care Records: A Study of Hospitalizations Due to Hypoglycemia and Other Conditions', *Pharmacoepidemiology and Drug Safety*, 3(1), pp. 15–21.

Wennberg, J., Roos, N., Sola, L., Scori, A. and Jaffe, R. (1987), 'Use of Claims Data Systems to Evaluate Health Care Outcomes: Mortality and Reoperation Following Prostatectomy', *Journal of the American Medical Association*, 257(7), pp. 933–36.

Westerholm, B. (1986), 'Therapeutic Auditing at the National and International Level', *British Journal of Clinical Pharmacology*, 22, 55S – 59S.

Wyshak, G., Burdick, E. and Mosteller, F. (1991), 'Technology Assessment in the Connecticut Tumor Registry', *International Journal of Technology Assessment in Health Care*, 7(2), pp. 129–33.

Chapter Four

Charging Ahead: The Policy and Practice of Health Charges in Britain

Allan Bruce

Introduction

Since their introduction into the National Health Service (NHS) in the early 1950s, health charges have consistently courted controversy. Imposed upon an NHS that the post-war Labour government had initially believed could deliver services free at the point of consumption, subsequent debates have tended to centre around the scope and intensity of charges than of whether to charge at all. Indeed, with the exception of a brief period in the mid-1960s when prescription charges were abolished, charges have been an inveterate feature of NHS finance. Crucially, however, while this analysis is not advocating that charges ought to be abolished, it questions the extent to which the imposition of charges represents an uncritical means of raising revenue and of limiting demand. Based upon data that has only recently become available, the analysis examines changes in the composition of health charges and of their role in the finance and delivery of health care. To begin with, the analysis seeks to contextualise the various debates surrounding imposition of health charges before moving on to examine the impact of these charges.

Health Charges in Perspective

General taxation currently accounts for 85.5 per cent of income available to the NHS, with National Insurance (NI) contributions providing a further 12.5 per cent. Of the remainder, only two per cent is now derived from the imposition of charges, with dental charges currently representing the largest single element (Office of Health Economics, 1999). In terms of the bigger picture, Figure

Health Policy and Economics: Strategic Issues in Health Care Management, M. Tavakoli, H.T.O. Davies and M. Malek (eds), Ashgate Publishing Ltd, 2001.

4.1 indicates that modest variations in the composition of income available to the NHS have been evident over the years but overwhelmingly, the service is financed, as it always has been, mainly from general taxation and largely free at the point of consumption. On the other side of the coin, however, the demands that are currently placed upon the NHS are substantially different and much more intense than in the past. This pressure upon resources has moved the rationing debate to a prominent position on the health care agenda (Hunter, 1997). A corollary of this has been a growing belief in some quarters that there may be limits to the extent that the NHS can continue to meet increasing demand without serious consideration being given to generating additional income through charges.

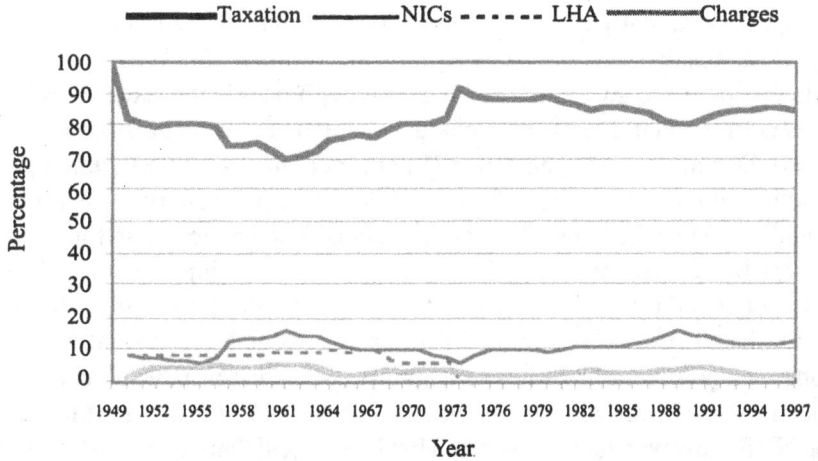

Figure 4.1 NHS income by source – expressed as a percentage of total income

Note

What is described as Local Health Authority (LHA) in official statistics refers to services that were funded and delivered by local government. In 1974, responsibility for funding and delivering these services was transferred to the NHS.

Source: Office of Health Economics, 1999.

Under the influence of Mrs Thatcher's premiership, the 1980s had been a relatively bullish time for increasing health charges. Prescription charges increased 15 fold between 1979 and 1990, rising from a per item charge of 20p to £3.05. Dental charges had also been increased in the same period, as had charges for the provision of spectacles. In 1985, however, the provision of spectacles became a matter for private finance, although in 1986 a voucher scheme was introduced to provide financial assistance from the social security system for those on low incomes to obtain spectacles or contact lenses at reduced cost. Furthermore, in 1989 free dental examinations and eye tests were abolished amidst considerable opposition from politicians of all political persuasions.

In addition to the 1980s witnessing substantial increases in existing charges, towards the end of this period, consideration had also been given to the possibility of extending the charging principle to other elements of the service (Butler, 1992; Bailey and Bruce, 1994). Yet even during the high tide of Thatcherism, the political arithmetic of extending the scope of charges failed to add up. Consequently the NHS entered the 1990s with its traditional means of financial support very much intact.

The Major years saw a much less aggressive approach being taken to health charges with per item prescription charges rising by 85 per cent (from £3.05 to £5.65). Dental charges remained at 75 per cent of treatment costs, although the maximum cost ceiling rose from £150 to £275. A corollary of this was that while revenue from prescription and dental charges expressed in cash terms rose by 525 per cent during Mrs Thatcher's premiership, it increased by only 41 per cent during the Major years (Office of Health Economics, 1999).

With the election of Labour in 1997, it remained to be seen what was to be done by a political party whose antagonism to increases in health charges had been so vociferous when in opposition. Labour's 1997 manifesto pledges on the NHS, however, had been somewhat less radical than in the past. Keen to shake off its tax and spend image, Labour was committed to adopting the Conservative's low-growth spending plans for their first two years in office. In addition, where their 1992 election manifesto had pledged to strengthen their commitment to health screening by restoring free eye tests (The Labour Party, 1992). No mention of this commitment was made in their 1997 manifesto (The Labour Party, 1997). Had 'New Labour' retreated from the ideological position characterised by 'Old Labour' that health charges were a tax upon illness?

Soon after their election victory, Labour came under pressure. The problems of widespread overspends (Brindle, 1997a), increased waiting lists and the imposition of bans on elective surgery (Healy, 1997) were amplified by a growing unease within the medical profession about the capacity of the NHS to meet the demands that were being placed upon it (Richards and Gumpel, 1997). This was closely followed by the then Secretary of State

Frank Dobson walking into a storm of protest regarding his impromptu announcement of a 'no holds barred review' of the NHS. It seemed nothing was to be ruled out in the search for additional income. This immediately stimulated rumours to the effect that the scope of charges would be widened with the possibility that existing charges would increase and the charging net might be expanded to include hitherto exempt groups such as old age pensioners not in receipt of income support (Brindle, 1997b).

The reality, however, was somewhat remote from the doom-laden scenario as 'New Labour' sought to identify with core principles that had for so many years sustained 'Old Labour'. The Prime Minister's Foreword to the 1997 White Paper – *Modern and Dependable* – emphasised the importance of fairness and a system based upon need, not the ability to pay. This was supported at a later stage by a belief in the advantages of a system financed through general taxation. 'The alternatives – rationing or a "charge based" system – would dissipate these advantages' (Department of Health, 1997, p. 9).

This position was to some extent reinforced with the publication of its comprehensive spending review (The Treasury, 1998). Not only did the Chancellor feel able to increase the income available to the NHS from general taxation by £21 bill over three years, but he went some way to allaying fears that the charging net was to be widened by restoring free eye tests to the over 60s. As far as existing charges are concerned, Labour has so far left dental charges undisturbed and prescription charge increases have been modest, rising by 4.5 per cent between April 1997 and April 1999.

More recently, the government has been presented with the recommendations of a Royal Commission in which there is no support for extending the charging principle to the provision of personal care for the elderly. The personal care component the Commission argued, 'should be available after assessment, according to need and paid for from general taxation. (Royal Commission, 1999). Furthermore, the Chancellor's pre-budget speech in November 1999 saw for the first time in Britain the earmarking of tobacco duty in order to provide additional revenue for the NHS (Sherman, 1999).

In spite of the government's relative generosity in its treatment of the NHS with the proceeds of general taxation, there were still those who saw this as a stop gap which, in the longer term, required more revenue to be raised from charges. Just days before the Chancellor's announcement of a cash bonanza for the NHS, *The Times* had joined the age old lament that without a more wide-ranging and coherent system of charging, the NHS would forever more be condemned to a future of feast to famine funding (Smith, 1998). This position has been supported elsewhere through criticisms that new concepts taking root in the NHS such as 'partnership' and the 'third way' are merely a means of fudging the issue. 'Thinking the unthinkable about introducing additional charges cannot be postponed much longer' (Crosby, 1999, p. 24). Indeed as a prelude to the next comprehensive spending review scheduled for 2000, in November 1999, the government had yet again come under considerable public pressure from the British Medical Association (BMA) and the Institute of Healthcare Management (IHM) to examine what the NHS should provide and how it ought to be funded (Gould, 1999).

Key Considerations in the Charging Debate

Since the early 1950s, two main considerations have been at the heart of the charging debate. Imposing charges, particularly upon prescribed medicines, is necessary in order to deter frivolous consumption and also, to provide additional revenue for the NHS. The background to these issues is fairly well documented elsewhere and need not be repeated here (Klein, 1995). Suffice to say that it was the Labour Government who introduced the Health (Amendment) Act 1949 which gave them the power to impose a one shilling (5p) prescription charge. Labour did not, however, impose the charge. This was left to the Conservatives in 1951. Indeed, it was also the Conservatives who made the necessary arrangements for the imposition of charges for dental and ophthalmic services in 1952.

Developments in the late 1940s and early 1950s may have set the tone for the rather stereotypical idea that the Conservatives are in favour of charging while Labour is opposed. The reality, however, is that whatever ideological ferment may be taking place on the back-benches, conviction politics invariably give way to pragmatism when in government (Bruce and Falconer, 1999). Consequently, however uncomfortable the Labour back-benches might be about the concept of charging, the reality is that charges are intended to dissuade the prescribing of low cost medicines that patients might purchase for themselves and of generating additional income for the NHS.

The down side to charging is of course the extent to which it interferes with the basic principles upon which the NHS was founded. A major consideration of the NHS is to pool societal risks both between rich and poor, between the healthy and the unhealthy and across an individual's life cycle. In a sense we are paying for the NHS when we are well and reaping the benefits if and when we become ill. In other words, health care is in principle at least, allocated on the basis of need and not the ability to pay.

In as much as charging runs contrary to securing access to health care on the basis of medically defined need, exemptions from charges have eased the conscience of politicians. Devised by Labour in 1968 when prescription charges were reintroduced, exemptions have been extended since then by both Conservative and Labour governments. Individuals who currently fall into one or more of the following categories are exempt from prescription charges:

- men and women over the age of 60;
- children under 16 or 19 if in full-time education;
- pregnant women and nursing mothers;
- individuals with valid exemption certificates;
- individuals and individuals with partners who in receipt of social security benefit;
- individuals who receive help under the low income scheme;
- individuals with a valid prepayment certificate – £13.80 for four months and £84.60 for one year. This is in effect a high cost ceiling.

Exemptions from prescription charges are more generous than their dental counterparts. Exemptions from dental charges relate largely to children and the poor. The elderly are not exempt from dental charges and the high cost ceiling is considerably higher for dental treatment (£275) than prescribed medicines. However, the imposition of charges for dental treatment (and ophthalmic services until 1985) has tended to court less controversy than prescription charges. Dental services, while important, are to some extent peripheral to the NHS.

Prescribed medicines on the other hand, represent a central feature of the NHS. Usually prescribed by a General Practitioner (GP) who is the gatekeeper to the NHS, prescribed medicines, more than dental treatment, have a life-saving or medical management element that engenders popular appeal. More controversial was in the imposition of a charge for dental checks and eye tests, both of which have a screening element and as such, represent a significant feature in preventive medicine. Nevertheless, exemptions from charges, particularly prescription charges, have important implications for charging both as revenue generating and rationing devices. This duality in the role of health charges is explored in greater detail in the analysis that follows.

The Impact of Health Charges

As a revenue generating device, income from charges has provided the NHS with additional income over the years but the amount has never been significant. From 1951 to 1964 the proportion of NHS income accounted for by charges averaged over 4 per cent and peaked at an all time high of 4.8 per cent in 1962. From 1965 to 1980, charge based income was much more modest, averaging 2.7 per cent per cent of total NHS income. The 1980s witnessed a slight increase to a high of 4 per cent in 1990, though subsequently the trend has been downwards and in 1997 stood at just 2 per cent.

It is significant to note, however, that in recent years there have been important changes to the composition of charge based income. These changes began in 1985 when ophthalmic services became a matter for private finance. As Figure 4.2 indicates, ophthalmic services were never high earners, but financial year 1985–86 saw some £50m disappearing from the NHS coffers. More noteworthy changes are evident in arrangements pertaining to hospital charges. These charges relate largely to pay beds and additional facilities on offer to both NHS and private patients. This income is generated by NHS Trusts and when they came on stream during the 1990s it was retained by them. Consequently, while this income still exists, it is no longer included as income available to the NHS nationally. This position is illustrated in Figure 4.3, where something in the order of £500m disappeared from this sector between 1992 and 1996. The net effect of all this has been to reduce substantially the income available to the NHS from charges and in addition, it has reduced the range of chargeable domains to prescriptions and dental services. Dental services remain the biggest earner and generated £475m in 1998.

As far as real income from charges is concerned, there has been a steady increase over the years but growth rates have been unremarkable. Using the Gross Domestic Product (GDP) deflator, the Office of Health Economics (1999) indicate that charge income adjusted to take account of inflation is only around twice its 1950s level. Admittedly, charge based income would have been greater had it not been for the loss of revenue associated with hospital charges. On the other hand, it is well known that the employment on an NHS specific deflator would reveal more modest growth rates than its more broadly based GDP equivalent. The explanation for this is that the NHS is exposed to higher levels of inflation due to wage increases and steeper rises in the cost of pharmaceuticals when compared to general inflation.

A difficulty in raising income from charges as they are imposed at present is that large increases in charge based revenue may tend to generate only

Charging Ahead: The Policy and Practice of Health Charges in Britain 61

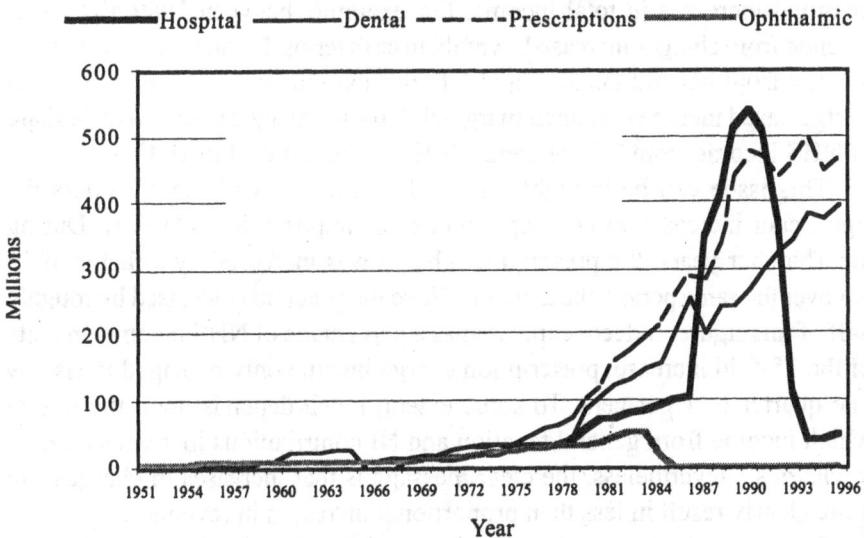

Figure 4.2　Payments by patients 1951–98

Source: Office of Health Economics, 1999.

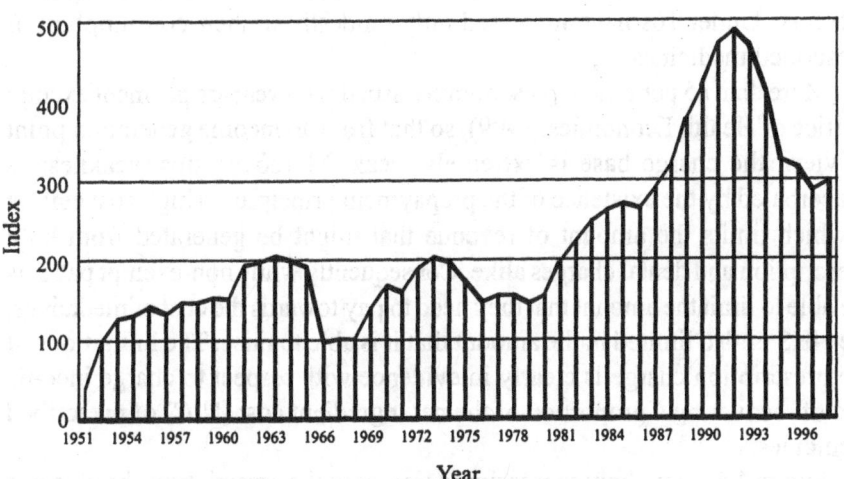

Figure 4.3　Real income from charges (1952=100)

Source: Office of Health Economics, 1999.

marginal increases in total income. For example, between 1980 and 1992, revenue from charges increased fivefold in cash terms. During the same period, income from general taxation and NI contributions increased threefold but charge based income remained marginal. It only managed to increase its share of NHS income from 2.3 per cent in 1980 to 3.6 per cent in 1992.

This issue can be brought into fairly sharp relief if one considers the significant increases to prescription charges imposed in the 1980s. During the Thatcher years, the prescription charge was increased by a factor of 15 but over the same period, the amount of revenue generated increased by roughly half of this figure. Indeed, expressed as a percentage of NHS income, in spite of the 15-fold increase, prescription charge income only managed to rise by one quarter of 1 per cent. To some extent, much depends upon the rate at which income from general taxation and NI contributions increases relative to charges. Nevertheless, the clear message is that increases in charges can quite clearly result in less than proportional increases in revenue.

The existence of exemptions is an influential explanation for the weaknesses of charging as a means of generating income and of limiting demand. If one examines prescription charges, for example, categorical exemption of the elderly plays a key role. Figure 4.4 shows that the number of prescriptions issued per capita for the elderly has increased substantially over the last 20 years, while a more significant decline has been observable in the chargeable category. Under 16s have increased only modestly in their consumption of prescribed medicines.

More than 85 per cent of prescriptions issued each year are payment exempt (Office of Health Economics, 1999), so that from an income generation point of view, the charge base is extremely weak. Moreover, this weakness is exacerbated by the existence of the prepayment principle – a high cost ceiling – which limits the amount of revenue that might be generated from both prescription and dental charges alike. Consequently while non-exempt patients are able to limit the amount that they need to pay towards the cost of medicines, the NHS is also limited in the amount that it is able to raise. The limitations of the prescription charge is clearly in evidence with respect to charge income and of recovering a proportion of the net ingredient cost (NIC) of prescribed medicines.

Figure 4.5 shows how successive increases in the prescription charge since 1979 has had the effect of increasing cost recovery when compared to the NIC of chargeable prescriptions. Remember, however, that the number of chargeable prescriptions has declined significantly and this, more than income raised through the prescription charge may serve as an explanatory variable.

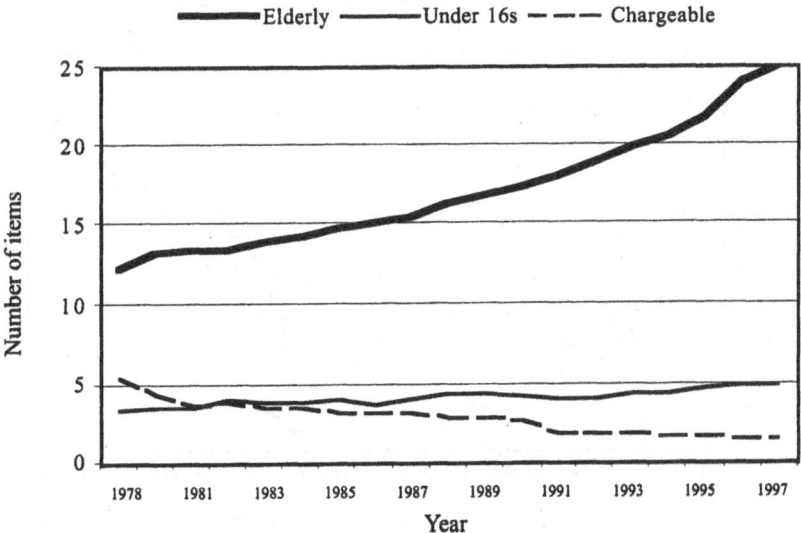

Figure 4.4 Prescription items dispensed per capital 1978–97

Note

Figures relating to the chargeable category should be interpreted with care as it includes an unknown number of individuals who are neither under 16 nor elderly but who nevertheless receive free prescriptions. In addition, the chargeable category does not include medicines dispensed to individuals who have prepayment certificates.

Source: Office of Health Economics, 1999.

In terms of the wider picture, the proportion of NIC recovered has decreased, particularly since the introduction of exemptions in 1968. Perhaps, therefore, this means that charging is neither a particularly effective means of generating additional income, nor is it terribly successful as a rationing mechanism as only a small percentage of the population are required to pay.

Is the solution to be found in reducing the number of people who qualify for free prescriptions? Why should the rich elderly receive free prescriptions and the working poor be required to pay? Notwithstanding the evidence that points to means testing being both stigmatising and expensive. In practice, the continued application of a high cost ceiling would limit the revenue that could be raised in this way. Besides, the heaviest users of prescribed medicines are those who are least able to pay by virtue of low income and/or chronicity of illness and in all likelihood would continue to be exempt – often the elderly.

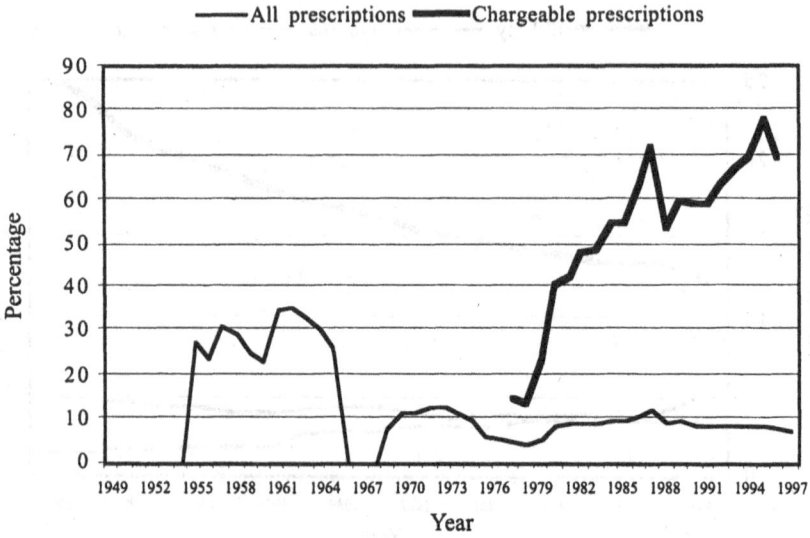

Figure 4.5 Percentage of net ingredient cost of prescribed medicines recovered from prescription charges

Source: Office of Health Economics, 1999.

Perhaps the reality of the situation requires an acceptance that the imposition of charges has played a limited role in generating income and of managing demand and will continue to do so in the future. This is not a case for abolishing charges. The longevity of charges within the context of the NHS is testament to their likely continuation. In any case, we in Britain are not prolific consumers of medicines. Japan, France, the United States, Belgium and Germany all spend twice the amount on prescribed and over the counter medicines than we do in Britain (Office of Health Economics, 1999). It is perhaps a feature of our culture to be parsimonious in the use of medicines regardless of whether a charge is imposed.

There is also a sense in which current and indeed future strategies for taming the drugs budget lies, not in imposing a charge upon patients, but in influencing the behaviour of the pharmaceutical companies. More potent measures of controlling the spiralling cost of medicines such as the limited list and GP fundholding have so far failed to stem the tide. Yet technological advance, as amply demonstrated in the case of Viagra, together with an overwhelming desire to maximise profits are of crucial importance (Boseley,

1998). The key question is how to succeed where others have failed. The Dutch government, for example, conscious of the rising cost of pharmaceuticals attempted, like Britain, to control costs and increase the use of generic drugs. Unfortunately, pharmaceutical companies are able to circumvent controls by introducing new similar products at higher prices. Moreover, in spite of attempts to encourage GPs to prescribe generics instead of branded drugs, drugs remained the fastest growing item of expenditure (Abel-Smith, 1992).

Conclusion

In spite of their somewhat controversial nature, sometimes branded as a tax upon illness, health charges have had a long if not illustrious connection with the NHS. At least one serious attempt had been made with regard to abolition but even given considerable ideological support, the Labour government was forced to reintroduce prescription charges in 1968 at a higher rate. The amount of revenue generated by charges has never been significant. Indeed, one might argue that charges, particularly prescription charges, have generated much higher levels of controversy. Yet in spite of this, the imposition of charges has a degree of pragmatic appeal. Perhaps, therefore, it is unlikely that we will see the demise of health charges, either now or in the foreseeable future.

Nevertheless, one must also be wary of seeing any expansion, intensification or extension of charges as a means of generating untold riches for the NHS. The truth is that charges have never managed to generate anything other than modest sums for a continually cash strapped NHS. Moreover, the widespread employment of exemptions, particularly for prescribed medicines, means that it is able only to exert an influence over the behaviour of a relatively small percentage of the population. There is little doubt, however, that the NHS is experiencing more intense demands upon its resources than at any time in the past. The number of prescribed medicines being consumed by the elderly has increased significantly and technological advance has brought with it an even greater range of medicines to be prescribed. Perhaps, therefore, if we are to find ways of rising to the challenge being imposed upon our health care system, we need to find new and more innovative ways of doing so. This does not mean to say that health charges are a spent force, but it may now be inappropriate to regard them as being part of a broader strategy for taking the NHS forward in the twenty-first century.

References

Abel-Smith, B. (1992), *Cost Containment and new Priorities in Health Care*, Aldershot, Avebury.
Bailey, S.J. and A. Bruce (1994), 'Funding the National Health Service: The Continuing Search for Alternatives', *Journal of Social Policy*, 23(4), pp. 489–516.
Boseley, S. (1998), 'NHS tries to stem cash haemorrhage', *The Guardian*, 21 September.
Brindle, D. (1997a), 'Scrutiny for NHS Cash', *The Guardian*, 9 June.
Brindle, D. (1997b), 'No Holds Barred Review for the NHS', *The Guardian*, 13 June.
Bruce, A. and P.K. Falconer (1999), 'The Politics of Health Charges in Britain: Rhetoric and Reality', *Policy and Politics*, 27(4), pp. 473–89.
Butler, J. (1992), *Patients, Policies and Politics: Before and After Working for Patients*, Open University Press, Buckingham.
Crosby, D. (1999), 'Archie's Enemies', *Health Service Journal*, 8 April, p. 24.
Department of Health (1997), *The New NHS: Modern and Dependable*, Cm 3807, The Stationery Office, London.
Gould, M. (1999), 'Split over future funding as £200m deficit looms', *Health Service Journal*, 18 November, pp. 2–3.
Healy, P. (1997), 'Pressure Soars', *The Health Service Journal*, 12 June, p. 15.
Hunter, D.J. (1997), *Desperately Seeking Solutions: Rationing Health Care*, Longman, London.
Klein, R. (1995), The New Politics of the NHS, Longman, London.
The Labour Party, (1992), *It's time to get Britain Working Again*, The Labour Party, London.
The Labour Party, (1997), *New Labour because Britain deserves better*, The Labour Party, London.
Office of Health Economics, (1999), *Compendium of Health Statistics*, 11th edn, Office of Health Economics, London.
Richards, P. and Gumpel, M. (1997), 'Save our Service', British Medical Journal, 314(14) pp. 1756–8.
Royal Commission on Long Term Care (Chair: Sir Stewart Sutherland) (1999), *With Respect to Old Age: Long Term Care – Rights and Responsibilities*, The Stationery Office, London.
Sherman, J. (1999), '£300m of Tobacco Duty Earmarked for the NHS', *The Times*, 10 November.
Smith, D. (1998), 'Charging is the Only Cure for a Sickly NHS', *The Times*, 28 June.
The Treasury, (1998), *Modern Public Services for Britain: Investing in Reform*, Cm 4011, The Stationery Office, London.

Chapter Five

Staging Type 2 Diabetes: Future Challenges in Cost of Illness Modelling, Health Policy and Global Health

Marsha A. Dowell, Billie R. Rozell and Matthew Dowell

Introduction

Market level transformations occurring within the United States health care management environment and the increasing emphasis on global health requires new and creative models for organisation, management, reimbursement and service (Cogswell et al., 1997). These newly created paradigms in decision-making and innovative management strategies will become stabilising forces in the new millennium. A variety of current internal and external organisational factors and characteristics both support and hinder paradigm changes in decision-making models for health care management for chronic diseases at national and international levels. Political astuteness, global environment, resource allocations, cognitive, behavioural and cultural patterns of health care providers and choice of decision support models are facilitators as well as barriers to paradigm changes. Current decision support models for chronic diseases such as diabetes, utilised for health policy decisions, are based upon assumptions that may no longer be valid and reliable nor the most effective in managing high-risk, high volume populations with chronic diseases. Many of the cost of illness models previously used by decision-makers are limited in their approach to design and/or use. In addition, no model specific to Type 2 diabetes exists to support informed decisions for management and reimbursement. This study describes foundational processes related to a secondary database for staging and costing out care of a large cohort population of Type 2 diabetics.

Health Policy and Economics: Strategic Issues in Health Care Management, M. Tavakoli, H.T.O. Davies and M. Malek (eds), Ashgate Publishing Ltd, 2001.

Diabetes

Diabetes is an incurable chronic disease characterised by high levels of blood glucose resulting in defects in insulin secretion, insulin action or both. There are two main types of diabetes, Type 1 (previously called insulin dependent or juvenile onset) and Type 2 (previously referred to as non-insulin dependent or adult onset).

Diabetes is a chronic disease that impacts multiple body systems. It has been called the 'silent killer' because of the multitudes who are unaware they have developed the disease until a life-threatening complication (primarily cardiovascular) forces them to seek help from a health care professional (Davidson, 1996). Significant co-morbidity complications are prevalent with this disease. In the United States, heart disease is the leading cause of diabetes related deaths; diabetes is the leading cause of blindness in adults 20–74 years of age; and the leading cause of end-stage renal disease (Douzdjian et al., 1998). Diabetes is also the most common cause of lower-limb amputation (Ollendorf et al., 1998; Davidson, 1999).

Diabetes is a global disease of increasing epidemic proportions. The World Health Organisation indicates that the problem diabetes poses to world health is widely under recognised (2000). The International Diabetes Federation states that diabetes is the fourth main cause of death in many countries (1997). The global prevalence of diabetes in adults was estimated to be at 4.0 per cent in 1995 and to rise to 5.4 per cent by the year 2025. The number of adults with diabetes in the world is expected to rise from 135 million in 1995 to 300 million in the year 2025, with the largest increase numbers in developing countries (King et al., 1998). Figure 5.1 is a graphic representation of the global incidence of diabetes.

Diabetes is one of the most prevalent diseases in the United States (US) with 15.7 million people suffering from the disease (National Diabetes Information Clearinghouse, 1998). Type 2 diabetes accounts for 90–95 per cent of all diagnosed cases of diabetes in the United States (ibid.). There are an estimated seven million people not yet diagnosed with the disease. Diabetes, although affecting all age groups, becomes increasingly prevalent with age. People over the age of 65 accounts for the majority of those diagnosed with the disease. As the seventh leading cause of death in the US, this disease has a significant impact on the health, quality of life and the longevity of people and has serious implications for all health care systems (Centers for Disease Control and Prevention, 1999).

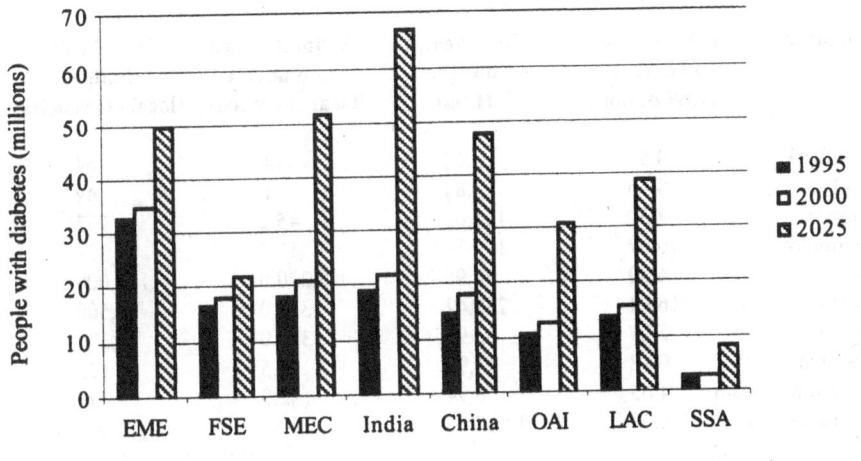

EME = established market economies   FSE = former socialist economies of Europe
MEC = Middle Eastern crescent   OAI = other Asia and islands
LAC = Latin America and the Caribbean   SSA = Sub-Saharan Africa

Note: an explanation of the regional groupings can be found in World Bank, 1993.

Figure 5.1 Global instances of diabetes

Source, King et al., 1998.

Costs for this one disease have been rapidly escalating. Direct US medical costs for this disease in the 1980s were estimated between $7.4–$11 billion dollars (Entmacher et al., 1985) and in 1997 these direct costs were estimated at $44.1 billion dollars (American Diabetes Association (ADA), 1998). Indirect costs have been estimated at $6.3–10.8 billion dollars in the 1980s and approximately $54 billion dollars in 1997. The economic burden of this disease is not confined to one nation, but felt throughout the world. The global impact of the economic consequences of the direct costs of diabetes is represented in Table 5.1.

As the disease state progresses and involves more body systems, diabetes becomes more costly in nature, and consumes a disproportionate amount of health care funds. Complications from the disease are both macrovascular and microvascular in nature. The macrovascular complications range from hypertension to myocardial infarctions to strokes while the microvascular complications range from retinopathy to neuropathies to nephropathies and include end stage renal disease (Rodby et al., 1996). By far the most common

Table 5.1 Global estimates of direct costs of diabetes

Country	Estimated cost of diabetes (US$ billions)	Total health budget (US$)	Estimated cost of diabetes (local currencies)	Total health budget (local currencies)
Denmark	0.54	9.12	3.8	64
Finland	0.46	7.84	2.6	44
France	7.30	121.66	45.2	753
Germany	10.67	179.36	19.7	331
Italy	4.50	74.95	8,220.0	137,000
Japan	16.94	282.42	320.0	34,500
Spain	2.04	33.93	320.0	5,330
Sweden	0.88	14.72	7.5	125
United Kingdom	4.65	76.94	2.9	48
United States	60.00	1,007.00	60.0	1,007

Note: the calculation of US$ sums is based on exchange rates as at 26 May 1999.

Source: adapted from Jönsson, 1998.

complications are macrovascular types, the leading cause of death and disability in Type 2 diabetics. The incidence of the three major macrovascular diseases (coronary artery, cerebrovascular and peripheral vascular) accounts for 80 per cent of the mortality for adults with diabetes (Meigs, 1999).

The economic consequences of the increasing numbers of Type 2 diabetics are wide spread. Not only do the disease and the complications consume appropriated monies for health care expenditures, but also the cost to societies for those not covered by some type of health care system is acute (Oberien et al., 1998). The total economic burden of this chronic disease on any and all societies is staggering.

Among adults with Type 2 diabetes in the United States, 92.0 per cent have some form of health insurance and most of those adults have been covered by a government sponsored health care plan such as Medicare or Medicaid (Harris et al., 1994). Government funded programmes are responsible for health care coverage for 57.4 per cent of adults with diabetes. A portion of this population has no coverage for health care with the primary reason of the expense of the coverage or they were unable to obtain health insurance because of their age (ibid.).

Costs of diabetes or any disease are commonly divided into direct and indirect costs. Most direct costs of diabetes in the United States are attributable to inpatient or hospitalisation care (62 per cent), outpatient services (25 per cent) and nursing home care (15 per cent) (Herman and Eastman, 1998;

Simonson, 1998). Indirect costs of diabetes are attributable to premature mortality, disabilities, loss of income and other quality of life issues. Indirect costs attributable to diabetes in the United States are far in excess of direct costs. Summation of both direct and indirect costs leads to the conclusion that the economic burden of diabetes is substantial. The approach of current models related to diabetes is to deal with diabetes as one entity, therefore little is understood about the costs of Type 2 diabetes as a discrete disease.

Economic Modelling

All models are wrong, but some are useful (George Box, 1979).

Economic models derived from cost of illness (COI) studies are critical to outcomes of disease management. These models provide a framework for organisational information on the impact of the disease and the efficiency and effectiveness of treatment (McCarty and Zimmet, 1994). These models influence policy makers regarding the prioritisation of funding for health care related research and care at national and international levels.

Decisions in health care management are often made in relative isolation and based on incomplete and small data sets. Efforts to focus management strategies on high cost illnesses have driven models of care that seek to reduce costs through prevention and early detection. These efforts commonly group small aggregates within individual health care systems and compare cost avoidance/reduction methods, which are internally benchmarked, thus reducing applicability to large populations. An important element that of aggregating and statistically predicting the comprehensive lifetime costs of populations within a service group has been attempted in fairly piecemeal fashion. In addition, data limitations, especially differences in methods of data collection make economic measurements and consequent decisions difficult.

Forecasting costs in health care through economic models has been accomplished primarily through national and state databases in which the disease model provides the framework for the cost model. Songer and Ettaro (1998) note major economic approaches that are useful for identifying direct and indirect costs for a specific entity. The COI studies approach for direct costs are designated as either 'top down' or 'bottom up'. The top down model uses data on total health expenditures using ICD-9 CM (International Classification of Diseases, Ninth Revision, Clinical Modification) codes for disease specific rates and cost estimates. The bottom up approach uses average costs of services provided and applies these costs to health care encounters in the aggregate. The indirect costs, the human capital approach, are recognised as willingness to pay and a friction cost approach. The friction approach measures the cost of replacement of workers and loss of productivity for ill employees.

Current models based on the human capital approach, which estimates costs for a cohort of those with a specific disease for a limited time period and extrapolates to other similar groups, tend to overemphasise the costs of the disease. Other models generate estimates based upon prevalence and cost out illness episodes to predict costs from disease onset until death. These models may underestimate the costs of the disease. Population based surveys to arrive at cost estimates are difficult to utilise in obtaining disease-specific estimates because of questionable validity (Rice et al., 1980). For example, in some models co-morbidity with a disease entity has been determined as an aetiological fraction and multiplied by the cost of treatment for that specific co-morbidity. This method adds to the total cost and may inflate the projected costs for the disease.

The current models are broad in their perspectives and based on relatively small data sets. Few studies glean data specific to Type 2 diabetes. Further, inflationary data coupled with the variability of co-morbidity leads to substantial risk for inaccurate forecasting and provides poor decision support information. In addition, many models evidence data limitations due to a wide variety of data collection methodologies, making decision-making for health care management problematic.

The Study

This research in progress describes the beginnings of a foundation for a decision support model useful in predicting chronic illness staging and costs at different points over the lifetime of individuals within a cohort population. The focus of the model is a costly chronic disease (Type 2 diabetes), which has attendant significant morbidity and mortality.

The study (funded by a private corporation) utilised the *HCUP–3 Department of Health and Human Services Healthcare Cost and Utilisation Project* database for the years 1988 through 1994. The study analysed specific variables in a nationwide inpatient sample (NIS) for the purpose of creating foundations for future decision models. The HCUP–3 database has a stratified probability sample of hospitals with sampling proportional in each stratum to the number of community hospitals and totalled about 6.4 million admission/ discharge records in 1994. Current variables considered included the client's age, gender, race, expected primary sources of payment, principal diagnosis and procedures (including validity indicators), length of hospital stay, and total charges as well as procedural charges. Appendix A provides an overview of the HCUP–3 database.

Research questions were formulated and the data are currently being analysed to respond to the posed questions.

1. What 'stages' for Type 2 diabetes can be identified with attendant costs per stage?
2. What are primary sources of payment and variance in the payments?
3. What are the total and procedural costs per age, gender and race per stage?
4. What are variances within populations associated with age, gender, race, hospital length of stay and costs?
5. What are health policy implications of costs per stage and lifetime costs for an aggregate population?

The basic premise of the model is predicting and identifying critical indicators in an aggregate large enough to establish trends in disease progression. Such identification of trends can augment the ability to prevent or delay more costly care. Outcomes of this model can provide the opportunity for more robust decision support systems.

Preliminary Findings

Cases included in the study were those identified by ICD–9 CM codes in the HCUP–3 1988–94 database and indicative of Type 2 diabetes or complications. Currently, however, only the 1994 data were used to 'stage' diabetes. One advantage to the use of this database is the standardised way of grouping and coding data from all participating hospitals. In 1988, 19 states participated in the gathering of the data, and 22 states participated in 1994. The American Diabetes Association recommends screening persons 45 years of age and older for Type 2 diabetes (ADA, 1998), and therefore only data for those adults 45 years and older were included in the study.

Preliminary findings indicated that of the total admissions to hospitals for Type 2 diabetes in 1988 (82,155) 41 per cent were male and 59 per cent were female. These gender differences remained relatively consistent through the seven years of collected data with a total admission of adults with Type 2 diabetes of 432,630 in 1994. Of the available data for 1994, over one half of the admissions and discharges were Caucasian and 11 per cent black. It is noted that these data reflects diagnostic categories while hospitalised and not numbers of patients admitted for that diagnosis.

The primary payer for all seven years was Medicare, paying approximately 31 per cent of the total costs of health care for the hospitalised population. In 1988, commercial health insurance companies and preferred provider organisations paid for approximately 27 per cent of the hospital costs, but in 1994 only paid for approximately 17 per cent of the costs. In 1988 Medicaid was the primary payer for approximately 12 per cent of the costs and in 1994 about 17 per cent of the costs. Health maintenance organisations and physician health plans paid approximately 5 per cent of the total hospital costs and this rose to approximately 12 per cent in 1994. All other sources of payment remained at relatively stable levels over the seven-year period.

Those diagnosed with diabetes accounted for approximately 1 per cent of all hospital admissions in each of the seven years (the vast majority of those records reflected Type 2 diabetes as a diagnosis), yet they account for only a portion of the total number diagnosed with the disease, and their attendant costs of care account for 11.9 per cent of the total US health care expenditures. While one percent may appear insignificant, it is the third highest overall admitting diagnosis. Other diagnostic categories that are significant to this study are congestive heart failure, acute myocardial infarctions, acute cerebrovascular disease and urinary tract infections. These diagnostic categories may well be co-morbid states with diabetes thus increasing the true number of hospital admissions with this specific disease. It is well documented that these more severe and debilitating events generate a greater financial burden than do early stage complications. Complications that are relatively low in cost such as microalbuminuria at $14 per event, progress to more costly advanced stages such as end stage renal disease at $53,659 per event.

Length of stay data indicate a decline of a mean of 6.34 days in 1988 to a mean of 6.27 days in 1994 with total charges increasing from $5,806.91 per hospital stay to $10,935. The most significant confounding variable affecting the length of stay is a diagnosis of cerebrovascular disease. Table 5.2 describes hospitalisations based on admission/discharge data from the HCUP–3 project for 1994.

Admissions by age per year also increased over the seven year period with the largest increase in admissions for people aged 65 and older. Preliminary findings indicate that for this population diagnostic testing for

Table 5.2 Type 2 diabetes admissions and discharges (1994)

Hospitalisations for 1994	Total discharges	% of total discharges	Mean (LOS)	Mean total charges
Uncomplicated DM	10,484	0.03	5.50	$04,626
Complicated DM	422,146	1.22	7.04	$10,935

Source: HCUP-3, 1994.

endocrine diseases (such as diabetes) were most common as opposed to a younger population (age 60) where diagnostic testing for diseases of the eye were more prevalent. Diagnostic testing for endocrine diseases was also prevalent in the age 40 groups. These findings are consistent with the literature related to the onset of diabetes and stages of disease progression. Table 5.3 describes 1994 outcomes by length of stay and mean total charges for those patients ages 45 years of age or older having a single level classification of 'Type 2 diabetes without complications'. It is noted that although the total admissions/discharges are similar for both age groups, the mean length of stay for the older group is significantly increased and, therefore, the mean total charges are also increased. It is also interesting that of the 2,186 admissions for the age group of 65 years of age and older, 14 per cent were discharged and needed some further follow-up home health care; 23 per cent of those patients needed some other form of institutionalised care (most commonly nursing home care). The lengths of stay statistics are similar for both males and females, and are at approximately four days (HCUP-3, 1994).

Table 5.4 describes the 1994 outcomes by length of stay and mean total charges for those 45 years of age and older having a single level classification of 'Type 2 diabetes with complications'. Statistics for this group are remarkably similar to those describes in Table 5.3, except surprisingly the mean length of stay for those with complicated diabetes is shorter than those with uncomplicated diabetes. However, a more substantial number of are discharged to home health care services and nursing homes. The mean total charges were relatively similar for both groups but the median charges for the 65+ age group are much higher.

A cross tabulation analysis was conducted on all variables. Of those analyses, one tabulation yielded interesting results. Cross-tabulations (see Table 5.5) were completed on the length of stay and age group for those with Type 2 diabetes with complications. Males had longer lengths of stay in the hospital than did females in the age ranges from 45–85+, and therefore the direct costs of the hospital stay were higher.

Table 5.3 Outcomes by client characteristics for Type 2 diabetes mellitus without complications (HCUP-3 1994)

		Total number of discharges	LOS, days (mean)	Charges, $ (mean)	In-hospital deaths	Routine discharge	Other institution	Home health care	Against medical advice
Age	45–64	2,526	3.8	4,685	12 (0.5%)	2,237 (88.6%)	76 (3.0%)	185 (7.3%)	16 (0.6%)
	65+	2,186	8.4	6,524	23 (1.0%)	1,348 (61.7%)	505 (23.1%)	305 (14.0%)	0 (0.0%)
Sex	Male	5,211	4.5	4,764	9 (0.2%)	4,500 (86.4%)	308 (5.9%)	336 (6.5%)	53 (1.0%)
	Female	4,643	4.3	4,555	26 (0.6%)	3,905 (84.1%)	317 (6.8%)	381 (8.2%)	15 (0.3%)
Payer	Medicare	2,200	7.2	6,725	23 (1.0%)	1,460 (66.4%)	452 (20.5%)	260 (11.8%)	0 (0.0%)
	Medicaid	1,410	4.5	4,743	6 (0.5%)	1,235 (87.6%)	45 (3.2%)	107 (7.6%)	17 (1.2%)
	Commercial	4,437	3.2	4,021	5 (0.1%)	4,079 (91.9%)	82 (1.8%)	247 (5.6%)	25 (0.6%)
	Uninsured	1,246	3.9	3,461	0 (0.0%)	1,112 (89.2%)	35 (2.8%)	82 (6.6%)	17 (1.4%)
	Other	523	3.2	4,155	0 (0.0%)	481 (92.0%)	12 (2.3%)	21 (4.0%)	9 (1.7%)
Median for zip code income	Low ($0–25,000)	3,710	4.3	4,635	5 (0.1%)	3,184 (85.8%)	261 (7.0%)	236 (6.4%)	25 (0.7%)
	Not low ($25,001+)	5,755	4.6	4,778	25 (0.4%)	4,857 (84.4%)	358 (6.2%)	469 (8.2%)	40 (0.7%)

Table 5.4 Outcomes by patient characteristics for Type 2 diabetes mellitus with complications (HCUP–3–1994)

		Total number of discharges	LOS, days (mean)	LOS, days (median)	Charges, $ (mean)	Charges, $ (median)
Total number of discharges		416,420	5.9	4.0	11,755	6,095
Age group	<1	*	*	*	*	
	1–17	22,968	3.1	2.9	5,164	12 (0.5%)
	18–44	105,629	4.4	3.1	9,873	23 (1.0%)
	45–64	133,030	6.3	4.0	13,059	*
	65–84	136,765	7.0	5.0	13,168	9 (0.2%)
	85+	17,885	6.9	5.2	10,835	26 (0.6%)
Sex	Male	197,918	6.2	4.0	11,339	23 (1.0%)
	Female	205,513	6.2	4.0	10,734	6 (0.5%)
	Missing	*	*	*	*	5 (0.1%)
Payer	Medicare	169,221	7.4	5.0	12,745	0 (0.0%)
	Medicaid	86,203	5.8	4.0	10,258	0 (0.0%)
	Commercial	114,807	5.1	3.0	9,668	*
	Uninsured	31,468	4.6	3.0	8,108	5 (0.1%)
	Other	14,729	5.1	3.0	10,351	25 (0.4%)
	Missing	700	3.9	2.0	7,462	*
Median income for zip code	Low ($0–25,000)	159,604	5.6	4.0	9.989	
	Not low (25,001+)	235,021	6.1	4.0	11,754	
	Missing	16,860	5.6	4.0	11,302	

In order to 'stage' Type 2 diabetes, several statistical analyses were conducted. Descriptive statistics for those patients diagnosed with complicated and uncomplicated Type 2 diabetes were complied and aggregated. The total costs for this aggregated data were summed. Correlation analyses were conducted on selected variables and a step-wise regression was conducted. The preliminary analysis indicated a significant correlation between mean total charges and specific ICD–9 diagnostic codes for complications of Type 2 diabetes.

Figure 5.2 demonstrates highest correlations among cardiovascular, renal, and neurological complications (ICD–9 codes for diabetes and complications). The correlations for the ICD–9 codes for Type 2 diabetes served as the basis for the preliminary staging of the disease. When submitted to step-wise regression analysis for costs and third party payers, a significance level of ($p<.02$) was noted for one commercial payer (HCUP–3, 1994).

Table 5.5 Number of discharges and mean LOS by age group and sex for clients with Type 2 diabetes mellitus without complications

		Total number of discharges	Male	Female
Age group	45–64	133,030	6.3	6.2
	65–84	136,765	7.2	6.9
	85+	17,885	7.6	6.6

Two aggregate variables substantially increased the costs of diabetes: cardiovascular procedures and subsequent co-morbid states, and renal procedures and subsequent co-morbid states. Admission cases where cardiovascular disease were evident and coded increased total charges from a mean of approximately $4,586 to $11,131 and when renal disease was evident, the mean total charges increased to approximately $23,899 (unadjusted 1994 dollars). Brown, Pedula and Bakst (1999) recently reported a similar study, and the outcomes were remarkably similar. Figure 5.3 indicates the costs per stage based on the HCUP–3 data for 1994.

A smaller number of admission/discharge records indicated renal complications as the most costly event. Approximately 80 per cent of the records reflected cardiovascular complications indicating that the total hospital costs for the aggregate are considerable for those with cardiac complications, but the impact on the health care system for individuals with renal complications is significantly higher.

This 'staging' of the disease supports previous clinical indicators reported in the literature that cardiovascular and renal complications increase costs, but this model graphically illustrates the rising costs associated with Type 2 diabetes. These preliminary findings are but a beginning to initial foundational constructs for new paradigms for decision-making models. Further analysis is continuing.

Limitations

Several limitations of this study are noteworthy and could influence the true direct costs of Type 2 diabetes in either direction (more or less expensive). The number of admissions/discharges that were the direct result of undiagnosed Type 2 diabetes is not known. Consequently the costs may be underestimated.

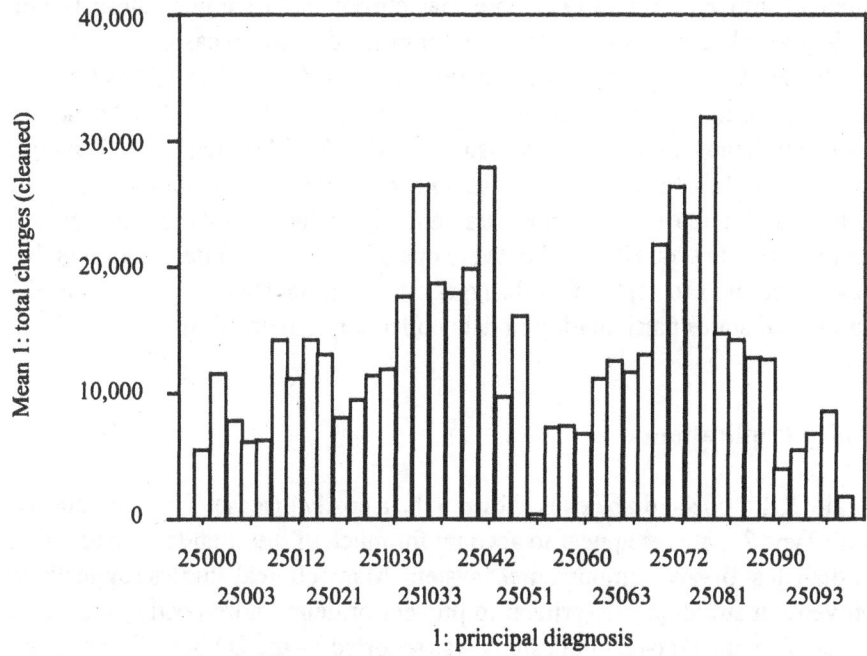

Figure 5.2 Relationship of total charges and diabetes diagnosis

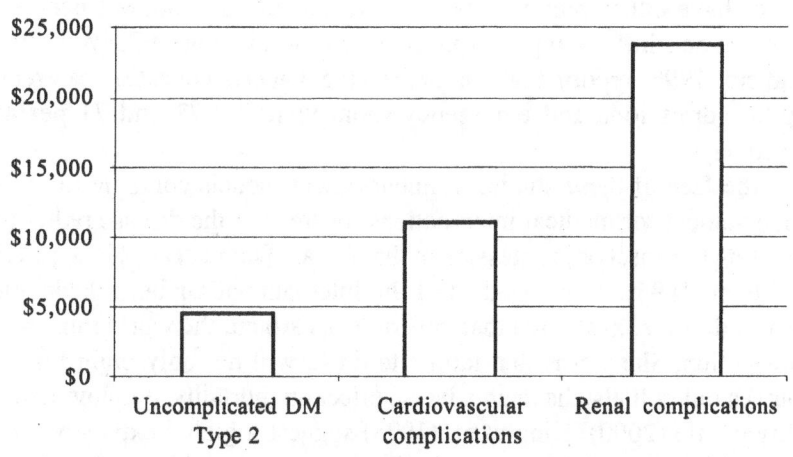

Figure 5.3 Staging of diabetes by incremental costs

Susman and Helseth (1997) note that current data suggest there is one undiagnosed case of Type 2 diabetes for every diagnosed case.

In addition, there are inherent problems of disease classification with secondary data sources where the disease specific estimate of direct costs are based on diagnostic information using the ICD-9 CM system. The fifth digit of the ICD-9 CM medical diagnosis indicates whether a patient is Type 1 or Type 2 and heretofore has been dramatically under-represented in previous secondary data sets. HCUP-3 data are one of the few secondary data sets that have attempted to report this disaggragation of diabetes diagnoses, but the number of states participating in data collection remains limited.

Policy Implications

In all COI models, diabetes is shown to be a costly disease. Those diagnosed with Type 2 diabetes appear to account for much of the attendant direct costs of diabetes for any reimbursement system. Many clinical studies suggest that prevention strategies are critical to prevent or delay more costly co-morbid states. The most far-reaching study was reported by the Diabetes Control and Complication Trail Research Group (1995) and showed that an intensive approach to glycemic regulation resulted in lowering the risk of progression in Type 1 diabetes. Studies related to intensive glycemic regulation in Type 2 diabetes have either produced negative results or have not yet been fully completed and little is reported in the scientific literature (Calwell, 1997). Caruthers (1996) reports that comprehensive diabetes education can reduce hospital admissions and emergency room visits by 72 and 71 per cent respectively.

In the face of these studies, reimbursement models continue to rely on reimbursement for medical interventions for treating the disease rather than preventing the onset or progression of that disease (Javitt et al., 1995; Levetan and Ratner, 1995). The President of the International Diabetes Federation, Maria L. de Alva, has stated that governments around the world must invest in prevention. She warns that failure to do so will not only drain financial resources but will also have an adverse effect on mortality, employment and quality of life (2000). King et al. (1998) suggest a global explosion of the disease with the largest increase in developing countries which makes diabetes one of the most costly health problems in the world. Various political leaders, health care providers, health care purchasers and patients continue to search for economic answers to the management of this chronic disease.

Diabetes places a substantial burden on societies as a whole and also places severe burdens on individuals and families. The classic COI analyses solely based on aggregate level national utilisation and expenditure data have provided little insight to the economic impact of the disease from the individual's perspective. This current staging model of diabetes is a beginning to bridge the gap between the economic impact on the aggregate and the individual. In the end, decisions about the management and reimbursement will be affected not only with this current and other COI studies, but also by the political, demographic, social and ethical values of those responsible for economic policies.

Conclusions

Whether in private or government sponsored arenas, use of new decision support system models may offer a heretofore unknown degree of predictability, especially in terms of costs and fiscal controls. From a policy perspective, as integrated systems have developed, governments have become more active purchasers of health care and have led in policy development. However, private sector initiatives with intense local competition have also fuelled policy decisions primarily related to health information and its use. Predictive models that use health indicators for risk identification and quantification such as the one described will engender new ethical, legal and policy ramifications.

Chronic diseases such as diabetes are very costly and have been identified and treated primarily on an individual basis utilising decision support system models with varying methodological difficulties. The preliminary model described with attention to large populations within health systems over time and identification of critical indicators (stages) can increase prediction of total costs over the lifetime of a population. In addition, identification of critical indicators may drive indicator-specific treatment, which can lead to lower lifetime individual and aggregate health care costs.

Acknowledgements

The authors would like to thank the following individuals for their expertise: David Brown, PhD, University of Alabama in Huntsville; Aurora Dunn RN, BSN, graduate student, University of Alabama in Birmingham; Sammye Bradley, RN, BSN, graduate student, College of Nursing, University of

Alabama in Huntsville; Sue Walters, Staff Assistant, College of Nursing, University of Alabama in Huntsville; Amy Shadoin, PhD, College of Nursing, University of Alabama in Huntsville; and the many other students and colleagues who assisted in the preparation of this manuscript.

References

American Diabetes Association (1998), 'Clinical practice recommendations', *Diabetes Care*, 21 (supplement 1) S, pp. 20–2.
Brown, J., Pedula, K. and Bakst, A. (1999), 'The Progressive Cost of Complications in Type 2 Diabetes Mellitus', *Archives of Internal Medicine*, 159, pp. 1873–80.
Box, G. (1979), 'Robustness in the Strategy of Scientific Model Building', in R.L. Launer and G.N. Wilkinson (eds), *Robustness in Statistics*, Academic Press, New York.
Calwell, J. (1997), 'Controlling Type 2 Diabetes: Are the benefits worth the costs?', *Journal of the American Medical Association*, 278, p. 1700.
Caruthers, C. (1996), 'Tallying the Cost of Diabetes', *Business and Health*, 14 (1A), pp. 8–14.
Centers for Disease Control and Prevention (1999), 'Economic Cost of Diabetes Mellitus in Minnesota, 1998', *Morbidity and Mortality Weekly Report*, 40(14), pp. 229–31.
Cogswell, M., Nelson, D. and Kaplan, J.P. (1997), ' Surveying Managed Care Members on Chronic Disease', *Health Affairs*, 16 (6) pp. 219–27.
Davidson, M.B. (1996), *Diabetes Mellitus: Diagnosis and treatment* (3rd edn), Livingstone, New York.
Davidson, M.B. (1997), Diabetes Update, International Diabetes Foundation, www.idf.org.
Davidson, M.B. (1999), 'Diabetes Related Lower Extremity Amputations Disproportionately Affect Black and Mexican Americans', *Southern Medical Journal*, 92(6), pp. 593–9.
Davidson, M.B. (2000), *Diabetes Newsletter*, 21 February, World Health Organisation.
Douzdjian, V., Ferrara, D. and Silvestri, G. (1998), 'Treatment Strategies for Insulin-dependent Diabetics with ESRD: A cost-effective decision analysis model', *American Journal of Kidney Diseases*, 5, pp. 794–802.
Entmacher, P.S., Sinnock, P., Bostic, E. and Harris, M.I. (1985), 'Economic Impact of Diabetes', in M.I. Harris and R.F. Hamman (eds), *Diabetes in America,* National Institutes of Health, Bethesda, Maryland.
Gonella, J.S., Hornbrook, M.C. and Louis, D.Z. (1984), 'Staging of Disease: A case-mix measurement', *Journal of American Medical Association*, 251(6), pp. 637–44.
Harris, M.I., Cowie, C.C. and Eastman, R. (1994), 'Health Insurance Coverage for Adults with Diabetes in the U. S. Population', *Diabetes Care*, 17, pp. 585–91.
Harris, M.I., Eastman, R.C. and Siebert, C. (1994), 'The DCCT and Medical Care for Diabetes in the U.S', *Diabetes Care*, 17, pp. 761–4.
Herman, W.H. and Eastman, R.C. (1998), 'The Effects of Treatment on the Direct Costs of Diabetes', *Diabetes Care*, Suppl. 3, C19–24.
Javitt, J.C., Aiello, P.I., Cheng, Y., Ferris, F.L., Canner, J.K. and Greenfield, S. (1995), 'Preventive Care in People with Diabetes is Cost-saving to the Federal Government', *Diabetes Care*, 17, p. 909.
Jonsson, A. (1988), 'The Economic Impact of Diabetes', *Diabetes Care*, 21, Supplement, C7–10.

King, H., Aubert, R. and Herman, W. (1998). 'Global Burden of Diabetes, 1995–2025', *Diabetes Care*, 21(9), pp. 1414–31.

Levetan, C. and Ratner, R. (1995). 'The Economic Bottom Line on Preventive Diabetes Care', *Practical Diabetology*, 5(6), pp. 10–19.

McCarty, D. and Zimmet, P. (1994), 'Diabetes 1994–2010. Global Estimates and Projections', paper presented at the International Diabetes Institute, Melbourne, Australia.

Meigs, J. (1999), 'Predictors of Complications and Death in Type 2 Diabetes', paper presented at the American Diabetes Assocation, 59th Scientific Session.

National Diabetes Information Clearinghouse (1998), *Diabetes Statistics*, NIH Publication No. 98–3926, Bethesda, Maryland.

O'Brien, J.A., Shomphe, L.A., Kavanagh, P.L., Raggio, G. and Caro, J.J. (1998), 'Direct Medical Costs of Complications Resulting from Type 2 Diabetes in the U.S', *Diabetes Care*, 7, pp. 1122–8.

Ollendorf, D.A., Kotsanos, J.G., Wishner, W.J., Friedman, M., Cooper, T., Bittoni, M. and Oster, G. (1998), 'Potential Economic Benefits of Lower-extremity Amputation Prevention Strategies in Diabetes', *Diabetes Care*, 8, pp. 1240–5.

Rice, D., Hodgson, P. and Kopstein, A.N. (1980), 'The Economic Cost of Illness: A replication and update', *Health Care Financing Review*, 7, pp. 61–80.

Rodby, R.A. and Firth, L.M. (1996), 'An Economic Analysis of Captopril in the Treatment of Diabetic Nephropathy', *Diabetes Care*, 19, pp. 1051–61.

Simonson, D (1998), 'The Economic Burden of Diabetes', *Clinical Diabetes*, 17(1), p. 47.

Songer, T. and Ettaro, L. (1998), 'Studies on the Cost of Diabetes', paper prepared for the Division of Diabetes Translation, Centers for Disease Control and Prevention, Atlanta, Georgia.

Susman, J. and Helseth, L. (1997). 'Reducing the Complications of Type 2 Diabetes: A patient centered approach', *American Family Physician*, 56, pp. 471–81.

The Diabetes Control and Complications Trial Research Group (1995), 'Lifetime Benefits and Costs of Intensive Therapy as Practical in the Diabetes Control and Complications Trial', *Journal of the American Medical Association*, 270, pp. 1409–18.

Appendix A: Healthcare Cost and Utilisation Project (HCUP)

HCUP-3
- Partnership among states, industry, and AHCPR
- All discharge data from 19 states (22 for 1997)
- Data available for 1988–96 (1997)
- Includes clinical, demographic, and resource use information
- Uniform database for cross-state study
- All-payer data; includes uninsured
- Captures all stays
- Reasonably current – gap closing
- Permits trend analysis
- Links to other databases
  - AHA hospital identifier —> AHA
  - Hospital county identifier —> ARF
- Permits state and sub-state focus
- Permits sub-population focus
  –Race/ethnicity
- Permits study of rare diseases or procedures
- Includes charge data
- Detailed, complete, electronic documentation
- Active public dissemination of data and tools
- Protects individuals and institutions confidentiality
- All community hospitals by AHA definition
  –All nonfederal short-term general and other specialty hospitals
- All discharges
- From 19 states (22 states)
  –Many formats to one format
  –Edit checks
- Over 56 per cent of US discharges
- Core data elements
  Hospital number, county
  Patient demographics
  Diagnoses and procedures
  Admission day of week, month
  Length of stay
  Admission/discharge status
  Expected payer
  Total charges
  Physician identifier (encrypted)
  Race

SECTION TWO
INEQUALITIES AND ACCESS

Chapter Six

Tackling Health Inequalities: Explaining the Outcomes of the Policy Process

Mark Exworthy, Martin Powell and Lee Berney

Introduction

This chapter explores the policy process relating to health inequalities (HI), an area of political interest and visibility in the late 1990s and early 2000s. Although HI have long existed (and since before the formation of the NHS in the UK), research has recently been demonstrating the causes and manifestations of such inequalities (Shaw et al., 1999). However, a lacuna in such research has been an examination of the way in which policies designed to tackle or reduce HI have been formulated and implemented. In a political climate which claims that 'what counts is what works' and unless the organisational and managerial aspects of the policy process are better understood, the success of the policies designed to tackle HI will inevitably be limited.

The chapter is divided into three main sections. The first deals with the current policy context in the UK as it applies to HI and inter-agency working. It employs the conceptual models of policy windows (Kingdon, 1995) and policy failure (Wolman, 1981). The second presents empirical evidence from three case studies collated between September and December 1999. It presents empirical evidence of the ways in which three health authorities have been translating national policies into local action and engaging with local agencies in implementing such policies. The third section concludes by making assessments of the value of the models used and the lessons that can be learnt from health authorities' strategies. As such, it also assesses the impact of current government policy.

Health Policy and Economics: Strategic Issues in Health Care Management, M. Tavakoli, H.T.O. Davies and M. Malek (eds), Ashgate Publishing Ltd, 2001.

Background

Health Inequalities Policy

The term 'health inequalities' refers to health status and health care. Health (status) inequalities are a persistent feature of all societies for which data are available. The pattern is one in which men and women in higher socioeconomic groups enjoy better health across longer lives than those in lower socioeconomic groups. The evidence for the UK suggests that these inequalities are widening (Shaw et al., 1999). *Health care* inequalities are also evident in terms of the distribution of expenditure, staffing, access and provision (among others) according to need; equity is thus often defined as equal access for equal need.

Health inequalities have been recorded since long before the NHS. However, it is recognised that the NHS has neglected its role in seeking equity (Klein, 1988) and that equity should be a more explicit priority in the future (Saltman, 1997). This is part of the Labour government's policy for the NHS. The government's strategy for the NHS (*The New NHS* in England and other documents for Scotland, Wales and Northern Ireland, published in 1997/98) emphasised the need to tackle HI. One of the key principles which underpinned Labour's proposals was the renewal of the NHS as a genuinely national services, characterised by 'fair access' to services, ending the 'unfairness', 'unacceptable variations' and 'two tierism' of the Conservative internal market (1991–97). Strategies to promote this equity agenda included national service frameworks, new institutions (e.g. National Institute for Clinical Excellence (NICE)) and health action zones (HAZs). HAZs will have certain flexibilities not enjoyed by other areas and reflect the emphasis placed upon inter-agency partnerships (see *Joined-up Government*, below).

The performance of NHS agencies would be measured according to an indicator of 'fair access'. The five other indicators used by the government are efficiency, health improvement, patient/carer experience, health outcomes, effective delivery of appropriate health care.

The policy thrust was enhanced by the 1998 NHS planning document *Modernising Health and Social Services* which identified a shared role for the NHS and local government in reducing HI. This priorities and planning guidance was more extensive than previous documents since it covered a three year period and established a policy direction which aimed to tackle causes of ill health and to encourage greater service flexibility. The document allocated responsibility to the NHS and local authorities. NHS has lead responsibility in the following areas:

- waiting list reduction;
- development of primary and community services;
- health improvement initiatives (particularly for heart disease); and
- improvements in the quality, effectiveness and speed of access to services.

The NHS and local authorities would share responsibility for:

- reducing HI by improving the health of the worst off at a faster rate than the rest of the population; and
- improving the mental health of the population.

The public health White Paper *Saving Lives: Our healthier nation* (1999) recognised the social and environmental determinants of health and the need to reduce HI. (It is seen as an update of the 1992 health strategy for England, 'The Health of the Nation'). Consistent with earlier documents, it recognises the social and environmental determinants of health and the need to tackle HI. The strategy included targets for four key areas: cancer, coronary heart disease and stroke, accidents and mental health. However, it did not include targets for reducing HI; this was left to local agencies.

Evidence for these policies was further supported by the Acheson inquiry into health inequalities (known as the Acheson Report) (1998). Commissioned soon after the election of the Labour government, the inquiry collected evidence about the causes and extent of HI. It took evidence across a number of areas such as taxation, food, transport, employment, child care as well as health care. Like the Black Report (1980) which preceded it, the Acheson Report highlighted many of the factors which influence health such as poverty and unemployment, most of which lie outside the scope of the NHS. The inquiry produced 39 recommendations but did not prioritise or cost them.

Locally, many agencies have tried to tackle HI but, for most of the time since the Black Report, the political climate has been hostile or unsympathetic to such initiatives. Nevertheless, many agencies (such as health and local authorities) have undertaken local equity audits to assess the impact upon equity of particular policies.

Joined-up Government

The government's strategy for HI also conforms to *joined-up government*, their approach to greater interdepartmental and inter-agency working. Such emphasis on collaboration and partnership is also indicative of Labour's third way (Powell, 1999). Joined-up government reflects the understanding that individual agencies, by themselves, are not able to solve or ameliorate complex problems. The causes of HI, for example, are thought to lie mainly outside the remit of the health service alone. Hence, collaboration and partnerships, termed horizontal government (Peters, 1998), with others are essential in order to meet the goals set in policy documents.

The policy emphasis on partnership – the collaborative discourse (Clarence and Painter, 1998) – is reinforced by the statutory duty to collaborate in order to tackle the causes of HI. The Health Improvement Programme (HImP) in each area will provide a strategic framework for such collaboration. Also, as part of the modernisation programme, documents such as *Partnerships in Action* (whose proposals were later incorporated in the 1999 Health Act) are designed to tackling deep-rooted and complex problems and yet partnerships and collaboration have been problematic in the past. *Partnerships in Action* proposed three main changes to inter-agency working:

- pooled budgets;
- lead commissioners; and
- integrated providers.

Lack of trust and openness, difficulties in resolving funding concerns and differing accountabilities between agencies (especially NHS and local authorities) have often hampered previous attempts at inter-agency collaboration (Hudson et al., 1999; Callaghan et al., 2000). However, shared strategies, shared goals and good relationships have fostered such collaborations. The balance between fostering and hindering factors is specific to local contexts. It is therefore important to understand the character of local (policy) networks and their governance arrangements in explaining local partnership working.

Theoretical Perspectives

Given the priority placed on tackling HI by central government and particularly the way in which this priority has precipitated action by local agencies, it is important to assess the intergovernmental relations (Rhodes, 1999). The transmission of policy from the centre to the periphery – the vertical dimension – may involve a readjustment and reinterpretation of priorities. This 'implementation gap' may affect the outcome of policy. Moreover, the emphasis on joined-up approaches and local governance means that there are significant local-local relations across agencies – the horizontal dimension. Two theoretical perspectives are useful to explaining the interaction between the vertical and horizontal dimensions. These are the models and frameworks proposed by Kingdon (1995) and Wolman (1981).

Kingdon (1995) employs the concept of 'policy windows' to explore the ways in which policy change and implementation occurs (windows equate to opportunities). He argues that such windows open (and close) by the coupling (or de-coupling) of three separate streams: problems, politics and policies. Conditions only become defined or recognised as 'problems' when they come to the attention of policy-makers through the publication of indicators, key events or feedback from current policies. The politics stream consists of interest group lobbying, elections, political manifestos and agendas. These factors are influenced by bargaining, consensus building, coalitions and compromises. Policies include a variety of proposals and solutions advanced by interest groups and policy makers. Kingdon argues that proposals float in the 'primeval soup', waiting to be selected. However, policies must meet criteria including technical feasibility, congruence with dominant values acceptability and anticipation of future constraints.

The three streams may remain separate until coupled by chance, the cycle of politics (such as elections) and organisations (such as staff turnover) or by the actions of a policy entrepreneur. These individuals act as key facilitating agents in the coupling process and thus help to open policy windows. They invest their resources to advance a particular cause or bring issues to the attention of others.

Wolman's model of 'policy failure' consists of ten stages which are thought to affect the likelihood of a 'successful' policy (Exworthy and Powell, 2000). Wolman divides the sections into policy formulation and policy implementation. Although there is much debate as to whether such a distinction is (or ever was) valid (e.g. Hill, 1997), it has some heuristic value in this context since policy formulated by central government may be in distinction to its implementation locally. This distinction also recognises the reformulation of policy locally. Wolman's sections are:

- policy formulation
  - problem conceptualisation
  - theory evaluation and selection
  - specification of objectives
  - programme design
  - programme structure.

- policy implementation
  - resource adequacy
  - management and control structure
  - bureaucratic rules and regulation
  - political effectiveness
  - feedback and evaluation.

Wolman poses a series of questions for each section. He does not argue that all ten sections need to be in place or sufficiently appropriate for policy to be 'successful'. He does, however, indicate points where a policy may 'fail.' Indeed Wolman argues that the model should be applied and adapted according to specific policy contexts. It is in this spirit that the model is applied here.

Kingdon looks at how issues get onto the agenda and Wolman looks at the implementation once on the agenda. As such, the models are complementary although inevitably there are some areas of overlap.

Empirical Evidence

Empirical evidence is drawn from three contrasting case studies which were chosen to highlight different policy processes to tackle HI. Each case study was based upon a single health authority (HA) in a rural, an urban and a mixed urban/suburban area. Each centred on the partnership network surrounding the HA. Forty-five semi-structured taped interviews were held with individuals in health authorities, NHS trusts, primary care groups, local authorities (LAs) and voluntary sector. Analysis of interview transcripts (using Nud*ist software) sought to sought identify themes across sectors, interest groups (Alford, 1975) and case study areas. Through triangulation of data sources, two themes became prominent in applying Kingdon's and Wolman's models. They are discussed here: policy imperatives, barriers and facilitators of implementation.

Policy Imperatives

Policy imperatives denote the strength of the policies emanating from central government and their transmission to the local levels – the vertical dimension. Hence, the coupling of the policy and politics stream determines the extent to which HI as accepted as a legitimate activity for local agencies. These imperatives were often termed the 'must-do's', the balance of which was tipped, according to interviewees, towards centralisation. A tension existed in the current imperatives between continuity and discontinuity with earlier policies. Discontinuity was manifest in the policy emphasis placed upon health inequalities which was attributed directly to the 1997 election of the Labour government. The emphasis involved an 'acceptance' of HI and a focus upon 'social inclusion' and inter-agency partnerships. The emphasis was evident, according to interviewees, in central government policy documents and statements. For example, a LA manager was supportive of national policy.

> I think it is a really positive statement of central government health policy; they recognise and state that health inequalities exist. That makes a refreshing change. And the fact that the central planks of the public health and the general health policy is to reduce those inequalities.

Whilst most welcomed this shift (probably because these individuals were associated with local HI policy, i.e. policy entrepreneurs), many were critical that this emphasis had not permeated much further than the Department of Health. Expectations had been raised by the new government but many in HAs and LAs were expressing disappointment that the government had either not done enough or gone further in tackling inequalities. Most of this criticism was directed towards the pace and direction of central government policy rather than the local policy process. This is exemplified by a HA director:

> Despite the fact that they have got a cabinet committee and so on, again they still haven't cracked that, that they can get these documents like 'our healthier nation' signed off by 12 ministers but, in terms of that flowing down at the DETR or the Home Office silos, it is just not happening yet.

These concerns bridge policy discontinuity and continuity. The (new) policy emphasis was being negated by the structural aspects of NHS and LA organisation which, in some ways, remain untouched. As the above quote illustrates, 'joined-up government' remained an aspiration, according to those at the local level. Also, the sheer number of imperatives was 'overwhelming' locally, many of which took precedence over HI. Imperatives such as waiting lists dominated local policy agendas and management time. This was most clearly evident in the way in which progress in tackling HI was not included as a measure of individual or organisational performance. One consequence was that, if individual managers failed to take action on tackling HI, then they would not 'lose their job'.

> My chief executive's head is not going to roll if we don't tackle health inequalities per se (HA director).

> I won't get that little tap on the shoulder if we don't make quite so much progress on our tackling of inequalities because we can always do that next year. That's the theory. Now I happen to think that is a strange set of priorities (HA chair).

Although HI were included in assessment criteria (such as 'fair access'), organisations were principally measured according to core imperatives (such as reduction of waiting lists). Reducing HI was not specifically one of these. Interviewees claimed that HI were not performance managed in the same way or to the same extent as other imperatives.

This approach accorded a lower priority to HI which was evident in performance management. Whilst 'hard' targets were related to the (apparently) 'precise' figures that were generated by waiting lists and financial statements, 'soft' targets were associated with HI policy because performance management was less able to define the association between policy and its outcome. Hence, performance management assessed managers according to 'process' factors such as the state of collaborative ventures which were *assumed* to reduce HI, albeit in the long term (Exworthy and Berney, 2000).

The greater emphasis placed on waiting lists, emergency pressures and financial balance, for example, compared to HI had a number of consequences which affected the 'policy stream' – that is, the formation and goals of policies. For example, not only did imperatives shape the internal organisational structure but it also meant that the main priorities took most of the management time and money.

> ... but at the end of the day, what do we spend 99.9 per cent of our management time on – the must be dones in terms of waiting lists ... and financial equilibrium (HA director).

As a result, few (human or financial) resources were devoted to tackling HI and so was left to the personal enthusiasm. It was thus argued that HI slipped down the list of priorities. It became a rhetorical priority, not backed by effective incentives. Inter-agency partnership working was the one imperative which coincided closely with HI but this was still superseded by other imperatives.

The tension between continuity and discontinuity in policy since 1997 was summarised by a HA manager.

> I certainly believe that the government is supporting the drive to address health inequalities, to eliminating gaps but I do not believe that they have done enough.

Barriers and Facilitators to Implementation

In assessing the likelihood of translating local policy towards HI into action, it is important to consider those factors fostering implementation and those hindering it. The Wolman model is useful in doing so. It is not necessarily possible to reach a conclusion about which Wolman stage will prevail since some might be significant and others will be prominent at different times and places. The local context is therefore crucial (Pettigrew et al., 1992).

Whilst most of the factors seen by interviewees as fostering implementation concerned social factors (such as willingness and vision), many of their hindering factors related mainly to material issues (such as resources and imperatives). Triangulation of data sources across case study areas, sectors and professions suggest that the fostering factors can be summarised into eight categories:

- permissive environment towards HI from government;
- partnership working seen as worthwhile;
- spirit of willingness to tackle HI;
- enthusiastic individual driving the local policy process;
- imaginative use of existing financial resources;
- ownership and inclusion in the policy process;
- clear strategic vision; and
- openness and transparency.

Hindering factors also fell into eight categories:

- resources;
- differing sets of local priorities;
- maintenance of enthusiasm among agencies;
- lack of clarity about how best to tackle HI;
- lack of data on extent of local HI;
- policy 'overload';
- short timescales; and
- lack of ownership of HI as an issue.

Although these respective sets of factors cover many of the issues facing HA and LA, three themes seem especially relevant in ascertaining the outcomes of the policy process in terms of the two models adopted. The themes are: policy context, organisational ownership, and individual enthusiasm. It should be noted that, at the time of writing, policy outcomes have not yet been realised and so the themes reflect the tension between fostering and hindering factors which must be resolved.

Policy context Through its statements and proposals, the government has created a 'permissive environment' in which HI are not only recognised but seen as legitimate. This signal from central government was especially important for local policy-makers. Unlike previous administrations, central government gave HI a status which indicated that time and effort could be spent on it, especially in terms of working with other agencies.

> We are allowed to use the word 'inequality' and we are encouraged to work with our partner organisations ... and there is a greater willingness to accept that variations in health are due to social determinants rather than health service actions. ... I think at the moment it is a permissive environment. We are not told that anything is off-limits. I think that our regional office, which is who we account to, are being very flexible in what they are allowing us to do (HA Director of Public Health).

For those who had been working on local HI initiatives, this shift was welcome. Under the banner of social exclusion/inclusion, HI was, to varying extents, applicable across all local agencies. Despite the support for the overall direction of government policy, serious concerns were raised about the continual process of reorganisation or further anticipated reforms. For example, many of those interviewed were also involved in the implementation of other health care reforms such as the commissioning framework, Primary Care Groups and the preparation for Primary Care Trusts. Combined with broad areas of policy such as clinical effectiveness/evidence-based medicine, many spoke of a 'policy overload'. The programme design and structure, according to Wolman, might thus have an adverse effect upon implementation. HI was seen as a competing priority for their time and, as shown earlier, the result was a downgrading of HI compared to other more pressing priorities:

> Their immediate short term priority has been that most of them [PCGs] have been overspending on prescribing and that's where they've got to focus their effort into because that's what they have to do *now*, whereas doing something with health and inequalities is always going to lose out if it's competing with that sort of issue (PCG Chief Executive).

> You just haven't been able to get it [i.e. inequalities] on the agenda because there have been these other major pressures that have to be resolved, a wealth of 'must be dones' (HA Director of Public Health).

Local policy makers argued that the few resources at their disposal meant that the policy context could not always be implemented as intended. Financial resources were not only scarce but devoted to other pressing priorities (see *Policy Imperatives*, above). Lack of resources was the most frequently cited factor hindering implementation and probably the most significant. It also accords most closely with Wolman's 'resource adequacy' category.

Policy inclusion and ownership Across different agencies, inter-agency partnerships were seen as a 'good thing' in themselves and which were seen as essential in tackling HI. The support that interviewees gave to both the principles of partnership working and the ends, to which they were currently being put (i.e. tackling HI), it was claimed, fostered local implementation.

> [People] are trying to work together and that is only a good thing. And in the past it was so strictly compartmentalised, you know, the acute trust worked separately, community group, GPs ... You would hear separate stories wherever you went, no one was talking to each other. At least now you feel there is a sense of people beginning to talk to each other (CHC Chief Officer).

This multi-agency consensus that HI were an important area of local action helped to foster a reasonably broad consensus and ownership of the 'problem'. A consistent conceptualisation of the (HI) problem is vital, according to Wolman and Kingdon. Moreover, in each case study area, many statutory agency respondents claimed an inclusive approach was being adopted.

> But the process we have adopted, not just on the HImP, on other things as well, is to be as inclusive as possible. We would produce internally an early draft which we would discuss, we would certainly discuss it informally with a number of our partners long before it went out to formal consultation (NHS chair).

However, this inclusiveness was contested by representatives of voluntary sector or those working closely with patients and communities.

> I think there is still a tendency for things to be done in a rather top-down way, and part of that is a central government pace, there's been a lot of change and not a lot of time to disseminate that. Part of it is that there are a lot of different

agencies who are involved, but part of it is also the issue of power; at a very real level we don't in the voluntary sector have a say in the kinds of money there is in the NHS or the council, nothing like it (Voluntary Sector Worker).

Fostering factors were being undermined by several hindering issues which were contrary to the inclusionary approach. For example, the agencies which were supposed to be collaborating in partnership have long histories of independence and so were sometimes resistant to agendas set by others. This had a practical manifestation in terms of their differing priorities, based in part on the 'management and control structure' required to meet the needs of their clients. Hence, a HA priority on addressing HI in terms of coronary heart disease, for example, had little immediate relevance to, say, a leisure services department in a LA. This was partly overcome by addressing specific aspects of CHD which made more relevance to such a LA department (such as the numbers taking regular exercise). However, a subsequent barrier emerged which was a lack of clarity about the issue under scrutiny and how best to tackle the issues. This was further compounded by a lack of appropriate data (which hampered 'feedback and evaluation'). These data were criticised for being out of data, being insufficient for aiding policy or covering different populations.

Enthusiasm Many interviewed were enthusiastic and willing participants in local strategies to tackle HI. This enthusiasm was not just found among those 'leading' the local HI and partnership strategies in different agencies (i.e. policy entrepreneurs) but also among those who were less closely associated with the policy process. Enthusiastic 'leaders' were found in each of the three case studies and had a key role in ensuring that HI got onto agencies' agendas and galvanising support for HI initiatives.

> Although I've made criticisms about it, actually it is quite a good partnership. It has a good feel and it has a lot of committed and willing individuals in it who I think will do their best to make sure that it does happen (LA Manager).

On their own, these policy entrepreneurs were probably insufficient to ensure effective implementation. Hence, it was fortunate that this enthusiasm was evident across agencies and other individuals.

> I mean the positive side is all agencies including both local authorities are totally committed to tackling inequalities in health (LA Manager).

Given the study's methodology, it was not possible to confirm interviewees' statements that enthusiasm had permeated the respective organisations. However, problems were anticipated in terms of maintaining this 'initial' enthusiasm for tackling HI. Unless progress could be shown in reducing local HI, it was feared that many individuals and agencies would not be so committed to strategies and initiatives in the long term. Thus sustaining interest in and commitment to the local process was seen as problematic. This will be a major issue as local programmes move into their second and subsequent years.

> People get very de-motivated, fed-up, if they think it is all, you know, people are always talking about talking shops and so they think this is just a lot of hot air and nothing happens (PCG Chair).

This question of interest and ownership was further complicated by the 'tight' timescales under which agencies were working. Tackling HI were seen as a long term initiative which would not always show progress in the time frame within which agencies were performance managed.

> My concern has been the government's push on wanting us to do it tomorrow, that what I would like to see is a commitment to the 10 years, that we have a process of really developing an organisational base (LA manager).

Discussion and Conclusions

Even though this study captured the policy process 30 months into the Labour government's term of office and some six months since the implementation of Primary Care Groups and associated structures, it does permit a preliminary assessment of the HI policy process. The application of the two conceptual models to these data enables a more detailed explanation of the outcomes of the policy process. It also highlights a number of trade-offs that are already evident but may become more acute over time.

Neither conceptual model is sufficient to account fully for outcomes in the policy process. However, they have been adapted to incorporate the vertical and horizontal dimensions. Kingdon's models of policy windows also has clear relevance to the local policy process. HI as a central government imperative was debatable because, although it was included in performance management processes, many respondents in the case studies argued that it was a marginal issue given the pressing concerns of waiting lists and financial balance. HI were claimed as a 'problem' by government but this was not supported by political and policy mechanisms. Though a significant 'condition' in each area, it had not yet become a *'problem'* across all agencies and departments sufficient to reduce HI (Kingdon, 1995). The local organisational *politics* meant that central government's imperatives shaped local policy process. These imperatives did not allow space for HI such that they became the province of local enthusiasts. Nevertheless, these individuals – policy entrepreneurs – were playing a key role in promoting, facilitating and organising inter-agency partnerships to address HI. They had managed to 'couple' the problem with 'politics'. However, the *'policies'* were still developing but early signs suggested a reasonable degree of ownership and inclusion. It is debatable whether such factors will persist over the whole length of time need to implement fully these HI policies. The policies being proposed related primarily to inter-agency partnerships since it was widely recognised that the determinants of HI lay outside the remit of health services alone. It is, as yet, unknown whether these policies will work. The government claims that what counts is what works but it is still unclear what works in specific contexts for particular populations. Thus, in short, the 'policy window' for HI was ajar but it was uncertain whether all streams had been coupled and hence whether this was sufficient to produce desired policy outcomes.

Wolman's (1981) model of policy failure illustrates the potential pitfalls for implementing HI policy. Certainly each of the five 'implementation' stages poses significant dilemmas for local policy makers. The 'adequacy of resources' was questioned by respondents and had a strong influence on the policy process. This was clearly applicable to financial resources in terms of the management capacity and funding for new initiatives. However, the adequacy of resources is a function to the definition of the problem being addressed by the policy. A subtle process whereby the scale of the problem was brought into line with available resources may have been taking place. This would illustrate the interconnectedness of Wolman's categories. The bureaucratic rules and regulation, as manifest through performance management, profoundly affected the local organisational structures and the management time available to address HI. Even initiatives to 'join-up' policies locally had to contend against the overarching accountability and governance arrangements. This was especially evident in LAs who tried to pull together health (and HI) issues across departments. The quasi-independent organisations in the NHS (such as NHS Trusts) made this 'political effectiveness' less apparent.

A number of trade-offs emerged from considering the local process which pose dilemmas for policy makers. The trade-offs may compromise their objectives to tackle HI. So they may determine whether the policy window remains open or whether policy failure or success occurs. A central trade-off was that between leadership (by policy entrepreneurs) and partnership working. Whilst the enthusiasm of individuals galvanised support and ensured HI did not slip off the local agenda, it did have the effect of excluding some individuals and agencies. Efforts were apparent to spread the ownership away from the 'leaders' and for maintaining support for HI. Ownership also raises a wider dilemma about HI policy among agencies whose primary purpose does not encompass 'health'. This strikes at the heart of governance issue in the UK public sector (Rhodes, 1999) since the number of agencies with a potential role in tackling HI was enormous but few had any authority over another organisation. Bargaining, compromise and persuasion was needed to ensure that HI policy was even on the agenda, let alone, making significant efforts towards its amelioration. It also means that the outcomes of the policy process will be contingent upon the character of local policy networks and especially policy entrepreneurs. These individuals still had to persuade those in LAs and some NHS Trusts that HI was an important 'problem'. Translating HI as a problem into a meaningful issues for, say, a housing department or a hospital was especially difficult. The national imperatives, emphasising financial balance, pointed towards a trade-off a more strategic level, viz. between equity, effectiveness and efficiency. Closure of a rural hospital, for example, may be on effectiveness and efficiency grounds but has a negative effect on equitable access. Interviewees indicated that the resolution of these trade-offs were invariably in favour of efficiency. The rewards and sanctions of individuals and organisations favoured efficiency (rather than equity and, to a lesser extent, effectiveness).

In short, the government's emphasis upon HI and partnership working was widely supported at the local level. This augured well for the 'success' of national and local policies. However, despite local enthusiasm, issues of ownership, inter-agency collaboration and competing imperatives (among others) suggest that local policy outcomes are unlikely to be easily generated. This study did not seek to identify what counted as 'good' practice or to ascertain what worked in reducing HI because it employed conceptual models to study the policy process. The combination of conceptual approaches and empirical evidence suggests that wider organisational and policy issues, let alone the embedded socioeconomic aspects, pose serious barriers to policy implementation.

Acknowledgements

The research upon which this chapter is based is funded by the Economic and Social Research Council under the Health Variations Programme (phase 2) (award ref. no. L128251039). We are grateful for their support.

References

Acheson, D. (Chair) (1998), *Independent Inquiry into Inequalities in Health*, The Stationery Office, London.
Alford, R. (1975), *Health Care Politics: Ideological and interest group barriers to reform*, University of Chicago Press, Chicago.
Black, D. (Chair) (1980), *Inequalities in health*, Penguin, London.
Callaghan, G., Exworthy, M., Hudson, B. and Peckham, S. (2000), 'Prospects for Collaboration in Primary Care: Relationships between social services and the new PCGs', *Journal of Inter-Professional Care*, 14 (1), pp. 19–26.
Clarence, E. and Painter, C. (1998), 'Public Services under New Labour: Collaborative discourses and local networking', *Public Policy and Administration*, 13 (3), pp. 8–22.
Department of Health (1992), *The Health of the Nation*, HMSO, London.
Department of Health (1997), *The New NHS: Modern, dependable*, The Stationery Office, London.
Department of Health (1998a), *Partnerships in Action*, The Stationery Office, London.
Department of Health (1998b), *Saving Lives: Our healthier nation*, The Stationery Office, London.
Exworthy, M. and Powell, M. (2000), 'Variations of a Theme: New Labour, health inequalities and policy failure', in A. Hann (ed.), *Analysing Health Policy*, Ashgate, Aldershot.
Exworthy, M. and Berney, L. (2000), 'What Counts and What Works? Evaluating policies to tackle health inequalities', paper presented to the ESRC seminar series on New Labour (no. 5), Cardiff Business School, September.
Hill, M. (1997), 'Implementation Theory: Yesterday's issue?', *Policy and Politics*, 25 (4), pp. 375–85.
Hudson, B., Exworthy, M., Peckham, S. and Callaghan, G. (1999), *Locality Partnerships: The early PCG experience*, Nuffield Institute for Health, Leeds University.
Kingdon, J.W. (1995), *Agendas, alternatives and public policy* (2nd edn), HarperCollins, New York.
Klein, R. (1988), 'Acceptable Inequalities' in D. Green (ed.), *Acceptable Inequalities*, IEA, London, pp. 3–20.
Peters, B.G. (1998), 'Managing Horizontal Government: The politics of coordination', *Public Administration*, 76 (2), pp. 295–311.
Pettigrew, A. et al. (1992), *Shaping Strategic Change*, Sage, London.
Powell, M. (1999), 'New Labour and the Third Way in the British NHS', *International Journal of Health Services*, 29 (2), pp. 353–70.
Rhodes, R. (1999), *Understanding Governance*, Open University Press, Buckingham.
Saltman, R. (1997), 'Equity and Distributive Justice in European Health Care Reform', *International Journal of Health Services*, 27(3), pp. 443–53.

Secretary of State for Northern Ireland (1998), *Fit for the Future: A consultation document on the government's proposals for the future of health and personal social services in Northern Ireland*, The Stationery Office, Belfast.

Secretary of State for Scotland (1997), *Desiged to Care: Renewing the National Health Service in Scotland*, Cmd. 3811, The Stationery Office, Edinburgh.

Secretary of State for Wales (1998), *NHS Wales: Putting patients first*, Cmd. 3841, The Stationery Office, Cardiff.

Shaw, M., Dorling, D., Gordon, D. and Davey-Smith, G. (1999), *The Widening Gap*, Policy Press, Bristol.

Wolman, H. (1981), 'The Determinants of Program Success and Failure', *Journal of Public Policy*, 1 (4), pp. 433–64.

Chapter Seven

Accessibility and Availability of Health Services: Has the Gap between the South and the Other Areas of Israel Diminished since Implementation of the National Health Insurance Law?

Nurit Nirel, Dina Pilpel, Bruce Rosen, Irit Zmora, Miriam Greenstein and Sima Zalcberg

Introduction

Inequity in the allocation and provision of health services is a subject that many health care systems in the modern world are concerned with. In Israel, this subject has been publicly discussed in regard to the impact of the National Health Insurance Law on increasing equity in health service provision between the south of the country and other regions.

The southern region is the largest geographic area of Israel, but the least densely populated. As of 1996, the region had 785,400 residents – 13.6 per cent of Israel's population – most of whom lived in medium-size cities. Relative to the centre of the country, the southern region has a high proportion of rural settlements. The region's population is relatively young, and its fertility rate is high. The area surrounding Beersheva, the region's largest city, is home to a large percentage of Bedouin Arabs – even though the total percentage of Arab residents of the region (15 per cent) is below the national average (20 per cent) (Central Bureau of Statistics, 1998). The economic status of the region's population is relatively low. An indication of this is the large percentage of work seekers (10 per cent, compared to the national average of 5 per cent), the large percentage of people who receive unemployment revenue (4.5 per cent, compared to the national average of 2.3 per cent), and the larger

---

Health Policy and Economics: Strategic Issues in Health Care Management, M. Tavakoli, H.T.O. Davies and M. Malek (eds), Ashgate Publishing Ltd, 2001.

proportion of people who earn less than minimum wage (42 per cent, compared to the national average of 38 per cent [data are for 1995] – Central Bureau of Statistics, 1997). Not surprisingly, the Central Bureau of Statistics places most of the region's towns and villages in the lower socioeconomic percentiles (Central Bureau of Statistics, 1997 and 1998).

It is important to note, however, that there are significant differences in income level among towns in the south. In 1995, the average per capita income in development towns (where the majority of the south's population is concentrated) was much lower than the national average: between NIS 500 and NIS 600 in two towns, and less than NIS 1,000 in the remainder, compared to a national average of NIS 1,011. In the three main cities, the average per capita income is similar to the national average, while in three small settlements (with concentrations of higher income earners), the average per capita income is greater than NIS 2,000. Data on Arab towns indicate extremely low economic status: the average per capita income is only NIS 200–300, and the unemployment rate is high (9–12 per cent) (Central Bureau of Statistics, 1997).

For many years, experts and health system activists in the south have claimed that insufficient resources are allocated to the south and that, consequently, the residents of the area receive a lower level of health services than do residents of other parts of Israel. Indeed, recently-published studies have found gaps between the national average and the south in the accessibility of services, the use of services, and other aspects of health, such as mortality rates (Chernichovsky et al., 1996; Tulchinski and Ginsberg, 1996; Central Bureau of Statistics, 1998; Weitzman et al., 1997).

The National Health Insurance Law, which was implemented in January 1995, created the possibility of increasing equity in the allocation of health services and improving the levels of service in the south and other peripheral areas. By mandating universal health insurance coverage, the law extended sick fund membership to population groups that were not insured prior to the law. Moreover, the law introduced 'capitation financing', whereby each sick fund's revenues are determined by the number of members and their age mix, but not their incomes. This is in contrast to the situation prior to the law, when sick funds whose members earned higher incomes received greater premium revenues. Thus, the introduction of capitation financing reduced the incentive to focus marketing efforts on population groups with higher incomes; this made the south, with its lower socioeconomic population, more attractive to the sick funds than it had been in the past. The ability to transfer among sick funds, mandated by the law, increased freedom of choice for consumers. This increase in freedom of choice, along with the change in sick fund incentives mentioned above, had the potential to lead to greater competition among sick funds. This, in turn, could lead to expansion of services and improvement in quality. Nevertheless, because the south is a peripheral region, experts and policy makers have expressed doubts as to whether the incentives offered by the capitation formula will succeed in raising the level of health services in the south to the national standard.

Our principal study question was whether gaps between the south and the rest of Israel in the allocation of resources and the accessibility of health services had diminished since implementation of the National Health Insurance Law.

The goals of our study were as follows:

1 to increase the information about gaps between the southern region and the centre of the country in the allocation of resources and the accessibility of health services prior to implementation of the National Health Insurance Law;
2 to discern changes in the sick funds' goals and provision of services in the south following implementation of the law;
3 to determine whether inequities in the availability and accessibility of health services in the south, diminished since implementation of the law.

Equity in the Health System: A Review of the Literature

Equity in the field of health may be defined as equivalent health status among variant population groups, fair allocation of services, and equal availability and accessibility of services. It is possible, then, to examine equity in this field from various perspectives: that of health status, that of the use of health services, and that of the availability and accessibility of services (Mooney, 1994). All of these concern what Wagstaff and Van Doorslaer (1992), call the 'horizontal equity of health services', or equal care for individuals with differing health needs. It is also possible to examine equity in financing (so-called 'vertical equity'), as reflected in the presence or absence of obstacles to payment for services.

Inequity in the health system due to geographic disparity is not unique to Israel. A broad study of the National Health System in the United Kingdom revealed a great deal of variance in health status and service accessibility among regions, despite the system's aim of providing equal health services for equivalent needs (Mooney and McGuire, 1987; Mohan, 1987; Illsley and Le Grand, 1993). Other researchers have examined inequity in the context of gaps between central and peripheral areas in the allocation of hospital beds, and in the supply of physicians, nurses and paramedical staff, as peripheral areas typically have a low physician–population ratio (Mohan, 1987; Bare et al., 1998; Politzer et al., 1998). In Israel, Chernichovsky and Shirom (1996) noted an inverse correlation between the accessibility of services, measured by the presence of medical manpower, and health needs, measured by weighted mortality rates for different areas of Israel.

The possibility of reducing inter-geographic inequity by allocating resources to regions according to need has been discussed at great length by various committees in the United Kingdom (Mays and Bevan, 1987). Age, weighted mortality rates, and measures that reflect gaps in socioeconomic levels among regions have been used in the allocation of resources by region. Additional studies examining formulas for the regional allocation of resources have also used parameters such as the proportion of the population of working age (or age 75 and over), and population density (Carr-Hill et al., 1994; Sheldon et al., 1994; RAWP, 1988), based on the assumption that inequity in health status is partly due to factors that are not directly tied to the system of services. Studies examining differences in health status, primarily as measured by morbidity and mortality rates, found a correlation between health status and socioeconomic level (primarily education and income) (Culyer, 1976; Carstair and Morris, 1989; Sihvonen et al., 1998). Studies conducted in Israel found a correlation between low socioeconomic status and high mortality rates (Barrell et al., 1988; Lusky et al., 1994; Anson, 1988).

In summary, the literature indicates that inequity in the field of health can result from factors that are not related solely to health services. Nevertheless, in Israel as elsewhere, an attempt has been made to reduce inequity among regions by reforming the health system. This study examines in depth the influence of the National Health Insurance Law on equity among regions of Israel in the availability and accessibility of services.

Study Method

We performed secondary analysis of data from several national sources. We also conducted open interviews with representatives of Israel's four sick funds.

Following we compare the southern and northern regions, and these two peripheral regions with the remainder of Israel (hereafter, the centre of the country). Data from the northern region provide an example of another peripheral area; however, we are primarily concerned with differences between the southern region (referred to hereafter as the south) and the centre of the country.

Sources of Data

1 Annual manpower surveys, conducted by the Central Bureau of Statistics: These surveys cover all permanent residents of Israel age 15 and over, or about 22,000 households annually. From these surveys and from data on population size we derived information on the proportion of physicians and nurses per capita, medical manpower work hours per thousand population, and average work hours of physicians and nurses. The number of physicians and nurses who are sampled each year is small, relative to the number of physicians and nurses employed. Published manpower surveys note that sampling errors are liable to be significant, as are errors arising from non-response, incorrect response, and biased analysis. In order to reduce the probability of such errors and increase the sample size, we used data from these surveys on employed health manpower in averages for groups of years, rather than for individual years. It should be noted that the numbers presented in this article were 'inflated' to suit the sample to the population by the Central Bureau of Statistics, based on their methods, before the data came into our hands.
2 Surveys of primary care physicians: data on primary care physicians come from two mail surveys conducted at different times on different samples of physicians. The first of these was conducted in 1993 (Gross et al., 1994). Of a sample of 872 physicians, 677 (77.6 per cent) were interviewed. The second survey was conducted in 1997 (Tabenkin et al., 1999). Of the 990 physicians sampled, 85.6 per cent were interviewed. These surveys provided demographic data, data on the employment conditions of physicians, and data on physician work load (weekly work hours, patient list size, and number of patients seen per day).
3 Hospital beds (1994, 1996 and 1997): data on hospital beds were taken from Ministry of Health publications concerning hospitals and outpatient clinics in Israel for the relevant years.
4 Survey of hospital patients – 1995: we used data from a mail survey of patients in 14 acute hospitals, which was conducted in the fall of 1995 (Yuval and Berg, 1997). The study population included all of the patients discharged during one month. In each hospital, 135 patients were sampled from each of two wards – internal medicine and surgery. A total of 3,780 patients from all of the hospitals were surveyed, with a response rate of 83

per cent. This survey gave us the patient's perspective on the length of time he waited to be hospitalised and on deferral of hospitalisation, his involvement in the choice of hospital, and his satisfaction with hospitalisation.
5 Population surveys for evaluation of the functioning of the health system, 1995 and 1997: two telephone surveys of a representative sample of the population were used. The first of these was conducted in 1995 (Berg et al., 1997), and the second in 1997 (Gross et al., 1998). The populations of both surveys included permanent residents of Israel over age 22. In 1995, 1,394 questionnaires were completed, giving a response rate of 85 per cent. In 1997, 1,205 questionnaires were completed, giving a response rate of 81 per cent. These surveys provided data on perceptions of the availability and accessibility of services, and satisfaction with the receipt of medical services.
6 Data on sick fund market shares: data on sick fund market shares up to 1993 were taken from health surveys of the Central Bureau of Statistics (see 4 above). For subsequent years, we used data from the main health file of the National Insurance Institute (Bendalk, 1998).

Statistical Analyses

For the secondary analysis of data, we unified only those files that examined identical variables – that is, the manpower surveys for the relevant years, the 1993 and 1997 surveys of primary care physicians, Ministry of Health data on hospital beds, and the 1995 and 1997 surveys of the population for the purpose of evaluating the health system. Data from other sources were analysed separately. Statistical analyses on individual years included cross-tabulated tables and examination of statistical significance using the χ^2 test, and examination of the independent influence of residence in the south on a series of dependent variables using logistic regression. Examination of the statistical significance of the cross-tabulated tables on the responses of the population at two points in time (in the survey conducted prior to and following implementation of the law) used the χ^2 test, which was appropriate because it used non-dependent population samples. In addition, we used an ANOVA analysis of variance to examine the statistical significance of means comparisons between two points in time. Gaps between the south and the centre of the country were measured by examining the ratios of the south to the centre of the country for different variables, and comparing these ratios from the periods prior to and following implementation of the law.

Limitations of the Data

The samples in the national surveys that we used for secondary analysis were not made according to geographic regions, and hence there was no over-sampling of the southern and northern regions. Since the proportion of respondents from these regions was similar to their proportion in the population, it was difficult, and at times impossible, to analyse unique groups in each region.

In addition, the study tools constructed for other surveys hampered our analysis of variables related to variance among regions, which were not included in those surveys. In addition, the definition of variables in discrete data bases differed; this also hindered analysis and comparison.

It must be remembered that some of the data bases were compiled from responses to questionnaires. In such cases, the responses reflect the subjective reports of respondents.

Findings

Medical and Nursing Manpower Inputs

Table 7.1 presents the data on employed medical and nursing manpower inputs, by region, for 1992–94 (prior to implementation of the National Health Insurance Law) and 1995–96 (following implementation of the law). It indicates that during the years examined, there was an increase in physicians per thousand population all over the county (due to the mass immigration of physicians from the former Soviet Union). However, during these years, the centre of the country had a clear advantage over the south (and over the north, which is also peripheral).

The ratio between the south and the centre of the country regarding medical and nursing manpower indicates that both prior to and following implementation of the law there were fewer employed physicians per population in the south (64 per cent of the physicians per population in the centre of the country), and the ratio of registered nurses per population declined from 0.74 per cent to 61 per cent of the registered nurses per thousand population in the centre of the country. In addition, there were fewer physician weekly work hours per population than in the centre of the country – about 68 per cent of the physician hours per population in the centre of the country before and after implementation of the law. Nurse weekly work hours per

Table 7.1 Physicians and registered nurses per 1,000 population, weekly physician and registered nurse work hours per 1,000 population and the average physician and registered nurse weekly work hours

	1992–94[1]	1995–96[2]
Employed physicians per 1,000 population		
South	2.06	2.62
Centre	3.22	4.07
North	1.67	2.19
National average	2.81	3.55
Ratio south: centre	0.64	0.64
Physicians' weekly work hours per 1,000 population		
South	98.51	132.66
Centre	147.57	194.20
North	74.93	105.23
National average	128.99	170.69
Ratio south: centre	0.67	0.68
Average weekly physician work hours		
South	47.75	50.69
Centre	45.84	47.72
North	45.00	48.04
National average	45.90	48.06
Ratio south: centre	1.04	1.06
Registered nurses per 1,000 population		
South	2.67	2.52
Centre	3.63	4.10
North	2.57	2.48
National average	3.33	3.61
Ratio south: centre	0.74	0.61
Registered nurses' weekly work hours per 1,000 population		
South	102.75	91.41
Centre	120.90	140.46
North	97.58	88.25
National average	114.63	124.90
Ratio south: centre	0.85	0.65
Average weekly registered nurse work hours		
South	38.51	36.20
Centre	33.20	34.22
North	37.89	35.60
National average	34.43	34.57
Ratio south: centre	1.16	1.05

Notes

1 Prior to implementation of the National Health Insurance Law.
2 Following implementation of the National Health Insurance Law.

Source: analyses of data from Central Bureau of Statistics' manpower surveys.

population declined from 85 per cent to 65 per cent of registered nurse hours, although the average hours they worked per week was higher in the south than in the centre of the country.

We found that in 1993 and in 1997, primary care physicians in the south and the north had greater work loads than did their colleagues in the centre of the country: more work hours, longer lists of patients, and greater average contact with patients per day (Table 7.2). Table 7.2 also indicates that between 1993 and 1997, there appears to have been a significant increase in the average length of the patient list per physician in the south (from 1,476 patients in 1993 to 1,529 patients in 1997). We found that the average number of patients seen per day increased in the south significantly: from 36 patients on average per day in 1993 to about 41 patients on average per day in 1997. In the centre of the country, in contrast, there was no change in the average number of patients per day.

Table 7.2 Primary care physicians: average weekly work hours, average length of patient list, and average number of patients seen per day, by region, in 1993[1] and 1997[2]

	Centre		North		South	
	1993	1997	1993	1997	1993	1997
Average weekly work hours	44.15	42.47	53.86*	39.43	51.86	46.57
Average length of patient list	1,376*	1,485	1,684	1,576	1,476*	1,529
Average number of patients per day	33.92	33.94	38.59	34.49	35.82*	40.44

Notes

1 Prior to implementation of the National Health Insurance Law.
2 Following implementation of the National Health Insurance Law.
* Difference between 1993 and 1997 for given regions is significant at a level of 0.05.

Source: analyses of data from studies on the role of the primary care physician (1993 and 1997).

Comparison between 1993 and 1997 reveals that there was a slight reduction in the gap between the south and the centre of the country in the average length of a primary care physician's patient list. However, the gap between the south and the centre of the country in the average number of patients seen per day increased: In 1993, the length of the average patient list in the south was 1.06 times greater than that in the centre of the country, while by 1997 it was 1.19 times greater than that in the centre of the country. In addition, in 1997 the average weekly hours worked by primary care physicians was still higher in the south than in the centre of the country – 1.10 times greater than the average weekly hours worked by a primary care physician in the centre of the country – despite the reduction in the gap between the two regions relative to 1993 (see Table 7.3).

Table 7.3   Primary care physicians: the ratio between the south and the centre of the country

	1993[1]	1997[2]
Average length of patient list	1.07	1.03
Average number of patients per day	1.06	1.19
Average weekly primary care physician work hours	1.17	1.10

Notes

1   Prior to implementation of the National Health Insurance Law.
2   Following implementation of the National Health Insurance Law.

Source: analyses of data from studies on the role of the primary care physician (1993 and 1997).

Hospital Bed Inputs

The proportion of hospital beds per thousand population in 1994, 1996 and 1997 was lower in the south, and even in the north, than the national average (see Table 7.4). When comparing the south to the centre of the country, we find that this is the case for all types of beds and wards. For example, in 1997, the proportion of beds per thousand population over age 45 in internal medicine wards was 2.3 in the south, compared to the national average of 3.0; the proportion of surgical beds per thousand population in the south was 0.55 compared to the national average of 0.88; and the proportion of maternity beds per thousand women of childbearing age (15–44) was 0.86 in the south, compared to the national average of 0.98. There are no rehabilitation beds at all in the south, and the proportion of beds for chronic illnesses per thousand population over age 65 is less than half of the national average (about 11 beds for chronic illness in the south, compared to the national average of 25.5 beds).

We also found that occupancy rates in selected wards were higher in the south than the national occupancy rates – particularly at Soroka Medical Centre

Table 7.4 Ratio of acute hospital beds (number of beds per thousand population), by region, in 1994, 1996 and 1997

	1994[1]	1996[2]	1997[2]
Nationwide	2.390	2.300	2.287
Jerusalem	3.270	3.080	2.994
North	1.680	1.580	1.587
Haifa	3.060	2.920	2.852
Centre	2.670	2.530	2.546
Tel Aviv	2.530	2.610	2.553
South	1.620	1.570	1.640

Notes

1 Prior to implementation of the National Health Insurance Law.
2 Following implementation of the National Health Insurance Law.

Source: Ministry of Health publications on hospitals and outpatient clinics for the relevant years.

Table 7.5 Occupancy rates in selected wards, national average, Barzilai Hospital and Soroka Hospital, 1996

Ward	National average	Barzilai Hospital*	Soroka Hospital**
Total acute wards	93.6	95.6	95.7
Internal medicine	101.3	114.3	117.8
Pediatrics	88.8	84.6	95.6
Maternity	101.3	100.5	118.4

Notes

*   Located in Ashqelon.
** Located in Beersheva.

Source: Ministry of Health, 1997.

in Beersheva, which is a multi-region hospital and the largest facility in the south (see Table 7.5). Table 7.6 indicates that between 1994 and 1997, the south maintained a smaller proportion of beds per population – only 72 per cent of the national average. Overall hospital occupancy rates remained higher in the south than the national average, at a ratio of 1.02.

Table 7.6 Ratio of the south to the national average in beds per thousand population and in hospital occupancy rates

	1994[1]	1997[2]
Beds per 1,000 population	0.68	0.72
Occupancy rates	1.03	1.02

Notes

1 Prior to implementation of the National Health Insurance Law.
2 Following implementation of the National Health Insurance Law.

Source: Ministry of Health publications on hospitals and outpatient clinics.

The Population's Perception of Accessibility and Availability of Services

A survey conducted in the autumn of 1995 (the third quarter of the first year of the law's implementation) among hospital patients, using multi-variate analysis (logistic regression), revealed that patients from the south were more likely to wait more than three months between setting a date for hospitalisation and actual admission than were patients from the centre of the country (see Table 7.7). This is most likely due to the small proportion of beds per population and the high hospital occupancy rates in the south. In addition, patients in the south and in the north were less likely than were patients from the centre of the country to be involved in the choice of hospital (see Table 7.8). This is due to the small number of hospitals in the south and to regional hospitalisation agreements, which obligate people living in a certain area to use a specific hospital. (We found evidence of this in the large percentage [36 per cent] of patients in the south who reported that their choice of hospital was a consequence of these regional hospitalisation agreements, compared to 20 per cent in the north and 15 per cent in the centre of the country who reported thus.) Furthermore, the proportion (62 per cent) of hospital patients from the south who expressed great or very great satisfaction with their hospital stay was lower than the proportion of those in the centre of the country (70 per cent) or the north (68 per cent) who reported thus.

In these multivariate analyses we used education and crowded housing conditions as measures of socioeconomic status. However, even when income was used as a measure of socioeconomic status (and even when used in a regression with education and crowding), socioeconomic status did not predict the likelihood of waiting more than three months for hospital admission or of

Table 7.7 Variables explaining the dependent variable, 'waited more than three months for hospital admission/surgery' (logistic regression)

Variable	B	Odds ratio	Basis
Age 60+	-0.22	0.80	Age 60–40
Age 18–39	-0.39	0.68	Age 60–40
Married	-0.12	0.89	Single/divorced/widowed
Not from North Africa/Middle East	-0.54*	0.58	From North Africa/Middle East
Arabic speaker	0.66	1.94	Hebrew speaker
Russian speaker	0.45	1.57	Hebrew speaker
Secondary education	-0.12	0.89	Elementary education or less
Crowded living conditions: fewer than seven people	0.52	1.68	More than 7 people
Surgical ward	1.23*	3.42	Internal medicine ward
Member of Leumit, Macabbi, or Meuhedet Sick Funds	-0.49	0.61	Member of Clalit Sick Fund
Woman	0.12	1.13	Man
North	0.05	1.06	Centre of the country
South	0.55*	1.73	Centre of the country
Has private medical insurance	0.31	1.37	No private medical insurance
Severe medical condition at admission to hospital	-0.10	0.91	Slight/moderate problem
Constant	2.96**		

Notes

* $p<0.05$
** $p<0.01$

Source: analyses of data from a patient survey, 1995.

being involved in the choice of hospital. In addition, the level of the coefficient for the variable 'south' did not change as a predictor of these variables. The regression analyses clearly indicate that delays in hospitalisation and inability to choose a hospital are a consequence of living in the south (where there is a lack of hospital beds), and not of socioeconomic status.

Analysis of two additional population surveys – from 1995 and 1997 – reveals that in 1997 there was an increase in the south, as in the rest of the country, in the proportion of patients who had a permanent physician, and in the length of time it took to reach the physician's office; reports on the convenience of service office hours were similar in the north and the centre of the country. We might have expected that implementation of the law, which

Table 7.8 Variables explaining the dependent variable, 'involved in choice of hospital' (logistic regression)

Variable	B	Odds ratio	Basis
Age 60+	-0.13	0.88	Age 60–40
Age 18–39	-0.02	0.98	Age 60–40
Married	-0.25*	1.28	Single/divorced/widowed
Not from North Africa/Middle East	-0.53*	1.27	From North Africa/Middle East
Arabic speaker	-0.18	0.84	Hebrew speaker
Russian speaker	-0.30*	0.74	Hebrew speaker
Secondary education	0.17	1.19	Elementary education or less
Crowded living conditions: fewer than seven people	0.25	1.29	More than 7 people
Surgical ward	0.55*	1.74	Internal medicine ward
Member of Leumit, Macabbi, or Meuhedet Sick Funds	0.22	1.25	Member of Clalit Sick Fund
Woman	0.15	1.17	Man
North	-0.33*	0.72	Centre of the country
South	-0.82*	0.44	Centre of the country
Has private medical insurance	0.31	1.36	No private medical insurance
Severe medical condition at admission to hospital	0.08	1.08	Slight/moderate problem
Constant	-0.73**		

Notes

* $p<0.05$
** $p<0.01$

Source: analyses of data from a patient survey, 1995.

generated competition for members among the sick funds, would have improved services and reduced waiting times to see a physician. Indeed, there was an increase (from 59 per cent to 69 per cent) in the proportion of those in the centre of the country who reported waiting a short time (up to 15 minutes) to see their family physician, and an increase in the proportion of those in the north (from 74 per cent to 81 per cent) and in the centre of the country (from 74 per cent to 76 per cent) who reported waiting less time to see a specialist. However, there was no improvement in the lengths of waiting times in the south.

Table 7.9 indicates that following implementation of the law, people in the south still had to wait more than 30 minutes to see a family physician – even though the ratio between the south and the centre of the country decreased, from 1.51 to 1.11. The ratio between the south and the centre of the country regarding waiting more than two weeks between making an appointment to see a specialist and actually seeing the specialist increased, from 1.05 to 1.41.

Table 7.9 **The ratio between the south and the centre of the country in perception of accessibility and availability of services and overall satisfaction with sick fund services**

	1995[1]	1997[2]
Proportion of those waiting to see a family physician more than 30 minutes	1.51	1.11
Proportion of those waiting more than two weeks for an appointment with a specialist	1.05	1.41
Proportion of those reporting specialist hours were convenient/very convenient	0.93	0.97
Proportion of those reporting that family physician hours were convenient/very convenient	1.01	1.00
Overall satisfaction with sick fund	0.93	1.02

Notes

1. Prior to implementation of the National Health Insurance Law.
2. Following implementation of the National Health Insurance Law.

Source: analyses of data from population surveys evaluating the health system, 1995 and 1997.

A multi-variate analysis (logistic regression) of 1997 data revealed that the variables predicting waiting longer than 30 minutes to see a family physician were not being a resident of the south, but having income below the average market wage (NIS 7,000 in 1997) and being over age 65 (see Table 7.10). Similarly, the probability of waiting more than two weeks to see a specialist was higher if the patient had an income below the average market wage and was over age 65. These findings indicate that the relatively large proportion of people in the south who wait a long time for physician services is not a consequence of their living in the south; rather, it is due to the large proportion of residents of the south who have low income, as noted above.

Between 1995 and 1997, there was a change for the better in satisfaction with sick fund services. During this period, there was an increase in the proportion of residents of the south who were satisfied with almost all aspects of sick fund services (see Table 7.11). This gap was thus closed: if in 1995 the proportion of those satisfied with sick fund services in the south was 93 per

Table 7.10 Variables predicting waiting times of up to 30 minutes to see a family physician in 1997 (logistic regression)

Variable	B	Odds ratio	Basis
Man	0.20	1.02	Woman
Maccabi sick fund	0.17	1.19	Clalit sick fund
Leumit sick fund	-0.14	0.86	Clalit sick fund
Meuhedet sick fund	0.80	2.22	Clalit sick fund
Russian-speaker	-0.16	0.85	Hebrew- or Arabic-speaker
North	0.36	1.43	Centre
South	-0.03	0.96	Centre
Up to age 44	0.27	1.32	Age 45–64
Age 65 and over	1.04**	2.82	Age 45–64
Income less than average wage	-1.01**	0.36	Income more than average wage
Excellent or good health status	0.14	1.15	Poor health status
Employed during the past three months	-0.34	0.70	Unemployed
Constant	2.34**	–	

Notes

* $p<0.05$
** $p<0.01$

Source: analyses of data from population survey evaluating the health system, 1997.

cent of those in the centre of the country who were satisfied with sick fund services, by 1997 the ratio had increased to 1.02 (see Table 7.9). In other words, in 1997, residents of the south were even more satisfied with their sick fund's services than were residents of the centre of the country.

Changes in Sick Fund Market Shares in the South

As can be seen in Figure 7.1, the 1993 market share of the Clalit Sick Fund – the largest of Israel's four sick funds, and formerly the primary provider of services in the south – was significantly greater in the south than its national market share: 77 per cent, versus 68 per cent. In contrast, the 1993 market share of the Maccabi Sick Fund in the south was significantly lower than its national market share: 9 per cent, versus 16 per cent. The market shares of the two other sick funds in the south were similar to their national market shares (see Figure 7.1).

Analysis of trends in changes in sick fund market shares in the south indicates that between 1993 and 1997, the market share of the Clalit Sick

Table 7.11 Comparison of proportions of respondents 'satisfied' and 'very satisfied' with sick fund services in 1995[1] and 1997,[2] by region (in %)

Service	Centre 1995	Centre 1997	North 1995	North 1997	South 1995	South 1997
Professional level of family physician	81.3*	87.4	85.3	87.6	75.4*	89.5
Attitude of family physician	90.0	91.1	91.0	92.0	85.1*	91.9
Attitude of nurses	87.2	88.0	86.1*	95.6	81.9*	94.4
Professional level of specialists	79.1*	86.4	79.5*	89.1	74.3*	85.7
Attitude of clerks	79.2	81.8	85.7	90.5	87.7	82.4
Selection of medications	74.6	75.9	73.4*	81.5	64.1*	78.8
Ease of getting referrals, payment coverage	79.3	79.0	78.7	82.4	80.2	81.1
Laboratory services	79.7	83.8	77.4	78.0	68.0*	83.9
Maintenance of facilities	92.9*	95.9	93.5	94.4	94.0*	100.0
Sick fund overall	83.9*	91.2	85.1	89.9	78.3*	93.4

Notes

1 Prior to implementation of the National Health Insurance Law.
2 Following implementation of the National Health Insurance Law.
* Difference between 1993 and 1997 for given regions is significant at a level of 0.05.

Source: analyses of data from population surveys evaluating the health system, 1995 and 1997.

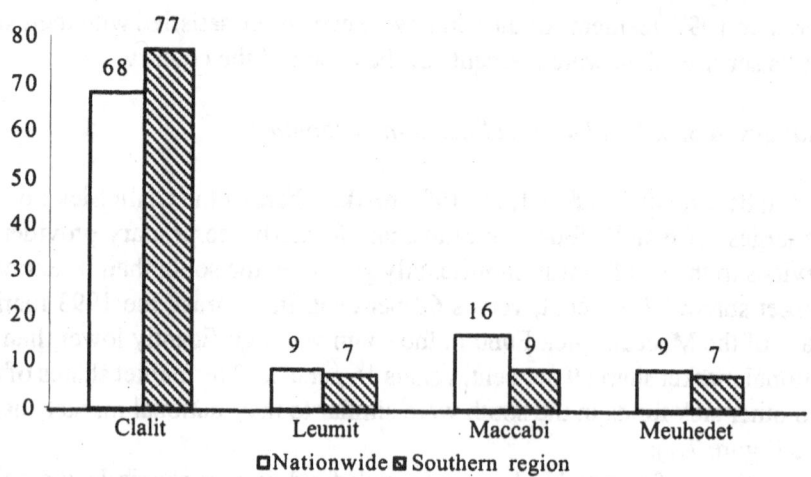

Figure 7.1 Market shares – 1993

Fund decreased by 13 percentage points in the south, compared to a decrease of nine percentage points in its national market share (see Figure 7.2). In contrast, the market share of the Maccabi Sick Fund increased by 11 percentage points in the south – far more than the five percentage-point increase in its national market share. The market share of the Leumit Sick Fund also increased in the south beyond that of its the national market share. This reflects member transfers from the largest to the smaller sick funds.

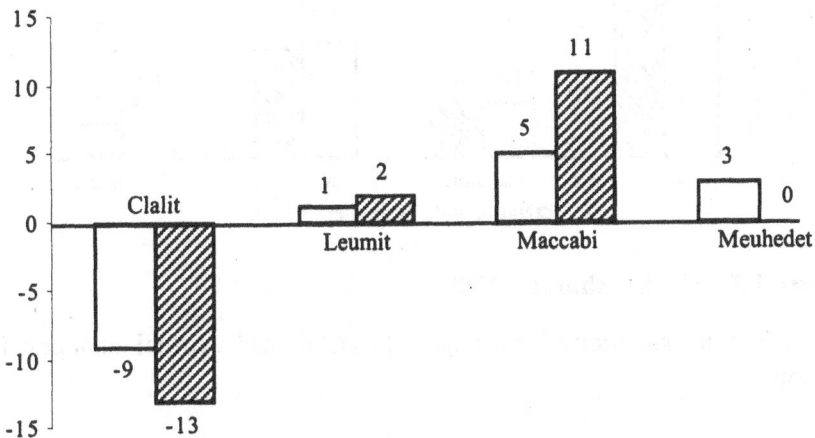

□ Nationwide ▨ Southern region

Figure 7.2   Changes in market shares between 1993 and 1997

Discussions with managers in some of the smaller sick funds revealed that, during this period, they did indeed make special efforts to increase their market share in the south, including initiating new services and improving existing ones. This was partly a response to the law's incentives, and partly because they realised that a significant segment of Clalit's membership was ready to consider alternatives. The discussions further revealed that once the smaller sick funds started making inroads in the south, Clalit also began expanding and developing its community services, in an effort to preserve its market share.

Figure 7.3 indicates that in 1997, the market share of the Clalit Sick Fund was still larger in the south than its national market share (64 per cent versus to 59 per cent), although the gap was smaller than it had been in 1993. The market shares of the Maccabi and Leumit Sick Funds that year were similar in the south to the their national market shares. Thus, the competitive dynamic in the south has become more similar to that in the centre of the country – a

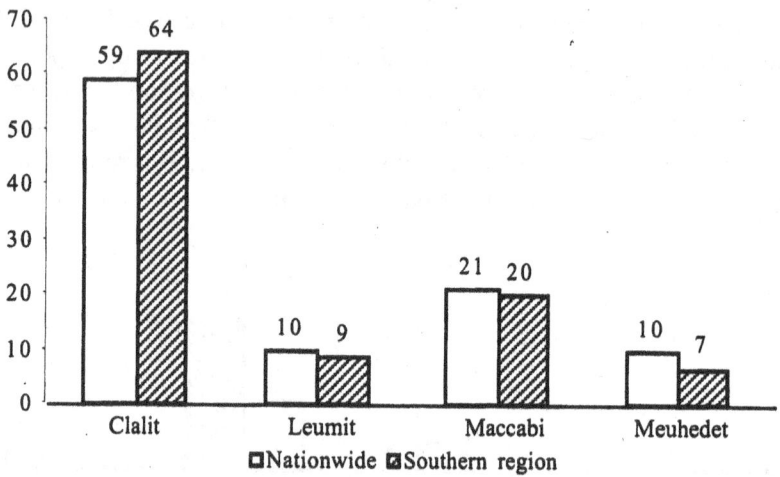

Figure 7.3 Market shares – 1997

far cry from the situation 10 years ago, when Clalit had a virtual monopoly in the south.

Summary and Discussion

The findings of this study indicate that, despite implementation of the law, the south is still at a disadvantage regarding medical and nursing manpower inputs, the proportion of hospital beds per population, and hospital occupancy rates, relative to the centre of the country.

Regarding level of services, health activists had expected that the competition for members among the sick funds, as a result of the implementation of the law, would result in an improvement. However, we found that while some gaps in the accessibility and availability of services were reduced, others increased. For example, in 1995 there was a greater chance that patients from the south would wait longer for hospitalisation than would patients from the centre of the country or even the north. This may be related to the small proportion of beds per population in the south, and the high occupancy rates. In addition, the length of time waited to see a family physician or specialist remained shorter in the centre of the country (and the north) than in the south. Thus, the accessibility of services in the south was still not equal to that in the centre of the country.

Interviews with key sick fund personnel and analysis of sick fund market shares indicate that the incentives offered by the law and its capitation formula have prompted some of the sick funds to invest in, expand and develop community services in the south, with the intention of expanding their market share there. These efforts, as well as the transfer of members from the largest to the smaller sick funds, may have contributed to increased satisfaction with sick fund services between 1995 and 1997 – to the point where sick fund members in the south were somewhat more satisfied than sick fund members in the centre and north of the country.

The findings of this study raise a number of issues of inequity. First, the findings indicate that the south still has fewer inputs in services, reflecting what Mooney (1994) identified as inequity in the supply and access to health services. However, as it was not the aim of this study to examine whether there is a connection between health services inputs and the process and outcomes of care, we cannot determine whether a lack of inputs in medical manpower leads to problems in health status. More in-depth examination of these issues requires a separate study.

The inequities we have highlighted spark discussion of the difference between the periphery and the centre. This study indicates that in the south there are indeed problems in the provision of health services. According to key sick fund personnel, some of these are the result of difficulties with above-average input prices (such as the salaries that sick funds must pay medical staff to work in a peripheral area). While the positive incentives created by the law enabled some sick funds to expand their services, they did not close the gaps in inputs and in the availability of services. Perhaps special resources should be allocated to peripheral areas to ensure equitable health service provision.

The findings of this study raise a question as to whether the gaps between the centre and the south of the country are related solely to the south's being peripheral, or whether they are related to other attributes. For example, as noted, some of the gaps in accessibility and availability of services are a consequence of the low income level of the south's population: Income below the average market wage predicts longer waiting times for the receipt of physician services. A possible explanation for this is that the poor are less aware of and less able to demand their rights. Other surveys examining gaps between poor and wealthy people in Israel (difficulties receiving service, forfeiting a necessary treatment, not purchasing medication because of its price; see Gross et al., 1999) found significant differences between those with low and those with high income. Thus, even if the law has helped improve some aspects of health service provision in the south, persistent differences in income levels, unemployment rates, and education levels between the south and the centre of Israel may preserve geographic inequity in health services availability and accessibility. Thus, in order to reduce this inequity, it may be necessary to include measures which reflect socioeconomic differences between regions in the capitation formula.

It appears that while the law has begun to improve the level of services in the south, it has only partly reduced inequity between the south and the centre of Israel in the allocation and level of health services. The processes the law was intended to affect are long-term ones; with time, the law may further close gaps and increase equity. However, our study also indicates that some form of direct government intervention – either in or outside the framework of the law – is necessary to closing the gaps between the south and the centre of the country, and diminishing inequity in the accessibility and availability of services.

Acknowledgements

This study was funded by the National Institute for Health Services and Health Policy Research. We thank our colleagues Ayelet Berg, Shuli Brammli-Greenberg, Revital Gross, David Chinitz, Hava Tabenkin, Dan Yuval, and Yona Yaphe, who made data from their research available to us. Without their willingness to do so, the lion's share of the study presented herein could not have been completed. However, responsibility for the findings that arose from the secondary analysis of the data rests with the authors alone.

References

Anson, J. (1988), 'Mortality and Living Conditions: Relative Mortality Levels and their Relation to the Physical Quality of Life in Urban Population', *Social Science and Medicine*, 27(9), pp. 901–10.

Bare, L.D., Ricketts, T.C., Konrad, T.R. and Mick, S.S. (1998), 'Do International Medical Graduates Reduce Rural Physician Shortages?', *Medical Care*, 36(11), pp. 1534–44.

Barell, V., Wax, Y. and Ruder, A. (1988), 'Analysis of Geographic Differentials in Infant Mortality Rates, the Or Yehuda Community', *American Journal of Epidemiology*, 128(1), pp. 218–30.

Bendalk, J. (1998), *Sick Fund Membership 1995–1997*, Periodic Paper No. 159, Research and Planning Authority, National Insurance Institute, Jerusalem (in Hebrew).

Berg, A., Gross, R., Rosen, B. and Chinitz, D. (1997), *Public Perception of the Health System Following Implementation of the National Health Insurance Law: Principal findings from a survey of the general population*, RR-284-97, JDC-Brookdale Institute, Jerusalem (in Hebrew).

Carr-Hill, R.A., Sheldon, T.A., Smith, P., Martin, S., Peacock, S. and Hardman, G. (1994), 'Allocating Resources to Health Authorities: Development of Methods for Small Area Analysis of Use of Inpatient Services', *British Medical Journal* 309, pp. 1040-9.

Carstairs, V. and Morris, R. (1989), 'Deprivation: Explaining Differences in Mortality between Scotland, England and Wales', *British Medical Journal*, 299, pp. 886-9.

Central Bureau of Statistics (1997a), *Characterization and Classification of Local Authorities by Socio-economic Level of the Population in 1995*, Publication No. 1039, Government Press Office, Jerusalem (in Hebrew).

Central Bureau of Statistics (1997b), *Demographic-health Profile of Towns and Cities in Israel, 1990-1994*, Publication No. 1959, Government Press Office, Jerusalem (in Hebrew).

Central Bureau of Statistics (1998a), *Natural migration 1994-1995, Part IV: Mortality*, Publication No. 1083, Government Press Office, Jerusalem (in Hebrew).

Central Bureau of Statistics (1998b), *1998 Statistical abstract for Israel*, Publication No. 49, Government Press Office, Jerusalem (in Hebrew).

Central Bureau of Statistics (1995), *Use of Health Services Survey, January-March 1993: Hospitalization and health insurance*, Publication No. 1001, Government Press Office, Jerusalem (in Hebrew).

Central Bureau of Statistics (1994), *Use of Health Services Survey, January-March 1993*, Publication No. 970, Government Press Office, Jerusalem (in Hebrew).

Chernichovsky, D. and Shirom, A. (1996), 'Equity in Health Systems in Israel', in Y. Kop (ed.), *Allocation of Resources to Social Services – 1996*, The Center for the Study of Social Policy in Israel, Jerusalem (in Hebrew), pp. 157-82.

Gross, R. and Brammli, S. (forthcoming), *Women's Health and Welfare in Israel*, JDC-Brookdale Institute, Jerusalem (in Hebrew).

Gross, R., Greenstein, M., Dubani, A., Berg, A., Yuval, D. and Rosen, B. (1998), *The Level of Service in Israel's Sick Funds Following the National Health Insurance Law: Principal findings from a 1997 members' survey and a comparison to the 1995 survey*, ES-17-98, JDC-Brookdale Institute, Jerusalem (in Hebrew).

Gross, R., Yuval, D., Japhe, Y. and Boerma, W. (1994), *The role of the primary care physician in Israel: preliminary findings from a national survey*, RR-216-94, JDC-Brookdale Institute, Jerusalem (in Hebrew).

Illsley, R. and Le Grand, J. (1993), 'Regional Inequalities in Mortality', *Journal of Epidemiology and Community Health*, 47(6), pp. 444-9.

Lusky, A., Gurvitz, R. and Barell, V. (1994), 'Variation in Mortality Rates in Tel Aviv Region Municipalities', *Israel Journal of Medical Science*, 30(9), pp. 690-8.

Mays, M. and Bevan, G. (1987), *Resource Allocation in the Health Services: A review of the methods of the resource allocation working party (RAWP)*, Occasional Papers on Social Administration No. 81, Social Administration Research Trust, Bedford Square Press/NCVO, London.

Ministry of Health (1995), *Hospitals and Out-patient cClinics in Israel: Statistics on patient mobility, by hospital and ward, 1994*, Government Press Office, Jerusalem (in Hebrew).

Ministry of Health (1997), *Hospitals and Out-patient Clinics in Israel: Statistics on patient mobility, by hospital and ward, 1996*, Government Press Office, Jerusalem (in Hebrew).

Ministry of Health (1998), *Hospitals and Out-patient Clinics in Israel: Statistics on patient mobility, by hospital and ward, 1997*, Government Press Office, Jerusalem (in Hebrew).

Mohan, J. (1987), 'Transforming the Geography of Health Care: Spatial Inequality and Health Care in Contemporary England', in A. Williams (ed.), *Health and Economics*, Macmillan Press, London, pp. 82–105.

Mooney, G. (1994), *Key Issues in Health Economics*, Harvester Wheatsheaf, New York.

Mooney, G. and McGuire, A. (1987), 'Distributive Justice with Special Reference to Geographical Inequality and Health Care', in A. Williams (ed.), *Health and Economics*, Macmillan Press, London, pp. 68–81.

Politzer, R.M., Cultice, J.M. and Meltzer, A.J. (1998), 'The Geographic Distribution of Physicians in the United States and the Contribution of International Medical Graduates', *Medical Care Research and Review*, 55(10), pp. 116–30.

Resource Allocation Working Party (RAWP) (1988), *Review of the Resource Allocation Working Party Formula: Final report by the NHS Management Board*, England.

Sheldon, T.A., Smith, P., Borowitz, M., Martin, S. and Carr-Hill, R. (1994), 'Attempt at Deriving a Formula for Setting General Practitioner Fundholding Budgets', *British Medical Journal*, 309, pp. 1059–64.

Sihoven, A.P., Kunst, A.E., Lahelma, E., Valkonen, T. and Mackenback, J.P. (1998), 'Socioeconomic Inequalities in Health Expectancy in Finland and Norway in the Late 1980s', *Social Science and Medicine*, 147(3), pp. 303–15.

Tabenkin, H., Gross, R., Brammli-Greenberg, S. and Shrira, S. (1999), *The Primary Care Physician as 'Gatekeeper': The perspectives of sick fund members, primary care physicians, and policymakers*, RR-336-99, JDC-Brookdale Institute, Jerusalem (in Hebrew).

Tulchinsky, T.H. and Ginsberg, G.M. (1996), *A District Health Profile of Beersheva Sub-district (the Negev), Israel, 1995*, Ministry of Health, Jerusalem.

Wagstaff, A. and Van Doorslaer, E. (1992), 'Equity in the Delivery of Health Care: Some International Comparisons', *Journal of Health Economics*, 11, pp. 389–411.

Weitzman, S., Sherf, M., Barak, N., Belmaker, E., Elhayany, A., Zmora, I., Porter, B., Bilenko, N., de Leeuw, D. and Katz, M. (1997), *Report of the Working Group on 'Health Needs of the Negev Population'*, The Faculty of Health Sciences, Committee for the Goldman Foundation, Beersheva.

Yuval, D. and Berg, A. (1997), *Hospitalization from the Patient's Perspective: Initial findings from a 1995 patient study*, RR-278-97, JDC-Brookdale Institute, Jerusalem (in Hebrew).

SECTION THREE
DEMAND

Chapter Eight

Demanding to Manage or Managing to Demand?

Annabelle Mark, David Pencheon and Richard Elliott

Demanding to manage is what health care organisations are trying to do in the provision of care, and managing to demand is what consumers or patients try to achieve when they access the formal health care system. At least that is how it first appears, but the two dimensions can also describe the differences between the UK and US health systems, and will affect how each country attempts to manage demand in the future.

The US health system is based on free markets dominated by the idea of consumer sovereignty so managing demand can be characterised as providers now demanding to manage the freedom of the consumer. In contrast the UK system is largely based on centrally controlled state provision where the patient/ consumer has had difficulty accessing the system or making their own demands felt: this now requires intervention to enable patients to gain more appropriate access to the system.

Identifying these differences helps in understanding why ideas now developing in both countries about managing demand in health care cannot be assumed as interchangeable or possibly even comparable. The reasons for managing demand are different, even if the outcomes required are the same.

In both countries there are increasing difficulties in managing the supply side alone to control health care. This has often been achieved by using, supply as a proxy for demand by changing access arrangements or reducing supply of services, one reason for this is that the interpretation of the problem has been largely economics based. Such interpretations although necessary are no longer sufficient to understanding and managing the problems. Different perspectives are now needed to influence the future; such perspectives emphasise alternative disciplinary interpretations, which taken together may provide some more sensitive and appropriate answers to these complex economic and behavioural problems.

Health Policy and Economics: Strategic Issues in Health Care Management, M. Tavakoli, H.T.O. Davies and M. Malek (eds), Ashgate Publishing Ltd, 2001.

Developing Interpretations

Differences in the interpretations in the USA and the UK for managing demand will not only determine the success of such strategies in the respective cultures, but also highlight the very different contexts for both organisations and individuals.

The leading exponent of demand management in the USA is Vickery, who has defined it as

> the support of individuals so that they may make rational health and medical decisions based on a consideration of benefits and risks. It is concerned with making more appropriate use of the health services not reducing it or making it cheaper – although both of these may occur (Vickery and Lynch, 1995, p. 551).

This definition represents what has been described as the third generation approach in the USA, the first generation being based on curtailment, the second generation combining this with a clinical focus to give it credibility, before the third approach emerged where consumer choice and participation where acknowledged as crucial to managing future resource utilisation (Marosits Mars, 1997).

Vickery presents a rationale for considering demand management as well as supply management. The concept of demand for medical services is examined within a theoretical framework of four components: morbidity, perceived need, patient preference and non-health motives. Two components, perceived need and patient preference, are suggested to offer considerable potential for making utilisation more appropriate and reducing costs. However, in the USA managing demand arises not only from the economic arguments, but also from the marketing perspective (Holleran, 1996; MacStravic, 1996), which respectively describe it as efficiently 'providing the right treatment at the right time to the right person' or 'steering consumers towards the most appropriate, cost effective response to perceived need'. These more consumer friendly approaches draw heavily on the expertise of the business marketing community to ensure that consumer satisfaction and confidence is maintained.

In the United Kingdom, people within the NHS began by identifying developments in this area in 1997. A series of articles also appeared in the *British Medical Journal* (Pencheon, 1998a) as well as other academic and practitioner contributions (Mark and Elliott, 1997; Rogers, Entwistle, and Pencheon, 1998). The work by Pencheon provides a working definition for the UK which attempts to reflect these current interpretations:

Demand Management is the process of identifying where, how, and why, people demand health care; and the best methods of curtailing, coping or creating this demand such that the most cost-effective, appropriate, and equitable health care system can be developed with the public; in short: how can supply and demand for health care be reconciled fairly?(Pencheon, 1998a, pp. 1665–6).

In the UK the first principles for demand management are thus based on normative definitions be they clinical or policy driven. It has yet to be shown how the patient/consumer population actually participates in, rather than just responds to this activity (ScHARR, 1998). Evidence of shared decision-making (Little and Williamson, 1997) is still rare and unless it becomes commonplace it could remain, in the eyes of consumers, just rhetoric. Without participation by patients or consumers, which places them at the centre, the emphasis will continue to be on 'management' rather than 'demand', which is why MacStravic and Montrose (1998) suggest the alternative paradigm of demand improvement, as this relocates the issue away from the professions and organisations towards the consumer.

The original USA definition from Vickery is predicated on the idea of individual freedom and responsibility to use health care appropriately, but also overtly assumes such use is based on rational acts. In contrast, the definition from the UK emphasises collective notions of fairness, which is the ethical and legal basis of the UK health system; what both definitions share is that they both remain largely outside the domain of the patient or consumer.

Demand in Progress

The progress of demand management in the USA provides contextual information which confirms the economic basis for the approach, but then goes on to demonstrate why economics alone cannot provide the answers (Sarel and Marmorstein, 1996). In contrast, within the UK, the centralised and normative developments to date are appropriate to the cultural context of health care, and have acknowledged the need for consumer involvement (Rogers, Entwistle, and Pencheon, 1998):

- to promote good self care of themselves by individuals;
- to manage the demand for utilisation of state services to which patients have free access.

This requires understanding of the patient's knowledge, culture, attitudes and experience of health care organisation, as these are key determinants of when, why and how people access the formal system. This will build on the ways in which people already take responsibility for managing health and illness, by additionally providing:

- information that is relevant, accessible, meaningful and integrated with other support systems;
- a culture in which risk, responsibility, control and uncertainties can be quantified, discussed and shared between providers, funders and users.

Without such shared ownership and participation in the appropriate use of health care some consumers – not always those most in need (Acheson, 1998) but often those most able to work the system – will find new ways to circumvent what they will continue to see as just failures in supply, rather than their inappropriate use of them, such as using emergency services when a later visit to primary care services would suffice.

Managing demand for health care is also about being explicit about what the formal health care system can provide, by offering a more graduated access to the system through developing levels of assessment, starting perhaps with nurse led or telephone triage. However, although a single point of entry/triage may have advantages (Salisbury, Dale, and Hallam, 1999), it also has some disadvantages, as experience in the USA suggests (MacStravic, 1996; MacStravic and Montrose, 1998), where some Health Maintenance Organisations (HMOs) have got into considerable difficulties by trying to restrict patient access in this way.

Drivers for Change

Within both the UK and USA, the drivers for change have developed beyond the economics and epidemiological to include three key areas, these can be summarised as:

1 technology in particular computer aided decision support and the development of the Internet. Examples are:
   – advice lines for health care, as well as the provision of various types of telephone triage where expertise is harnessed to sort individuals and target them towards the appropriate setting for their health needs, before

leaving home (Mark and Elliott, 1997);
- information relating to health on the Internet, which is influencing the use of existing health resources (Castells, 1996), although its effects on demand are not documented (Gillam and Pencheon, 1998).

These changes are part of a more general move away from relationships to encounters between patients and professionals in health care (Gutek, 1997) which will require new understanding and behaviours by both parties.

Technology is also developing fast and may be further enhanced by the introduction of emotional understanding within computer based systems (Epstein, 1998), further changing the potential for health encounters;

2 consumerism – a growing understanding of the differing interpretations of the consumer which influences responses to and behaviour by them. Gabriel and Lang (1995) distinguish the consumer as chooser, communicator, explorer, identity seeker, hedonist or artist, victim, rebel, activist or citizen. Consumers /patients are no longer passive but active participants who have been 'educated' in other spheres to a sophisticated understanding of how their behaviour affects and is affected by others, and how this can be changed to fit the context they are in (Martin, Knopoff, and Beckman, 1998). Problems occur because of differing assumptions about the consumer's role, making communication (O'Connell, 1996) increasingly problematic;

3 organisational behaviour – examines redefined professional roles and role boundaries; as well as changes in how health care is managed. This has been critical for both the USA and UK systems in recent years, as they have both struggled with alternatives which have proved politically and/ or culturally unacceptable (Mechanic, 1995; Department of Health, 1997). The behaviour of organisations affects the behaviour of users, both in relation to when and how they use it. What is apparent as an ongoing theme is the gap between expectation (Mark, 1992; Tudor Hart, 1998; Smith, 1999) of the myth and the reality of what happens when people interact with the system.

One organisational response to the perceived gaps has been the development of risk analysis (Alaszewski, Harrison, and Manthorpe, 1998). Joint professional and organisational responses have been found in audit and accreditation (Scrivens, 1995), and more recently the Evidence Based Medicine (EBM) movement, a powerful force in individual and organisational decision-making both in the UK and US systems (Davidoff et al., 1995).

Assimilating New Perspectives

A broader range of disciplines is now needed to analyse the expression and management of demand for health care, than the rationally based contributions made by public health and health economics. Managing demand properly can only be understood by investigating the interaction at both an organisational and consumer level (MacStravic, 1996) to discover why and how changes occur both intentionally and unintentionally.

To explain the interaction of these disciplines it is useful to look at examples in demand management: for example the growth in telephone help lines which use technology to mediate interactions with consumers for example the UK NHS Direct whose success to date is assessed by effects on clinical outcomes and the ability to coordinate and integrate services, (Lattimer et al., 1996) (Pencheon, 1998b; Munro et al., 2000). At the same time innovation via the Internet includes the government sponsored NHS ONLINE: http://www.nhsdirect.nhs.uk/main.jhtml.

A wider perspective is now needed to explore how context has shaped organisation and delivery, and how implementation and provision reshapes consumer behaviour. This will need to explore not only health services, but also the alternatives such as complementary therapies, because, as Lupton (1998) suggests, individuals are continually shaped and reshaped via discourse, embodied sensations, memory, personal biography and interactions with others and objects.

The speed at which the UK government has implemented NHS Direct in the UK suggests this wider perspective is not of prime importance. Yet the need for consumer involvement to illuminate these issues at an early stage in the development of the services, is evident (Kennelly and Dale, 1998).

Such omissions in evaluation are in part because these systems have developed rapidly worldwide as an alternative to direct patient care (Mark and Elliott, 1997). Their effect on future behaviour in response to the whole health care system is relatively unknown and unexplored (Pencheon, 1998c), yet may in part account for some of the increased utilisation of some facilities. For example, in the UK accident and emergency services have developed telephone help lines (British Association for Accident and Emergency Medicine, 1992; Eagleston et al., 1994; British Association for Accident and Emergency Medicine Clinical Services Committee, 1992) partly in response to problems of increased utilisation. Patients have seen such centres as the most logical place to go (Singh et al., 1991) even when, as American experience suggests (Verdile, 1989), it may not have been the most effective way of receiving help.

Crossing Cultures

The cultural context of demand management strategies in the USA and UK shares problems in how these new strategies combine facts and feelings.

Social science methodologies used in consumer behaviour and the study of health behaviour are the same; but the perception of the problems differs because of the different purposes of medicine and marketing. In simple terms the primary task of medicine is to meet clinical needs while the primary task of marketing is to manage and often create desires. Health care now crosses both such domains, but neither patients nor professionals necessarily recognise or wish to acknowledge where the boundaries are. The breadth of understanding in health remains narrower (Connor and Norman, 1995), confined more often to the cognitive approach, rather than that now being developed in consumer behaviour (Elliott, 1998; Firat, 1993; Thompson, Locander and Pollio, 1990) and organisational behaviour (Weik, 1995, Fineman, 1993). This is reflected in the new health help lines which seek to address demand for health care through rational responses, persuading individuals that their emotionally driven health seeking behaviour can be met more appropriately through rational analysis. Their development and evaluation by medicine and economics largely reinforces this linear deductive approach. However this is inadequate and not representative of the process of behaviour (Keren, 1996). It is devised as a rational proxy for decisions, because the knowledge base is encapsulated in protocol or algorithmically driven processes. However, the outcomes of these two rational processes themselves differ; protocols provide automated checklists of clinical guidelines, which are seen as less reliable in terms of both safety and effectiveness than the alternative clinical algorithms (physician developed binary logic pathways that assess specific medical complaints) (Wolcott, 1996). However neither can incorporate the individual patient's memory and personal biography (Lupton, 1998), which influences both their health seeking behaviour and responses to health provision.

How we interpret new information about our health is thus strongly influenced by our previous experience. We find it much easier to believe what we want to believe – i.e. what fits with our pre-existing worldview – and hence alter our behaviour. The conclusion is that information needs to be presented in a way that people will want to believe because it is both consistent with what they already know and provides what could be termed both cognitive and emotional assonance.

Closing the Rational/Emotional Gap

It is necessary to explore the dynamics of organisations, individuals and their interactions, and acknowledge the uncertain link between cognition and emotion (Zajonc, 1980; Lupton, 1998). This is important because emotions in mass industrial societies have been neglected to devastating effect (Mestrovic, 1997) particularly in their separation from action. This divide has a profound effect through all sorts of daily living experiences, be it news reporting, advertising or life in organisations. Individuals transfer experiences as carriers of meaning between a whole range of interactions with others. These differences and their transfer are relatively unexplored yet increasingly recognised as profoundly influential.

From these interactions personal meaning and the meaning of our social context are symbolised. A model for understanding this has now been developed (Elliott, 1998) in relation to how we make choices.

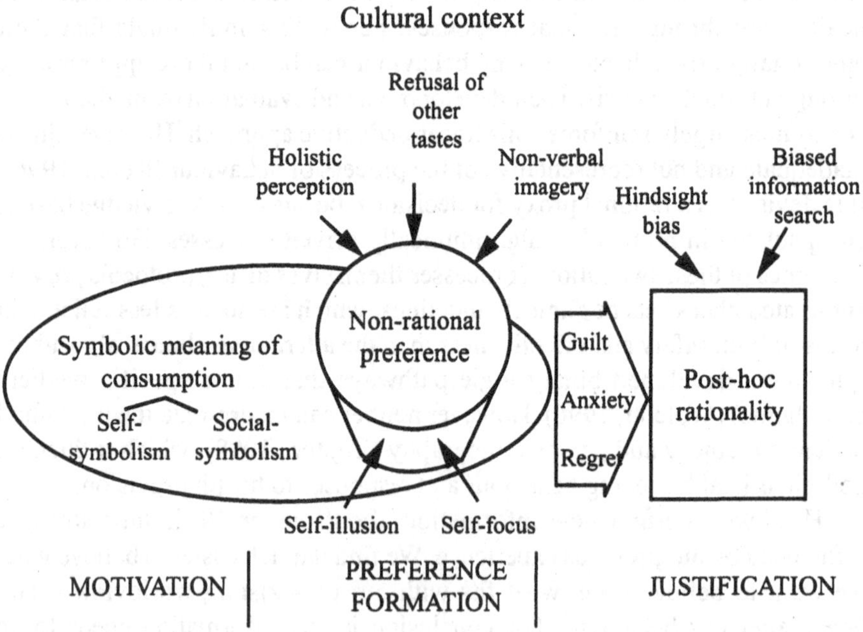

Figure 8.1 A model of emotion-driven choice

The problem with emotion used in most consumer research is that it refers to a personal and individual phenomenon, when in fact the most important aspects of emotion are social (Parkinson, 1995; Burkitt, 1997). Interpersonal communication theory proposes that 'emotion is constructed on-line as part of the developing relationship emerging from a real-time encounter between people' (Parkinson, 1995). This is particularly relevant to how we understand health encounters mediated by technology. Emotions are not simply internal events but are interactions addressed to specific audiences, and are thus partly defined according to conventional cultural representations (Hochschild, 1983). describes how we learn the local 'feeling rules' in a social situations so that our emotions are appropriate to local circumstances and meet the expectations of other people.

In health care, the individual patient also has recourse to professional opinion the interpretation of which is more complex than it first appears. Such opinion may falter on two counts, firstly because there are few definitive scientifically based answers, as the EBM movement has revealed, and secondly because of the negative and unacknowledged effects of 'emotional labour' (Hochschild, 1983) on the interaction. Emotional labour is broadly interpreted now as managing emotions for a wage (Grandey, 2000), and will involve both the conscious and subconscious management of emotions in the self and others to achieve organisational and professional goals. Medicine has yet to sufficiently acknowledge its own role in this, or consider the effects of emotion on health (Stewart Brown, 1998; Pennebaker, 1995), which is seen as diametrically opposed to the deductive rationality at the heart of scientific medicine. In contrast, nurses acknowledge the high degree of emotional labour involved in their work (Jones, 1994) and this in part accounts for their primary use in telephone triage and help lines, where much health seeking behaviour can be satisfied by the reassurance and emotional support they can provide rather than any medical intervention (Munro et al., 2000). Emotional labour is used in health care both to act out expressions of feeling to patients to elicit particular responses from them (Jones, 1994), but also has a major part to play as a defence for the worker against stress and burnout. However, in so doing it often separates emotion from action by decoupling what is felt from what is expressed (Martin, Knopoff and Beckman, 1998) and is in reality recognised by patients as a fake response. They feel the disconnection and so seek alternative confirmation of their needs through second opinions and other multiple utilisation of resources, thus increasing demand. New behavioural solutions to this growing problem of health interactions may need to be explored for example the use of 'bounded emotionality' which encourages the constrained expression of real emotion (ibid.). Because bounded emotionality is based on real feelings, it may help to re-establish the trust lost in part through the abuse of emotion by society in general (Mestrovic, 1997).

Changing cultures

Maintaining only explicitly rational responses to emotionally triggered demand is no longer sufficient or sustainable in the longer term. Demand is significantly an emotional process and any response to it must take account of this.

Three different approaches will be needed because of the way in which demand is separately manifested:

1. curtailing the demand for ineffective and the least cost effective services;
2. coping better with demand for effective services;
3. creating demand for services which are known to be cost effective but under-used.

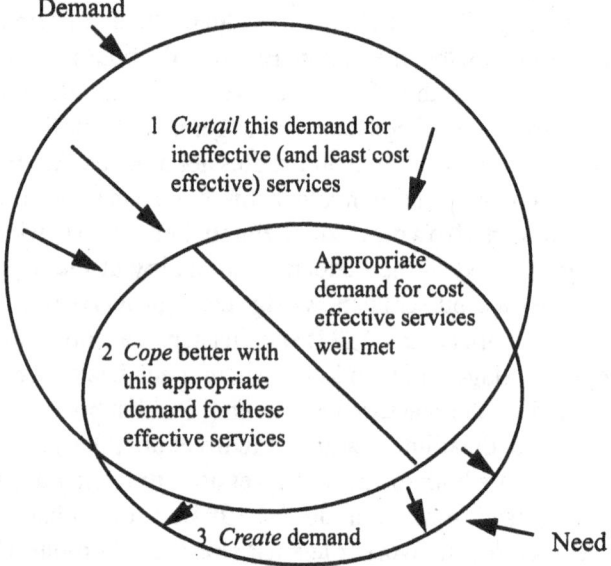

Figure 8.2 The relationship between demand and need

Curtail, Cope and Create

The process of managing demand better is not simply about reducing activity. Too much emphasis on overuse may well distract attention from the probable under-use elsewhere in health care by specific groups such as the elderly, in both the US (Dolinsky, 1995) and the UK, where low utilisation of NHS Direct by those aged over 65 (ScHARR, 1998) has been observed.

The primary concern of health care has been to cope and curtail or demarket health care (Mark and Elliott, 1997) because of what Kotler and Levy (1971) termed 'chronic over popularity' expressed for example by politicians in the UK through the contentious issue of the length of waiting lists for hospital appointments. Yet disparities – for example of social class (Acheson, 1998) – mean that there are areas where demand must also be created, for example in the need for better uptake of screening and prenatal services within certain groups in the population.

Whose Demands

Managing demand within health care is not a simple two party relationship, although politicians who wish to meet every-ones demands wish it was, it is influenced by:

- demand from the public for services to be available in case they are needed; for example access to emergency services without the prospect of waiting hours to be seen or having to travel long distances. This is often expressed negatively through public protests at attempts to close local services;
- demand from patients for services as they are needed; for example going to see a GP and gaining fast access or being provided with an alternative resource such as the immediate attention of a nurse practitioner, the main purpose being to satisfy the lay or patient concept of need;
- demand from professionals acting as agents for patients; for example ensuring that primary care doctors can refer to hospital consultants and get a response for patients within acceptable timeframes.

Demand from the public needs to be better understood and is influenced by a range of factors. Firstly, in the UK health has historically been a right and in the USA it has been portrayed as a commodity. Some convergence of these perspectives has taken place in each country (Tudor Hart, 1998) because of the flaws revealed in each. Secondly, through the influence of the media (Rogers, Entwistle, and Pencheon, 1998) and the way its interpretation has changed boundaries.

A third factor is that arising from patients' interpretation of their own needs for services that are shaped by their peer group, acting as a means of social control (Mestrovic, 1997), and factors which produce lay concepts of health and illness (Mark and Elliott, 1997; Rogers, Hassell and Nicolaas, 1999).

Finally, demand from professionals, acting as both patient's advocate and promoters of their professional groups and specialities influence the agency relationship, which exists between professionals and those for whom they are acting.

Demand is thus a function of culture. Decisions about making demands for health are also based on lifestyle choices, rather than a strict definition of clinical need. Dealing with the boundaries between these becomes increasingly important. A recent example of this has been the controversy over the use of Viagra in the UK (Smith, 1998), where the boundaries between health and lifestyle have become less clear and more dynamic. Maffesoli (1996) suggests that in what he calls 'the time of the tribes' individuals associate with lifestyle groups or 'neo-tribes' which are based on affinities of emotional response, the personal and emotional form the basis for ethical and moral judgements. Demand for health care can therefore be seen in this context as being based on lifestyle seeking behaviour through emotion, not rationality. So if we continue to seek only rational justification for this behaviour we miss the point in terms of managing demand and seeking cooperation with patients.

Shifting the Boundaries

Making progress in managing demand requires a shift in perspective from individuals, organisations and publics. However it may prove easier to shift attitudes in the whole population than in subgroups such as doctors. Huang (1998) suggests that 'basic emotions' such as fear are universal and are the target for the former group, while for doctors there is a need to appeal to 'social emotions' which are unique constructions of a number of basic emotions by specific groups. Doctors will thus require an approach which takes them through the social emotions constructed by their organisational and professional contexts towards these new attitudes.

Managing to demand (UK) and demanding to manage (USA) may however have a significant influence on changing the boundaries between these two cultures. Evidence is emerging in the USA that the boundary between health need (Holleran, 1996) and supplier induced demand are less clear (Lester and Breudigam, 1996) and conversely, that demand strategies may be leading to improvements to access for health care for those most in need (Henderson and Hahn, 1998), although there is little data to support this at present.

Managing demand may increase the convergence between the two systems to the benefit of both. In the UK attempts are being made by some to involve patients in the decision process more practically; an RCT on the use of antibiotics for sore throats (Little and Williamson, 1997) shows that reducing fear by allowing patients access to drugs can actually reduce their uptake of services. The experiment gave some patients immediate access to drugs and some the choice of picking up a prescription already written if no improvement occurred within a given period.

The latter group, feeling safe in the knowledge that what they thought they needed was available, found in many cases that it was not required and so reduced the uptake of prescribed drugs by not using the prescription. They also potentially learnt from the experience in a way which may influence their future demands in similar circumstances. These objectives and outcomes are similar to those attempted in the use of video information for patients on the consequences of taking up surgery for prostatic hypertrophy (Flood and Wennberg, 1996). They have been influential as a strategy to reduce demand in both the UK and the US (MacStravic, 1996), where it is referred to as decision management. Reducing fear by increasing choices may reduce demand; the reverse of this, increasing fear by reducing choices – as we know from both US and UK attempts to control access to demand have shown (MacStravic and Montrose, 1998; Smith, 1998) – will only increase demand.

The World Turned Upside Down

What these approaches share is an attempt to turn the idea of supplier induced demand on its head, instead of continuing to assume that availability and utilisation are synonymous, demand management strategies seek to exploit the gap between them, so that participants can reinterpret them.

As a phenomenon it seems that it could result in the opposite of panic buying: it uses information plus emotion (the reduction of fear) to bring about change, because offering more can reduce demand if individuals participate in the decision-making process by for example controlling their own uptake. Dowrick (1997) confirms that more control by patients, more expression of emotion and more information sought and provided leads to better health. To do this successfully we need to understand the boundaries between emotion and rationality in the health decision process to give people more control when they want it.

There are risks for both individuals and organisations in shifting these boundaries, but what the examples do confirm is the need for professionals and health care organisations to move from paternalism to participation.

Participation must now be taken one step further so that people become co-producers of health by being key players in these decision processes. This also implies that they will become co-risk takers, but this is both an essential part of the move from paternalism to participation and a recognition that few definitive answers exist in medicine. In this way patients', rather than just professional and organisational, values can be incorporated. Such a shift is essential in both the UK and USA, given the consequences of the increased prevalence of chronic disease and the cultural fantasy of perfect health. While it may not be possible to satiate consumer demand – because the gap between the fantasy world of perfect consumption and the disappointments of reality results in limitless wants and a permanent state of frustration (Campbell, 1987) – it may be possible to alter patient expectation and experiences through participation with professionals in the health process.

Explicitness in moving the locus of control from professionals towards patient/consumers will highlight both the rights and responsibilities and the costs and benefits of these shared risks. This would have implications not just for resource use and demand management, but for other more common features of twenty-first century health care in both the UK and USA, such as litigation.

Demanding health care is a far bigger activity than supplying it, yet we still know so little about it. The emphasis on the role of health care providers must now shift towards a better understanding of users and what influences their responses. The way forward must therefore be, for both the UK and USA, to bring together interdisciplinary expertise to better assimilate the role of rational and emotional process in the production of health.

References

Acheson, D. (1998), *Report of the Independent Inquiry into Inequalities in Health*, HMSO, London.

Alaszewski, A., Harrison, L. and Manthorpe, J. (1998), *Risk, Health and Welfare Policies*, Open University Press, Milton Keynes.

British Association for Accident and Emergency Medicine Clinical Services Committee (1992), *Guidelines on the Handling of Telephone Enquiries in Accident and Emergency Departments*, British Association for Accident and Emergency Medicine, London.

Burkitt, I. (1997), 'Social Relationships and Emotions', *The Journal of the British Sociological Association*, 31, 1, pp. 37–55.

Campbell, C. (1987), *The Romantic Ethic and the Spirit of Modern Consumerism*, Blackwell, Oxford.

Castells, M. (1996), *The Rise of the Network Society*, Blackwell, Oxford.

Connor, M. and Norman, P. (1995), *Predicting Health Behaviour*, Open University Press, Milton Keynes.

Davidoff, F., Haynes, B., Sackett, D. and Smith, R. (1995), 'Evidence Based Medicine' (editorial), *British Medical Journal*, 310, 6987, pp. 1085–6.

Department of Health (1997), *The New NHS – modern, dependable*, Cm 3807, HMSO, London.

Dolinsky, A. (1995), 'Complaint Intensity and Health Care Services: A framework to establish priorities for quality improvements can be used to improve patient satisfaction', *Journal of Health Care Marketing*, 15, 2, pp. 42–8.

Dowrick, C. (1997), 'Rethinking the Doctor–Patient Relationship in General Practice', *Health and Social Care in the Community*, 5, 1, pp. 11–14.

Elliott, R. (1998), 'A Model of Emotion Driven Choice', *Journal of Marketing Management*, 14, pp. 95–108.

Epstein, J. (1998), 'Computers with Emotions', *Futurist*, 32, 3, p. 12.

Firat, A.F. (1993), 'The Consumer in Postmodernity', *Advances in Consumer Research*, 18, pp. 70–6.

Flood, A. and Wennberg, J. (1996), 'The Importance of Patient Preference in the Decision to Screen for Prostate Cancer – Prostate Patient Outcomes Research Team', *Journal of General Internal Medicine*, 11, 16, pp. 342–9.

Gabriel, Y. and Lang, T. (1995), *The Unmanageable Consumer – Contemporary Consumption and its Fragmentation*, Sage, London.

Gillam, S. and Pencheon, D. (1998), 'Managing Demand in General Practice', *British Medical Journal*, 316, pp. 1895–8.

Grandey, A.A. (2000), 'Emotional Regulation in the Workplace: A new way to conceptualise Emotional Labor', *Journal of Occupational Health Psychology*, 5, 1, pp. 95–110.

Gutek, B. (1997), 'Dyadic Interactions in Organisations,' in C. Cooper and S. Jackson (eds), *Creating Tomorrow's Organisations – a Handbook for Future Research in Organisational Behaviour*, John Wiley, Chichester, pp. 139–56.

Henderson, M. and Hahn, W. (1998), 'Can Demand Management Programs Increase Access to Care While Controlling Costs', 31st edn of the AHSR and FHSE Annual Meeting, Vol. 13, Abstract Books.

Hochschild, A.R. (1983), *The Managed Heart: Commercialisation of human feeling*, University of California Press, Berkeley.

Holleran, M. (1996), 'Who Needs a Needs Assessment? You do!', *Journal of Health Care Marketing*, 16, 3, pp. 32–4.

Huang, M.H. (1998), 'Exploring a New Typology of Advertising Appeals: Basic versus social, emotional advertising in a global setting', *International Journal of Advertising*, 17, 2, pp. 145–68.

Jones, L.J. (1994), *The Social Context of Health and Health Work*, Macmillan, Basingstoke.

Kennelly, C. and Dale, J. (1998), 'Direct Enquiries', *Health Services Journal*, 5615, pp. 24–5.

Kotler, P. and Levy, S.J. (1971), 'Demarketing Yes Demarketing', *Harvard Business Review*, 49, 6, pp. 74–80.

Lattimer, V., Smith, H., Hungin, P. and George, S. (1996), 'Future Provision of Out of Hours Primary Medical Care: A survey with two general practitioner research networks', *British Medical Journal*, 312, 7027, pp. 352–6.

Lester, J.A. and Breudigam, M. (1996), 'Nurse Triage Telephone Centres: Key to demand management strategy', *NAHAM Management Journal*, 22, 4, pp. 13–14.

Little, P. and Williamson, G. (1997), 'Open Randomised Trial of Prescribing Strategy in Managing Sore Throat', *British Medical Journal*, 315, 7104, pp. 350–2.

MacStravic, S. (1996), 'Marketing or Management: Which way the future?', *Journal of Health Care Marketing*, 16, 2, pp. 10–14.

MacStravic, S. and Montrose, G. (1998), *Managing Health Care Demand*, Aspen Publishers, Gaithersburg, Maryland.

Maffesoli, M. (1996), *The Time of the Tribes: The decline of individualism in mass society*, Sage, London.

Mark, A. (1992), 'How has the Symbol Changed – a Community Care Consumer's Dilemma', *Health Services Management*, 88, 1, pp. 29–31.

Mark, A. and Elliott, R. (1997), 'Demarketing Dysfunctional Demand in the UK NHS', *International Journal of Health Planning and Management*, 12, pp. 297–314.

Marosits Mars, J. (1997), 'Improving Financial and Patient Outcomes: The future of demand management', *Healthcare Financial Management*, 51, 8, p. 43(2).

Martin, J., Knopoff, K. and Beckman, C. (1998), 'An Alternative to Bureaucratic Impersonality and Emotional Labor: Bounded emotionality at The Body Shop', *Administrative Science Quarterly*, 43, pp. 429–69.

Mechanic, D. (1995), 'Failure of Health Care Reform in the USA', *Journal of Health Services Research Policy*, pre-launch issue.

Mestrovic, S.G. (1997), *Postemotional Society*, Sage, London.

Munro, J., Nicholl, J., O'Caithain, A. and Knowles, E. (2000), *Evaluation of NHS Direct First Wave Sites – Second Interim Report to the Department of Health*, ScHARR Medical Care Research Unit, University of Sheffield, Sheffield.

O'Connell, M.J. (1996), 'Marketing-driven Change Management (Healthcare Market Transition)', *Journal of Health Care Marketing*, 16, 1, pp. 11–14.

Parkinson, B. (1995), *Ideas and Realities of Emotion*, Routledge, London.

Pencheon, D. (1998a), 'Matching Demand and Supply Fairly and Efficiently', *British Medical Journal*, 316, pp. 1665–7.

Pencheon, D. (1998b), 'NHS Direct: Evaluate, integrate or bust', *British Medical Journal*, 317, pp. 1026–7.

Pencheon, D. (1998c), 'NHS Direct: Managing demand', *British Medical Journal*, 316, 7126, pp. 215–16.

Pennebaker, J.W. (1995), *Emotion, Disclosure and Health*, American Psychological Association, Washington, DC.

Rogers, A., Entwistle, V., and Pencheon, D. (1998), 'A Patient Led NHS: Managing demand at the interface between lay and primary care', *British Medical Journal*, 316, pp. 1816–19.

Rogers, A., Hassell, K. and Nicolaas, G. (1999), *Demanding Patients? Analysing the Use of Primary Care*, Open University Press, Milton Keynes.

Salisbury, C., Dale, J. and Hallam, L. (1999), *24 hour primary care*, Radcliffe Medical Press, Oxford.

Sarel, D. and Marmorstein, H. (1996), 'Identifying New Patient Prospects', *Journal of Health Care Marketing*, 16, 1, pp. 38–44.

ScHARR (1998), *Evaluation of NHS Direct First Wave Sites – First Interim Report to the Department of Health*, Medical Research Unit School of Health and Related Research, University of Sheffield.

Scrivens, E. (1995), *Accreditation – Protecting the Professional or the Consumer?*, Open University Press, Milton Keynes.

Smith, R. (1998), 'Viagra and Rationing. Let the Sunlight in, Let the People Speak', *British*

Smith, R. (1998), 'Viagra and Rationing. Let the Sunlight in, Let the People Speak', *British Medical Journal*, 317, pp. 760–61.
Smith, R. (1999), 'The NHS: Possibilities for the endgame', *British Medical Journal*, 318, pp. 209–10.
Stewart Brown, S. (1998), 'Emotional Well Being and its Relation to Health', *British Medical Journal*, 317, pp. 1608–9.
Thompson, C.J., Locander, W.B. and Pollio, H.R. (1990), 'The Lived Meaning of Free Choice: An existential–phenomenological description of everyday consumer experiences of contemporary married women', *Journal of Consumer Research*, 17, pp. 346–61.
Tudor Hart, J. (1998), 'Expectations of Health Care: Promoted, managed or shared', *Health Expectations*, 1, pp. 3–13.
Vickery, D.M. and Lynch, W.D. (1995), 'Demand Management: Enabling patients to use medical care appropriately', *Journal of Occupational and Environmental Medicine*, 37, 5, pp. 551–7.
Zajonc, R. (1980), 'Feeling and Thinking: Preferences need no inferences', *American Psychologist*, 35, pp. 151–75.

Chapter Nine

Citizen, Consumer or Both? Re-conceptualising 'Demand' in Health Care

Richard D. Smith and Brian Salter

Introduction

The NHS symbolises the essence of the welfare state 'equation' regarding the universal rights of citizens and the absolute duties of the state. However, for exactly that reason the NHS also faces a fundamental, and chronic, problem: that of disequilibrium, the most visible result of which is the 'waiting list' (Salter, 1998). Although disequilibrium simply refers to the excess of demand relative to the capacity of supply to meet it, discussion and policy reforms to address it focus, almost exclusively, upon the nature of the *supply* of health care services; variously referred to as 'efficiency gains' or 'cost-containment' (ibid.). However, unless demand is fixed and stable (which, it would appear, it is not), improvements in the supply-side alone will not resolve this fundamental imbalance in the demand-supply equation (DHSS, 1976; Department of Health, 1995a).

Attempts to consider the demand side have been largely unsuccessful, as they have been based on a narrow 'neoclassical' economic view of health care demand. However, within the NHS, the individual has a dual role of both 'consumer' and 'citizen', which has become increasingly ambiguous over recent years. Although the NHS remains fundamentally based on the citizen model, there has been active promotion of the 'consumer' role. This creates confusion over just who the 'patient' is in health care – citizen or consumer?

This chapter argues that, if the *principles* of the NHS are to remain and this disequilibrium is to be tackled, the answer is *both*. However, this requires the development of a new paradigm of demand which encompasses this 'dual role' of the individual. The purpose of this chapter is, therefore, to establish

Health Policy and Economics: Strategic Issues in Health Care Management, M. Tavakoli, H.T.O. Davies and M. Malek (eds), Ashgate Publishing Ltd, 2001.

the need for such a paradigm shift, and to begin the process of developing it. Thus, the chapter explains in some detail the reasoning behind why such a reconceptualisation of demand is required, and proposes briefly an approach to such reconceptualisation. It is envisaged that future papers will expand and develop this model further.

The chapter begins by outlining the nature of disequilibrium in the health care market and critiquing the current application of the neoclassical theory of demand to health care. The importance of the citizen, and the growth of 'consumerism' in health care, are then presented, before an alternative conceptualisation of demand is proposed.

Disequilibrium in the Market *and* in Policy Response

The fundamental problem within the health care market in the UK is a chronic state of disequilibrium, where demand is consistently, and significantly, greater than the supply of services devoted to meet it (MacPherson, 1988). In other markets the price mechanism would adjust the levels of demand and supply until equilibrium was reached. In the absence of a price mechanism such equilibrium requires alternative 'non-price' interventions to adjust demand and supply; most notably waiting lists' (Department of Health, 1995a, p. 1).

Within health care in the UK the ideological context of the welfare state foundations of the NHS dominates discussion, precluding significant intervention in the demand-side of the equation. Debate and policy therefore focus, almost exclusively, on the supply side, which is reflected in the language of that debate: that there is a 'cost explosion' in health care, or that 'inefficiency' or 'cost containment' is the overriding issue (Normand, 1998). In other words, the demand issue is sidestepped and presented in terms of its consequences. As a result, access to the policy agenda is restricted to policies which do not confront demand, but instead seek to reconfigure the supply-side response, which is more tractable politically than trying to curtail or manage demand in any explicit manner (even the 'internal market' reforms of 1990s addressed only supply-side issues).

This stress on (technical) efficiency in the production of services does not appear to accept that efficiency savings must at some stage reach a saturation point (or at least incur severe diminishing returns), where all (worthwhile) efficiency savings have been made. Yet even at this point there will still be excess demand, which can be met neither through increased expenditure nor efficiency savings in production.

However, although it is clear, we would argue, that demand issues should be addressed, current analyses based on the traditional neoclassical economic concept of demand may be inadequate.

Inadequacy of the Current (Economic) Model of Demand

In the analysis of heath care the term 'consumer' is typically viewed as synonymous with that of 'patient' in referring to the *users* of health care services. However, there is a critical distinction to make here.

The 'patient' is 'a person who receives medical care' (*Collins Concise Dictionary*, p. 979), which emphasises individual *use* of health care services. In contrast, 'consumer' refers to 'a person who *purchases* goods and services for his own personal needs' (ibid., p. 283, emphasis added), which emphasises the *purchase*, rather than the *use*, of services (although the confusion between the terms no doubt stems from the act of 'consumption' referring to the 'using up' of something [ibid., p. 283]).

In standard economic theory (including that applied to health care) the 'consumer' is considered to be a fully informed and sovereign agent in the market who seeks to maximise their 'utility' (well-being) from their personal resources by deciding upon consumption of a mix of available goods and services. This decision is based on the relative price (i.e. full cost to the consumer, comprising price of the commodity and related expenses involved in purchase and consumption) between them and the utility gained by the individual from their consumption. Critical in this market is the price mechanism, which is the means by which the consumer communicates with producers to determine the mix and level of supply (and therefore consumption) of various commodities. In this sense, 'demand' reflects an individual's willingness and ability to pay for a commodity at a given price (McGuire et al., 1988).

From a purely theoretical perspective, therefore, the 'consumer' in the NHS does not actually exist because they do not have to make a direct 'purchase' based on willingness and ability to pay, as the price is reduced to zero (noting of course that the opportunity cost is not necessarily zero, but that the important function of price as an allocation tool has been removed) (Toth, 1996).

One may, of course, conceive of the individual *acting* as a consumer faced with a zero price at point of use, and there have been modifications to standard theory to reflect anomalies of the health care market such as this, as well as others, such as the agency relationship. However, the fundamental basis of analysis remains this neoclassical model of the individual as a 'consumer' (McGuire et al., 1988). Thus, analyses and predictions relating to policies, such as increasing user-charges, have been made with respect to this model in estimating the impact on the 'demand' for services.

The inadequacy of analyses and predictions based on such a model recently led some leading economists to debate whether the 'demand' for health care actually exists at all (Reinhardt et al., 1999; see also: Evans, 1997a, 1997b; Gaynor and Vogt, 1997; Pauly, 1997; Rice, 1997a, 1997b). While this may be a little extreme, we would suggest that the traditional model is certainly *misspecified* by failing to incorporate the political demand generated in a citizen-based model of health care finance and delivery. In the UK at least, individuals are, at best, 'quasi-consumers', as they engage in a 'public contract' with the NHS as 'citizens'. It is this role as 'citizen' which is not reflected in the traditional economic model and which is vital for examining demand in health care.

Importance of the 'Citizen' in Health Care

A citizen is, broadly speaking, a 'member of a State or Commonwealth [and] member of a political community' (*Collins Concise Dictionary*, p. 242). More specifically, 'citizenship' refers to a reciprocal relationship between individual and state. As a citizen the individual has rights which the state guarantees to fulfil, and has duties which he/she must carry out for the state. Importantly, there is a distinction between civil rights necessary for individual freedom, political rights necessary in order to participate in political power and social rights. Whereas civil and political rights are generally formulated in a *negative* way, in terms of freedom from something, social rights are formulated in a *positive* way, requiring an interventionist state to give citizenship a material foundation (Marshall, 1950). Furthermore, social rights are given an absolute status, with their fulfilment not seen as conditional upon the *ability* of the state, primarily its economic ability, to provide them, but as the state's absolute *duty* to deliver the welfare component of citizenship regardless of the costs (Van Steenbergen, 1994).

The NHS reflects such a 'social rights' model (e.g. Smith et al., 1999). Here price regulation is removed in order to provide citizens with the health care 'right' of access to services free of charge at point of use, with the necessary obligation on the state to generate the appropriate supply. This is made in exchange for a duty on the citizen to pay toward this through taxation, *and* accept non-price rationing. 'Demand', in the economic sense, is therefore replaced with the concept of the 'right' for health services (when 'needed') and an incumbency on the state to respond to this 'right' (Salter, 1998).

In the absence of price signals, demand (and supply) is thus determined by a political rather than price basis, and the allocative mechanism changes from that of price to the political process of lobbying. Citizens, in activating their rights, generate a 'political' demand on government. To survive, politicians must generate a response which deals with, or at least placates, this demand. An alternative option is to remove the right(s) and thus the demand. However, as discussed, this alternative option is at present prohibited by the prevailing welfare state hegemony which insists that welfare rights can be expanded but not contracted (ibid.).

In exercising his/her rights the citizen might therefore *appear* to act as a consumer (although only of course expressing a *preference*, not demand as defined earlier) and generates a 'want' for a service, which is perceived as if it were economic 'demand'. The NHS therefore becomes subject to both 'political' and 'economic' demands at the same time. When citizens find that their political and 'economic' demands are not met (they don't get the health care they think they have the 'right' to) they can then if they so wish activate a separate set of citizenship rights: the 'right' to choose their health care from the private sector. They then, of course, become a 'legitimate' consumer registering a real economic demand on the private sector (ibid.).

Thus, in the absence of price, it is therefore not necessarily consumer demand which is of importance but 'political' demand upon the polity by the individual as 'citizen'. Significantly, it is this 'political' demand made by citizens which has grown, and has been encouraged, over the last 10 to 20 years.

Growth of Citizen 'Rights'

As outlined, 'free at point of access' health care is part of the practical status of citizenship in the UK. However, the concept of such 'social rights' is one which is infinitely expandable, flexible and never exclusive, with no nation finding a consensus on what might be called core or basic social rights in the same way that there are core or basic human rights.

In defining what it is *exactly* that the public may expect from the health service, and indeed what the health service expects from them, citizenship is a weak concept. Citizenship emphasises rights of access to services, but leaves vague the detail of what actually can be expected, and, more importantly, it leaves out the detail of what is expected of the individual. Nowhere is there a definition of the nature of health, or illness, or indeed care, that is, and is not, the responsibility of the state. The health service has no core definition of the citizens' social rights to which it is to respond. Thus, as health care services have expanded so it has been politically difficult to exclude them from the promise of free comprehensive health care from cradle to grave (Toth, 1996).

Combined with this, it is electorally ever popular to increase the range of rights which a citizen has, and correspondingly always unpopular to decrease them. This has meant that in the 50 years since the erection of the welfare state, there has been a general expansion of these social rights, rather than any reduction or limitation on them. In health care in particular there has been active expansion of these 'rights'. For example, outlined in the White Paper, *Working for Patients* (1989), and subsequently more fully in the Patient's Charter (Department of Health, 1992), which promises that '... every citizen has the right: 1. To receive health care on the basis of clinical need ... 3. To receive emergency medical care at any time' (p. 8). Furthermore, the Patient's Charter guaranteed seven existing and three new rights (on information availability, waiting times for treatment and complaints). In 1995 a new version called *The Patient's Charter and You* (Department of Health, 1995b) was published containing 26 rights (which all patients will receive all the time) and 47 expectations (standards of service which the NHS is aiming to achieve). The industry of patients' rights has clearly grown and we have an expansion of charters, including The Maternity Charter and The Children and Young People Charter. The net effect of these charters has been to create new areas of 'demand', politicise them, and construct new measures for assessing the states' ability, or more frequently inability, to meet those demands.

Combined with this expansion of citizen rights, however, has been the simultaneous growth in the perception, and portrayal, of the patient as a 'consumer' of health care services, both generally in society and more specifically in health care, which has compounded this growth in political demand.

Growing 'Consumerisation' of the Citizen

Over the last decade or so, as a part of the general political move toward the right, there has been a general societal move toward 'consumerism' (Toth, 1996). Here we are using 'consumerism' to refer to the advocacy of the 'libertarian' philosophy of the individual's 'sovereignty' in decisions concerning consumption, based on improvements in the availability of information and in allocation according to each individual's preferences (willingness to pay) and resources (ability to pay). Reflecting this is the increase in the

> organised movement to protect the interests of consumers ... developed in response to the growing market power of large companies and the increasing technical complexity of products [embracing] bodies such as the Consumers Association in the UK (*Collins Dictionary of Economics*, p. 90).

Of particular importance is the increase of 'consumerism' in the NHS, as a result of government policy, and the role for the public as 'consumers' of NHS products which, prior to 1979, did not exist. Examples of 'consumer' initiatives includes such things as 'drop-in centres', 'NHS Direct', patient satisfaction surveys and the plethora of league tables of hospital performance (a similar feature of which has been seen in other sectors of the welfare state, such as education), many following the Patient's Charter revolution several years ago (Toth, 1996).

The importance of this for demand analysis is that the 'psychology' of the citizen has been changed, and the nature of the 'public contract' implicitly changed, fuelling demand side pressures (Lupton et al., 1991). The perception of the 'patient' has changed from one of a passive recipient of his/her health care 'rights' to one in which they are 'active citizens' (quasi-consumers), with an associated imbalance in perceived 'rights and responsibilities' (Thornton, 1999). That is, the 'patient' operates *as if* they were a consumer in a 'traditional' market, with an expectation of the same level of responsiveness of supply and quality of service (McIntosh and White, 1999). However, this is not matched with a corresponding reduction in the citizen 'rights' basis of health care and thus increase in 'responsibility' of the patient to pay. The net effect of this is a compounding of the level of demand on the system, both of an 'economic' and political form.

This has led to, for example, individuals making more decisions within that 'consumer' frame of mind, such as on initial consultations, elective treatments, and diagnostic tests. Many of these entail significant waiting time in the NHS, and an increasing number of people are opting to undertake privately the initial consultations, and diagnostic tests, in order to speed their way through the system, even though their final treatment will be provided and paid for through the NHS. There has also been a rise in the number of individuals paying directly for elective surgery, with BUPA alone claiming a 61 per cent increase in non-insured operations since 1995 (Barron, 1999). Thus there is a growth of the perception of the individual as a 'consumer' in health care, as in other markets, with only those without the necessary ability to pay for specific services in monetary terms being restricted totally to the NHS (bearing in mind that this will, of course, vary across different services according to their cost).

This growth in what we might term 'active-citizenship', created by the expansion of 'rights' and the growing 'consumerisation' of health care, creates problems, however, for the analysis of health care based on the 'traditional' concept of demand, and highlights the need for a new paradigm, or conceptualisation, of demand in health care.

Reconceptualising Demand: the 'Dual-utility' Function?

The importance of citizenship in health care means that predictions and evaluations made of policies based on the narrow theory of demand, as representing 'consumers', will not account for the impact that the citizen role has upon the overall level of demand. The model will therefore be under-specified, and analysis partial. Importantly, such a model is under-specified in terms of the constraints and incentives acting upon both the individual and the producer/supplier, which becomes acute when we have a mixed demand function based on the interaction of the individual as simultaneously consumer and citizen, which has increasingly occurred over recent years. There therefore needs to be a reconceptualisation of demand which accounts for this 'dual role' of the individual as simultaneously citizen and consumer, reflecting the respective political and economic components.

The model we would propose is one based on an explicit specification of the dual-role, expressed in terms of a 'dual utility function' for the individual. 'Utility function' in this context is an approach to identifying and assessing the dimensions of importance to the individual in guiding their actions, typically in their decision-making within a market context. Thus, major dimensions in the utility function are usually considered to be the price of the commodity, prices of substitute and complementary commodities, 'satisfaction' gained from consumption of each commodity, income etc. (McGuire et al., 1988). These functions are generally based on the model of the 'self interested consumer', and there has been little work on specifying such a utility function for the individual as a 'citizen'.

We would propose that explicit consideration of the dual role of the individual requires development of such a 'dual utility function' approach to demand, with interdependent utility functions for consumer and citizen. Each function would express different parameters effecting that element of demand, allowing factors influencing 'economic' demand by the 'consumer' to be combined with those representing 'political' demand by the 'citizen', to create a 'unified' theory of demand. For example, the consumer utility function may incorporate dimensions such as those mentioned, with the citizen function incorporating issues of utility from community participation, sense of duty and responsibility, equity constraints/objectives, 'rights' etc., with some specified interaction between the two operating in parallel within the individual.

An early suggestion of the possible usefulness of such a 'dual utility function' approach was made by Buchanan (1965) in considering health care funding. He highlighted the conflict of the individual in acting as 'consumer' and 'citizen' with respect to the overall health care funding decision; that as consumers their incentive is to maximise consumption (which is free at point of use), and as citizen to minimise investment in health care (i.e. taxation) which funds its availability. That is, at the same time as the public 'demand' increases through additions and extensions of social rights, their revealed preference is for reduction in the very taxation income which is necessary to fund those increased demands. Indeed, Klein (1989) goes further in suggesting that a 'service for the people' must undertake *only* to invoke such a 'citizen' utility function, implying that 'the real justification of the NHS lies precisely in the fact that it does not respond readily to consumer demands: that it is a device for compelling collective altruism' (p. 158).

Although the existence, and usefulness, of multiple utility functions has been subjected to limited debate (see for example Lutz, 1993; Brennan, 1989, 1993), a recent variation on this theme was proposed by Mooney (1998), who suggests that a 'multiple' utility function approach might be used in establishing an alternative basis for allocating health care resources than one based on 'need'. In essence he proposes a personal utility function nested within a community one. He then defines the 'personal' utility function as one reflecting 'the individual desire for own health', and the 'community' utility function as reflecting 'the individual as a citizen', with the role of the citizen to 'set the procedural rules' by which the health care system is run (p. 1173). Mooney's argument is therefore for a 'principal-agent' relationship on a societal level, with the individual as citizen setting the principles by which resource allocation decisions should occur, and then the nominated 'agent' (bureaucrat), with information concerning relevant costs and benefits, making decisions consistent with these principles and applying them to the individual at a 'patient' level.

Although our proposal would build on, and could incorporate, Mooney's suggestion, it differs in that the dual utility function we propose recognises that the roles of consumer and citizen coexist *at all times* in the individual's interaction and relationship with the health care system, and cannot be differentiated in to discrete levels whereby one utility function is invoked at 'high level' development of principles and the other at the level of individual use of services.

Conclusion

This chapter has proposed three things: 1) that the 'dual role' of the individual in their relationship with the health care system should be explicitly acknowledged; 2) that this 'dual role' may be modelled through the application of a 'dual utility function' approach; and 3) that this would allow the integration of both 'consumer' and 'citizen' demands in the analysis of health care. We believe that this will allow an open debate to begin on the demand side issues of the 'market' in health care in the UK, and will facilitate a structured and comprehensive analysis of the working of the 'market', and the impact of changes to that 'market'. What is required now, of course, is development of the model itself, assessment of the dimensions within each utility function, and, critically, the specification of the interdependency between them. We hope to pursue this in the future.

Acknowledgements

The authors would like to express their appreciation to Dr Joanna Coast, of the University of Bristol, for comments on earlier drafts of the paper. Any errors or omissions are, of course, the author's responsibility.

References

Barron, P. (1999), 'Patients Prepared to Pay as they Go', *The Times*, 18 September.
Brennan, T.J. (1989), 'A Methodological Assessment of the Multiple Utility Frameworks', *Economics and Philosophy*, 5, pp. 189–208.

Brennan, T.J. (1993), 'The Futility of Multiple Utility', *Economics and Philosophy*, 9, pp. 155–64.
Buchanan, J.M. (1965), *The Inconsistencies of the National Health Service*, Occasional Paper 7, Institute of Economic Affairs, London.
Collins Concise Dictionary (1997), HarperCollins Publishers, Glasgow.
Collins Dictionary of Economics (1988), HarperCollins Publishers, Glasgow.
Department of Health and Social Services (1976), *Priorities for the Health and Personal Social Services*, HMSO, London.
Department of Health (1992), *The Patient's Charter*, HMSO, London.
Department of Health (1995a), *Statement of Responsibilities and Accountabilities*, HMSO, London.
Department of Health (1995b), *The Patient's Charter and You*, HMSO, London.
Evans, R.G. (1997a), 'Going for the Gold: The redistributive agenda behind market-based health care reform', *Journal of Health Politics Policy and Law*, 22(2), pp. 427–65.
Evans, R.G. (1997b), 'Coarse Correction – and Way Off Target', *Journal of Health Politics Policy and Law*, 22(2), pp. 503–8.
Gaynor, M. and Vogt, W.B. (1997), 'What does Economics have to Say about Health Policy Anyway?', *Journal of Health Politics Policy and Law*, 22(2), pp. 475–96.
Klein, R. (1989), *The politics of the National Health Service*, Longman, London.
Lupton, D., Donaldson, C. and Lloyd, P. (1991), 'Caveat Emptor or Blissful Ignorance? – Patients and the consumerist ethos', *Social Science and Medicine*, 33, pp. 559–68.
Lutz, M.A. (1993), 'The Utility of Multiple Utility: A comment on Brennan', *Economics and Philosophy*, 9, pp. 145–54.
MacPherson, G. (1988), '1948: A turbulent gestation for the NHS', *British Medical Journal*, 316, p. 6.
Marshall, T.H. (1950), *Citizenship and Social Class*, Cambridge University Press, Cambridge.
McGuire, A., Henderson, J. and Mooney, G. (1988), *The Economics of Health Care: An introductory text*, Routledge, London.
McIntosh, K. and White, C. (1999), 'Spiral of Demand Hits Summertime 999 Services', *Health Service Journal*, 26 August.
Mooney, G. (1998), 'Communitarian Claims as an Ethical Basis for Allocating Health Care Resources', *Social Science and Medicine*, 47(9), pp. 1171–80.
Normand, C. (1998), 'Ten Popular Health Economic Fallacies', *Journal of Public Health Medicine*, 20, pp. 129–32.
Pauly, M.V. (1997), 'Who Was that Straw Man Anyway? Comment', *Journal of Health Politics Policy and Law*, 22(2), pp. 467–73.
Rice, T. (1997a), 'Can Markets Give us the Health System We Want?', *Journal of Health Politics Policy and Law*, 22(2), pp. 383–426.
Rice, T. (1997b), 'What Does Economics have to Say about Health Policy Anyway – Reply?', *Journal of Health Politics Policy and Law*, 22(2), pp. 497–501.
Reinhardt, U., Evans, R.G., Rice, T., Pauly, M., Sloan, F. and Zweifel, P. (1999), panel discussion of 'The Demand Curve (for medical care) Should be Abolished', 2nd World Conference of the International Health Economics Association, Rotterdam, 6–9 June.
Salter, B. (1998), *The Politics of Change in the Health Service*, Macmillan Press Ltd, London.
Scotton, R. (1995), 'Managed Competition: Issues for Australia', *Australian Health Review*, 18, pp. 82–104.
Scotton, R. (1999), 'Managed Competition', in G. Mooney and R. Scotton (eds), *Economics and Australian Health Policy*, Allen & Unwin, Sydney, pp. 214–31.

Smith, R. (1999), 'The NHS: Possibilities for the endgame', *British Medical Journal*, 318, pp. 209–10.

Smith, R., Hiatt, H. and Berwick, D. (1999), 'Shared Ethical Principles for Everybody in Health Care: A working draft from the Tavistock Group', *British Medical Journal*, 318, pp. 248–51.

Thornton, H. (1999), 'Today's Patient: Passive or involved?', *The Lancet*, 354, p. 48.

Toth, B. (1996), 'Public Participation in Health Care: An historical perspective', in J. Coast, J. Donovan and S. Frankel (eds), *Priority-setting: The health care debate*, John Wiley & Sons Ltd, Chichester, pp. 169–202.

Van Steenbergen, B. (1994), 'The Condition of Citizenship: An introduction', in B. Van Steenbergen (ed.), *The Condition of Citizenship*, Sage, London, pp. 3–15.

Chapter Ten

Income, Income Distribution and Hospitalisation: an Ecologic Study in Rome, Italy

Laura Cacciani, Enrico Materia, Giulia Cesaroni, Giovanni Baglio, Marina Davoli, Massimo Arcà and Carlo A. Perucci

Introduction

Although low socioeconomic status is a strong determinant of early mortality and excess morbidity (Marmot and Wilkinson, 1999), health care financing systems do not usually consider the socioeconomic status of the target population. With regard to socioeconomic status and hospitalisation, in the United States it has been shown that the socioeconomic level of a community is inversely correlated with hospitalisation rates and that this correlation explains a large part of the geographical variations in hospital use (McMahon et al., 1993). Moreover, it has been shown that residents of lower and middle income areas are more likely than those of high income areas to be hospitalised because of conditions for which hospitalisation is potentially avoidable (Pappas et al., 1997).

Few studies have focused on the association between relative deprivation as measured by income heterogeneity indexes (Huang and Joseph, 1999) on hospitalisation, whereas more studies have focused on the association between income distribution and mortality. For example, studies conducted in the United States have shown that those States with greater inequality have increased mortality from several causes (Kennedy et al., 1996; Kaplan et al., 1996) and that the potential factors in this association include chronic stress associated with the psychosocial effect of social comparison, level of insecurity and frustration (Wilkinson, 1997), disinvestment in human capital, and the erosion of social capital (Kawachi and Kennedy, 1997a; 1999).

Health Policy and Economics: Strategic Issues in Health Care Management, M. Tavakoli, H.T.O. Davies and M. Malek (eds), Ashgate Publishing Ltd, 2001.

In the United States, emphasis has also been placed on the association between patients' socioeconomic status and the use of hospital resources. Some studies have shown that for at least some conditions, hospital care for poor patients entails longer stays and requires a greater use of resources (Epstein et al., 1988; Jencks et al., 1990; Epstein et al., 1990). Possible explanations are that patients of lower socioeconomic status might not receive early treatment and might therefore be more severely ill at the time of admission or they might not have a sufficiently supportive environment. Consequently, more resources would need to be allocated to hospitals whose patients are mostly persons of lower socioeconomic status.

In Italy, the prospective system of hospital payment based on Diagnosis Related Groups (DRG) and adopted by the National Health Service in 1995 does not take into account the degree of socioeconomic heterogeneity within patient groups, and little emphasis has been placed on the effect of income and income distribution on hospitalisation and the use of hospital resources. The objective of the present study, conducted in Rome, Italy, was to evaluate the effect of both income (considered as a proxy of socioeconomic status) and income distribution on acute hospitalisation rates and the effect of income on the use of hospital resources.

Methods

The study was conducted in the city of Rome, which is located in the Lazio Region (central Italy; Italy is divided into 20 geographic regions). Rome is divided into 19 districts, each of which is divided into a varying number of census tracts.

The specific objectives of this study were as follows:

1 hospitalisation and income: to evaluate the relationship between acute hospitalisation rates and mean per capita income among districts;
2 hospitalisation and income distribution: to evaluate the relationship between acute hospitalisation rates and income distribution (as measured using income heterogeneity indexes), among districts; and
3 length of hospital stay and income: to evaluate the relationship between the use of hospital resources (as measured by length of stay for acute hospitalisation) and mean per capita income (categorised into levels of socioeconomic status) among census tracts.

Data on hospitalisations were taken from the Lazio Region Hospital Information System, which since 1995 has collected data on all hospital discharges in the Lazio region (both private and public hospitals). To calculate the district level hospitalisation rates (age standardised and gender specific) and to determine the length of hospital stay, we used data on all residents of Rome hospitalised in 1997 in the Lazio region, excluding hospitals not receiving remuneration from Italy's National Health System (i.e., strictly private hospitals). We also calculated the association between length of hospital stay and hospitalisations for appendectomy (DRGs 164–167) and diseases and disorders of the circulatory system (Major Diagnostic Category [MDC: 5]; DRG Classification System), which were the most prevalent surgical diagnosis and the most prevalent MDC, respectively.

To calculate income and income distribution, we used data aggregated by census tract on taxable income earned in 1993 (declared in 1994) (data provided by the Italian Tax Register). To calculate the mean per capita income of each district, we used as denominator the total population of the district, as opposed to the number of taxpayers. To calculate the district level income distribution, we used two commonly used indicators of inequalities in income (i.e., the Gini coefficient and the decile ratio) (Kawachi and Kennedy, 1997b), with higher values representing greater heterogeneity in income distribution. To calculate the mean per capita income for each census tract, we used as denominator the total population of the census tract. The mean per capita income by census tract was categorised into four levels (levels I–IV), using as cut-off the 20th, 50th, and 80th percentiles. The socioeconomic status indicated by these levels ranged from very well-off (level I) to very underprivileged (level IV). A deterministic record linkage procedure was used to link the individual codes of the Rome Census Bureau to the episodes of hospitalisation in order to attribute the census tract code and the income aggregated by census tract to discharge records.

All population figures were taken from a 1996 estimate based on the 1991 census. The population ranged from one inhabitant to approximately 16,000 inhabitants for the census tracts and from approximately 59,000 to 211,000 inhabitants for the districts; the population of Rome was 2,825,663 inhabitants.

Statistical Analysis

The Pearson coefficient (r) was used to examine the presence of a linear correlation between district-level hospitalisation rate and: 1) mean per capita income; 2) the Gini coefficient; and 3) the decile ratio. Ordinary multiple least squares regression models were used to examine the relationship between the length of hospital stay and the income level, separately for both genders. To correct for non-normality of the distribution for length of stay, log transformation was used. Violations of assumptions of linearity, equality of variance and normality were checked by plotting residuals against standardised predicted values and by constructing histograms of standardised residuals. To establish the goodness of fit of the models, we calculated the R^2 coefficient. All t-tests for the regression coeffiecients were two-tailed. For overall hospitalisation, to control for confounding, adjustments were made for age, type of discharge institute (teaching, non-teaching, and private hospitals, among others), DRG weight, type of discharge (home, transfer, voluntary, decease, supervised discharge), type of DRG (medical, surgical, other), MDC, and the number of readmissions (defined as the next subsequent admission of a patient to any hospital in the Lazio region for the same MDC during 1997). For hospitalisations for appendectomy, adjustments were made for age, type of discharge institute, and DRG. For diseases and disorders of the circulatory system, adjustments were made for age, type of discharge institute, type of discharge, type of DRG, and DRG weight. A separate category, corresponding to missing values for the income indicator, was used to describe patients whose income level was unknown.

Results

In 1997, there were 546,223 episodes of hospitalisation in the Lazio region among residents of Rome (all types of hospitalisation and of hospitals); of these, 358,243 were episodes of acute hospitalisation in hospitals receiving remuneration from Italy's National Health System and thus were included in the present analysis: 2,851 were episodes of appendectomy and 51,107 were episodes of diseases and disorders of the circulatory system. Information on income was not available for 16,411 of the overall hospitalisations (4.6 per cent), for 146 of the hospitalisations for appendectomy (5.1 per cent), and for 2,247 of the hospitalisations for diseases and disorders of the circulatory system (4.4 per cent).

Hospitalisation and Income

The mean district level per capita annual income ranged from 8,280,000 to 23,950,000 Italian lira. We observed a negative bivariate correlation between mean per capita annual income and overall acute hospitalisation rates (for males: r=-0.89, p=0.00; for females: r=-0.95, p= 0.00) (Figures 9.1 and 9.2).

Hospitalisation and Income Distribution

The district-level Gini coefficient varied from 0.12 to 0.29; the decile ratio varied from 2.8 to 8.9. Neither of these measures was found to be significantly associated with hospitalisation rates (Gini coefficient: for males, r=-0.19, p=0.42; for females, r=-0.21, p= 0.38 for females; decile ratio: for males, r=-0.23, p=0.34; for females, r=-0.26, p= 0.29).

Length of Hospital Stay and Income

Table 10.1 shows the crude mean length of hospital stay and the mean age of patients by income level (levels I–IV) and gender for overall hospitalisations, appendectomy, and diseases and disorders of the circulatory system. Table 10.2 shows the exponential regression coefficients, and their confidence intervals, of the regression models adjusted for confounding variables (the necessary assumptions to perform the regression models were met).

Length of Hospital Stay for Overall Hospitalisation

Of the 358,243 overall hospitalisations included in the analysis, 163,671 (45.7 per cent) were among males and 194,572 (54.3 per cent) among females. After adjustment for age, type of discharge, type of discharge institute, type of DRG, MDC, DRG weight, and number of readmissions, we observed an increase in the length of hospital stay with decreases in socioeconomic status. Specifically, among males, the increase was 7.7 per cent (p=0.00) for level II, 13.1 per cent (p=0.00) for level III, and 17 per cent (p=0.00) for level IV, when compared with level I (highest socioeconomic status) (R^2=0.29). Among females, the increase was 5.2 per cent (p=0.00), 9.6 per cent (p=0.00), and 13.7 per cent (p=0.00), respectively, with respect to level I (R^2=0.32).

Length of Hospital Stay for Appendectomy

Of the 2,851 hospitalisations for appendectomy that were included in the analysis, 1,264 (44.3 per cent) were among males and 1,587 (55.7 per cent) among females. After adjustment for age, type of discharge institute, and DRG, we observed an increase in the length of hospital stay with decreases in

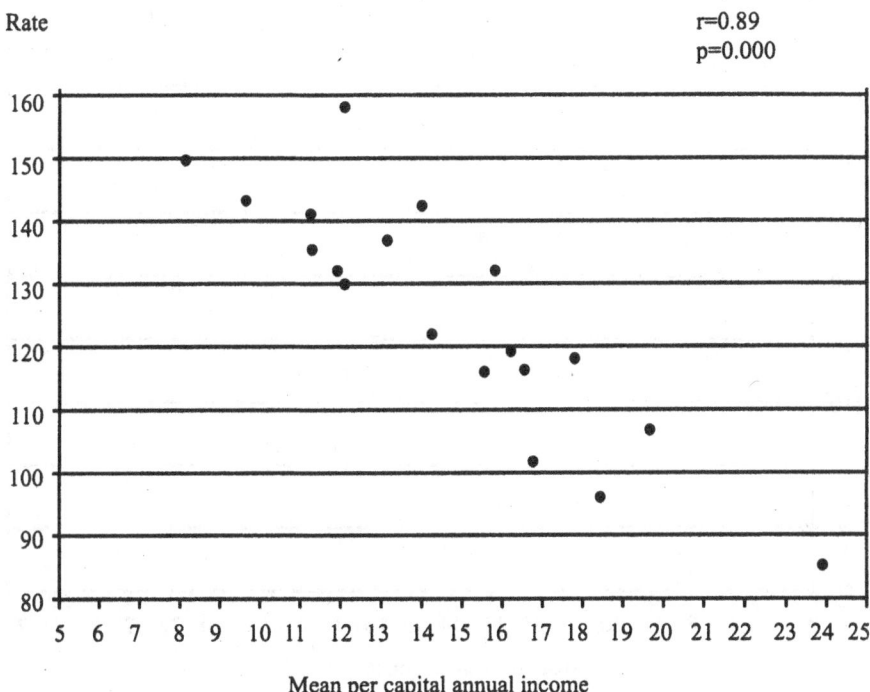

Figure 10.1 Relationship between age-standardised hospitalisation rates (x 1,000) and mean per capita annual income (in millions of Italian lire) by district; males, Rome, 1997

socioeconomic status, yet only among females: 7.1 per cent (p=0.02) for level II, 9.1 per cent (p=0.00) for level III, and 13.9 per cent (p=0.00) for level IV, when compared with level I (R^2=0.21). Among males, no statistically significant associations were observed between income level and length of hospital stay.

Length of Hospital Stay for Diseases and Disorders of the Circulatory System

Of the 51,107 hospitalisations for diseases and disorders of the circulatory system that were included in the analysis, 26,759 (52.4 per cent) were among males and 24,348 (47.6 per cent) among females. After adjustment for age, DRG weight, type of discharge, type of discharge institute and type of DRG, we observed an increase in the length of hospital stay for lower socioeconomic

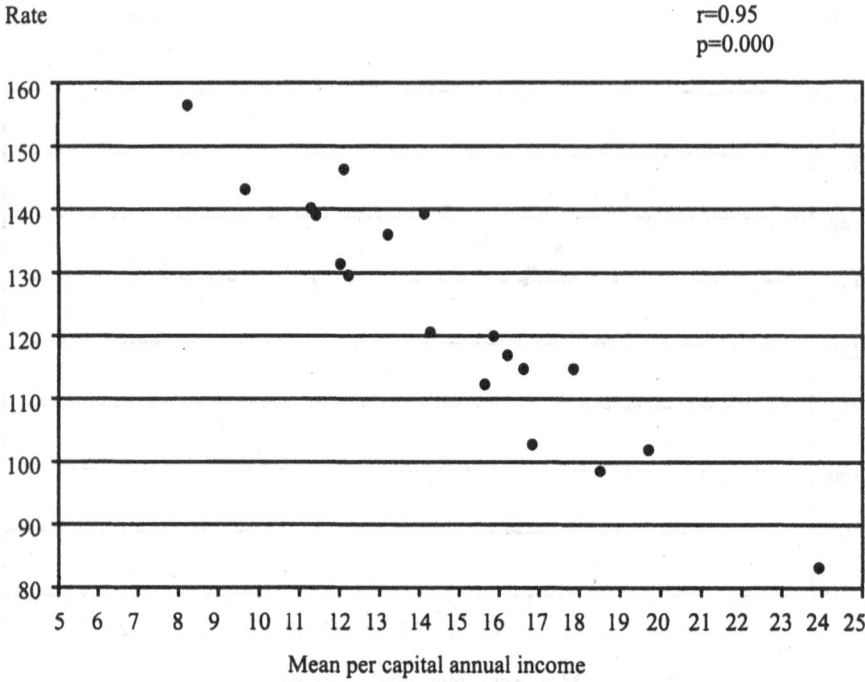

Figure 10.2 Relationship between age-standardised hospitalisation rates (x 1,000) and mean per capita annual income (in millions of Italian lire) by district; females, Rome, 1997

status. Among males, the increase was 5.3 per cent (p=0.00) for level II, 10.5 per cent (p=0.00) for level III, and 17.7 per cent (p=0.00) for level IV, when compared with level I (R^2=0.28). Among females, the increase was 2.9 per cent (p=0.00), 6.1 per cent (p=0.00), and 9.2 per cent (p=0.00), respectively (R^2=0.29).

Discussion

We observed an inverse correlation between district level income and hospitalisation rates in Rome, for both males and females. By contrast, no association was found between income distribution (as measured by the Gini coefficient and decile ratio) and hospitalisation rates, and the values provided by these indexes were much lower than those reported in a study conducted in the United States (Kawachi and Kennedy, 1997b), suggesting that aggregated

Table 10.1 Number of discharges, mean length of hospital stay and mean age by income level and gender; Rome, 1997

Overall hospitalisation (n=358,243)

	Males				Females			
Income level	No.	(%)	Mean length of stay	Mean age	No.	(%)	Mean length of stay	Mean age
I High	20,711	(12.7)	8.5	55	25,447	(13.1)	8.3	55
II Medium – high	49,384	(30.2)	8.9	54	59,785	(30.7)	8.4	54
III Medium – low	55,737	(34.1)	9.2	52	66,017	(33.9)	8.4	51
IV Low	29,965	(18.3)	9.0	48	34,786	(17.9)	8.2	48
Missing	7,874	(4.8)	8.9	48	8,537	(4.4)	7.9	48
Total	163,671		9.0	52	194,572		8.3	52

Appendectomy (n=2,851)

	Males				Females			
Income level	No.	(%)	Mean length of stay	Mean age	No.	(%)	Mean length of stay	Mean age
I High	179	(14.0)	6.1	26	206	(13.0)	5.2	25
II Medium – high	377	(29.8)	6.1	27	458	(28.9)	5.8	25
III Medium – low	391	(30.9)	5.9	24	509	(32.1)	5.6	23
IV Low	245	(19.4)	6.0	23	340	(21.4)	5.7	19
Missing	72	(5.7)	5.5	27	74	(4.7)	5.7	25
Total	1,264		6.0	25	1,587		5.7	23

Diseases and disorders of the circulatory system (n=51,107)

	Males				Females			
Income level	No.	(%)	Mean length of stay	Mean age	No.	(%)	Mean length of stay	Mean age
I High	3,643	(13.6)	9.7	67	2,997	(12.3)	10.0	70
II Medium – high	8,468	(31.6)	10.0	66	7,673	(31.5)	9.8	69
III Medium – low	9,020	(33.7)	10.2	64	8,392	(34.5)	9.9	67
IV Low	4,380	(16.4)	10.3	62	4,287	(17.6)	9.8	65
Missing	1,248	(4.7)	9.7	61	999	(4.1)	9.8	65
Total	26,759		10.0	65	24,348		9.9	68

Table 10.2 Exponential regression coefficients of the natural logarithm of length of hospital stay and their 95% confidence intervals by income level and gender; Rome, 1997

Overall hospitalisation[a]

Income level	Males Exp(B)	Exp(95% CI)		Females Exp(B)	Exp(95% CI)	
I High	1	–	–	1	–	–
II Medium – high	1,077	1,064	1,091	1,052	1,041	1,064
III Medium – low	1,131	1,117	1,145	1,096	1,084	1,107
IV Low	1,170	1,154	1,186	1,137	1,123	1,150
Missing	1,133	1,111	1,156	1,095	1,076	1,115

Appendectomy[b]

Income level	Males Exp(B)	Exp(95% CI)		Females Exp(B)	Exp(95% CI)	
I High	1	–	–	1	–	–
II Medium – high	1,002	0,936	1,074	1,071	1,010	1,138
III Medium – low	0,996	0,930	1,066	1,091	1,029	1,157
IV Low	1,038	0,963	1,119	1,139	1,070	1,213
Missing	0,950	0,856	1,057	1,139	1,035	1,252

Diseases and disorders of the circulatory system[c]

Income level	Males Exp(B)	Exp(95% CI)		Females Exp(B)	Exp(95% CI)	
I High	1	–	–	1	–	–
II Medium – high	1,053	1,021	1,087	1,029	0,996	1,064
III Medium – low	1,105	1,071	1,139	1,061	1,026	1,095
IV Low	1,177	1,137	1,219	1,092	1,053	1,133
Missing	1,132	1,075	1,191	1,090	1,031	1,153

Notes

a   Regression model adjusted by age, DRG weight, type of discharge, type of discharge institute, type of DRG, MDC and number of readmissions.
b   Regression model adjusted by age, type of discharge institute, and DRG.
c   Regression model adjusted by age, DRG weight, type of discharge, type of discharge institute, and type of DRG.

data are not the most appropriate source for calculating income distribution indexes. We also observed an inverse correlation between income and mean length of hospital stay for both males and females for overall hospitalisation and for hospitalisation for diseases and disorders of the circulatory system, and for females only for hospitalisations for appendectomy.

Heterogeneity in hospital use could partly depend on differences in health status among socioeconomic groups, as shown by differentials in mortality between well-off and disadvantaged persons in Rome (Michelozzi et al., 1999). However, low socioeconomic groups may also be at greater risk of inappropriate hospitalisations (Materia et al., 1999) and may be more likely to be hospitalised for episodes that would be avoidable with better access to primary health care services (Pappas et al., 1997).

The results of this analysis confirm previous findings from a study conducted in Rome on hospitalisation and socioeconomic status (Materia et al., 1999), which showed an excess of acute hospitalisation risk among persons of lower socioeconomic status when compared with more affluent persons. In that study, a composite, geographic, census-based (1991 census) index of the socioeconomic status was used (Michelozzi et al., 1999). The results of the present study are also consistent with those of studies conducted in North America (McMahon et al., 1993; Mustard and Frohlich, 1995) and Europe (Keskimaki et al.; Chenet and Mckee, 1996).

With regard to the finding of no association between hospitalisation rates and income distribution, this may have depended on the method used to calculate the indexes. Although there exists evidence of an effect of income distribution on total mortality (Kennedy et al., 1996; Kaplan et al., 1996) and on self-rated health status (Kennedy et al., 1998), there are still few studies related to hospitalisation (Huang and Joseph, 1999). Moreover, although hospitalisation rates reflect morbidity, hospitalisation is a complex phenomenon potentially influenced by supply-dependent factors that could mask the real relationship between income distribution and health status.

The inverse association observed between the length of hospital stay and the level of mean per capita annual income may be explained by the fact that low-income patients are more severely ill at the time of admission (Vineis et al., 1993; Eachus et al., 1999) and receive less timely and lower quality care (Fiscella, 2000). Our results are consistent with those of studies conducted in the United States, which showed an inverse effect of the income level on the length of stay (Epstein et al., 1988 and 1990).

Some limitations of our study should be considered. The study design is ecologic; thus the ecologic fallacy is one of its major problems (Greenland

and Robins, 1994; Piantadosi, 1994; Cohen, 1994), even though the objective was to describe ecologic associations between hospitalisation and income in Rome, not to infer a causal link on an individual basis. Moreover, there are both advantages and disadvantages to using geographic indexes as measures of socioeconomic status, as opposed to individual indexes. Specifically, although small area based geographic indicators tend to underestimate the effect of the individual socioeconomic level, they do measure the environmental effect of the geographic area under study at the individual level (Haan et al., 1987; Anderson et al., 1997). Moreover, it has been shown that the impact of socioeconomic characteristics on hospitalisation rates is consistent when measured by individual- or community-level measures (Hofer et al., 1998) and that geographic indicators can approximate individual measures (Krieger, 1992; Geronimus et al., 1991; Geronimus and Bound, 1998).

Some limitations in the calculation of the income distribution indexes should also be considered. These indexes are usually based on household income figures, whereas we calculated them on the basis of income aggregated by census tract. The lack of analytic information on household income could hide substantial differences in income distribution and be potentially responsible for the lack of an association observed between hospitalisation and income distribution.

Information on potential strong determinants of hospitalisation, such as smoking and drug use by district, were not available. Moreover, it was not possible to adjust the analysis of the length of stay for confounders such as disease severity; it was only possible to adjust for the weight of DRG, as a measure of hospital resource consumption.

As far as missing data are concerned, data on income were missing for 4.6 per cent of the overall hospitalisations. We considered these as a separate category of the indicator to take into account its effect on the length of hospital stay.

In conclusion, the results of our study suggest, in confirmation of previous evidence, that persons with lower income are more likely to be hospitalised and spend more time in the hospital. As a consequence, both hospital case mix and income level should be taken into account by hospital financing systems. The analysis between relative deprivation and hospitalisation cannot be considered conclusive; it should be replicated when household income-based indexes are available.

Acknowledgments

We acknowledge the collaboration of the Working Group of SOGEI – Ministry of Finance (Guilio Bugarini, Ursula Herr, Maria Paola Mirale, Guiseppe Simeone and Loredana Vergine) for providing income data.

References

Anderson, R.T., Sorlie, P., Backlund, E., Jonshon, N. and Kaplan, G.A. (1997), 'Mortality Effects of Socioeconomic Status', *Epidemiology*, 8, pp. 42–7.
Cadum, E., Costa, G., Biggeri, A. and Martuzzi, M. (1999), 'Deprivation and Mortality: A deprivation index suitable for geographical analysis of inequalities', *Epidemiologia e Prevenzione*, 23, pp. 175–87.
Chenet, L. and Mckee, M. (1996), 'Challenge of Monitoring Use of Secondary Care at Local Level: A study based in London, UK', *Epidemiology and Community Health*, 50, pp. 359–65.
Cohen, B.L. (1994), 'In Defense of Ecologic Studies for Testing a Linear No-threshold Theory', *American Journal Of Epidemiology*, 139(8), pp. 765–8.
Davey Smith, G. (1996), 'Income Inequality and Mortality: Why are they related?', *British Medical Journal*, 312(7037), pp. 987–8.
Eachus, J., Chan, P., Pearson, N., Propper, C. and Davey Smith, G. (1999), 'An Additional Dimension to Health Inequalities: Disease severity and socieconomic position', *Journal of Epidemiology and Community Health*, 53(10), pp. 603–11.
Epstein, A.M., Stern, R.S., Tognetti, J., Begg, C.B., Hartley, R.M., Cumella, E. and Ayanian, J.Z. (1988), 'The Association of Patients' Socioeconomic Characteristics with the Length of Hospital Stay and Hospital Charges within Diagnosis-related Groups', *The New England Journal Of Medicine*, 318(24), pp. 1579–85.
Epstein, A.M., Stern, R.S. and Weissman, J.S. (1990) 'Do the Poor Cost More? A Multihospital Study of Patients' Socioeconomic Status and Use of Hospital Resources', *The New England Journal Of Medicine*, 322(16), pp. 1122–8.
Fiscella, K., Franks, P., Gold, M.R. and Clancy, C.M. (2000), 'Inequality in Quality', *The Journal of the American Medical Association*, 283(19), pp. 2579–84.
Geronimus, A.T., Bound, J. and Neidert, L.J. (1996), 'On the Validity of Using Census Geocode Characteristics to Proxy Individual Socioeconomic Characteristics', *Journal Of The American Statistical Association*, 91(434), pp. 529–37.
Geronimus, A.T. and Bound, J. (1998), 'Use of Census-based Aggregate Variables to Proxy for Socioeconomic Group: Evidence from national samples', *American Journal Of Epidemiology*, 148(5), pp. 475–86.
Greenland, S. and Robins, J. (1994), 'Ecologic Studies – Biases, Missconceptions, and Counterexamples', *American Journal Of Epidemiology*, 139(8), pp. 747–60.
Greenland, S. and Robins, J. (1994), 'Accepting the Limits of Ecologic Studies: Drs Greenland and Robins replay to Drs. Piantadosi and Cohen', *American Journal Of Epidemiology*, 139(8), pp. 769–71.
Haan, M., Kaplan, G.A. and Camacho, T. (1987), 'Poverty and Health. Prospective Evidence from the Alameda County Study', *American Journal Of Epidemiology*, 125, pp. 989–98.

Hofer, T.P., Wolfe, R.A., Tedeschi, P.J., McMahon, L.F. and Griffith, J.R. (1998), 'Use of Community versus Individual Socioeconomic Data in Predicting Variation in Hospital Use', *Health Services Research*, 33(2), pp. 243-59.

Huang, J.Z. and Joseph J.G. (1999), 'Does Small Area Income Inequality Influence the Hospital Utilisation of Children? A Disease-specific Analysis', in Proceedings of the Conference on *Socioeconomic Status and Health in Industrial Nations: Social, psychological and biological pathways*, organised by the New York Academy of Sciences, New York.

Jencks, S.F, Stern, R.S and Weissman, J.S. (1990), 'Do Frail, Disabled, Poor and Very Old Medicare Beneficiaries have Higher Hospital Charges?', *Journal Of American Medical Association*, 257(2), pp. 1122-8.

Kaplan, G.A., Pamuk, E.R., Lynch, J.W., Cohen, R.D. and Balfour, J.L. (1996), 'Inequality in Income and Mortality in the United States: Analysis of mortality and potential pathways', *British Medical Journal*, 312(7037), pp. 999-1003.

Kawachi, I. and Kennedy, B.P. (1997a), 'Socioeconomic Determinants of Health: Health and social cohesion: Why care about income inequalitiy?', *British Medical Journal*, 314(7086), p. 591.

Kawachi, I. and Kennedy, B.P. (1997b), 'The Relationship of Income Inequality to Mortality: Does the choice of indicator matter?', *Social Science Medicine*, 45(7), pp. 1121-7.

Kawachi, I. and Kennedy, B.P. (1999) 'Income Inequality and Health: Pathways and mechanisms', *Health Services Research*, 34(1), pp. 215-27.

Kennedy, B.P., Kawachi, I. and Prothrow-Stith, D. (1996), 'Income Distribution and Mortality: Cross sectional ecologic study of the Robin Hood index in the United States', *British Medical Journal*, 312(7037), pp. 1004-7.

Kennedy, B.P., Kawachi, I., Glass, R. amd Prothrow-Stith, D. (1998), 'Income Distribution, Socioeconomic Status and Self rated Health in the United States: Multilevel analysis', *British Medical Journal*, 317(7163), pp. 917-21.

Keskimaki, I., Salinato, M. and Aro, S. (1995), 'Socioeconomic Equity in Finnish Hospital Care in Relation to Need', *Social Sciences in Medicine*, 41, pp. 425-31.

Krieger, N. (1992), 'Overcoming the Absence of Socioeconomic Data in Medical Records: Validation and application of a census-based methodology', *American Journal of Public Health*, 92, pp. 703-10.

Marmot, M. and Wilkinson, R.G. (eds) (1999), *Social Determinants of Health*, Oxford University Press, Oxford.

Materia, E., Spadea, T., Rossi, L., Cesaroni, G., Arcà, M. and Perucci, C.A. (1999), 'Health Care Inequalities: Hospitalizazion and socioeconomic position in Rome', *Epidemiologia e Prevenzione*, 23, pp. 197-206.

McMahon, L.F., Wolfe, R.A., Griffith, J.R. and Cuthbertson, D. (1993), 'Socioeconomic Influence on Small Area Hospitalization', *Medical Care*, 5, YS29-36.

Michelozzi, P., Perucci, C.A., Forastiere, F., Fusco, D., Ancona, C. and Dell'Orco, V. (1999), 'Inequality in Health: Socioeconomic differentials in mortality in Rome, 1990-95', *Journal of Epidemiology and Community Health*, 53(11), pp. 687-93.

Mustard, C. and Frohlich, N. (1995), 'Socioeconomic Status and the Health of the Population', *Medical Care*, 33, SD43-DS54.

Pappas, G. Wilbur, C.H., Kozak, L.J. and Fischer, G.F. (1997), 'Potentially Avoidable Hospitalizations: Inequalities in rates between US socioconomic groups', *American Journal of Public Health*, 87, pp. 811-16.

Piantadosi, S. (1994), 'Ecologic Biases', *American Journal Of Epidemiology*, 139(8), pp. 761-4.

Vineis, P., Fornero, G., Magnino, R., Giacometti, R. and Ciccone, G. (1993), 'Diagnostic Delay, Clinical Stage, and Social Class: A hospital based study', *Journal of Epidemiology and Community Health*, 47, pp. 229–31.

Wilkinson, R.G. (1997), 'Socioeconomic Determinants of Health: Health inequalities: relative or absolute material standards?', *British Medical Journal*, 314(7080), p. 591.

Chapter Eleven

Health Care Tax Relief and the Demand for Private Health Care for the Over-60s

Manouche Tavakoli and John O.S. Wilson

Introduction

In recent years, there has been an increased interest among health economists and health care policy makers in explaining the rising health care expenditures in various developed countries. It has been argued that health care expenditure depends primarily on the health care organisation and delivery systems, the level of economic development, the structure of the population, and the quality demanded and supplied (Gerdtham, 1992; Murillo et al., 1993; Hitiris, 1997).

Since late 1970s the rising cost of National Health Service (NHS) has put huge strain on the public purse. In the UK the share of government health expenditure to total public expenditure rose from 10.8 per cent in 1976 to 14.5 per cent in 1997. Also the share of public health expenditure to GDP has been rising steadily since 1960, from 3 per cent to 5.6 per cent in 1998. Consequently the funding of NHS has become one the major challenges that various governments have to deal with.

Much of the funding for the NHS has been met by taxation, while in other countries similar health schemes have been funded by earnings-related contributions and social contributions. However, numerous factors (reviewed below) have meant that the funds raised for the supply of health care fall short of satisfying demand. This shortage is particularly acute for the elderly sections of the population. To alleviate this shortage and reduce the burden on scarce financial resources, policy makers have encouraged the elderly (by offering tax concessions) to take up private health insurance policies. In this chapter we examine the extent to which such policies have been effective in terms of reducing the demands on NHS resources.

Health Policy and Economics: Strategic Issues in Health Care Management, M. Tavakoli, H.T.O. Davies and M. Malek (eds), Ashgate Publishing Ltd, 2001.

Motives for Encouraging Private Health Care

The supply of health care services differs between member countries of European Community in both quantity and quality. Although most EC member states tend to provide comprehensive health care coverage, they differ substantially in organisation, financing and delivery. Medical costs (medical care, ambulatory and medical goods) in the EC member states are provided through two systems: National Health Service (NHS) and Social Sickness Funds (SSF). NHS is a state-run institution providing universal free coverage, financed mainly through taxation (e.g. in the UK since 1948, in Denmark since 1973, and Greece, Italy, Portugal and Spain in the late 1980s). The other system, Social Sickness Funds (SSF) is characterised by insurance, usually compulsory, financed by contributions paid by employers and employees (e.g. France and Germany) (Hitiris, 1997).

In general, compulsory earnings-related contributions, social contributions and taxation finance health care expenditures. As a result, there is no direct link between contributors, consumers and producers of health care. As it has been shown elsewhere (Hitiris, 1997) that irrespective of economic structure and health care delivery systems, the growth of heath care expenditures are well above the growth rates of GDP in EC member states. This has meant a gradual shift of resources to health care over time. The evidence seems to suggest that despite various governments' reforms and cost-containment policies (e.g. in the UK, Belgium and Spain) health care expenditure has been rising faster than income. A number of explanations have been forward for this observation in the developed economies. One is that both public and private health expenditures are not constrained by budgetary considerations as the users of health care do not directly and fully pay for such services. Also advances in cost-increasing medical technology, improvements in medical diagnosis and rising proportion of the elderly in the population have resulted in rising demand over time. Finally, political and social pressures have also led to increases in the supply of health care.

Improvements in medical diagnosis and the rising proportion of the elderly in the population mean that this segment of the population will need more additional health care provision. The Conservative Party has recently pledged to restore private health related tax concessions. The implicit assumption being that incentives are required for elderly segments of the population to take up private health care in order to alleviate and reduce a potential financial crisis in the NHS. Consequently, it is thought that health expenditure saved from such policies will outweigh the lost tax revenues given in tax relief. The aim of this chapter is to raise some of the issues related to the effectiveness of health care tax relief policies introduced by the Conservative government in April 1990. The chapter examines the extent to which such policies have been successful in reducing the rising demand for publicly provided health care. We examine the relationship between health care tax relief and total health care expenditure, and the impact on the private health care expenditure. We shall also propose the theoretical links between various key factors and highlight some of the difficulties in estimating such relationships.

Determinants of Health Expenditure

Consumption of health in most cases is not like other conventional goods, where the individual's demand for a good is directly related to the amount that individual is willing to spend (see for example Andersen and Benham, 1970; Grossman, 1972; Newhouse and Phelps, 1974; Muurinen, 1982; Wagstaff, 1986). This is because in most advanced economies health care is centrally organised (either through NHS or SSF) and heavily subsidised. While an individual's demand depends partly on his/her health condition (which is to some extent stochastic), he/she only pays part of the cost (through tax, or buying an insurance policy) but receives the full benefit of health care. Therefore, in most cases an individual's demand for health care is not constrained by the patient's ability to pay (Pauly, 1986). Furthermore, as there are always social and political pressures on the supply side, the supply considerations can also determine the size of the health care expenditure. So as income rises total expenditure is expected to rise, but as income falls (e.g. due to recession or slow growth) downward pressure on health care expenditures will be resisted.

A number of empirical studies based on country specific time-series data (Murthy and Ukpolo, 1994) and on international cross-section data (Newhouse, 1977; Leu, 1986; Newhouse, 1987; Parkin et al., 1987; Gerdtham and Jonsson, 1991; Milne and Molana, 1991; Warshawsky, 1991; Gerdtham, 1992; Hitiris and Posnett, 1992; Gerdtham and Jonsson, 1992a and b) have attempted to identify factors which make health care expenditures differ among countries. All these studies have attempted to calculate the price and income elasticities, with various degrees of success, and found that per capita income, age of the population, number of practising physicians, and public financing of health care are important determinants. This chapter assess some of the issues of financing total health care expenditure especially for the over-60s in the UK.

As we have stated previously, one way to alleviate the pressure on the public health care has been to encourage private heath care by providing generous tax relief incentives. Table 11.1 provides statistics relating to private and total health care expenditures. It shows that the proportion of private health care in total health care expenditure has increased, from 9.2 per cent in 1976 to 14.4 per cent in 1998. It also shows a rising proportion of private health insurance to total health expenditure for the same period. These statistics seem to suggest that private health care has started to play a supplementary role, as a complement and not as a substitute for the public health care expenditure.

Table 11.1 Selective health statistics

Year	Public health care expenditure to total government expenditures %	Share of public health care expenditure to GDP (%)	Number of patients on the waiting list ('000)	Private consumption on health to GDP %	Private consumption on heath to total health expenditure %	Private health insurance to total health expenditure %
1976	10.8	5.0	700.8	0.5	9.2	1.2
1981	11.0	5.3	736.6	0.6	10.3	1.5
1983	11.2	5.3	854.5	0.7	11.6	2.2
1984	10.9	5.2	854.5	0.7	12.1	2.4
1985	10.9	5.1	854.5	0.7	12.5	2.5
1986	11.0	5.0	830.6	0.8	13.1	2.7
1988	12.0	5.0	827.7	0.8	13.6	2.9
1990	12.0	5.1	841.6	0.8	14.0	3.3
1991	12.7	5.4	830.1	0.9	14.7	3.4
1993	13.2	6.0	995*	1.0	14.2	3.4
1994	13.3	5.9	n/a	1.0	14.6	3.4
1996	15.1	5.9	1,200	1.0	14.4	3.3
1997	14.5	5.6	1,200*	1.0	14.4	3.5
1998	n/a	5.6	1,452	1.0	14.4	3.5

* England only.

Sources: OECD Health Data, 2000; *Social Trends*, various issues.

Since the middle of the 1970s there has been a series of health care reforms in the European Union (EU) member states. In the UK the health care internal market reform of 1991 was aimed to increase efficiency through restructuring the NHS and by targeting needs making both providers and purchasers respond to the needs of patients. The reforms were aimed to control the rising health care expenditure, reduce waiting lists and respond to patients' needs. However, although the internal market reform may have improved waiting lists in some areas and dealt with patients' needs, the overall public health care expenditure has been rising steadily (see Table 11.1). The question has been how to control this rising health care expenditure. This becomes more severe at times of low growth rates and recession. In the UK since 1980, one way to control the rising cost of health care expenditure and to reduce demand on NHS has been to encourage people to take up private health care by providing tax relief. This tax subsidy was viewed as a cost-containment strategy and also providing choice in the health care sector.

It was thought that by providing tax incentives/subsidy for the over-60s to take up private health care the rising demand on NHS services would be slowed down. This then raises the question whether forgone tax revenue would be lower than the expenditure saved which would be otherwise spent on such patients in the absence of such tax relief.

Given that in the UK, NHS provides the great bulk of medical care, those who purchase private health care (health insurance policies) are not, therefore, expected to be poor. It is argued that this tax subsidy is correlated with income (Mitchell and Vogel, 1975; Pauly, 1986). The health tax subsidy is perceived to redistribute income from the poor to the rich, as virtually the entire tax subsidy goes to those who cannot be classified as poor. The debate over health tax subsidy has not involved considerations of the welfare of low-income people and is not the subject of this chapter. We are mainly interested in raising the question as to what degree it could be considered as successful in controlling rising demand.

One way of looking at this issue is to develop an econometric model in order to assess the key relationships empirically. However, such models are, although, very useful, they demand substantial amount of data over a long period of time, where data for some variables such as tax relief are only available for a short period. While there has been a relatively large literature on the determinants of total health expenditure, there has been very little research on the factors responsible for the take-up of private health care via insurance or out-of-pocket payments in the UK.

There exists a long-term association between public financing and heath care expenditure, but it is not clear whether public financing will increase or decrease the level of health care expenditure. On one hand Buchanan (1965) and Bird (1970) have argued that public finance in health care acts a restraining factor in health care expenditure, while Leu (1986) argues the opposite that health care expenditure rises with increasing share of public finance. In contrast to both these views, Newhouse (1975 and 1977) suggested that income per capita is the most important variable and other variables are of negligible importance (Culyer, 1988). Unfortunately, there is no straightforward theory of the determinants of public health spending, but some general hypotheses regarding both public and private health care can be formulated and tested. A simplified version of such a framework is presented below. However, the complexity of such relationships between the key variables (health care expenditure and tax incentive policy) requires substantial amount of data, which at the present time is unavailable.

$THC_t = PBHC_t + PRHC_t$
$PBHC_t = f(PRHC_t, PCGDP_t \text{ or } PCTTAX_{t-1}, RPHC_t, DEPR_t, NDOC_t, NBEDS_t)$
$PRHC_t = h(PBHC_t, PDY_t, RACHI_t, TAXS_{t-1}, GWAITL_{t-1}, HIP_t)$
$HIP_t = k(RAPHI_t, PDY_t, GWAITL_{t-1})$

Where f( ) is a function whose mathematical form will be specified later,
THC_t = total health care expenditure, in constant prices
$PBHC_t$ = public health care expenditure, in constant prices
$PRHC_t$ = private health care expenditure, in constant prices
$PCGDP_t$ = per capita GDP, in constant prices
$PCTTAX_{t-1}$ = per capita total tax, in constant prices
$RPHC_t$ = relative price health care (health services and medical care price index to GDP deflator)
$DEPR_t$ = the dependency rate, the proportion of population aged 0 to 19 and 65 plus to population aged 20 to 64
$NDOC_t$ = number of doctors
$NBEDS_t$ = number of beds
PDY_t = per capita disposable income, in constant prices
$RACHI_t$ = average cost of heath insurance, in constant prices
$TAXS_{t-1}$ = health care tax subsidy, in constant prices
$GWAITL_{t-1}$ = general waiting list, in constant prices
HIP = health insurance premiums, in constant prices
$RAPHI$ = real average price of health insurance policy.

The concerns about tax subsidies are twofold. One is that it results in government income tax revenue loss, and secondly the exclusion effectively reduces the price of insurance to consumers and thereby provides an incentive for employees to purchase more insurance than they would if they were using taxable income (Taylor and Wilensky, 1983). The resulting increased level of insurance may then exacerbate the inflation rate in the health care sector. The evidence suggests that tax subsidy is likely to have increased substantially the demand for health insurance (Feldstein and Friedman, 1977; Taylor and Wilensky, 1983). In the case of UK, all the available data are of aggregated nature and consequently not suitable for such empirical analysis. Modelling the private health cares expenditure and to examine the subscribers' behaviour with respect to tax rates and income will require data at the individual level. This will then enable the policy decision makers to predict changes in expenditures for health insurance that would result from specified changes in the tax laws.

In the absence of relevant data to estimate an econometric model, here we make use of some aggregate health data to provide a tentative and rather a general picture of the likely success of such health policy. Table 11.2 shows the actual number of contracts, the individual covered, and the cost of tax relief over the period 1990/91 to 1996/97.

Table 11.2 Tax relief on private medical insurance contracts for individuals aged 60 or over

Year	Approximate number of contracts	Approximate number of individuals covered	Cost of tax relief (£ million)
1990–91	350,000	500,000	40
1991–92	350,000	500,000	60
1992–93	350,000	500,000	70
1993–94	375,000	550,000	80
1994–95	375,000	550,000	95
1995–96	400,000	600,000	100
1996–97	375,000	550,000	110

Source: Inland Revenue, 1997.

The Conservative government first introduced tax relief on private medical insurance premiums in the 1989 Finance Bill, and private medical insurance tax relief started in April 1990. In a White Paper *Working for Patients*, published in January 1989, the government announced its decision to introduce legislation to give income tax relief from April 1990 on premiums for private medical insurance for the over-60s.

The tax relief was not given on premiums payable in respect of insurance contracts made, or renewed, on or after the announcement were, however, subject to certain exceptions. The exceptions applied to those people who made arrangements, before the announcement, to renew an existing contract or to enter into a new one but who did not yet have the contract in place. The exceptions only applied where the contract was finally made, and payment of the whole or some part of the premium due was received by the insurer, before 1 August 1997. Existing contracts, which had attracted tax relief, would continue till their expiry dates.

In 1997 it was estimated that about 550,000 individuals were covered by private medical insurance contracts attracting tax relief. The Exchequer cost of the relief for 1996–97 was estimated at £110 million (see Table 11.2). If the relief were not abolished the cost would rise in 1997–98 to approximately £120 million (Inland Revenue, 1997). It was expected that the cost of the tax relief would fall during 1998–99, as existing annual contracts would come to an end. The savings were estimated to be about £120 million in 1998–99 and then rising to £140 million in 1999–2000. Despite tax relief amounting to some £560 million since its introduction on 6 April 1990 to 5 April 1997, there is little evidence that the relief led to any significant increase in the purchase of private medical insurance for the over-60s during that period. This could be explained by the fact the private health care insurance has been rising since 1976 and the rise in private health care subscriptions between 1990 and 1994 has been very modest and is in line with upward trend in taking up private health care.

However, in July 1997 with the Labour government in power, the tax relief on premiums for private medical insurance for the over-60s was to be abolished, with the existing annual contracts to continue to benefit from relief until they fell due for renewal. The aim was to free up public money to finance the package of proposals in the 1997 Budget to help a much wider section of the sick and elderly.

Conclusions

We have argued in this chapter that improvements in technology, increased life expectancy along with political and economic pressures have increased the costs of providing health care in developed countries. These increased costs have placed an even greater burden on many health care systems. Tax relief policies, aimed at encouraging elderly segments of the population to take up private health insurance, with the view to reduce the burden on the NHS in the UK, were examined. Initial indicators suggest that such policies have been ineffective given the nature and the quality of health service provided in the UK. This perhaps suggests that policy makers should adopt a long-term funding strategy to ensure the NHS is adequately funded. In the meantime, however, the private sector could be used as an effective short-term measure to alleviate pressure in areas where there is a serious shortage of health care provision.

References

Andersen, R. and Benham, L. (1970), 'Factors Affecting the Relationship between Family Income and Medical Care Consumption', in H. Klarman (ed.), *Empirical Studies in Health Economics*, Johns Hopkins University Press, Baltimore and London.

Bird, R.M. (1970), *The Growth of Government spending in Canada*, Toronto, Canadian Tax Foundation.

Buchanan, J.M. (1965), *The Inconsistencies of the National Health Service*, Insistute of Economic Affairs, London.

Culyer, A. (1988), *Health Expenditures in Canada: Myth and reality; past and future*, Canadian Tax Paper No. 82, Canadian Tax Foundation, Toronto.

Feldstein, M. and Friedman, B. (1977), 'Tax Subsidies, the Rational Demand for Insurance and the Health Care crisis', *Journal of Public Economics*, 7, pp. 155–78.

Gerdtham, U. (1992), 'Pooling International Health Care Expenditure Data', *Journal of Health Economics*, 1, pp. 217–31.

Gerdtham, U. and Jonsson, B. (1991), 'Price and Quantity in International Comparisons of Health Care Expenditure', *Applied Economics*, 23, pp. 1519–28.

Gerdtham, U. and Jonsson, B. (1992a), 'An Econometric Analysis of Health Care Expenditure: A cross-section study of the OECD countries', *Journal of Health Economics*, 11, pp. 63–84.

Gerdtham, U. and Jonsson, B. (1992b), 'International Comparisons of Health Care Expenditure-conversion Factor Instability, Heteroscedasticity, Outliers and Robust Estimators', *Journal of Health Economics*, 11, pp. 189–97.

Grossman, M. (1972), *The Demand for Health: A theoretical and empirical investigation*, Columbia University Press, New York.

Hitiris, T. (1997), 'Health Care Expenditure and Integration in the Countries of the European Union', *Applied Economics*, 29, pp. 1–6.

Hitiris, T. and Posnett, J. (1992), 'The Determinants and Effects of Health Expenditure in Developed Countries', *Journal of Health Economics*, 11, pp. 173–81.

Inland Revenue (1997), *Budget 97*, Inland Revenue Press Office, London.

Leu, R.E. (1986), 'The Public-private Mix and International Health Care Costs', in A.J. Culyer and B. Jonsson (eds), *Public and Private Health Services: Complementarities and conflicts*, Basil Blackwell, Oxford, pp. 41–63.

Milne, R.G. and Molana, H. (1991), 'On the Effect of Income and Relative Price on Demand for Health Care: EC evidence', *Applied Economics*, 23, pp. 1221–6.

Mitchell, B.M. and Vogel, R. (1975), 'Health and Taxes: An assessment of the medical deduction', *Southern Econ. Journal*, 41, pp. 660–72.

Murillo, C., Piatecki, C. and Saez, M. (1993), 'Health Care Expenditure and Income in Europe', *Econometrics and Health Economics*, 2, pp. 127–38.
Murthy, N.R.V. and Ukpolo, V. (1994), 'Aggregate Health Care Expenditure in the United States: Evidence from cointegration tests', *Applied Economics*, 26, pp. 797–802.
Muurinen, J.M. (1982), 'Demand for Health: A generalised Grossman model', *Journal of Health Economics*, 1, pp. 5–28.
Newhouse, J.P. (1975), 'Development and Allocation of Medical Care Resources: Medico-economic approach', 29th World Medical Assembly, Japanese Medical Association.
Newhouse, J.P. (1977), 'Medical Care Expenditures: A cross-national survey', *Journal of Human Resources*, 12, pp. 115–25.
Newhouse, J.P. (1987), 'Cross-national Difference in Health Spending – What do They Mean?', *Journal of Health Economics*, 6, pp. 159–62.
Newhouse, J.P. and Phelps, C.E. (1974), 'Price and Income Elasticities for Medical Care Services', in M. Perlman (ed.), *The Economics of Health and Medical Care*, Macmillan, London and Basingstoke.
OECD Health Data (2000), Organisation for Economic Cooperation, Paris.
Parkin, D., McGuire, A. and Yule, B. (1987), 'Aggregate Health Care Expenditures and National Income: Is health care a luxury good?', *Journal of Health Economics*, 6, pp. 190–27.
Pauly, M.V. (1986), 'Taxation, Health Insurance, and Market Failure in the Medical Economy', *Journal of Economic Literature*, 24, pp. 629–75.
Social Trends (various issues), Office for National Statistics, The Stationery Office, London.
Taylor, A.K. and Wilensky, G.R. (1983), 'The Effect of Tax Policies on Expenditures for Private Health Insurance', in J. Meyer (ed.), *Market Reforms in Health Care*, American Enterprise Institute, Washington, DC, pp. 163–84.
Wagstaff, A. (1986), 'The Demand for Health: Some new empirical evidence', *Journal of Health Economics*, 5, pp. 195–233.
Warshawsky, M.J. (1991), *Factors Contributing to Rapid Growth in National Expenditures on Health Care*, Finance and Economics Discussion Series, Board of Governors of the Federal Reserve System.

SECTION FOUR
PERFORMANCE

Chapter Twelve

Comparative Costs and Hospital Performance

Diane Dawson, Maria Goddard and Andrew Street

Introduction

In England, the setting of performance targets has become a primary tool for management of public sector activities. The Treasury, as custodian of the public purse, has played a central role in this development. The Treasury's interest has focused on two problems. First, the elimination of X-inefficiency as reflected in observed differences in unit costs between providers at any one point in time; and second, providing incentives for public sector organisations to seek out and adopt productivity enhancing technical change. In the private sector, competition is expected both to eliminate inefficient producers and to drive industry wide productivity improvement. In the public sector, some alternative mechanism may be required. The mechanism currently adopted for use in the public sector in England is the setting of targets for the reduction of unit costs.

The usefulness of this mechanism depends on answers to two key questions:

1 are the techniques used to measure relative efficiency and productivity improvements sufficiently reliable that we can have confidence that they are correctly distinguishing between efficient and inefficient producers and that they effectively distinguish productivity improvements from changes in quality or mix of outputs;

2 what are the incentives for providers to meet the targets they have been set?

Health Policy and Economics: Strategic Issues in Health Care Management, M. Tavakoli, H.T.O. Davies and M. Malek (eds), Ashgate Publishing Ltd, 2001.

The importance of securing more efficient production of health care has been widely recognised as all countries have tried to deal with the growing demands on public resources of rising health care costs. While we have been primarily concerned to examine the evolving system for improving the efficiency of English hospitals, we also wanted to examine the approach to hospital efficiency measurement and creation of incentives in other countries. The hope was that experience elsewhere might be of use in dealing with problems emerging in the English system.

The chapter is organised as follows. First, we outline the main economic issues related to the use of comparative cost information for setting efficiency targets in the health sector. Next we describe the comparative cost data sets developed in the NHS and present our analysis of the conflicting messages on relative performance generated by the data. We then discuss the use of the data in setting efficiency targets in the NHS, focusing on the importance of incentives for changing behaviour. We then offer a summary of experience from outside the UK and, in the final section, present our conclusions.

Economic Issues

If comparative cost information is to be used as a means of setting efficiency targets for hospitals, a number of important economic issues need to be addressed before concluding whether this is likely to bring about the desired improvements in hospital performance. Some of these relate to measurement issues and others to the incentive effects of target setting in a sector such as the NHS.

Hospital Cost and Production Functions

The first issue relates to whether the cost functions generated from data on hospital expenditure reflect an underlying production function. Only if there is an underlying production function does it make sense to examine technical properties such as economies of scale or scope or productive efficiency. Evans, in an early paper, distinguished a 'behavioural cost function' from a technical cost function when dealing with hospital expenditure on inputs and any measured outputs (Evans, 1971). When the basic data are expenditure by publicly funded organisations like NHS hospitals, what we may be observing is the influence of funding formulae rather than underlying cost functions (Ashford et al., 1981; Lave et al., 1992). McGuire stressed the role of public sector property rights and transaction costs in determining the feasible frontier for hospital production (McGuire, 1987). Cost studies based on observed expenditure may reveal something about allocative efficiency but can tell us little about productive or technical efficiency. These debates have not been resolved and current practice is to assume hospital cost studies reveal something about underlying cost functions and technical efficiency (Butler, 1995; Van der Merwe, 1999a).

Measurement of Hospital Efficiency

Second, even if we assume an underlying production function, we need to be confident that the way in which costs are measured produces a reliable measure of relative hospital efficiency. This issue has been widely debated for a number of years and there is still no consensus about the merits of alternative techniques for estimating relative cost efficiency of hospitals. The traditional means of obtaining estimates of the relative importance of factors expected to influence cost is to use multivariate regression analysis. Explanatory factors of interest usually include economies of scale and scope, factor prices, casemix, teaching activity and market power. A number of researchers have adopted the translog specification as a more flexible functional form to the Cobb-Douglas when estimating the cost function (Fried, 1993; Butler, 1995; Rosko, 1996; Scott and Parkin, 1995). When interest is focused on obtaining measures of the relative efficiency of hospitals, stochastic frontier analysis (SFA) and data envelopment analysis (DEA) have been employed. These techniques seek to identify an efficiency frontier defined by the hospitals (or schools or other producers) that achieve the highest level of output for the inputs employed or the least cost mix of inputs for a given output. All units not on the frontier are deemed 'inefficient' and the degree of inefficiency can be measured as the distance of the unit from the frontier. Both techniques are particularly suited to analysis of multi-product firms and SFA has the additional advantage of allowing for the stochastic nature of activity and costs in units like hospitals (Rosko, 1999; Maniadakis et al., 1999; Van der Merwe, 1999b). However, the efficiency rankings and the size of measured inefficiency is highly dependent on which technique is used. The estimates are significantly different depending on whether one uses multivariate regression, SFA or DEA. Techniques for estimating relative inefficiency can only – at best – offer insights into performance. Newhouse argued against use of frontier techniques on the grounds that we understood too little about the quality differences of hospital outputs to be able to specify the models in ways that separated differences in quality from differences in cost when estimating inefficiency (Newhouse, 1994). However, this criticism applies to all known techniques for measuring relative inefficiency and not just to frontier methods. The main argument of the Newhouse paper is that regulators should not be over reliant on using the efficiency scores of these studies to set reimbursement rates. The results may not be sufficiently robust for that purpose.

Target Setting and Incentives

There are some potential problems associated with the use of comparative cost information to set targets within a system like the NHS as opposed to the use of similar information to set prices in a system such as US Medicare. Economic theory predicts that in particular circumstances there is a strong case for improving efficiency through the use of price regulation based on the relative costs of similar firms within an industry. This holds most especially where firms act as local monopolists, limiting the extent to which competition can serve to reduce costs (Shleifer, 1985). Whilst there are many variations, the essence of the argument is that some form of 'yardstick competition' can simulate the incentives of competition by encouraging each firm to improve its cost performance in the following way: the profit (surplus) that it is allowed to retain is a direct function of its ability to outperform other firms. A maximum unit price (or total revenue) is set for each firm, enabling it to generate a rate of return equal to the firm's cost of capital as determined by capital markets. This regulated price is based on costs observed in other firms within the same industry, not just on the individual firm's costs. Making the regulated price partly or entirely independent of a firm's own costs is the key to maximising incentives for cost reduction. This requires the regulator to observe at least two firms in identical circumstances so that the price cap for one can be related to the cost of the other. Being able to observe costs from other firms allows the regulator to infer more about the conditions faced by particular firms within an industry and about the level of effort behind each particular firm's cost level, thereby reducing information asymmetry. However, this implies that differences in the operating conditions facing each firm are either identical or are taken account of systematically. If not, differences in observed costs will not be a good signal of effort but may well be related to exogenous factors over which the firms have little control. Where firms or their environments are heterogeneous, Shleifer argues for 'reduced-form' regulation based on regression analysis allowing correction for exogenous characteristics (Shleifer, 1985).

The example used by Shleifer was the DRG-based reimbursement of hospitals in the USA under the Medicare system. However, for this form of regulation to work, hospitals must have sufficient incentives to respond to the cost-related prices or targets by improving their efficiency. In the USA the incentive is obvious. If a hospital's actual costs are higher than the comparative costs used to set prices, bankruptcy would result if cost performance could not be improved. If a hospital's costs are lower than the centrally set DRG price, the incentives are less clear. Hospital management could attempt to expand activity and increase market share or could decide not to expand, but to direct the surplus to increased quality or other activities that generate professional satisfaction (e.g. research).

It is not immediately obvious what the incentives are to meet efficiency targets that are set by a central authority if success or failure to meet the targets is unlikely to affect the income of the hospital or reward professionals within the organisation.

In the following section, we describe the comparative cost data collected in the UK and examine the extent to which it deals adequately with the problems identified in the economics literature. At the end of the chapter we return to the important question of incentives to respond to cost targets.

Comparative Cost Data in the NHS

The government elected in May 1997 announced a policy of developing and publishing detailed information on the costs of individual treatments provided by each and every hospital in the NHS. These treatment costs would be based on the allocation of accounting costs by health care resource groups (HRGs). HRGs are, with some important differences, the UK version of DRGs and, as in other countries, are used to adjust hospital activity and costs for casemix. Cost weighted HRGs are used in the UK just as resource weighted DRGs are used in other countries to ensure that indices of activity and cost take some account of the resource implications of differences in casemix.

Description of the Data

The first set of accounting costs of individual treatments by hospital was published as the *National Schedule of Reference Costs* in November 1998 (NHS Executive, 1998). The intention is that data on hospital costs by procedure be published annually and the second cost data set was released in

December 1999 (NHS Executive, 1999). Data reported for both years suggest that the costs of providing similar treatments may vary considerably among Trusts. Although it is possible that this variation might stem from differences in efficiency, other explanations should be considered. For instance, clinical coding and accounting practices are highly influential in determining the costs reported for individual treatments (Dawson and Street, 1998). There will always be a substantial element of discretion in how to allocate the majority of hospital costs to specific clinical activities and patients as many resources are shared between a variety of uses. For example, this issue of joint costs would arise in obstetrics and gynaecology if consultants provide services in both specialties or patients have conditions coded to both specialities. Methods of allocating such shared resources will vary between hospitals and thus unit cost estimates will vary also.

As well as providing a list of costs by HRG, the treatment cost data are aggregated to provide a summary of each Trust's overall casemix weighted costs. The reference cost index is a weighted summary of all HRG costs in each Trust relative to the national average and is adjusted for differences in the cost of land, building and labour in the NHS using the market forces factor (MFF) (see Table 12.1). This index was used to compare the performance of one hospital with another in terms of whether the hospital as a whole, after adjusting for casemix, was more or less expensive than other NHS hospitals.

There were grounds for scepticism in regarding the original RCI as a valid measure of hospital unit costs. The fact that, even though it purported to adjust for casemix, the two Trusts providing the most and least complicated procedures (Walton Centre for Neurology and Neurosurgery and Moorfields Eye Hospital) were respectively least and most 'efficient' according to the index suggests that factors explaining cost differences were not adequately dealt with.

Criticism focused on three major deficiencies. First, the RCI related to surgical activity and failed to account for outpatient, accident and emergency (A&E), and non-acute activity. Second, it used finished consultant episodes (FCEs) to measure activity, a measure with known deficiencies, in view of the amount of local discretion over what constitutes the time spent in the care of a consultant (Clark and McKee, 1992). Third, although there was an attempt at clustering similar hospitals into family groups, the index itself failed to take into account factors known to influence costs such as the severity of cases treated and hospital configuration.

Attempts to deal with these problems resulted in three alternative cost indices produced by the Department of Health (DoH) and the Audit

Table 12.1 The NHS cost indices published in 1998/9

Reference cost indices

RCI The national reference cost index is compiled using data provided by Trusts about their unit costs by health care resource group (HRG) for their main surgical specialties. The RCI is a weighted average of all HRG costs in each Trust relative to the national average. The market forces factor (MFF) is then added to account for differences in local factor costs. The index was published in November 1998.

RCI+ The RCI covers only acute activity. The RCI+ attempts to provide a comprehensive indication of activity, by including non-surgical, outpatient and accident and emergency (A&E) activity.

Casemix cost indices

CCI The casemix cost index (CCI), unlike the RCI, includes mental health services and day care costs. The index is a ratio of actual to expected costs, taking into account hospital casemix. Activity in the CCI is summarised as a weighted combination of HRG based inpatient spells, outpatient first attendances and A&E first attendances.

2CCI The casemix costliness cost index (2CCI) builds on the CCI, incorporating adjustment for other variables hypothesised to explain cost differences among trusts. These variables included hospital transfers, multi-episode spells, and the proportion of elderly or female patients, student numbers, research revenue and the MFF. The extent of the adjustment for each of these variables is estimated through regression analysis.

3CCI The 3CCI – the casemix costliness and configuration index – attempts to take into account differences in hospital configuration, over and above the adjustments made in the 2CCI. These include the costs of multi-site working, hospital size, and capacity utilisation.

Commission in early 1999 (Audit Commission and Department of Health, 1999). The three casemix cost indices (CCIs) used patient 'spells' rather than FCEs as a measure of hospital activity, with spells corresponding to hospital admissions. Furthermore, they were based on data from the hospital episode statistics rather than the non-routine returns used for the RCI. The three new indices were derived by calculating an index of expected to actual costs and then regressing this index against a succession of explanatory factors. The 3CCI included the most comprehensive set of adjustments.

The casemix cost index (CCI) was calculated for each hospital by dividing expenditure by the number of patients treated. Activity was weighted to take account of casemix, so if a hospital admits patients with above average care requirements it is accorded a higher casemix weight.

Casemix is not the only factor that might influence the level of costs. The casemix costliness cost index (2CCI) built on the CCI, incorporating adjustment for other variables hypothesised to explain cost differences among Trusts. Hospital transfers, multi-episode spells, and the proportion of elderly or female patients were included to account for cost differences over and above the HRG casemix adjustment. In addition, the 2CCI made allowance for possible cross-subsidisation between patient care and teaching or research which may not have been adequately dealt with in the funding allocations, and for differences in local factor costs, assessed using the MFF.

The 2CCI was described as a long-run cost index in that it implied that hospital re-configuration is feasible in the long term. In reality, hospitals may appear relatively inefficient on the 2CCI because of factors beyond immediate managerial control. The 3CCI (casemix costliness and configuration index) attempted to take some of these factors into account, over and above the adjustments made in the 2CCI. These included the costs of multi-site working, measured by the number of sites with more than 50 beds; hospital size, measured by the number of beds; and capacity utilisation, reflected by the number of patients treated.

Does Cost Variation Reflect Differences in Hospital Efficiency?

The availability of alternative measures of relative hospital efficiency for the *same* hospitals, using data for the *same* time period, provides an opportunity to study the impact of measurement technique on reported relative efficiency. While we would expect differences in efficiency rankings, what is surprising is the extent of movement experienced by individual hospital Trusts. Of the 213 Trusts for which full data are available, only ten remain in the same decile across all indices. Trusts move an average of 80 places from one index to the next – equivalent to a third of the 'league'. At the extreme, The Queen Victoria Hospital Trust moves from near the bottom of the RCI (206/213) to third most 'efficient' on the 3CCI.

This variability in league positions ranks across indices can be represented by 'Adjustment Intervals'.[1] Figure 12.1 shows the adjustment interval for the family group of small/medium acute hospitals outside London as an illustrative example.

The scale ranges from 1 to 213, with 1 indicating the lowest cost provider according to each index. The lines indicate the range in ranks for each Trust across the RCI, CCI, 2CCI and 3CCI (data for the RCI+ are unavailable). The length of the line reflects the impact on each Trust's league position of the

Comparative Costs and Hospital Performance

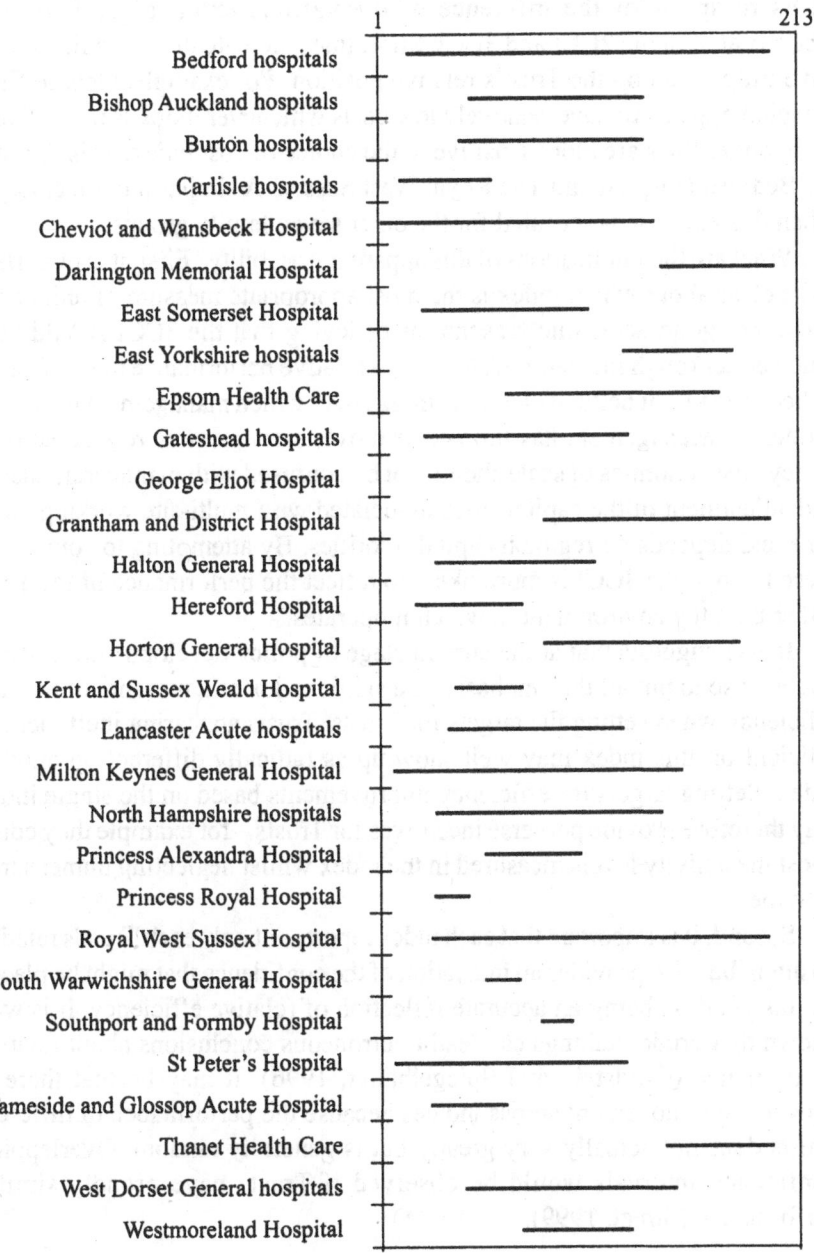

Figure 12.1 Variations in ranks across NHS cost indices

adjustments used in the construction of each index, such as the move from FCEs to spells or the influence of the various explanatory variables incorporated in the 2CCI and 3CCI. Short lines indicate that the adjustments have little effect on the Trust's relative position. For example, George Eliot Hospital appears to have relatively low costs whichever index is used. Trusts with longer lines are more sensitive to the choice of cost index, as is the case for Bedford Hospital and The Royal West Sussex. A similar picture emerges when this exercise is repeated for the other seven family groups.

What are the implications of this apparent variability? First, it is important to be clear about which index is the most appropriate measure of unit costs. There are good economic reasons for believing that the 3CCI should be a much better rough indicator of short-term relative performance than the other indices because it better isolates the things over which management may have influence. Management has little control over size, mergers reflect national policy, diseconomies of scale should not be confused with managerial 'slack' and adjustment of the capital stock associated with multi-site working takes time and depends on regional capital priorities. By attempting to control for these factors, the 3CCI is more likely to reflect the performance of the Trust rather than the environment in which it operates.

It also suggests that at the current stage of policy development, it would not be wise to put all the emphasis on a single index as a measure of relative efficiency when setting the targets for Trusts. Trusts appearing inefficient or efficient on this index may well show up as radically different on another index. Setting targets for efficiency improvements based on the single index may therefore provide perverse incentives for Trusts – for example they could boost the activity levels measured in the index whilst neglecting unmeasured activities.

Second, it is important that each index reports not only each Trust's relative position, but also provides an indication of the confidence that might be placed on this position being an accurate reflection of relative efficiency. It is well known that crude rankings can lead to erroneous conclusions about relative performance (Goldstein and Spiegelhalter, 1996). It may be that there is considerable movement across indices because the performance of different Trusts does not actually vary greatly but is generally random. Overlapping confidence intervals would be observed if Trusts have broadly similar performance (Street, 1999).

Using Cost Data to Set Efficiency Targets in the NHS

As described earlier, the economic rationale behind regulatory regimes which set price caps based on comparative cost is that of creating incentives to reduce costs. Organisations benefit directly from improving cost efficiency and suffer financially if they do not. However, in the NHS there is a weaker link between performance and rewards or penalties, so the incentives for Trusts to meet the cost reduction targets will not be as powerful. For example, it is not clear whether there have been any sanctions associated with the failure of Trusts to meet efficiency targets in the past and the Department of Health has not set out what the position will be under the new performance framework. Similarly, in a public sector service governed by rules which limit retention and reinvestment of savings and by annual rather than periodic targets, the financial rewards associated with making efficiency gains are limited. Nevertheless current policy is to set targets. For the last two financial years hospital trusts have been set cost efficiency targets ranging from a minimum of 2 per cent per annum for the most 'efficient' Trusts up to 4.5 per cent for the 'least' efficient Trusts (NHS Executive, 2000).

Another problem within any system with multiple outcomes is that measurement in one area may encourage organisations to reduce their effort in areas which are not measured. The National Performance Framework attempts to overcome this in part by incorporating measures along a number of different dimensions. However as far as we know, the 'efficiency' targets are being set mainly in relation to the comparative cost data rather than reflecting any quality or other performance measures. This creates the potential for Trusts to achieve cost reductions at the expense of other important dimensions such as quality of care.

There is some experience from UK regulatory agencies operating in sectors other than health care that may be of relevance to the development of efficiency regulation for the hospital sector of the NHS. The Office of Water Trading (OFWAT) (1999), the regulator of the water industry, uses comparative cost data to set price caps for firms in the UK water supply industry. In this sector the regulator has recognised the danger of firms responding to cost reduction targets by reducing quality. OFWAT has now introduced a direct link between price limits and quality performance. The existence of quality measures in the NHS (even where these relate to process rather than outcome) in theory provide a basis for a similar approach to be taken. Indeed, the Department of Health (1997) has stated an intention that clinical information will be taken into account by regional offices when targets are set. However, it may not be politically acceptable to penalise financially those Trusts that are providing the poorest quality care as this may further disadvantage patients. Recognising this problem, the government has announced a strategy that rewards hospitals doing well on quality measures by giving them greater autonomy and access to new funds (Department of Health, 2000).

This sort of tension will always arise in the NHS because penalising Trusts that are doing badly will raise issues of whether it is ultimately the patients who suffer, rather than those responsible for poor performance (management, clinicians or GPs).

In the private sector, OFWAT has taken a fairly tough line in setting efficiency targets, believing that the greatest gains can be made by those who are least efficient but also rejecting claims from the most efficient companies that further efficiency savings are not possible. As well as commissioning extensive research on the potential for future efficiency gains, the director of OFWAT took advice from a panel of senior industrialists and concluded that challenging assumptions (on efficiency) would be a powerful stimulus to achieve even greater improvements (OFWAT, 1999). The outcomes of previous price reviews have shown that companies with the most demanding expectations are likely to outperform the targets the most. While this may also be true in the NHS, research would be required to investigate whether Trusts for whom the most demanding efficiency targets have been set in the past were in fact the hospitals making the greatest efficiency gains. Like OFWAT, the NHS expects even the most efficient hospitals to make efficiency gains (2 per cent per annum) but, unlike OFWAT, no research has been published on the reasons for assuming that industry specific efficiency gains of 2 per cent per annum are feasible.

Experience from outside the UK

The evidence presented above suggests that setting efficiency targets for hospitals based on available comparative cost data may present some difficulties from an economic perspective. However, as the collection of hospital cost data is becoming a more common feature of health care systems outside the UK, we explored the nature and use of such data in several other countries in order to see if there were any insights to be gained for the UK approach to improvement of hospital performance.

Based largely on a wide range of government and academic personal contacts (as much of the information does not appear in published documents), we investigated a number of issues relating to collection, analysis and use of hospital cost data in countries and in states of federal countries where we understood there to be active research or policy interest in hospital efficiency.

It is not possible to present the full results here but Table 12.2 summarises some of the results relevant to this chapter.

We found that, with the exception of New South Wales, there was no evidence of governments setting performance targets with respect to comparative hospital cost along the lines introduced in England. In all countries, Ministries of Health or research institutes are involved in developing systems for defining hospital products by (often local) DRGs and attempting to adapt imported, or to generate local, resource weights for their DRGs. There is universal appreciation of the importance of improved measures of casemix for the analysis and management of hospitals but little agreement on how such information is best incorporated in measurement of relative hospital efficiency.

The uses to which governments are putting the casemix weighted cost data, or the uses to which they hope to put the data when coverage is sufficient, are quite diverse. In some systems the casemix data is being used to implement policies of moving from historic hospital budgets to some form of complexity and equity weighted formula budgets. Elsewhere, resource-weighted DRGs are being used to generate prices that can be used with the introduction of competition into the hospital sector. It is striking that there is little information available at all on the impact of various measures on behaviour of providers.

It may be useful to think of a 'policy cycle' or 'policy matrix' (if it is not linear) that runs from focus on: 1) cost containment to; 2) allocating budgets for equal access to; 3) stimulating efficiency through competition to; 4) stimulating efficiency through performance management. The use to which information on resource weighted DRGs is put will depend on where a country happens to be in this policy matrix. In the UK, costed HRGs were originally intended as the basis for pricing in the internal market but their use now, with a different policy focus, is for performance management. Ministry officials and researchers in countries not currently using resource-weighted DRGs to measure and target relative hospital efficiency are interested in this performance management approach but it is not the current policy priority.

Conclusions

The NHS seems almost unique in its approach to improving efficiency through setting targets based on comparative cost estimates. In our second section, we

198 Health Policy and Economics: Strategic Issues in Health Care Management

Table 12.2 Summary of experience outside the UK

Countries/ states*	Method and format of cost comparison	Uses of comparative cost data	Impact on efficiency
Norway	DRG costs allocated in similar way as UK. Index created at hospital level. DEA also used.	Available in public domain for voluntary benchmarking and for use by purchasers. Proposals to use it for reimbursement based on DRGs in future.	Preliminary research shows expensive hospitals not penalised by purchasers but allowed increase in budgets instead – perceived as 'soft' budgets. No systematic tendency for dispersion of cost variation to increase or decrease.
New South Wales, Australia	DRG level and hospital level costs calculated. Multiple regression and DEA modelling also undertaken.	Used by government to set 'efficient provider costs' as an efficiency benchmark/ target. Used on voluntary basis by purchasers to compare costs. Used to distribute efficiency savings between hospitals.	Not known although initial evidence suggests some overall reduction in average cost following benchmarking, but not necessarily attributable to the target setting process.
Manitoba, Canada	Index of hospital costliness based on DRGs, aggregated to hospital level.	Initiative of academics not government.	When hospital budgets were cut, biggest cuts targeted at teaching hospitals which were most expensive on the index. Mixed evidence on whether those with biggest cuts became less costly on the index.
Ontario, Canada	Casemix adjusted cost index produced at hospital level.	Developed in order to facilitate new system of budget setting for hospitals. Aim was to have funding better reflect type of patients treated. Also some element of yardstick competition as increased activity was reimbursed at the average level of costs for peer group, not actual hospital costs.	Some evidence that the new system of funding produced desired changes in activity.

Countries/ states*	Method and format of cost comparison	Uses of comparative cost data	Impact on efficiency
New Zealand	No hospital level comparative cost data exist. DRG-type analysis is undertaken but not clear how it is developed.	Regulatory bodies are responsible for monitoring performance but no information on relative cost performance was available.	Not known
Sweden	Comparative costs calculated at level of cost per patient are published but the basis of reporting costs is under review in order to produce a uniform system of costing activity by DRG.	Not used for promoting efficiency/setting targets. Some use in remuneration but varies between areas.	Not known
Finland	Research institute has developed DEA analysis to identify changes in hospital productivity over time. Benchmarking project has identified several indicators, including cost per DRG which are disseminated via the internet to hospital managers.	Analysis suggested most change in productivity over time was dominated by technical change rather than efficiency change. Some purchasers have used data to set target budgets for hospitals.	The impact of dissemination of cost information via the internet is being evaluated currently.
Victoria, Australia	Considerable interest in hospital cost data at DRG-type level.	Used only as basis for casemix funding formulae to date, although development of performance systems in Victoria indicates they intent to use some measures of efficiency at hospital level in future.	Not known

Note

We also looked at various schemes within the USA (e.g. prospective pricing; Pennsylvania Health Care Cost Containment Council, HEDIS etc.) but these are not reported here. The conclusions on the UK system are not altered by the US experience, especially as the main use made of cost data in the US is for remuneration purposes.

outlined some of the main reasons why such a policy may face difficulties: 1) for it to work we have to be confident that relatively high costs reflect inefficiency rather than other unmeasured factors; and 2) that there are appropriate incentives in place for encouraging hospitals to meet efficiency targets once they are set. In our third section, we indicated the ambiguity of existing measures of efficiency in English hospitals. We also pointed out that in the NHS there is no direct relationship between the achievement of cost targets and rewards for management or clinicians. Whilst it is possible that managers may lose their jobs if they fail to meet centrally set targets, there is no evidence that this regularly occurs or whether such sanctions have improved hospital performance.

In health care systems where hospitals receive prospective reimbursement for patients treated and where there is some excess capacity, the scope exists for creating strong incentives for lower cost production. The problems of how to monitor the quality implications of such 'efficiency' drives are as serious in the market transaction oriented systems as they are in more centralised and planned health care systems such as the English NHS. The English system would appear to have less scope for incorporating the now relatively abundant information on relative cost performance into mechanisms with strong incentives to respond to relatively poor/good performance. The market approach of allowing hospitals to compete for patients has been firmly rejected by the present government. This severely limits the role of using comparative cost information to set prices at which hospitals trade. An alternative mechanism, employed in some countries with more planned systems, is to use comparative cost information to allocate resources to hospitals in different parts of the country. In the UK there has been a strong tradition of allocating budgets to areas based on the needs of the resident population rather than the relative efficiency of the hospitals in the area. Equity of access has been a fundamental principle of resource allocation. If the government began reducing the allocation of resources to areas where hospitals were relatively expensive or 'inefficient' and if incentives to reduce costs were not strong, then the local population would receive even less health care than before the 'efficiency' measures were introduced. At present, using the comparative cost data in resource allocation does not appear a viable policy option.

The casemix adjusted cost data currently being collected in England may be very good relative to that available in many other non-market health care systems. What is missing is a clear view of how most effectively to use it. This is essentially a question of what incentives to create for its use. At present it is not acceptable for a hospital to close if it is not supplying services at costs close to the median for all hospitals. Nor is it acceptable to direct funds away from 'expensive' areas to the benefit of patients in 'lower cost' parts of the country. In presenting the model of yardstick competition, Shleifer emphasised the importance of living with the consequences of the system:

> It is essential for the regulator to commit himself not to pay attention to the firms' complaints and to be prepared to let the firms go bankrupt if they choose inefficient cost levels. Unless the regulator can credibly threaten to make inefficient firms lose money ... cost reduction cannot be enforced (Schleifer, 1985, p. 323).

In the 1990s when the internal market was first introduced, there was general agreement that a major shortcoming of the system was the lack of information on the costs of services provided by different hospitals. We have now made considerable progress in generating information on comparative cost but that has merely highlighted another deficiency of the system: the lack of incentives to act on the information.

Acknowledgements

We are grateful for the excellent secretarial assistance of Helen Parkinson. We acknowledge funding from the Department of Health and the MRC but all opinions expressed are our own and do not necessarily reflect those of the funders.

Note

1   This follows the terminology adopted in a paper by Goldstein and Spiegelhalter (1996) discussing statistical issues in institutional performance, in which it was recommended that confidence intervals be constructed around ranks to capture uncertainty, and that adjustment procedures be conducted on the raw scores (in this case, unit costs).

References

Ashford, J., Butts, M. and Bailey, T. (1981), 'Is There Still a Place for Independent Research into Issues of Public Policy in England and Wales in the 1980s', *Journal of the Operational Research Society*, 32, pp. 851–64.

Audit Commission and Department of Health (1999), *NHS Trust Profiles Handbook: 1997/8*, Audit Commission, London.
Butler, J.R.G. (1995), *Hospital Cost Analysis*, Kluwer Academic Publishers, Dordrecht.
Clarke, A. and McKee, M. (1992), 'The Consultant Episode: An unhelpful measure', *British Medical Journal*, 305, pp. 1307–8.
Dawson, D. and Street, A. (1998), *Reference Costs and the Pursuit of Efficiency in the New NHS*, Discussion Paper 161, Centre for Health Economics, University of York.
Department of Health (1997), *The New NHS: Modern, Dependable*, HMSO, London.
Department of Health (2000), *The NHS Plan*, The Stationary Office, London.
Evans, R. (1971), 'Behavioural Cost Functions for Hospitals', *Canadian Journal of Economics*, 4(2), pp. 198–215.
Fried, H., Lovell, C. and Schmidt, S. (1993), *The Measurement of Productive Efficiency*, Oxford University Press, Oxford.
Goldstein, H. and Spiegelhalter, D. (1996), 'League Tables and their Limitations: Statistical issues in comparisons of institutional performance', *Journal of Royal Statistical Society*, 159A (part 3), pp. 385–43.
Lave, J., Jacobs, P. and Markel, F. (1992), 'Transitional Funding: Changing Ontario's global budgeting system', *Health Care Financing Review*, 13(3), pp. 77–84.
Maniadokis, N., Hollingsworth, B. and Thanassoulis, E. (1999), 'The Impact of the Internal Market on Hospital Efficiency, Productivity and Service Quality', *Health Care Management Science*, 2, pp. 75–85.
McGuire, A. (1987), 'The Measurement of Hospital Efficiency', *Social Science and Medicine*, 24(9), pp. 719–24.
Newhouse, J. (1994), 'Frontier Estimation: How useful a tool for health economics?' *Journal of Health Economics*, 13, pp. 317–22.
NHS Executive (1998), *Reference Costs*, Leeds.
NHS Executive (1999), *The New NHS 1999 Reference Costs*, Leeds.
NHS Executive (2000), *NHS Efficiency Targets 2000–01: A plain English guide*, Leeds.
Office of Water Trading (1999), *Future Water and Sewerage Charges 2000–05: Draft determinations*, OFWAT.
Rosko, M. (1996), 'Understanding Variations in Hospital Costs: An economic perspective', *Annals of Operations Research*, 67, pp. 1–21.
Rosko, M.(1999), 'Impact of Internal and External Environmental Pressures on Hospital Efficiency', *Health Care Management*, 2, pp. 63–74.
Scott, A. and Parkin, D. (1995), 'Investigating Hospital Efficiency in the New NHS: The role of the translog cost function', *Health Economics*, 4(6), pp. 467–78.
Shleifer, A. (1985), 'A Theory of Yardstick Competition', *Rand Journal of Economics*, 16(3), pp. 319–27.
Street, A. (1999), *Interpreting the NHS Cost Indices for Acute Trusts*, Discussion paper 175, Centre for Health Economics, University of York.
Van der Merwe, R. (1999a), *The Economics of Hospitals and Hospital Cost Behaviour: A Review*, Department of Economics and Related Studies, University of York.
Van der Merwe, R. (1999b), *Efficiency as a Factor in Hospital Cost Variation: A report for the Department of Health on efficiency in NHS acute Trusts*, Department of Economics and Related Studies, University of York.

Chapter Thirteen

Turkish Hospital Managers' Perceptions of their Job Satisfaction and Job Abandonment

Yavuz Yıldırım and Gülsün Erigüç

Introduction

Job satisfaction in general and in the health sector in particular has emerged as an important area to pursue. Several studies aimed at measuring job satisfaction levels at different levels of organisations have been conducted. Hospitals and hospital personnel have also been subject to such attempts. However, although a large body of literature has been developed especially for the developed world, in Turkey this area of organisational behaviour has not attracted wide attention for hospitals. Studies of hospital managers in particular are rare. The study presented below aims at investigating the issue from hospital managers' perspective. To this end, first a general framework for job satisfaction will be presented in order to draw the attention to the study's contextual background. Later, the results of the study will be presented.

Job Satisfaction: General Framework

Job satisfaction, as a concept, has been subject to in-depth analysis in organisational literature. The concept as a term, its meaning and ways of measurement and consequences of its varying degrees have attracted the attention of managers and social scientists.

So far as the definition is concerned, as in other concepts of social sciences, an agreed definition has not yet been reached. Robbins (1994), for example, defines job satisfaction as an individual's attitude towards his/her job. Similarly Newstrom and Davis (1993) define the concept as the employees' favourable or unfavourable feelings and emotions about their job. These definitions indicate that job satisfaction implies the attitudes and feelings of the employees towards their job and job related environment in general.

Locke (1976) bases his definitions of job satisfaction on the wants (desires, values and perceived amount of the value provided by the job) of the employees about certain dimensions of their job. In his value-percept discrepancy model, Locke differentiates between needs, expectancy and values. According to the model, there are certain differences between the concepts of need and value. Value is defined as the desires and wants that a person consciously or subconsciously seeks to attain. Values are acquired by the person through his/her experiences in life while needs are inborn. It is the values that differ from person to person and determine his/her actual choices and emotional reactions towards job. Locke, in this context, regards job satisfaction as the contentment feeling of the person from his perceptions about the opportunities provided by the job. According to the model, job satisfaction level is determined by the difference between individual's values about certain dimensions of the job such as payment, working conditions and opportunities for promotion, and perceptions about the fulfilment of his/her values. Job satisfaction results from the values and perceptions that are consistent but in the case of discrepancy between them dissatisfaction is unavoidable. In brief, Locke defines job satisfaction as a function of the discrepancy between the person's values (desires, wants, importance) and perceptions about the fulfilment of these values in job environment. In other words, this definition could be formulised as follows:

satisfaction = the values − the perceived amount of the value provided by the job.

As can be seen from above, a variety of definitions of job satisfaction have been provided. In line with these definitions, there are also various ways of measuring it as well. One way of measuring job satisfaction is to assess the individual's overall satisfaction level by using a single global rating. Another method is to enquire about job satisfaction levels from different dimensions of the job. These dimensions could include the nature of work, supervision, payment, promotion opportunities and relations with co-workers. An overall job satisfaction score could be reached after rating the results on a standardised scale (Robbins, 1994).

Another view proposes to measure job satisfaction by investigating the current perception levels of individuals of certain dimensions of the job.

However, according to Vroom (in Wanous and Lawler, 1972), not only the perceptions about certain dimensions of the job but also the value attached to these dimensions by the individual should also be pursued. He also added the concept of valence to the literature. Porter (ibid.), on the other hand, proposes that job satisfaction levels are determined by the difference between the two types of items (should be – is now). However, according to Locke (1976), job satisfaction can be measured not only by involving their expectations and needs but their desires as well. In this view, the discrepancy between the individual's desires and perceptions about fulfilment reveals his/her level of satisfaction.

As the discussion above manifests, certain dimensions of the job influence the overall job satisfaction levels of the individual to certain degrees. Job satisfaction is a multidimensional concept, encompassing financial rewards, supervision, working conditions, fellow workers, the job itself, etc. (Newstorm and Davis, 1993; Longenecker and Pringle, 1981; Robbins, 1994). These dimensions can be grouped under dimensions related with job content (the nature of the job) and those related with the job context (the supervisor, co-workers and organisation) (Newstorm and Davis, 1993). Locke (1976), on the other hand, analyses these dimensions under two headings as: 1) events and conditions; and 2) agents. Factors such as work, pay, promotion, verbal recognition and working conditions are grouped under the 'events and conditions' heading. Under the 'agents' heading, the self, supervisors, co-workers and subordinates, company and management are included. The satisfaction level of the individual from these dimensions would inevitably differ from one to the other from time to time, offsetting the benefits gained from a high level of satisfaction in a particular dimension.

As stated elsewhere, in an era of increasing competition and scarce resources, maximising employees' productivity, job satisfaction and commitment to the organisation is crucial for managers in all organisations, not just in health care organisations (McNeese-Smith, 1996). In service organisations where the services provided are usually individualistic and require intensive efforts, a high level of satisfaction among employees is a prerequisite for effectiveness (Curry et al., 1986). Hospitals are among this type of organisation. Hospital managers are the key actors in creating a satisfactory environment among the personnel and meeting the needs of the patients, personnel and the community as a whole (Bennett, 1976). The manager's role is so crucial that unless s/he can get the people in the organisation to do what must be done neither s/he as a manager nor the organisation as a whole would be successful (Rakich et al., 1977).

At this point, managers' contribution to the job satisfaction level should be elaborated upon. As stated above, the manager has a key role in directing the efforts of the people towards achieving the goals of the organisation through using his/her skills on leadership, motivation and communication. However, this crucial role aside, the job satisfaction levels of managers themselves should also be taken into account.

It could be claimed that the managers' satisfaction levels from their job environment is as important as those working under their control. This reality is, unfortunately, sometimes ignored and satisfaction surveys have more usually focused on the employee component of the organisation. It has been claimed that if managers are dissatisfied, their unhappiness can spread throughout the whole department, and even organisation, and influence the levels of satisfaction of the employees as well (Newstorm and Davis, 1993). This clarifies the importance attached to job satisfaction studies of managers. Based on this argument, the study presented below attempts to analyse the job satisfaction levels of hospital managers in Turkey.

Job Satisfaction: Views of Turkish Hospital Managers

Hospitals within the Health System

The Turkish health system is quite complicated and fragmented in terms of finance and provision. Multiple providers and financiers attempt to solve the health problems of the population with varying degrees of quality, availability and accessibility. In 1998, there were 1,120 hospitals, of which 63 per cent were Ministry of Health (MoH), 10 per cent were the State Insurance Organisation (SIO), 3 per cent were university, 22 per cent were other public institutions and 19 per cent were private hospitals. The MoH, as a major provider of health services, owns 50 per cent of all hospital beds followed by the SIO (16 per cent of total beds) (Sağlık Bakanlığı, 1999).

So far as their management structure is concerned, as stated elsewhere (Tatar et al., 1998), a highly centralised structure in terms of management dominates the current style of hospital administration. Within this centralised structure, the hospital managers' role is restricted to administering the institution according to the rules and guidelines issued from the centre. In terms of administration of hospitals, another feature that can be generalised for all hospitals is the dominance of the medical profession. Chief Medical Officers (CMOs) and hospital managers are the major actors in the administrative structure. However, CMOs hold the major responsibility for the management of all activities within the hospitals, both clinical and administrative. In practice, the CMO delegates some of his/her authority and power to hospital managers and head nurse, but at the end of the day, the CMOs have the ultimate responsibility of management.

The Research

The aims of this study were threefold: 1) to determine job satisfaction levels of hospital managers; 2) to inquire their views about quitting the job; and 3) to determine the relationship of these views with their job satisfaction levels. Job satisfaction was defined as emotional reactions of hospital managers arising from the discrepancy between the managers' desires from their job/job environment and perceptions about the fulfilment level of these desires. Accordingly, job satisfaction and dissatisfaction are situated at opposite ends of a continuum. An increase on one side leads to a decrease on the other.

The study population was hospital managers of the MoH general hospitals. In the research, managers titled as hospital managers and vice-managers were included. The manager of a hospital is mainly responsible for the general managerial activities in the hospital. S/He is accountable to the CMO of the hospital, who is the ultimate authority in the organisation. Vice-hospital managers (their numbers vary according to the size of the hospital) assist managers in their managerial function. They are accountable to the managers. 167 general hospitals having 100 or more beds were included which comprised 40 per cent of all general hospitals in 1996 (Sağlık Bakanlığı, 1997). All the managers and vice-managers were included (167 and 426 respectively) without using a sampling method. A questionnaire designed to meet the aims of the research was posted to hospitals. Fifty-six hospital managers (33.5 per cent) and 115 hospital vice-managers (27 per cent) responded to the questionnaire, with an overall response rate of 28.8 per cent.

The questionnaire was adapted from an instrument developed for managers in education and its reliability and validity were already tested (Balcı, 1985). It was composed of three sections and in the first section, questions to describe the general characteristics of the managers were asked.

Job dimensions expected to contribute to the job satisfaction levels of managers were determined as:

1) job and job content (10 items);
2) management and supervision (10 items);

3) payment (seven items);
4) promotion opportunities (six items);
5) working conditions (seven items);
6) co-workers (five items);
7) organisational environment (10 items).

The model was based on Locke's value-percept discrepancy model mentioned earlier. The questions were designed to measure job satisfaction through the discrepancy between the desires (values, wants) and their fulfilment levels. In other words, each question was asked in two stages, where first the desire levels of the managers were questioned, followed by their fulfilment level. In the second section of the questionnaire, the questions were about desires regarding job satisfaction dimensions and in the third section perceptions of managers about their fulfilment level were investigated. Answers were scaled on a Likert type scale from 1 to 5, where 5 was associated with 'too much' and 1 with 'too little'. The answers were evaluated by the numeric values. In addition to these questions, the managers were also asked if they were planning to quit their job. A pilot study was conducted to amend the questions.

So far as the job dimensions are concerned, the questions were formed according to Locke's (1976) causal factors in job satisfaction. The *job and job content* dimension comprised variables such as learning new things on the job, opportunities to improve skills, ability utilisation, balance between authority and responsibilities, independence and creativeness. Support from CMOs (that is, CMOs for managers; managers and CMOs for vice-managers), interaction with CMOs, objective and consistent decisions by CMOs, clear and written guidelines, participation in decisions related to themselves, and constructive criticisms towards themselves have formed the *management and supervision* dimension. Under the *payment* dimension, variables such as a payment level consistent with the level of education and requirements of the job, a level sufficient to meet basic needs, adequacy of pension, other payments and social assistance and compatibility with the payments in the private sector were included. The *promotion* dimension, on the other hand, comprised occupational competence and provision of opportunities for promotion, objectivity of the promotion policies, in-service training opportunities and chances to follow recent occupational developments. The *working conditions* dimension included adequacy of buildings in terms of security, heating, lightning, ventilation, transportation and environmental conditions and sufficiency of equipment. The *co-workers* dimension covered variables such as the unity among workers, involvement in management and occupational competency. Last but by no means least, the *organisational environment* dimension comprised variables such as having a balance between the organisational and individual needs, adhering to teamwork, delegation of power, good relations with supervisors, exchanging information, pride in the hospital and participation in decisions.

Findings

The data were analysed by paired samples 't' test. The difference between the decisions to quit by managerial position was tested by chi-square test. As far as the personal characteristics of hospital managers are concerned, their average age was 38 (X: 38.06, SD 6.37), average working duration in the hospital was 12 years (X: 12.42, SD: 6.98) and average working years as a hospital manager was 8.6 years (X: 8.68, SD: 7.66). One hundred and forty-three hospital managers were male (83.6 per cent) and 28 were female (16.4 per cent).

Table 13.1 Discrepancy between desires from job satisfaction dimensions and their fulfilment level

Job satisfaction dimensions	Desire X±SD	Fulfilment X±SD	Discrepancy X±SD	t	p
1 Job and job content	45.04±4.37	30.03±7.86	15.01±9.00	21.81	$p<0.05$
2 Management and supervision	43.84± 4.94	28.08 ±7.63	15.76±9.27	22.21	$p<0.05$
3 Payment	32.61± 3.25	12.10±5.18	20.50±6.43	41.66	$p<0.05$
4 Promotion	27.72± 2.74	13.55±5.53	14.16± 6.42	28.83	$p<0.05$
5 Working conditions	31.92± 3.18	19.45±4.85	12.47± 6.23	26.19	$p<0.05$
6 Co-workers	22.87± 2.22	14.98±3.62	7.88±4.29	24.02	$p<0.05$
7 Organisational environment	45.01± 4.49	30.83±7.35	14.17± 8.14	22.76	$p<0.05$
Total	249.04±19.42	149.04±32.51	99.99±37.85	34.51	$p<0.05$

Table 13.1 shows the discrepancy between desires in job satisfaction dimensions and their fulfilment level. Any increase in the discrepancy between desires and fulfilment level indicates a higher level of dissatisfaction and vice versa. In this context, analysis of the table reveals that the desires of the hospital

managers were high, but their fulfilment levels were lower. When the discrepancy in each dimension is analysed, it can be seen that the hospital managers were dissatisfied in all job satisfaction dimensions. This dissatisfaction was lower for the co-workers dimension but highest for the payment dimension. Analysis of the discrepancy for total job satisfaction revealed that the hospital managers were dissatisfied in all dimensions and this discrepancy was statistically significant ($p<0.05$).

Table 13.2 Hospital managers' satisfaction level in job satisfaction dimensions by managerial position

Job satisfaction dimensions	Managerial position		t	p
	Manager X±SD	Vice-manager X±SD		
1 Job and job content	14.64±7.8	15.19±9.53	0.37	$p>0.05$
2 Management and supervision	15.33±8.83	15.96±9.52	0.41	$p>0.05$
3 Payment	18.87±6.82	21.30±6.11	2.35	$p<0.05$
4 Promotion	14.27±5.87	14.12±6.70	0.14	$p>0.05$
5 Working conditions	12.11±6.46	12.66±6.13	0.54	$p>0.05$
6 Co-workers	8.05±3.93	7.81±4.47	0.35	$p>0.05$
7 Organisational environment	14.37±7.60	14.08±8.43	0.22	$p>0.05$
Total	97.66±36.71	101.13±38.57	0.56	$p>0.05$

Table 13.2 presents the relationship between job satisfaction dimensions and managerial position. As the table shows, so far as the payment dimension is concerned, hospital vice-managers were more dissatisfied than their manager counterparts and this difference was statistically significant ($p<0.05$). The same conclusion was not valid for the total job satisfaction level. As far as total job satisfaction is concerned, hospital vice-managers were more dissatisfied than their manager counterparts and this difference was statistically insignificant ($p>0.05$).

Table 13.3 Hospital managers' views about quitting their job by managerial position

Managerial position	Wants to quit		Doesn't want to quit		χ^2	p
	N	%	N	%		
Manager	25	45.5	30	54.5	1.29	$p>0.05$
Vice-manager	38	36.2	67	63.8		

Table 13.3 shows the views of hospital managers about quitting their job, by managerial position. As seen from the table, 45.5 per cent of hospital managers were considering quitting their jobs and 54.5 per cent were not. So far as the hospital vice-managers were concerned, these figures were 36.2 per cent and 43.8 per cent respectively. The differences were statistically insignificant ($p>0.05$).

Table 13.4 The difference between hospital managers' views about quitting their jobs and job satisfaction

Job satisfaction dimensions	Wants to quit Yes X±SD	No X±SD	t	p
1 Job and job content	18.13±10.09	13.17±8.06	3.43	p<0.05
2 Management and supervision	18.98±9.66	13.76±8.62	3.57	p<0.05
3 Payment	21.67±6.70	19.69±6.44	1.87	p>0.05
4 Promotion	16.76±6.43	12.35±5.97	4.43	p<0.05
5 Working conditions	12.92±6.83	12.11±5.88	0.80	p>0.05
6 Co-workers	9.65±5.05	6.95±3.44	4.03	p<0.05
7 Organisational environment	17.68±9.04	12.32±7.08	4.19	p<0.05
Total	115.79±41.92	90.36±33.09	4.27	p<0.05

Table 13.4 reveals the relationship between the hospital managers' views about quitting their jobs and their satisfaction levels from job satisfaction dimensions. As seen from the table, job satisfaction levels of hospital managers were lower for those considering quitting their jobs in dimensions such as job and job content, management and supervision, promotion, co-workers and organisational environment and this difference was statistically significant ($p<0.05$). Although the satisfaction level in payment and working condition dimensions were also lower for those considering quitting their jobs, the difference was statistically insignificant ($p>0.05$). So far as total job satisfaction was concerned, the managers considering quitting their job were more dissatisfied than others and the difference was statistically significant ($p<0.05$).

Results

The hospital managers' perceptions about the discrepancy between their desires (values, wants) and fulfilment levels from each job satisfaction dimension were found to be statistically significant (Table 13.1). As seen from the above section, hospital managers were dissatisfied in all job satisfaction dimensions. The payment dimension has been stated as the most unsatisfactory dimension for hospital managers, i.e. the managers were primarily dissatisfied in this dimension. In a number of other studies, using similar methodology, it was found that the payment dimension was the most dissatisfactory dimension for nurses (Aksayan, 1990), nurses and doctors (Özaltın, 1997) and managers of education (Balcı, 1985). By the same token, in another study enquiring into sources of stress for hospital managers, insufficient salary and economical conditions were found to be the most important stress sources (Şahin and Erigüç, 1999). Bodur et al. (1996) in their research covering hospital managers, as well as other managers, have also found the positive effect of sufficient payment on job satisfaction. However, this is not surprising as payment dimensions in other parts of the public sector is also dissatisfactory. Austerity measures in recent years have added an extra burden on people working in the public sector.

The second job satisfaction dimension that hospital managers were dissatisfied with was management and supervision (Table 13.1). When the indicators of this dimension were analysed, it was found that hospital managers were dissatisfied with the support provided from their CMOs (that is CMOs for managers; managers and CMOs for vice-managers), interaction with CMOs and supervisors, participation in decisions related to themselves, supervision system and clear and written guidelines (role ambiguity). In another study, Erigüç and Kavuncubaşı (1996) also found that role ambiguity had a direct and negative effect on job satisfaction levels of nurses.

The most satisfactory dimension for hospital managers was co-worker dimension, followed by working conditions (Table 13.1). These findings are important in an organisation where teamwork constitutes the backbone of efficiency, effectiveness and quality. A similar conclusion was also reached by Özcan (1991) who stated that interaction among co-workers was the most satisfactory dimension for managers and employees in a public organisation outside the health sector. On the other hand, the job and job content dimension was found to be the most satisfactory dimension for nurses (Aksayan, 1990), doctors (Özaltın, 1997) and managers of education (Balcı, 1985). However, in our research, job and job content was the other less satisfactory dimension followed by payment, management and supervision. But Özcan (1991) found that the least satisfactory dimension was job and job content.

When the managerial positions of hospital managers were taken into account, hospital vice-managers were found to be more dissatisfied than their manager counterparts, but this difference was statistically insignificant (Table

13.2). The vice-managers were found to be more dissatisfied with the payment dimension and this difference was statistically significant. For instance, research on public and private bank employees (Güney et al., 1996), on employees of the public economic enterprises (İncir, 1990), on ministerial and governmental managers and employees (İncir, 1984) have reached similar conclusions.

As stated earlier, this study also enquired into hospital managers' views about quitting their job. The results revealed that the number of hospital vice-managers who do not want to leave their jobs was higher than hospital managers, but this difference was statistically insignificant (Table 13.3). Expectations of promotion to manager in the future, having no choice in career movement and being at the first stages of their career might have influenced their decisions. Some restrictions on career movement are valid for managers as well.

Analysing the views of hospital managers regarding quitting their jobs revealed that those who were considering leaving their jobs were more dissatisfied than others. This difference was statistically significant (Table 13.4). When hospital managers' satisfaction levels from job satisfaction dimensions were taken into account it was found that those considering leaving the hospital were more dissatisfied than those who would prefer to stay. In another study, Erigüç-Kaygın (1994) found that the doctors and nurses were less inclined to consider leaving their jobs with the increase in job satisfaction. Similarly in another study, a positive effect of job satisfaction on decreasing the propensity of leaving the job was also found (Erigüç and Kavuncubaşı, 1996).

Conclusion

The human aspects of an organisation are the crucial element in achieving organisational goals. Hospitals as labour intensive organisations established to meet the health needs of the society are not distinct from this. Hospitals are complex organisations embracing various occupations with varying degrees of education, knowledge, need and expectations. This complexity requires a fully motivated managerial team to adopt management practices geared to the attainment of overall goals. However, this can easily be achieved by managers with a high degree of job satisfaction. So far as management is concerned the concept of job satisfaction is a two-sided concept. First of all, the manager has to meet all job satisfaction requirements of the workforce working under his/her control. Second, and maybe more importantly, s/he should reach a satisfaction level compatible with the roles expected from him/her.

Job satisfaction as a managerial issue to be studied has attracted wide attention in Turkey in recent years. A number of studies have been conducted for differing occupations and organisations. In the health sector, job satisfaction levels of nurses and doctors have been particularly studied, but hospital managers have rarely been the subject of such studies. This study, aimed at analysing the job satisfaction levels of hospital managers, is a rare example of its kind.

A number of conclusions can be drawn from the above discussion. First of all, the low level of job satisfaction among hospital managers is alarming; especially when the chain reaction between the satisfaction of managers and employees mentioned above is taken into account. Hospital managers in Turkey need to be motivated in order to motivate their employees. Second, payment emerges as an important job dimension contributing to the overall satisfaction levels of managers. In developed countries, it could be claimed that payment has already lost its importance as a source of job satisfaction (İncir, 1990). Increases in payment without increases in intrinsic rewards may have little effect on job satisfaction (Mottaz, 1994). This proposition was also supported by McCloskey, Everly and Falcione (in Mottaz, 1994) who emphasised the role of intrinsic factors in job satisfaction. However, in Turkey the payment dimension still plays an important role on job satisfaction. This issue has to be tackled at higher levels as a policy for the whole public management area. Third, it has also been found that although the managers were dissatisfied with their jobs they were not considering quitting. This point has to be further researched to find out if this was a result of their commitment to the organisation or their lack of opportunities in seeking alternative employment. It could be concluded that job satisfaction of hospital managers in Turkey requires new and provocative research as a whole.

References

Aksayan, S. (1990), *Koruyucu ve Tedavi Edici Sağlık Hizmetlerinde Çalışan Hemşirelerin İş Doyumu Etkenlerinin İrdelenmesi*, unpublished PhD thesis, Istanbul University, The Institute of Health Sciences, Istanbul.

Balcı, A. (1985), *Eğitim Yöneticisinin İş Doyumu*, unpublished PhD thesis, Ankara University, The Institute of Social Sciences, Ankara.

Bennett, C.A. (1976), 'Effective Manager Must Have Both Vision and Purpose', *Hospitals*, 50 (April), pp. 67–70.

Bodur, S., Güler, S. and Güler, S. (1996), 'Sağlık Yöneticilerinde İş Doyumu', in *Ulusal Halk Sağlığı Kongresi Bildiri Kitabı*, Istanbul.
Curry, J.D., Wakefield, S.D., Price, J.L. and Mueller, C.W. (1986), 'On the Causal Ordering of Job Satisfaction and Organizational Commitment', *Academy of Management Journal*, 19 (4), pp. 847–58.
Erigüç-Kaygın, G. (1994), *Hastanelerde Personelin İşle İlgili Tutumları, Personel Devri, Ankara İli Örneği*, unpublished PhD thesis, Hacettepe University, The Institute of Health Sciences, Ankara.
Erigüç, G. and Kavuncubaşı, Ş. (1996), 'Hemşirelerde İşten Ayrılma Eğilimine Nedensellik Yaklaşımı', *Hacettepe Üniversitesi Hemşirelik Yüksekokulu Dergisi*, 3 (2), pp. 32–42.
Güney, S., Varoğlu, A. and Aktaş, A.M. (1996), 'Özel ve Kamu Bankalarında İş Tatminine Yönelik Bir Araştırma', *Verimlilik Dergisi*, (3), pp. 53–76.
İncir, G. (1984), 'Çalışanları İsteklendirmede Etkili Birkaç Özendirici', *Verimlilik Dergisi*, (4), pp. 82–97.
İncir, G. (1990), *Çalışanların İş Doyumu Üzerine Bir İnceleme*, Milli Prodüktüvite Merkezi, Publication No. 401, Ankara.
Locke, E.A. (1976), 'The Nature and Causes of Job Satisfaction', in M.D. Dunnette (ed.), *Handbook of Industrial and Organizational Psychology*, Rand McNally College Publishing Company, Chicago.
Longenecker, J.G. and Pringle, C.D. (1981), *Management*, 5th edn, Charles E. Merrill Publishing Company, Columbus.
McNeese-Smith, D. (1996), 'Increasing Employee Productivity, Job Satisfaction, and Organizational Commitment', *Hospital and Health Services Administration*, 41 (2), pp. 160–75.
Mottaz, C.J. (1994), 'Work Satisfaction among Hospital Nurses', in A.R. Kovner and D. Neuhauser (eds), *Health Care Management, Readings and Commentary*, 5th edn, Aupha Press, Health Administration Press, Ann Arbor, Michigan.
Newstrom, J.W. and Davis, K. (1993), *Organizational Behavior: Human Behavior at Work*, 9th edn, McGraw-Hill, New York.
Özaltın, H. (1997), *Türk Silahlı Kuvvetlerinde Görev Yapan Muvazzaf Tabip ve Ordu Hemşirelerinin İş Doyumlarının Analizi*, unpublished MSc thesis, Gülhane Military Medical Academy, The Institute of Health Sciences, Ankara.
Özcan, H. (1991), *Yüksek Öğrenim Kredi ve Yurtlar Kurumu Ankara Bölge Müdürlüğü Yurtları Yönetim İşgörenlerinin İş Doyumu*, unpublished MSc thesis, Ankara University, The Institute of Social Sciences, Ankara.
Rakich, J.S., Longest, B.B. and O'Donovan, T.R. (1977), *Managing Health Care Organizations*, Saunders Series in Health Care Organization and Administration, W.B. Saunders Company, Philadelphia.
Robbins, S.P. (1994), *Organizational Behavior. Concepts, Controversies and Applications*, 4th edn, Prentice-Hall International Editions.
Sağlık Bakanlığı (1997), *Yataklı Tedavi Kurumları İstatistik Yıllığı 1996*, Sağlık Bakanlığı, Ankara.
Sağlık Bakanlığı (1999), *Yataklı Tedavi Kurumları İstatistik Yıllığı 1998*, Sağlık Bakanlığı, Ankara.
Şahin, H. and Erigüç, G. (1999), 'Yönetsel Pozisyonlarına Göre Hastane Yöneticilerinin Yönetsel Stres Kaynakları', in K. Ersoy and Ş. Kavuncubaşı (eds), *II. Ulusal Sağlık Kuruluşları ve Hastane Yönetimi Sempozyumu Bildiri Kitabı*, Başkent University, Ankara.

Tatar, F., Tatar, M., Şahin, İ., Çelik, Y., Özgen, H. and Ökem, G. (1998), 'Turkish Hospital Management At A Crossroads: Prospects for the Year 2000', *The Journal of Health Administration Education*, 16 (3), pp. 283–96.

Wanous, J.P. and Lawler III, E.E. (1972), 'Measurement and Meaning of Job Satisfaction', *Journal of Applied Psychology*, 56 (2), pp. 95–105.

SECTION FIVE
REFORMS

Chapter Fourteen

What Structures Health Care Reforms? A Comparative Analysis of British and Canadian Experiences

Damien Contandriopoulos, Jean-Louis Denis and Ann Langley

Introduction

Health care systems in developed countries are experiencing a rapid pace of reform and restructuring. This restructuring is generally seen to be the product of pressures at the financial, technological and political levels (Angus, 1991, 1994; Mhatre and Deber, 1992; Glennerster and Matsaganis, 1994; Ham and Brommels, 1994; Garpenby, 1995; WHO/OMS, 1996; Saltman and Figueras, 1997, 1998). In this chapter, we will use a comparative analysis of the reforms in the health care systems of the UK and Canada to suggest that beyond these common macro pressures, other forces, such as managerial and political trends or fashions, greatly influence the form of restructuring.

The health care systems in the UK and Canada share important structural characteristics and values, including tax-based, universal, public insurance. During the 1990s, in both countries the health sector experienced deep restructuring that took the form of the internal market in the UK and a strong regionalisation of management in the Canadian provinces (Denis et al., 1998; Dorland and Davis, 1996, Church and Barker, 1998; Canadian Medical Association, 1993; Casebeer and Hannah, 1996; Casebeer et al., 1998). As we will see, restructuring in both countries was stimulated and legitimated by very similar rhetorical discourses. In addition, both sets of reforms had comparable sets of objectives and were mainly targeted to the relationship between regional management and hospitals. However, while the UK decided to implement an internal market that implies a purchaser-provider split, eight Canadian provinces out of 10 decided to implement an integration of regional management and hospitals. We will use the contrast between these positions

– given the similarity in the context, objectives and rhetoric – to argue that health sector reforms are far from being determined by a rational value free analysis of problems and solutions.

We will begin with a brief description of the Canadian reforms, and by summarising the logic of the purchaser–provider split in the UK's internal market. We will then analyse the similarities between both sets of reforms. However, before proceeding we must acknowledge that this comparison and analysis of logical grounds involves two very broad and complex health care reforms in two countries divided into subsystems. In this chapter, we will simplify somewhat the situation and limit our discussion to the hospital sector, leaving aside general practice and private production. In this respect, our discussion is based on an 'ideal-type' analysis of the reforms. Finally, reasons of space constrain us to a somewhat preliminary analysis. Nevertheless, we believe that we offer an original and fairly critical perspective on an old topic.

The Canadian Health Care System and its Reforms

Canada is a federation of 10 provinces and three territories and while health care is a provincial responsibility, the provinces must abide by five principles of the *Canada Health Act* if they are to receive federal funding transfers (roughly a third of provincial health expenditures [CIHI, 1998]). These principles are: public administration (hospital and medical plans must be administered on a public, non-profit basis), comprehensiveness (provincial health care systems must insure all medically necessary services), universality (all residents of the province must be included), portability (individuals must be covered while they are temporarily out of province), and accessibility (no user fees may be charged for medically necessary services). Health care systems differ according to province, but all comply with these principles. As a country, Canada spends approximately 9 per cent of its GDP on health care and 70 per cent of that spending is public and tax-financed (CIHI, 1999). The remaining 30 per cent is derived from (among other things) over the counter drugs, out-of-hospital dental services, some home-care, non-medically necessary services, and many 'borderline' interpretations of the federal principles which allow for private practice or, in some circumstances, user fees.

During the 1990s, nine of the provinces regionalised the management of their health care systems (Ontario being the exception). This regionalisation is a two-sided movement that can be analysed both as centralisation and decentralisation (Church and Barker, 1998; Casebeer and Hannah, 1996; Canadian

Medical Association, 1993). Local producers view this shift as centralisation, since many of their responsibilities were thereby transferred to the regional level. On the other hand, from the vantage point of central government, this is clearly a decentralisation since responsibilities that were once provincial are delegated to regional boards. In eight of the nine 'regionalising' provinces, some or all of the hospital boards were abolished and their duties transferred to regional bodies (in this respect, Quebec is the exception). As a result, regional boards are often directly responsible for the management and operation of hospitals. For example, Alberta abolished 200 hospital boards and transferred their responsibilities to 17 Regional Health Authorities (Alberta Health, 1993a, 1996); in Saskatchewan, 30 District Health Boards replaced over 450 local boards (Kouri, 1996); in Nova Scotia four regional boards took over the duties of 36 hospital boards (Nova-Scotia Health, 1998); and so on. In Table 14.1 we summarise the principal changes in management structures after regionalisation.

Although the alternative solutions of Ontario and Quebec are in themselves interesting, especially since Ontario and Quebec represent roughly 60 per cent of the Canada's population, we will focus here on the eight provinces that transferred responsibility from hospitals to regional bodies and abolished hospital boards. In these eight provinces, the regional tier is responsible for planning, providing, and evaluating all health services produced in its region. These range from operating hospitals to ambulance services and home-care. For these purposes, regional bodies are allotted a fixed budget by the provincial government, which includes everything except physicians' remuneration (that responsibility is still assumed by provincial Departments of Health on a fee-for-service basis). Importing British vocabulary, regionalisation in these provinces can be qualified as a purchaser–provider integration (Ellis, 1993) since hospitals (providers) are directly integrated as an internal component of the organisations responsible for financing and evaluating health services (the purchasers). Despite the absence of an internal market, and therefore the existence of no true 'purchaser', the regional bodies have the responsibility of paying for the health services of the population, which identifies them as a kind of 'purchaser'.

Purchaser–Provider Split in the NHS: an Overview

Without providing a detailed review of all the NHS reforms of the last decade, we will first rapidly recall the background to the creation of the purchaser–provider split.

Table 14.1 Structural regionalisation of the health care system in Canada

	British Columbia	Alberta	Saskatchewan	Manitoba	Ontario	Quebec	New Brunswick	Nova Scotia	Prince Edward Island	Newfoundland
Regionalised management	yes	yes	yes	yes	no	yes	yes	yes	yes	yes
Beginning of regionalisation process	1996	1994	1992	1996–97	—	19989–92[1]	1992	1996	1993–94	1992
Number of regional boards	11	17	33	10[2]	16	18	8[3]	4	5	6
Abolition of hospital boards: purchaser/provider integration	most of them	yes	yes	most of them[4]	no	no	yes	most of	yes	yes
Mean population/region	86,000	164,099	31,000	114,350	703,000	410,506	95,313	196,000	27,460	143,000
Regional financing formula		capitation	capitation	historical	—	historical	mix	historical	historical	
Regional financing mode	programme	global	global		—	programme	global	programme	global	global

Notes

1 In its present form.
2 Plus three northern/rural health associations (NRHA).
3 There are eight regional boards but seven regions because one regional has one French board and one English board.

To build a more efficient and consumer-centred NHS, the Thatcher government tried to reorganise the system to emulate market mechanisms which were thought to allow an optimal allocation of goods (Shackley and Healey, 1993). In this process the District Health Authorities were granted the responsibility of buying services from public or private hospitals. The public hospitals were given an independent 'Trust' status and were expected to compete in terms of price/quality for Health Authority contracts. Health Authorities and Trusts were no longer hierarchically linked, and this separation was labelled purchaser-provider split. The logic was that to freely shuffle contracts in search of the best deal, purchasers must be distinct from providers (Enthoven, 1985, 1988, 1991, 1993, 1994). As Walsh et al. (1997, p. 100) put it, 'manufacturing financial crisis within units for which one is directly responsible is a strange, if not masochistic, activity'. In the logic of internal competition, purchasers and providers are conceptualised as having distinct interests: providers seek greater revenues and a better market position, while purchasers seek the best deal in terms of quality price ratio (Hart, 1995). Both parties are also concerned with two distinct kinds of efficiency (Ratcliffe, 1993; Shackley and Healey, 1993): providers are concerned with technical efficiency, while purchasers are concerned with efficiency of allocation (maximising the population health produced for a given amount).

Even though Blair's government officially 'abolished' the internal market in 1997 (Labour Party, 1996; Department of Health, 1997), many of its fundamental characteristics remained (Boyce and Lamont, 1998; Ham, 1998; Klein, 1998; Le Grand, 1999). More specifically, the Health Authorities lost their purchasing role as it was transferred to primary care groups (PCG), but the purchaser-provider split persisted between PCG and Trusts (Le Grand, 1999). This separation is still seen to allow for more systematic and rational management (Maynard and Bloor, 1996) and a clearer delineation of responsibility and accountability (Ham, 1997; Le Grand, 1999).

As we have seen, while purchasers and providers were split in the UK, the majority of Canadian provinces took initiatives to integrate both roles. At first glance, the contrasts between the two approaches are striking. And yet intriguingly, the objectives were very similar in both contexts: clearer roles, streamlined structural organisation, more power for the patient seen as a consumer, and more efficiency and value for money. In the following section we propose a comparative analysis of some important characteristics of the reforms that will emphasise the similarities between them.

Comparative Analysis

According to the literature, the acknowledged principal objective of the internal market reform was to produce better 'value for money ' in the NHS (Klein, 1995a; Maynard and Bloor, 1996; Filinson, 1997; Ratcliffe, 1993; Edgar, 1995). Similarly, official documents in the Canadian provinces strongly emphasised the need for more efficient use of existing resources (Saskatchewan Health, 1992), or even reduced health care expenditures, while maintaining the level of service produced (Alberta Health, 1993a; Capital Health Authority, 1994; New Brunswick Health, 1996; Newfoundland Health, 1994; British Columbia Health, 1993; Manitoba Health, 1997; Nova Scotia Health, 1995; PEI Health Transition Team, 1993).

> The challenge facing Manitoba's health system, as in other provinces, is to preserve the principles of the Canada Health Act in the face of increasing cost, increasing demand for health services and constrained financial resources (Manitoba Health, 1997, p. 2).

The fact that reforms in both countries emphasise efficiency gains may seem elementary given that efficiency is a rather consensual goal, but it is also a shared characteristic of all managerial fashions (Abrahamson, 1996).

In both countries, the underpinning logic is founded on a 'businesslike' philosophy and New Public Management (NPM) paradigm (Ferlie et al., 1996; Walsh et al., 1997; Le Grand and Bartlett, 1993; Metcalfe, 1993). While the goal in the UK was to manufacture (or imitate) the functioning of a market as a whole, the proclaimed goal in many Canadian provinces was to emulate the 'businesslike' operation of individual private firms. The integration of all health related organisations within a given territory produced vertically integrated organisations directly responsible for the production of care. According to the rhetoric presented in government documents, such entities, while publicly financed and directly accountable to the provincial government, are deemed to be more streamlined, efficient, and businesslike than the old structures were (Alberta Health, 1993a; British Columbia Health, 1993; Capital Health Authority, 1994; Manitoba Health, 1992).

Nevertheless it is true that the 'market' approach in the UK created incentive-based regulation between hospitals and district management (though not between hospital physicians and management), which is in stark contrast to the hierarchical or structural-based regulation implemented in Canada. However, two factors cast doubt on the absoluteness of this divergence. First, the incentives in Britain were theoretically strong but their practical condition of use rendered them quite weak (Light, 1997; Ham, 1997). Second, in both cases the new structures of management created a (perceived) need for more and better information and an emphasis on accountability, which seems to be a general characteristic of NPM (Ferlie et al., 1996).

In both contexts the reforms' emphasis on efficiency gains was backed by an 'anti-bureaucracy' discourse. In the NHS, inefficiencies and bureaucracy were the 'straw man' to explain both the perceived problems of the old system, and why the new system would be better (Light, 1997). The same targets were publicised in Canada, with the goal to 'Reduc(e) bureaucracy waste and duplication' (British Columbia Health, 1996, p. 4). The fact that bureaucracy is an intrinsic facet of large organisations, and that in both cases new (bureaucratic) managerial structures were created, was not particularly stressed in the official discourse.

De-politicising Decisions

Even though the centralised structure of the NHS afforded good cost control, this was done at the expense of intense political pressure (Maynard and Bloor, 1996). In this context, the internal market scheme was thought to protect politicians from operational level pressures by de-politicising the system (Tuohy, 1999; Klein, 1995a; Young, 1996; Enthoven, 1985; 1991). Decisions were to be made according to pure economic rationality.

In Canada, the situation was somewhat different: rather than suffering from under-financing (as the NHS probably did [Light, 1990; Abel-Smith, 1992; Secretary of State for Health, 2000]), the health care system was targeted by governments for major cutbacks. Federal transfers had dropped, as had provincial revenues, and zero-deficit was the objective. Since health care expenditures account for 25–30 per cent of provincial budgets, it was clear that those expenditures would be frozen, or even cut. In this context, the decentralisation of responsibility for hospital closures or staff lay-offs – away from the minister's office – seems a clever strategy; such decisions were to be taken by regional boards on the grounds of technocratic rationality. In this way, regionalisation in Canada can also be seen as an attempt to de-politicise the system.

Purchaser–Provider Relations

Another important commonality between British and Canadian reforms is their focus on relations between hospitals and management bodies. The real financial (market driven) incentives in the NHS were supposed to take place between hospitals and Health Authorities. Similarly, in Canada the biggest managerial upheaval was the integration of hospital and Regional Boards. However, we should not forget that, in both cases, the shift in relations between management bodies and hospitals was drastic, but was only implemented as a means toward an 'ultimate' goal: a change in the internal practice of providers. This goal is not in itself surprising since the implementation of new modes of delivery of care seems one of the biggest challenges facing health care systems in developed countries (Fitzgerald and Dufour, 1997). What is surprising is, in both cases, the somewhat indirect path to this objective.

In the case of Britain's internal market, it was clear even from the outset (Enthoven, 1985) that the ultimate goal was to influence the production side (Saltman, 1994). According to logic, a purchaser–provider split allows a quasi-market scheme to produce competition, which in turn fuels 'natural selection' where only the best providers survive. This natural selection is seen as a powerful incentive for providers to reorganise their internal functioning, and, at the macro level, it should have produced a better, more cost-efficient health care system in the country (Enthoven, 1985, 1988). It is not our purpose here to emphasise the glaring gap between this theoretical and hypothetical scenario and the real operation of the quasi market – others have done it better than we could (Klein, 1995a, 1998; Light, 1997, 1998; Le Grand, 1999). What is pertinent to our analysis is the fact that the internal market reform was, even at the logical level, a very roundabout way to influence the internal functioning of hospitals.

The Canadian reforms also targeted the relations between hospitals and management to induce a transformation at the production level. The biggest upheaval was the abolition of hospital boards and the transfer of power that followed the creation of regional bodies. The official rhetoric claims that this transfer will produce a better health care system because more funds would be devoted to patient care.

> Why Regionalize Health care? ... to make the system more efficient by devoting a larger share of health care spending to patient care ... while reducing management and support cost (Nova-Scotia Health, 1998).

However, the abolition of hospital boards could, at best, only produce rather symbolical savings. In the same way, official documents often contain very simplistic arguments that a simplified organisational chart in itself warrants more efficiency (Alberta Health, 1993a; Nova Scotia Health, 1998; Capital Health Authority, 1994; PEI Cabinet Committee on Government Reform, 1992). More realistically, it is the internal restructuring of providers in conjunction with a broader, system-wide restructuring (which includes hospital closures, development of ambulatory care, etc.) that could produce the expected changes. Here again, what is relevant for our analysis is the fact that the reforms targeted the relations between hospitals and regional management as a means to produce changes at the production level. We are not saying that this approach is inappropriate, but we would like to point out it is not the only one. The integration of hospitals and regional boards is surely not an absolute prerequisite to a reorganisation in the delivery of care.

In both countries we observe that the biggest structural upheaval involved the relations between hospitals and regional management. This is interesting since the official objectives were aimed at the production level and mainly related to the internal functioning of the hospitals. In both cases, the logical relations that linked the changes in the management structure to the official objectives were quite circuitous. Moreover, whereas the UK chose to split hospitals from regional management, the majority of Canadian provinces favoured their integration. We thus observe that while there was a somewhat surprising consensus on the fact that the relations between purchasers and providers were the logical focus of the reforms, the direction of those reforms was directly opposed.

Give the System Customer Focus

Following the internal market reform, the NHS was supposed to shift from a patient-driven orientation to a customer one (Melville, 1997; Klein, 1995a; Filinson, 1997, Ferlie et al., 1996). In one sense that could mean a more proactive role for the customer (Klein, 1995b) since he or she could influence the organisation of the system by exercising both 'voice' and 'exit' rather than 'voice' and 'vote' (Hirschman, 1995; Schachter, 1995; Sharp, 1984; Cope, 1997; Mintzberg, 1996). On the other hand, this seems more a rhetorical debate than a real change in practices since patients' choices could have little impact on providers in the NHS (Klein, 1995a; Melville, 1997).

In all Canadian provinces the objective was also to give citizens a stronger voice in health care management (Charles and DeMaio, 1993; Singer, 1995; Church and Barker, 1998; O'Neill, 1992; Brassard, 1987; Alberta Health, 1993b, 1994). In some provinces (particularly Alberta), this objective was implemented through a consumer-centred philosophy: 'A new Alberta health system must place the needs of consumers as a priority' (Alberta Health, 1993a, p. 5). In the Canadian context, this is a radical shift in vocabulary; whereas the health care system was founded on 'patients' needs', it was restructured according to 'consumers' desires' and the creation of such concepts as 'one-stop shopping' (ibid., p. 13). On the other hand, the implemented reforms had minimal impact on patients' day-to-day interactions with the health care system. The patient was (and still is) able to select the physician, clinic, or hospital of his or her choice anywhere in the province – or in the country for that matter – since physicians are paid on a fee for service basis and since hospitals accept patients wherever they live. Apart from this shift in vocabulary, it is still the case that each province that has regionalised its management has emphasised the need for more public participation in health care management (Alberta Health, 1993a, 1993c; British Columbia Health, 1993, 1997; Manitoba Health, 1992, 1997; Newfoundland Health, 1994, 1997; New Brunswick Health, 1996; Nova Scotia Health, 1995, 1997, 1998; PEI Cabinet Committee on Government Reform, 1992; Saskatchewan Health, 1992, 1998). However, the way in which this participation will influence the system still remains unclear. Although many regional boards were initially expected to include some elected citizen representation, only Saskatchewan pursued this goal. And while each board retains the responsibility to consult the population and study its needs, this is a rather small revolution considering the huge emphasis given to this issue in official documents.

Discussion

We have seen in the preceding section that health care reforms of the nineties in the UK and Canada shared many important characteristics. Among other things a strong recourse to 'businesslike' vocabulary and New Public Management concepts; a vivid 'anti-bureaucracy' discourse concomitant with the introduction of new managerial (bureaucratic) structures; a claim that the reforms could 'de-politicise' decisions, a claim that can be understood as a wish that the political pressure could be lowered; a somewhat surprising consensus on the fact that the best way to maximise the efficiency of the system was to deeply reorganise the relations between hospital and regional management (providers and purchasers); a strong 'consumer centred' rhetoric which had very little impact on the day to day interaction in the system; more generally, deeper transformations on the rhetorical level than on the production level; and we could continue with a discussion of accountability, rational decision-making or decentralisation. Our first main conclusion is that these common points seem far too numerous to be explained by pure chance.

One possible explanation may be that the similar pressures both systems were facing structurally determined the reforms. On the other hand, if the reforms were simply determined by the context (taken in the narrow sense of care production problems), how can opposite solutions can be explained? As we have seen, even though both reforms are very similar, if we look at their rhetorical justification and their objectives, they are also directly opposed in some major respects. While the UK chose to implement a market like, incentive based, regulation that implied splitting purchasers and providers, the majority of Canadian provinces chose a hierarchical based integration of hospitals and regional management. We believe that a pure rational policy making perspective which considers that policy is (should be?) a value free response to a context (either a set of problems or a list of objectives) would be unable to provide a coherent explanation for the observed similarities and differences in British and Canadian health care reforms.

This analysis in fact seems to show that there is only a weak link between perceived problems, official objectives, and the choice of means in the management of such a complex system as health care production. And although such observations are far from new (Cohen et al., 1972; Kingdon, 1984; March and Olson, 1995), factual and supporting observations remind us of this reality. Notwithstanding the partisan rhetoric, there is no clear and obvious managerial recipe to attain the desirable official goals of both sets of reforms. In both cases, the logic that supports the reforms is often simplistic, and at times suspect. This suspicion is particularly clear here since the structural reforms in management take opposite directions although they rest on very similar rhetoric, and claim similar objectives.

We can also describe this phenomenon using the concepts of 'managerial fashions' (Abrahamson, 1996). It is self evident that the health care system reforms of, for example, New Zealand and the UK, are the products of a common managerial fashion. The same is true between the Canadian provinces. On the other hand, the health care reforms in the UK and Canada are not identical, and they are not the products of a shared fashion. Nevertheless, we have shown that the common points between the two contexts are too obvious to be ignored. To account for these observations we suggest the hypothesis that these common points are the products of a general trend in the management field which, in turn, influences every fashion in the field. The reforms in the UK and in Canada can then be seen as the product of two distinct managerial fashions that share the basic components of the macro trend that was structuring the management field at that time. This particular case, then, is noteworthy since, without any direct (visible) emulation we can still observe that health care management policy seems strongly influenced by changes in social and managerial perspectives.

Due to communications capabilities, academic fields are becoming more and more unified at the transnational level (major journals are read everywhere, international conferences bring participants together, and so on). In turn, this transnational unification of the management field fuels a parallel convergence in the evolution of policy making. In our view, the health care reforms in the UK and Canada share many common points simply because they were influenced by the same macro trends in the field of management and policy making. These similarities can be analysed as an example of what Bennett (1991, p. 254) calls 'policy convergence': 'Convergence in this sense results from the existence of shared ideas amongst a relatively coherent and enduring network of elites engaging in regular inter-actions at the transnational level'. This explanation also accounts for the fact that in both countries the changes in the structure of the managerial structure as well as is the managerial vocabulary were much more impressive than the changes at the care production level.

The hypothesis we suggested here has two major implications. First, it suggests that managerial and policy making fashions could influence the formulation of health care reforms as much as objective problems in health care delivery. Secondly, and more substantially, we can suggest that, at a given period, reforms in health care management need to be in minimal harmony with the structuring of the health care management and policy making field. This in turn could explain why so many health care systems around the world are facing continual reforms. The new NHS plan (Secretary of State for Health, 2000) or, in Canada, the never-ending federal provincial rounds of negotiations concerning health care are examples of this phenomenon.

In our view, the fact that health care reform could be influenced more by a new vision of management than by the appearance of new managerial needs throws an interesting light on health care policy analysis. In this respect, policy making seem quite far from being a value-free exercise of rational thinking.

Conclusion

In this chapter we summarised the structural reforms of the nineties in the management of the health care systems in Canada and the UK which allowed for a comparative analysis of their principal characteristics. Even if the internal market implemented in the UK is very different from the regionalisation process that was chosen in Canada, we saw that both sets of reforms share many common points. As we argued, these common points are too similar to be unrelated. In our view, the existence of managerial trends and policy fashions is a plausible hypothesis that could explain why these reforms share many common point even though they are structurally so different.

In other words we suggest that social and managerial trends can (internationally) structure and influence the way in which we perceive and analyse health care systems, and therefore, structure a common basis of reform characteristics that will be objectified and implemented in each country. We do not claim to have proved this hypothesis here, but the facts presented give the proposition at least some face validity and remind us of the inherent subjectivity in the perception of system problems and in the construction of managerial solutions.

The hypothesis we presented is attractive in the sense that it offers an alternative to very rational perspectives where health care reforms are supposed to be determined by the pressures or constraints the systems are facing. Without undermining the power of external pressures such as demographic transition, technological progress or budgetary constraints, we think that they can be seen more as contributing to create a sense of political need for change than as determining the characteristics of the reforms. Moreover, the endless cycle or reforms in the UK and Canada (as well as many developed countries) suggests the possibility that, at a given time, policy needs to be in a minimal harmony with the managerial and policy making trends which structure our perception of problems and solutions.

Finally, we can currently observe a growing interest in the notion of evidence-based policy making. Although it is probably very reassuring for policy makers to imagine that they can rely on the rational analysis of evidence to orient policies and reforms, we believe that academic policy analysts should be more cautious before proceeding too far in this direction.

> In this sense policy forms a highly functional part of a continuing political theatre designed to keep the audience absorbed and committed. And insofar as it takes policy-making at face value, academic study merely plays the role of the sympathetic critic who legitimates the performance (Salter, 1994, p. 47).

The analysis we presented here can be seen as a modest step in the direction Salter (1994) indicates.

References

Abel-Smith, B. (1992), 'The Reform of the National Health Service', *Quality Assurance in Health Care*, 4 (4), pp. 263–72.
Abrahamson, E. (1996), 'Management Fashion', *Academy of Management Review*, 21(1), pp. 254–85.
Alberta Health (1993a), *Starting Points: Recommendations for creating a more accountable and affordable health system*, Health Planning Secretariat, Edmonton.
Alberta Health (1993b), *Regionalization of Health Services Planning and Management: A Canadian Perspective*, Health Planning Secretariat, Edmonton.
Alberta Health (1993c), *Getting Started: An orientation for RHAs*, Health Planning Secretariat, Edmonton.
Alberta Health (1994), *Regionalization of Health Services Planning and Management: A Canadian Perspective. Update January 1994*, Health Strategy and Evaluation Division, Edmonton.
Alberta Health (1996), *Understanding Alberta's Restructured Health System*, Alberta Health, Edmonton.
Angus, D. (1991), *Significant Health Commissions and Task Forces in Canada since 1983–1984*, Canadian Nurses' Association, Ottawa.
Angus, D. (1994), *Update of 'Significant Health Commissions and Task Forces in Canada since 1983–1984*, Canadian Nurses' Association, Ottawa.
Bennett, C.J. (1991), 'What is Policy Convergence and What Causes It ?' (review article), *British Journal of Political Science*, 21, pp. 215–33.
Boyce, J. and Lamont, T. (1998), 'The New Health Authorities: Noving forward, moving back?', *British Medical Journal*, 316, p. 215.
Brassard, L. (1987), *La Participation* (dossier thématique), Commission d'Enquête sur les Services de Santé et les Services Sociaux, Québec.
British Columbia Health (1993), *New Directions for a Healthy British Columbia*, Ministry of Health and Ministry Responsible for Seniors, Province of British Columbia, Vancouver.
British Columbia Health (1996), 'Report of the Regionalization Assessment Team', Ministry of Health, Province of British Columbia, Vancouver, http://www.health.gov.bc.ca.
British Columbia Health (1997), *Better Teamwork, Better Care. Regionalization Implementation*, Ministry of Health and Ministry Responsible for Seniors, Province of British Columbia, Vancouver.
Canadian Medical Association (1993), *The Language of Health Care Reform*, report of the Working Group on Regionalization and Decentralization, Ottawa.
Capital Health Authority (1994), *A New Direction for Health* (health business plan), Capital Health Authority, Edmonton.
Casebeer, A.L. and Hannah, K.J. (1996), *The Process of Change Related to Health Policy Shift (Regionalizing Alberta's Health Care System), A Summary Document*, research report, Department of Community Health Sciences, University of Calgary.
Casebeer, A.L., Scott, C. and Hannah, K.J. (1998), *Transforming a Health Care System: Managing change for community gain*, paper presented at the Annual Meeting of the Academy of Management, San Diego.
Charles, C. and DeMaio, S. (1993), 'Lay Participation in Health Care Decision Making: A conceptual framework', *Journal of Health Politics, Policy and Law*, 18(4), pp. 881–904.

Church, J. and Barker, P. (1998), 'Regionalization of Health Services in Canada: A critical perspective', *International Journal of Health Services*, 28(3), pp. 467–86.
CIHI (1998), *National Health Expenditure Database*, Canadian Institute for Health Information, Ottawa.
CIHI (1999), Canadian Institute for Health Information website, http://www.cihi.ca.
Cohen, M.D., March, J.G. and Olsen, J.P. (1972), 'A Garbage Can Model of Organizational Choice', *Administrative Science Quarterly*, 17, pp. 1–25.
Cope, G.H. (1997), 'Bureaucratic Reform and Issues of Political Responsiveness', *Journal of Public Administration Research and Theory*, 7, pp. 461–71.
Denis, J.-L., Contandriopoulos, D., Langley, A. and Valette, A. (1998), *Les Modèles Théoriques et Empiriques de Régionalisation du Système Socio-sanitaire* (R98–07), GRIS, Montreal.
Department of Health (1997), *The New NHS: Modern, Dependable*, Department of Health, London, http://www.official-documents.co.uk/document/doh/newnhs/forward.htm.
Dorland, J.L. and Davis, S.M. (1996), *How Many Roads? Regionalization and Decentralization in Health Care*, proceedings of a conference held at Queen's University, Kingston, Ontario, June, 1995.
Edgar, A. (1995), 'Enterprise Association or Civil Association? The UK National Health Service', *Journal of Medicine and Philosophy*, 20(6), pp. 669–88.
Ellis, P. (1993), 'Purchaser Versus Providers – Defining Roles in a Regionalized Health System', *Healthcare Management Forum*, 6(1), pp. 53–5.
Enthoven, A.C. (1985), *Reflections on the Management of the National Health Service*, Nuffield Provincial Hospital Trust, London.
Enthoven, A.C. (1988), 'Managed Competition: An agenda for action', *Health Affairs*, 7 (Summer), pp. 25–47.
Enthoven, A.C. (1991), 'Internal Market Reform of the British National Health Service', *Health affairs*, 10 (Fall), pp. 60–70.
Enthoven, A.C. (1993), 'The History and Principles of Managed Competition', *Health Affairs*, 12 (supplement), pp. 24–48.
Enthoven, A.C. (1994), 'On the Ideal Market Structure for Third-party Purchasing of Health Care', *Social Science and Medicine*, 39(10), pp. 1413–24.
Ferlie, E., Ashburner, L., Fitzgerald, L. and Pettigrew, A. (1996), *The New Public Management In Action*, Oxford University Press, Oxford.
Filinson, R. (1997), 'Legislating Community Care: The British experience, with U.S. comparisons', *Gerontologist*, 37(3), pp. 333–40.
Fitzgerald, L. and Dufour, Y. (1997), 'Clinical Management as Boundary Management: A comparative analysis of Canadian and UK health care institutions', *International Journal of Public Sector Management*, 10(1/2), pp. 5–20.
Garpenby, P. (1995), 'Health Care Reform in Sweden in the 1990s: local pluralism versus national coordination', *Journal of Health Politics, Policy, and Law*, 20(3), pp. 695–717.
Glennerster, H. and Matsaganis, M. (1994), 'The English and Swedish Health Care Reforms', *International Journal of Health Services*, 24(2), pp. 231–51.
Ham, C. (1997), 'Replacing the NHS Market', *British Medical Journal*, 315(7117), pp. 1175–6.
Ham, C. (1998), 'The New NHS: Commentaries on the White Paper. From Command Economy to Demand Management', *British Medical Journal*, 316, p. 212.
Ham, C. and Brommels, M. (1994), 'Health Care Reform in The Netherlands, Sweden, and the United Kingdom', *Health Affairs*, 13(5), pp. 106–19.

Hart, J.T. (1995), 'Clinical and Economic Consequences of Patients as Producers', *Journal of Public Health Medicine*, 17(4), pp. 383–6.
Hirschman, A.O. (1995), *Défection et Prise de Parole*, Fayard, Paris.
Jérôme-Forget, M., White, J. and Wiener, J.M. (eds) (1995), *Health Care Reform through Internal Markets: Experience and proposals*, IRPP, Montréal.
Jost, T.S., Hughes, D., McHale, J. and Griffiths, L. (1995), 'The British Health Care Reforms, the American health Care Revolution, and Purchaser/Provider Contracts', *Journal of Health Politics, Policy and Law*, 20(4), pp. 885–908.
Kingdon, J.W. (1984), *Agendas, Alternatives, and Public Policies*, HarperCollins Publishers, New York.
Klein, R. (1995a), 'Big Bang Health Care Reform – Does it Work?: The Case of Britain's 1991 National Health Service Reforms', *The Milbank Quarterly*, 73(3), pp. 299–337.
Klein, R. (1995b), 'La Réforme du Service National de Santé Britanique: le consommateur introuvable', *Revue Française d'Administration Publique*, (76), pp. 619–28.
Klein, R. (1998), 'Why Britain Is Reorganizing Its National Health Service – Yet Again', *Health Affairs*, 17(4), pp. 111–25.
Kouri, D. (1996), *Assessing Board Decision-Making Needs: Saskatchewan District Health Boards* (Occasional Paper No. 1). HEALNet, Saskatoon.
Labour Party (1996), 'Renewing the National Health Service: Labour's agenda for a healthier Britain', *International Journal of Health Services*, 26(2), pp. 269–308.
Le Grand, J. (1999), 'Competition, Cooperation, or Control? Tales from the British National Health Service', *Health Affairs*, 18(3), pp. 27–39.
Le Grand, J. and Bartlett, W. (1993), *Quasi-Markets and Social Policy*, Macmillan Press, London.
Light, D.W. (1990), 'Learning from their Mistakes?', *The Health Service Journal*, 100, 4 October, pp. 1470–2.
Light, D.W. (1997), 'From Managed Competition to Managed Cooperation: Theory and lessons from the British experience', *The Milbank Quarterly*, 75(3), pp. 297–341.
Light, D.W. (1998), 'Is NHS Purchasing Serious? An American perspective', *British Medical Journal*, 316, pp. 217–20.
Manitoba Health (1992), *Quality Health for Manitobans: The Action Plan*, Manitoba Ministry of Health, Winnipeg.
Manitoba Health (1997), *Next Steps, Pathways to a healthy Manitoba*, Manitoba Ministry of Health, Winnipeg.
March, J.G. and Olsen, J.P. (1995), *Democratic Governance*, Free Press, New York.
Maynard, A. and Bloor, K. (1996), 'Introducing a Market to the United Kingdom's National Health Service', *New England Journal of Medicine*, 334(9), pp. 604–8.
Melville, M. (1997), 'Consumerism: Do patients have power in health care?', *British Journal of Nursing*, 6(6), pp. 337–40.
Metcalfe, L. (1993), 'Public Management: From imitation to innovation', in J. Kooiman (ed.), *Modern Governance: New government–society interactions*, pp. 173–89, Sage Publications, London.
Mhatre, S. and Deber, R. (1992), 'From Equal Health Care Access to Equitable Access to Health: A review of Canadian provincial health commissions and reports', *International Journal of Health Services*, (22), pp. 645–68.
Mintzberg, H. (1996), 'Managing Government, Governing Management', *Harvard Business Review*, May–June 1996, pp. 75–83.

New Brunswick Health (1996), *Plan Ministériel – Santé et Services Communautaires*, Ministère de la Santé et des Services Communautaires du Nouveau-Brunswick, Fredericton, http://www.gov.nb.ca.

Newfoundland Health (1994), *Reform Initiatives: Responding to changing health needs*, Newfoundland Department of Health, Saint John.

Newfoundland Health (1997), *The Evolving Health System*, Newfoundland Department of Health, Saint John.

Nova Scotia Health (1995), *From Blueprint to Building*, Nova Scotia Department of Health, Halifax.

Nova Scotia Health (1997), *Nova Scotia Health System Regionalization*, Nova Scotia Department of Health, Halifax.

Nova Scotia Health (1998), *Health Care Update: Regionalization*, Nova Scotia Department of Health, Halifax.

O'Neill, M. (1992), 'Community Participation in Quebec's Health System: A strategy to curtail community empowerment?', *International Journal of Health Services*, 22(2), pp. 287–301.

PEI Cabinet Committee on Government Reform (1992), *Health Reform: A vision for change*, Prince Edward Island Health Task Force, Charlottetown.

PEI Health Transition Team (1993), *Structure of our Health System: Working group report*, Prince Edward Island Health Task Force, Charlottetown.

Ratcliffe, J. (1993), 'Extra-market Incentives in the New NHS', *Health Policy*, 25, pp. 169–83.

Salter, B. (1994), 'Change in the British National Health Service: Policy paradox and the rationing issue', *International Journal of Health Services*, 24(1), pp. 45–72.

Saltman, R.B. (1994), 'The Role of Competitive Incentives in Recent Reforms of Northern European Health Systems', paper presented at the conference *Health Care Cost-Control: Internal market mechanism*, Institut de Recherches en Politiques Publiques, Montreal.

Saltman, R.B. and Figueras, J. (1997), *European Health Care Reform: Analysis of current strategies*, WHO Regional Office for Europe, Copenhagen.

Saltman, R.B. and Figueras, J. (1998), 'Analysing the Evidence on European Health Care Reform', *Health Affairs*, March/April, pp. 85–108.

Saskatchewan Health (1992), *A Saskatchewan Vision for Health: A framework for change*, Saskatchewan Health, Regina.

Saskatchewan Health (1998), *Health System Directions, Part 1: Continuing the vision*, Saskatchewan Health, Regina.

Schachter, H.L. (1995), 'Reinventing Government or Reinventing Ourselves: Two models for improving government performance', *Public Administration Review*, 55, pp. 530–7.

Secretary of State for Health (2000), 'The NHS Plan: A plan for investment, a plan for reform', London, http://www.nhs.uk/nationalplan/nhsplan.pdf.

Shackley, P. and Healey, A. (1993), 'Creating a Market: An economic analysis of the purchaser-provider model', *Health Policy*, 25, pp. 153–68.

Sharp, E.B. (1984), '"Exit, Voice, and Loyalty" in the Context of Local Government Problems', *The Western Political Quarterly*, 37, pp. 67–83.

Singer, M.A. (1995), 'Community Participation in Health Care Decision Making: Is it feasible?', *Canadian Medical Association Journal*, 153(4), pp. 421–4.

Smyth, J.D. (1997), 'Competition as a Means of Procuring Public Services: Lessons for the UK from the US experience', *International Journal of Public Sector Management*, 10(1–2), pp. 21–46.

The Economist (1997), 'Democracy at a Price', 20 September.
Tuohy, C.H. (1999), 'Dynamics of a Changing Health Sphere: The United States, Britain and Canada', *Health Affairs (Project HOPE)*, 18(3), Internet version.
Walsh, K., Deakin, N., Smith, P., Spurgeon, P. and Thomas, N. (1997), *Contracting for Change: Contracts in health, social care and other local government services*, Oxford University Press, Oxford.
WHO/OMS (1996), *European Health Care Reforms Analysis of Current Strategies*, WHO Regional Office for Europe, Copenhagen.
Young, A.P. (1996), 'Marketing: A flawed concept when applied to health care?', *British Journal of Nursing*, 5(15), pp. 937–40.

Chapter Fifteen

Lessons from the Provincial Health Care Reforms in Canada: When the Same Objective of Cost Containment Leads to Heterogeneous Results

Astrid Brousselle, Marc-André Fournier and François Champagne

Introduction

Canada is a confederate nation consisting of 10 provinces and two territories. Under the Canadian constitution, it is the provinces who are responsible for the organisation and management of the health care system. After several attempts to introduce a national, universal health insurance plan, the federal government finally garnered the compliance and support of all provinces in 1968. The federal government undertook to assume half of the cost of insured services and the provinces, in turn, agreed to comply with the federal principles of public administration (non-profit organisation, public authority), comprehensiveness (all 'medically required' hospital and physician services), universality (all residents of the province are covered), portability (individuals can received insured services in another province), and accessibility (no geographical and financial barriers, e.g. no extra billing or user fees).

Although the federal government's financial contribution is limited to medical and hospital services, all provinces assume public funding (totally or in part) for drugs for elderly and indigent populations, and most of them (although in a decreasing way) included other services (like optometric services and dental services for children) in the health services to be publicly funded.

Over the past 25 years, the federal government has repeatedly reduced its financial participation. The last important chapter occurred at the beginning of the nineties, when the federal government decided to reduce its spending in an attempt to eliminate its long-standing budgetary deficit. One facet of this policy was the reduction of financial transfers to those provinces also wanting to re-establish their fiscal situation. These new circumstances created great pressures on governmental expenses. Between 1990 and 1995, all provinces adopted measures to slow the increase of, or reduce, their global spending, i.e., reducing the number of personnel and controlling wage increases. These measures, which affected the entire public sector, focused on particular aspects of the health sector and led to an appeal for reform in the health care system to reduce (or at least maintain) public health care costs while implementing an important structural reform that would respond to population needs and technology development.

Between 1992 and 1997, the percentage of GDP allocated to health expenditures dropped from 10 per cent to 9.0 per cent, representing a 10 per cent reduction. This might represent relatively important reductions in health expenditures in the different provinces. In this article we will analyse if public expenditures were reduced after the implementation of reforms and examine the experience of the private sector. All provinces claimed to reduce health care costs, but the idea of concentrating only on public health care costs was implicit. First, the discourse on cost control is directly associated with the reduction of federal transfers and the control of governmental expenses. Second, the government cannot expect to reduce expenses it does not control directly without completely reforming the funding system. It might have been accomplished through the control of private funding by enlarging public insurance, but the discourse would have been on the creation of wider insurance coverage rather than cost control. And all provinces emphasise the impossibility of increasing public funding through taxes for fear of the unpopularity that would ensue. Third, all measures proposed concern essentially, if not completely, the public sector. The desire to control public health care costs by reducing or stabilising them is evident from the provinces' discourse.

The provinces wanted to highlight the importance of determinants of health and of community resources. There was a clear resolve, as in other countries, to reorient the health system towards prevention and health promotion. At the same time, the need to develop ambulatory care (to decrease the hospitalisation of patients who could be treated on an outpatient basis) was expressed. The idea consisted of augmenting hospital specialisation and in reducing costs. Five provinces decided to convert or close hospitals, and four encouraged or forced hospital mergers in urban areas. These measures often came with staff dismissals and reductions in the numbers of beds. All provinces expressed their will to reduce medical expenses. Finally, governments decided eliminate insurance (either in part or entirely) for certain non-medical or hospital services like optometric and dental care and aesthetic services. At the same time, three provinces officially decided to grant the private sector a greater role: in Alberta, direct fees for services are authorised for certain procedures; Manitoba wanted to privatise home care services and allows private clinics to receive fees for certain services; in New Brunswick, new legislation permits the creation of private hospitals. This trend toward privatisation can also be noted in other provinces, but it is not stressed (for the time being) in official guidelines.

The first striking point is the general perception in all provinces that these reforms were necessary. The other salient issue is the homogeneity of discourse concerning the generally proposed orientation of reforms. Reforms were organised around two themes: first, to reduce public health care costs; second, to improve accessibility and quality of services through organisational measures. This article will concentrate on the first objective – to discover if it was attained, and to understand what happened to health care expenses. Now, a few years after the implementation of these reforms, we can answer some of the questions that have arisen. Was the objective of public cost containment reached? If so, was it done through volume or price control? Has the private sector benefited from these reforms? We will answer these questions by examining the evolution of public and private expenditures in each province, controlling for the evolution of price and volume.

Methodology

All data in this chapter has been gathered from the Canadian Institute for Health Information and Statistics Canada. We have examined the variations in current and constant dollars, public and private health expenditures. All expenditures are considered per capita. Expenditures in constant dollars (real expenditures) are calculated using implicit price indices: one for the public sector, the other for private.

The use of price indices is an interesting means by which to separate the price effect from the quantity effect (McGuire, 1994; Statistics Canada, 1990). Implicit price indices are calculated by associating a price index with different sectors (medical, hospital, etc.). Then, to control for the relative importance of the different sectors, a weight is allocated to each price index. However, some problems arise from the calculation of price indices.

First, there is no price for non-commercial activities as no product is exchanged on a commercial market where prices are fixed by supply and demand. This difficulty is circumvented by estimating prices from costs. The sector's production is considered proportional to costs, which are separated into remuneration costs and non-remuneration costs (Statistics Canada, 1990). However, using this method, the price index becomes a resource cost index. This is not an issue until production is really proportional to costs. Problems occur when, for example, new work charges are imposed after reducing the workforce in a labour intensive sector. Let us consider that production is unchanged. The workforce productivity increases (produced quantity/number of workers) but the volume of services estimated through the level of resources is reduced, and the real volume of services is constant. The difference between the estimated volume of services and the real volume of services produced shows that productivity gains render price indices estimated from costs problematic.

Second, weights of each sector are not revised annually. Thus, the more distant we are from the reference year, the greater the risk that they become inadequate. The CIHI (CIHI, 1999, 1998) presented two implicit price indices for government expenditures; the old index was revised and the weights changed (see Tables 15.1 and 15.2). The change of weighting in the public sector gives more importance to the Labour Income Index, and reduces that of the Hospital Commodity Index and of the Physician Price Index. (The first index was calculated until 1995 and the new one until 1996.) To control for differences between the two indices, we represented both on our graphs. Differences exist but they do not change the variation of expenditures calculated in constant dollars, except in two cases: Ontario and British Columbia. We attempted to solicit an explanation for these variations from Statistics Canada and the Canadian Institute of Health Information (CIHI), but unfortunately, we were unable to elicit a reasonable response. Access to raw data was also denied. We then decided to include these provinces in the analysis of cost control, but to exclude them from the volume or price reduction analysis. The price index was revised in 1992, and is now alleged to offer appropriate representation of the relative importance of the different sectors. Yet, since the revision of the weights was not done for the years previous to 1992, only the old index is available for this period. So we decided to use the old index until 1992 and the new one from 1992 to 1996.

The calculation of two indices adds validity to the variations observed, even if we cannot ascribe absolute importance to the values of the rates of variations. The use of two indices plays the role of a sensibility analysis, which shows the constancy of results. We control for the important differences between the two indices for Ontario and British Columbia by excluding them from the price/volume analysis. On the other hand, variations observed in real expenditures are valid variations since they are confirmed by the calculation of two slightly different indices.

Table 15.1 Health care price index – public sector

Component	Price index	Weight pre-1992	Weight 1992
Hospitals – labour income	Labour Income Index	0.529	0.462
Hospitals – residual	Hospital Commodity Index	0.087	0.083
Hospitals – capital cost allowance	Capital Cost Allowance Index (CCA)	0.0033	0.0029
Residential care – labour income	Labour Income Index		0.088
Residential care – capital cost allowance	Capital Cost Allowance Index (CCA)		0.003
Medicare expenditure	Physician Price Index	0.351	0.315
Other health care – Labour income	Labour Income Index		0.020
Total – government		1.00	1.00

Source: Statistics Canada, implicit price index for government expendifure on medical and health care, cited in CIHI, 1998, p. 56.

Table 15.2 Health care price index – private sector

Component	Price index	Weight pre-1992	Weight 1992
Drugs and drug sundries	CPI	0.326	0.351
Special care facilities (SCF)	SCF Labour Income Index, Commodity and CCA Indices	0.214	0.104
Hospital care	Labour Income Index, Commodity and CCA Indices	0.139	0.067
Medical and dental care	CPI Dental Care and Physician Index	0.114	0.251
Other health care	Service Price Index	0.148	0.107
Accident and health insurance (other medical care)	Insurance Price Index	0.059	0.120
Total – personal health		1.00	1.00

Source: Statistics Canada, implicit price index for government expendifure on medical and health care, cited in CIHI, 1998, p. 57.

Results

Was the Objective of Public Cost-containment Reached?

Canada's health care system is primarily public financed. In 1998, 69.7 per cent of the health system's resources came from public sources, and 30.3 per cent from private funds (CIHI, 1999). In 1998, Canada spent 9.1 per cent of its GDP in the health sector: that means $1,613 Can. (about £680) per capita (CIHI, 1999). The expenses were concentrated in the hospital sector (34.3 per cent), with 14.3 per cent of the budget financing medical practice (physicians' remuneration) and 13.6 per cent spent on drugs (CIHI, 1999).

Over a period of four years (1986–90), before the federal decision to reduce its financial participation, health care expenditures grew, on average, 8.2 per cent annually. The public expenditures experienced a growth of 8.0 per cent compared with 9.0 per cent for private expenditures. So, if the public sector represents a bigger proportion of health sector expenditures, it grows more slowly than the private sector. When we examine expenditures calculated in constant dollars and rates of growth for price indices, we observe that the volume of services grew 2.8 per cent annually in the public sector, compared with 2.4 per cent for real private expenditures, so that the volume of services in the public sector grew more rapidly than in the private sector. The growth rate of price indices shows that prices in the private sector grew faster (6.0 per cent per year on average) than in the public sector (4.7 per cent). This data offers us quite useful information about the factors which represent pressures to health care expenditures. The private sector is the first sector responsible for total expenditure growth. Furthermore, private sector prices increase more rapidly than volume. The public sector grows each year, but at a lesser rate; both volume and price increase, but prices show a more rapid rhythm of growth. Notwithstanding that private financing increases more rapidly, the official guidelines expressed the desire to control public expenditures and not total health care expenditures.

The reforms began at different times in each of the provinces. To know if the official objective controlling of public expenditures was implemented, we decided to calculate average rates of growth over a two-year period after the beginning of reforms. This shows us if public expenditures have been controlled a few years after implementation of the reforms. Six out of 10 provinces decreased public health expenditures over the two-year period following reform: Alberta (-6.3 per cent), Quebec (-3.9 per cent), Ontario (-1.3 per cent), Nova Scotia (-1.1 per cent), Prince Edward Island (-0.7 per cent) and Saskatchewan (-0.6 per cent). It was confirmed by the graphic analysis that this rate of growth represents a general trend of attrition in the public sector, except for Prince Edward Island, where public expenditures increased after 1995 (reforms here began in 1993). The public health care expenditures are still increasing in four provinces, those being: Manitoba (+3.6 per cent), Newfoundland (+3.1 per cent), New Brunswick (+1.8 per cent) and British Columbia (+0.7 per cent). The case of British Columbia is somewhat unusual because the rate of growth is close to 0 per cent and this province did not want to decrease public health care expenditures, but to stabilise them. We can also note that Ontario officially stated the same objective of reduced public health care expenditures. Again, the evolution during this period reflects a trend more than a punctual evolution.

These results show that despite the generally declared objective of controlling public health care expenditures, not all provinces succeeded in reducing or stabilising them. The homogeneity of objective led to heterogeneity in outcomes. Yet, it is also important to note that while public expenditures continue to grow in four provinces, their rate of increase is much slower than prior to 1990. That is to say, if there were no stabilisation or reduction in public expenditures, at least efforts were made to reduce their rate of increase.

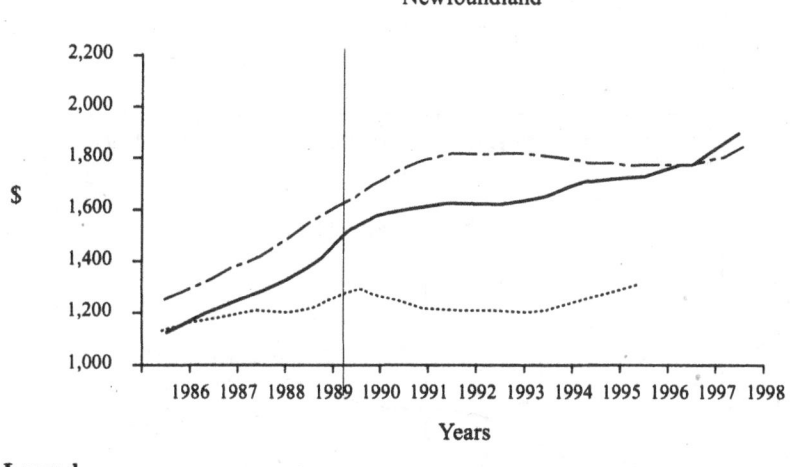

Legend

– · – ·   Canada's current public health care expenditures (per capita)
─────   Province's current public health care expenditures (per capita)
·········   Province's real public health care expenditures (per capita)

Figure 15.1 Public health care expenditures (per capita)

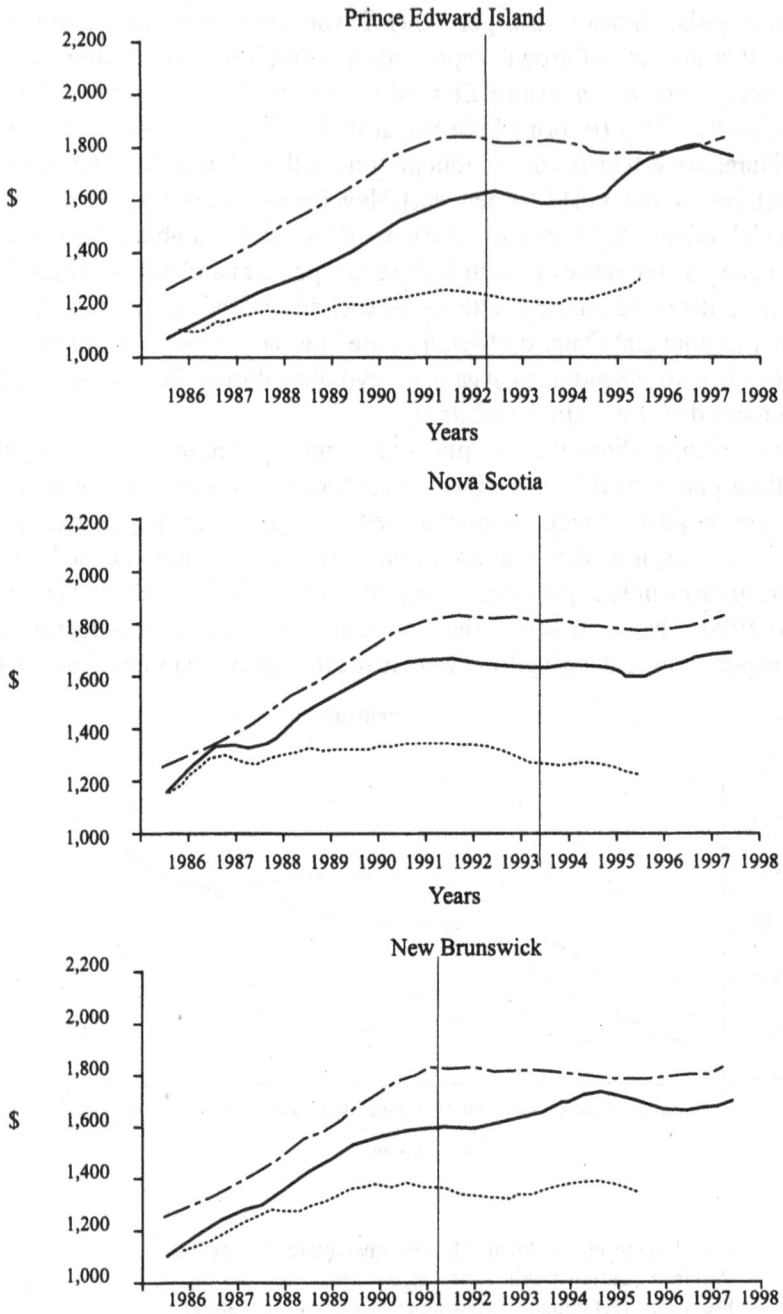

Figure 15.1 cont'd

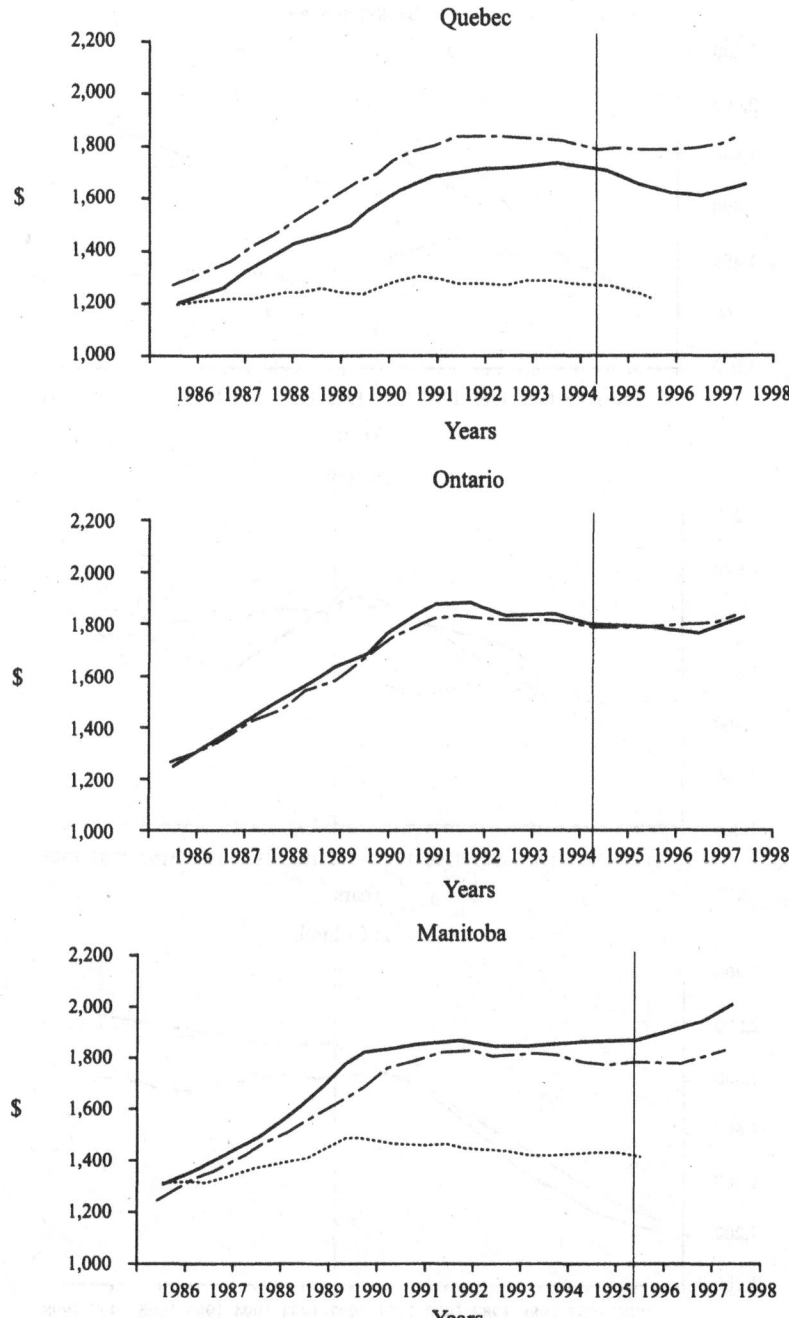

Figure 15.1 cont'd

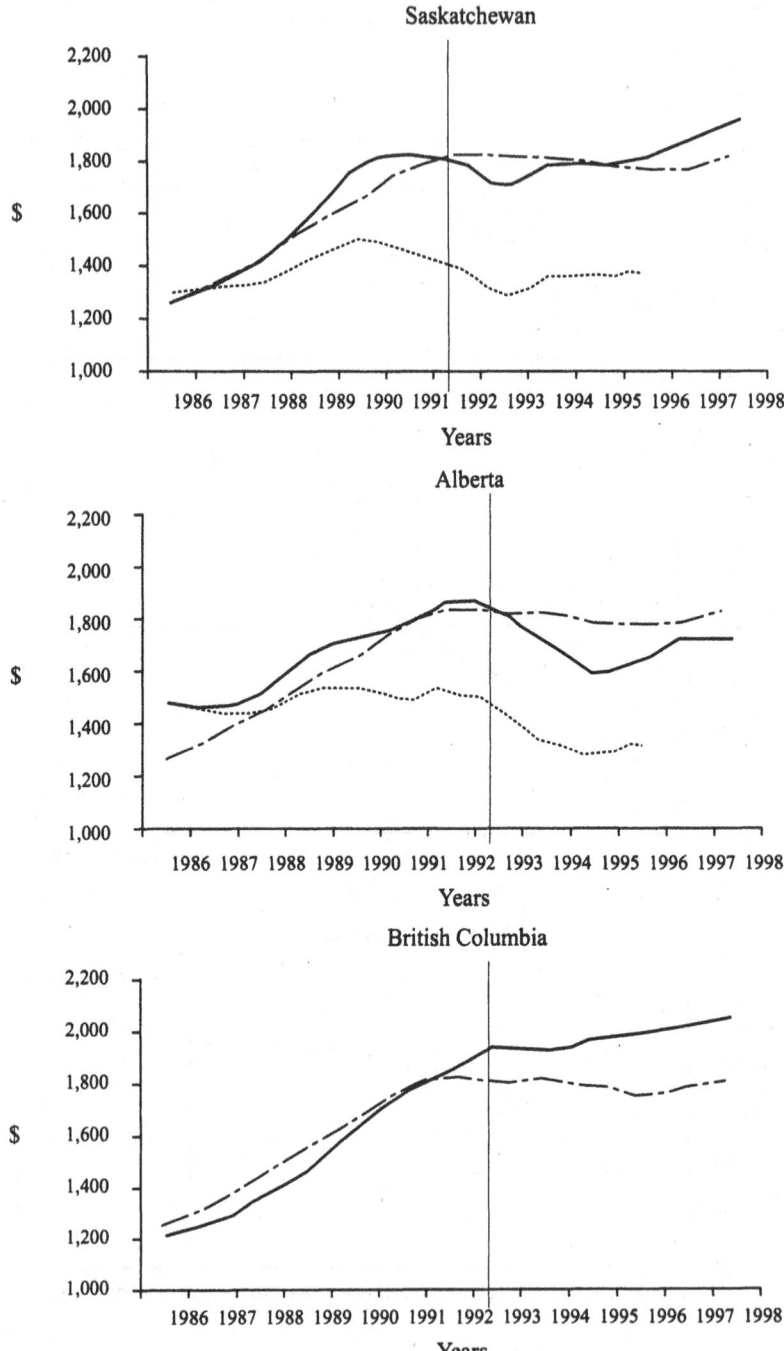

Figure 15.1 cont'd

Furthermore, examining the evolution of public costs on the graphs, we can see that in most cases, the control of public expenditures does not seem to be associated with health care reforms. In the majority of provinces it began before the implementation of the official guidelines. This poses questions regarding the link between implementation of reforms and cost-control.

Was Public Cost-containment Reached Through Volume or Price Control?

Six provinces have reduced their public health care expenditures, but all provinces have reduced the growth rate of public health care expenditures. Using implicit price indices we can determine if this control was accomplished through a control of prices or of the volume of services (real public health care expenditures). Ontario and British Columbia were not considered for this part of the analysis because of the extreme variation between both price indices. We also excluded Manitoba because health reforms occurred there in 1996 and no price indices were available for 1997 and 1998. The variation for Quebec is calculated over one year because of the reform date (1995).

When examining the growth rate of real public health care expenditures, we can note that all provinces reduced the volume of services. The reductions ranged from −0.1 per cent for Prince Edward Island to −6.0 per cent for Alberta (see Table 15.3).

Table 15.3 Public health care expenditures over a two year period after reforms began

	Nfld	PEI	NS	NB	Que	Ont	Man	Sask	Alta	BC
Date of the beginning of reforms	1990	1993	1994	1992	1995	1993	1996	1992	1993	1993
Annual growth rate of real public expenditures	-2.29	-0.06	-1.07	-0.55	-3.30	–	–	-1.72	-6.02	–
Annual growth rate of implicit price index	5.63	-0.64	-0.04	2.42	-0.59	–	–	1.12	-0.28	–

Among the six provinces which reduced public health care expenditures, Alberta, Quebec, Nova Scotia, and Prince Edward Island have reduced both prices and the volume of services. We can comment that, excluding the case of Prince Edward Island, the price reduction is inferior to volume reduction. Saskatchewan reduced volume of services but the prices still increase.

The remaining provinces which did not reduce public health care expenditures (New Brunswick and Newfoundland) show a reduction in the volume of services, but prices still increase. Thus increases in the public budget finance price increases, rather than increases in the volume of services.

In all provinces the rate of growth of prices has decreased, which means they increased at a slower rate; the exception is Newfoundland where prices increase more rapidly than before the reduction in federal transfers.

The reforms had a clear effect on volume of services in all provinces. The effect on prices is heterogeneous in the different provinces. In some provinces prices decreased and, in others, prices still increase but in general at a slower rate than before the reforms.

Has the Private Sector Benefited from these Reforms?

Financing modalities in the public and private sectors differ considerably. Public financing is essentially derived from taxation. In 1996, private financing was composed of out-of-pocket payment (54.6 per cent), private health insurance (35.2 per cent), and non-consumption expenses (10.2 per cent) ('non-consumption expenditure includes a number of heterogeneous sources, such as hospital non-patient revenue, capital expenditures for privately owned facilities, and health research' (CIHI, 1999, p. 37)). In 1996, private funds were used to finance 9.7 per cent of hospitals costs, 30.6 per cent of costs induced by other institutions (residential care types of facilities), 1.1 per cent of physician remuneration and 89.6 per cent of other professional services (dental services, vision care services and other professional services (CIHI, 1999). Contrary to what we can see in many health care systems, there is no hospital private sector in Canada so that no substitution is possible for acute care. Nevertheless, some provinces nowadays challenge this point especially for surgery services. In the Canadian system, the limits of what is financed by public funds and what is financed by private funds are well defined. Nevertheless, there are grey zones concerning billing rights, which can be modified by reforms. Furthermore, as reorganisation often creates dissatisfaction, we could expect that the private sector could benefit from the changes that occurred. To answer this question we have used two indicators: first, we examined the evolution of the proportion of private spending in total health care expenditures; second, we observed the evolution of private expenditures.

The proportion of total expenditures financed by private funds grew from 25 per cent in 1986 to 30 per cent in 1996. This proportion grew in all provinces except British Columbia. At first glance, it seems that private funding takes importance. But is it a real trend? We have seen that public spending has been controlled in almost all provinces. The calculation of the proportion depends directly on the amount of public funds spent in the health sector. It would be normal to observe a growing proportion of private funds if public spending decreased, without attributing this increase to a funding transfer (public to private funds). In 1990, when public expenditures began to bend after the reduction of federal transfers, the proportion of private funding was 25.4 per cent – close to that of 1986 (24.9 per cent). We can say that public and private expenditures grew at a rate that maintained the share of funding between the two sectors. Per capita private expenditures continued to grow at the same rhythm, whereas public expenditures began to decrease. The balance between the public and private sector began to shift. This analysis is confirmed by the observed evolution of private expenditures: they continue to grow and seem unaffected by reforms. In 10 years (1986–96), nominal private expenditures have grown 81 per cent, and prices increase more rapidly than the volume of services (46 per cent compared with 24 per cent over the same period). As we can see, real private expenditures have grown of 24 per cent in 10 years.

Discussion

In blueprints for health care reforms, all provinces expressed the desire to control public health care expenditures, eight provinces sought reductions, and two aspired to stabilisation. We have seen that the evolution of public expenditures is far from homogeneous, as not all provinces attained their goal. However, a trend of cost control is noticeable in the reduced rhythm of growth of expenditures. Furthermore, we have observed that the control of health care expenditures has, in general, a weak association with the implementation of reforms; control generally began before implementation. It seems to be more a consequence of the fiscal restrictions in the entire governmental sector that preceded implementation of reforms in the health care sector than the effect of the reforms. Yet in most provinces where public health care expenditures were effectively controlled, reforms seem to have accentuated an existing trend. In these provinces, control of public health care costs has meant a reduction in the volume of services. Prices seem to have been more minimally affected.

Since the price indicator for the public sector is estimated through costs of production, the volume indicator (real public values) is a direct indicator of resources. The observed reduction could represent the effective reduction of resources in the health sector (employment reduction, hospitals mergers, bed closings, etc.). However it is not possible to draw any conclusion on services received by patients or waiting times and waiting lists. A recent study by Canadian health services experts concluded that even if there are many anecdotes no reliable data exist on waiting times and waiting lists in Canada (Lewis et al., 2000). We have some information about different punctual situations across Canada but reliable general data is difficult to find. A Canadian study showed clearly that the repercussions of the decline in acute care resources for elderly people in the province of British Columbia between 1986 and 1995 was not so important, the changes in capacity were absorbed by decreasing the amount of care received by each individuals (Sheps et al., 2000). Data from the region of Winnipeg (Manitoba), where 21 per cent of hospital beds were closed between 1992 and 1995, provided other interesting facts : stays were shortened and many inpatient procedures were moved to outpatient care, but we did not observe any effect on death rates, readmissions and consultations in emergency departments or physician offices. Yet, we observed an important increase in high-profile surgical procedures (Brownell et al., 2000). Therefore it is difficult to draw any conclusion on how access and technical aspects of care were affected by the reforms, however the human aspects of health care seem to have been affected (quality in human relations, confidence in having the best quality of care, need of more support coming from the relatives, etc.). Increasing dissatisfaction of Canadians in regard to their health care system is certainly a consequence of this situation.

We must remember that in the health sector, cost containment is income containment (Evans et al., 1991). Controlling expenditures often means reductions in remuneration, reductions in employment, or both. On the other hand, reductions in the volume of services can be less critical if productivity gains occur. And this is what certainly occurred when we pay attention to the complaints of the health care employees about heavy workload and burnout (Dussault et al., 1999).

The results found regarding the link between reforms and the control of public expenditures suggest two interpretations: 1) the control occurred a few years before the institution of health care reforms and was initiated by federal transfer reductions and the will of most provinces to reduce their deficit; or 2) reforms which produce meso and micro reorganisation have a limited effect on macro financial trends. In the first case, reforms might express a need for rationalisation and reorganisation of care after the occurrence of budgetary restraints and drastic cuts in production costs. Then the objective of cost control would have no reasonable justification for appearing in blueprints as it would be rather a cause than an objective. In the second case, to justify their implementation we expect that the micro objectives of reforms have a rationale different from that of cost control; if not, as we see no obvious trend in the control of health care expenditures in the different provinces, it would at the very least demonstrate their inadequacy for attaining this objective. They may be more adequate for attaining the other objectives of reforms which are increased quality of care, efficiency and accessibility.

We have observed that private expenditures increased markedly over ten years (+81 per cent in nominal terms, +24 per cent in real terms). Before public costs were controlled, public and private expenditures increased at a rate that maintained their proportional share. Now that public costs have been controlled, private expenditures represent a growing proportion of health care funding. Categories where private funding took importance between 1990 and 1996 are administrative costs (+85.2 per cent), prescribed drugs (+53.4 per cent), health institutions other than hospitals (+34.9 per cent) and professional services other than physicians (+33.6 per cent). Nevertheless, as we can see no modification in the evolution of private expenditures, it would seem that there were no noticeable transfers from public to private payments. The evolution was observed a short term after the implementation of health care reforms, and the private sector may need more time to adapt to new rules and regulations. Another explanation may be that organisational change in the public sector does not affect the private sector. Technological change (for example, drugs) and insurance coverage are elements more likely to affect private expenditures than organisational changes in the public sector. Finally, there may be transfers from public to private funding in certain sectors (such as professional services) since certain services were excluded from the Canadian public health insurance; per capita public health expenditures for dental care and vision care services have decreased and private funding has increased significantly. Yet we do not have the data to associate this trend with real transfers in the funding of particular services.

Private expenditures constituted a smaller proportion of total health expenses, nevertheless it showed a rate of growth, in the period previous to federal decision to reduce its financial participation, superior to the one of public expenditures. Yet, provincial governments decided to reduce public expenditures. This is defensible with respect to a budget derived from taxes; but when one claims that public expenses increase too rapidly, what is the rationale for not applying this reasoning to private expenditures? Let us remember that in the private sector, increases in prices are more important (+46 per cent between 1986 and 1996), even if volume increases at a good rhythm (+24 per cent in 10 years). The augmentation in volume of services can express a new demand for certain health care services. In 1996, the private sector financed 94.7 per cent of dental services, 90.5 per cent of vision care services, and 57.0 per cent of prescribed drugs. Should we not examine in detail the demand for services that are privately financed to consider their inclusion in public insurance? Health insurance creates a redistribution of income from people with good health to those who are ill. A public health insurance redistributes resources in the same way, but additionally from rich people to those who are financially deprived (Evans, 1987). Public management is also a means to invoke control measures, and to avoid the costs of swollen administrative structures, as is the case in health systems that give a greater place to the private sector (Evans et al., 1991; Conseil de la Santé et du Bien-être, 1997). In Canada, administrative costs grew 85.2 per cent between 1990 and 1996 in the private sector, compared to 7.2 per cent in the public sector.

These days, there is a tendency in all provinces to reduce health insurance coverage to a limited number of defined medical and hospital services (Conseil de la santé et du bien-être, 1997). Restrictions have been imposed on certain services and on rights to access certain health programs. We must be careful to conserve the distributive advantages of public health care insurance while striving to reduce public health care costs. The difficulty is all the more important when reorienting the health care system to ambulatory and outpatient care. The stakes of cost control go beyond the realisation of objectives. They concern the very foundations of our health care systems.

References Cited

Brownell, M.D., Roos, N.P. and Burchil, C.l (1999), 'Monitoring the Impact of Hospital Fownsizing on Access to Care and Quality of Care', *Medical Care*, 37(6), JS135–50.
Conseil de la Santé et du Bien-être (1997), *Évolution des Rapports Public–Privé dans les Services de Santé et les Services Sociaux*, Québec.
Dussault, G., Fournier, M.-A., Zanchetta, M. S., Kérouac, S., Denis, J.-L., Bojanowski, L., Carpentier, M. and Grossman, M. (1999), *The Nursing Labour Market in Canada: Review of the Literature*, report presented to The Invitational Roundtable of Stakeholders in Nursing.
Evans, R.G. (1987), 'Public Health Insurance: The collective purchase of individual care', *Health Policy*, 7, pp. 115–25.
Evans, R.G, Barer, M.L. and Hertzman, C. (1991), 'The 20-year Experiment: Accounting for, explaining, and evaluating health care cost containment in Canada and the United States', *Annual Review of Public Health*, 12, pp. 481–518.
Lewis, S., Barer, M.L., Sanmartin, C., Sheps, S., Shortt, S.E.D. and McDonald, P.W. (2000), 'Ending Waiting-list Mismanagement: Principles and practice', *Canadian Medical Association Journal*, 162(9), pp. 1297–300.

McGuire, A. (1994), 'Is there Adequate Funding of Health Care?', in A.J. Culyer and A. Wagstaff (eds), *Reforming Health Care Systems. Experiments with the NHS*, Edward Elgar Publishing Ltd., Aldershot.
Sheps, S.B, Reid, R.J., Barer, M.L., Krueger, H., McGrail, K.M., Green, B., Evans, R.G. and Herzman, C. (2000), 'Hospital Downsizing and Trends in Health Care use among Elderly People in British Columbia', *Canadian Medical Association Journal*, 163(4), pp. 397–401.

Other References

Alberta Health, *Getting Started II: Health Business Plan Guidebook*.
Alberta Health, *Getting Started: An orientation for RHAs*.
Alberta Health (1993), *Starting Points: Recommendations for creating a more accountable and affordable health system*, Health Planning Secretariat.
British Columbia Health (1993a), *New Directions for a Healthy British Columbia*, Ministry of Health and Ministry Responsible for Seniors, Province of British Columbia.
British Columbia Health (1993b), *Processes, Benchmarks and Responsibilities for Developing Community Health Councils and Regional Health Boards*, Ministry of Health and Ministry Responsible for Seniors, Province of British Columbia.
British Columbia Health (1996), 'Changes to Health Plan put Services for People First' (news release), Ministry of Health, Province of British Columbia: http://www.health.gov.bc.ca.
Canadian Institute for Health Information (1997), *National Health Expenditure Trends, 1975–1998*, National Health Expenditure Database.
Canadian Institute for Health Information (1998), *National Health Expenditure Trends, 1975–1998*, National Health Expenditure Database.
Denis, J.-L., Contandriopoulos, D., Langley, A. and Valette, A. (1998), *Les Modèles Théoriques et Empiriques de Régionalisation du Système Socio-sanitaire*, Groupe de Recherche Interdisciplinaire en Santé, Faculté de Médecine, Université de Montréal, R98-07.
Evans, R.G. (1990), 'Tension, Compression, and Shear: Directions, stresses and outcomes of health care cost control', *Journal of Health Politics, Policy, and Law*, 15(1), pp. 101–27.
Government of Newfoundland and Labrador (1994), *Newfoundland Department of Health Reform Initiatives: Responding to Changing Health Needs*, Department of Health.
Manitoba Health (1992), *Quality Health for Manitobans: The Action Plan*, Manitoba Ministry of Health, Winnipeg.
Manitoba Health (1995a), *Annual Report 1994–1995*, Manitoba Ministry of Health, Winnipeg.
Manitoba Health (1995b), *Recommendation to the Minister of Health on the Governance of Health Services Delivery in Northern/Rural Manitoba*, Northern/Rural Health Advisory Council, Winnipeg.
Manitoba Health (1996a), *Annual Report 1995–1996*, Manitoba Ministry of Health, Winnipeg.
Manitoba Health (1996b), *Annual Report 1996–1997*, Manitoba Ministry of Health, Winnipeg.
Manitoba Health (1997a), 'A Planning Framework to promote, Preserve and Protect the Health of Manitobans', http://www.gov.mb.ca/health/documents/planning.pdf, Manitoba Ministry of Health.
Manitoba Health (1997b), 'Community Health Needs Assessment Guidelines', http://www.gov.mb.ca/health/documents/chnag.pdf, Manitoba Ministry of Health.
Manitoba Health (1997c), 'Core Health Services in Manitoba', http://www.gov.mb.ca/health/documents/core.pdf, Manitoba Ministry of Health.

Manitoba Health (1997d), 'Neighourhood Resources Networks: Primary Health Care Working Document', http://www.gov.mb.ca/health/documents/nrn.pdf, Manitoba Ministry of Health.

Manitoba Health (1997e), *Next Steps, Pathways to a healthy Manitoba*, Manitoba Ministry of Health, Winnipeg.

Naylor, D. (1999), 'Health Care in Canada: Incrementalism Under Fiscal Duress', *Health Affairs*, May/June 1999, http://www.projhope.org/HA/mayjun99/Canada.htm.

Newfoundland and Labrador Department of Health (1997), *The Evolving Health System*.

Newfoundland Health (1994), *Reform Initiatives: Responding to changing health needs*, Newfoudland Department of Health, Saint John.

Newfoundland Health (1997), *The Evolving Health System*, Newfoudland Department of Health, Saint John.

Nouveau-Brunswick, *Vers une Stratégie Globale en Matière de Santé. Santé 2000, vision, principes et objectifs*, Ministère de la santé et des Services Communautaires du Nouveau-Brunswick, Fredericton.

Nouveau-Brunswick Santé et Services Communautaires, *Plan des Services de Santé et des Services Communautaires pour le Nouveau-Brunswick*, Ministère de la santé et des Services Communautaires du Nouveau-Brunswick, Fredericton.

Nouveau-Brunswick Santé et Services Communautaires (1996a), 'Health and Community Services: Legislative statement' http://www.gov.nb.ca/hcs/spendesp.htm', Ministère de la santé et des Services Communautaires du Nouveau-Brunswick, Fredericton.

Nouveau-Brunswick Santé et Services Communautaires (1996b), 'Plan Ministériel – Santé et Services Communautaires', http://www.gov.nb.ca, Ministère de la santé et des Services Communautaires du Nouveau-Brunswick, Fredericton.

Nova Scotia Health (1995), *From Blueprint to Building*.

Nova Scotia Health (1998), *From the Ground Up: Community Health Board Development in Nova Scotia 1994–1997*, Community Health Planning and Evaluation Working Group.

Nova Scotia Health (1998), *Health Care Update: Regionalization*, Nova Scotia Department of Health.

Ontario Health (1996), 'Ontario Ministry of Health Business Plan 1996', Ontario Ministry of Health, Toronto, http://www.gov.on.ca/health.

Ontario Health (1997a), 'Ontario Ministry of Health – Putting the Patient First: What are the problems?', Ontario Ministry of Health, Toronto, http://www.gov.on.ca/health.

Ontario Health (1997b), 'Ontario Ministry of Health – The Rural and Northern Health Care Framework', Ontario Ministry of Health, Toronto, http://www.gov.on.ca/health.

Ontario Health (1997c), 'Ontario Ministry of Health – Who Does Want?', Ontario Ministry of Health, Toronto, http://www.gov.on.ca/health.

Ontario Health (1997d), 'Ontario Ministry of Health Business Plan 1997–1998', Ontario Ministry of Health, Toronto, http://www.gov.on.ca/health.

Ontario Health (1997e), 'Ontario Ministry of Health Future Shape: A new structure for the Ministry of Health', Ontario Ministry of Health, Toronto, http://www.gov.on.ca/health.

Ontario Premier's Council, *Challenging Assumptions: Restructuring health systems across Canada – devolution or dog's breakfast?*, The Ontario Premier's Council, Toronto.

P.E.I. Health Transition Team (1993a), *Community Needs Asseeement: Working Group Report*, Transition Team on Health Reform.

P.E.I. Health Transition Team (1993b), *Partnership for Better Health*, Transition Team on Health Reform.

P.E.I. Health Transition Team (1993c), *Provincial Health Policy Council: Working Group Report*, vol. 1, Transition Team on Health Reform.

P.E.I. Health Transition Team (1993d), *Provincial Health Policy Council: Working Group Report*, vol. 2, Transition Team on Health Reform.

P.E.I. Health Transition Team (1993e), *Structure of our Health System: Working Group Report*, Transition Team on Health Reform.

P.E.I. Health Transition Team (1993f), *Utilization Management: Working Group Report*, Transition Team on Health Reform.

Prince Edward Island Cabinet Committee on Government Reform (1992), *Health Reform: A vision for shange*, Health Task Force.

Provincial Health Council of Alberta (1997), *Final Report on Alberta Health and Regional and Provincial Health Authorities Business Plan Review for 1997–98 to 1999–2000*, Edmonton, Provincial Health Council of Alberta.

Québec (1996), *La planification régionale des services sociaux et de santé. Enjeux politiques et méthodologiques*, Les publications du Québec.

Santé Canada, *Réforme du système de santé au Canada*.

Santé Canada (1996a), *La réforme des soins de santé à l'Île du Prince Édouard*.

Santé Canada (1996b), *La réforme des soins de santé à Terre-Neuve*.

Santé Canada (1997a), *La réforme des soins de santé à l'Ile du Prince-Édouard*, Santé Canada.

Santé Canada (1997b), *La réforme des soins de santé a Terre-Neuve*, Santé Canada.

Santé Canada (1997c), *La réforme des soins de santé au Manitoba*, Santé Canada.

Santé Canada (1997d), *La réforme des soins de santé au Nouveau-Brunswick*, Santé Canada.

Santé Canada (1997e), *La réforme des soins de santé au Québec*, Santé Canada.

Santé Canada (1997f), *La réforme des soins de santé en Alberta*, Santé Canada.

Santé Canada (1997g), *La réforme des soins de santé en Colombie Britanique*, Santé Canada.

Santé Canada (1997h), *La réforme des soins de santé en Nouvelle-Ecosse*, Santé Canada.

Santé Canada (1997i), *La réforme des soins de santé en Saskatchewan*, Santé Canada.

Santé Canada (1997j), *La réformes des soins de santé en Ontario*, Santé Canada.

Saskatchewan Health (1992), *A Saskatchewan Vision for Health: A framework for change*, Regina: Saskatchewan Health.

Saskatchewan Health (1994), *Introduction of Need-Based Allocation of Ressources to Saskatchewan District Health Boards for 1994–95*, Saskatchewan Health.

Saskatchewan Health (1996), *Health Renewal is Working: Progress Report October 1996*, Saskatchewan Health.

Saskatchewan Health (1998), *Health System Directions, Part 1: Continuing the Vision*, Saskatchewan Health, Regina.

Statistique Canada (1990), *Guide des Comptes des Revenus et Dépenses*, Série des sources et méthodes, catalogue 13–603, n°1- hors série.

Statistique Canada (1999), communication privée, *Public Sector Health Expenditure Price Index Ealculation*, National Accounts and Environment.

Chapter Sixteen

The Process of Health Priority Setting in France: an Attempt at Critical Analysis

Pascal Jarno, Françoise Riou, Jean Pascal, Christophe Lerat,
Christine Quelier, Jacques Chaperon and Pierre Le Beux

Introduction

In France, public health policy has undergone a change of paradigm over the last few years: previously focused on the financial management of curative health care, public health policy is now grounded in a process which includes conducting needs assessments, setting objectives and priorities, and evaluating interventions.

Since the introduction of the French medical insurance system in 1945, health expenditures have grown steadily. The simultaneous increase in economic activity in France made such growth affordable. Since 1975, however, national economic decline has led successive political leaders to take cost-containing measures. This has included controlling the medical insurance budget by increasing insurance premiums while reducing the number of services provided, and reducing costs by implementing measures such as limiting the number of medical students. These measures, however, have had a limited impact on medical insurance systems and the growth of expenditures.

Needs assessment was introduced at the beginning of the 1960s (Jobert, 1981) for the regulation of hospital bed capacity. In the 1970s, the national health map (*Carte Sanitaire*), which establishes the number of hospital beds and equipment per inhabitants, was introduced. The process reached a new dimension with the creation in 1991 of the regional plans for health organisation, Schéma Régional d'Organisation Sanitaire (SROS), intended to establish the number of hospital beds according to more precise indicators of needs.

Since 1996, the French parliament has voted each year the target revenues and expenditures of the medical insurance (Objectif National des Dépenses

---

Health Policy and Economics: Strategic Issues in Health Care Management, M. Tavakoli, H.T.O. Davies and M. Malek (eds), Ashgate Publishing Ltd, 2001.

d'Assurance Maladie (ONDAM)). The voting of these amounts have to take into account the annual report on the health status of the French population compiled by two authorities: the High Committee for Public Health (Haut Comité de Santé Publique (HCSP)) and the National Health Conference (Conférence Nationale de Santé (CNS)). The HCSP, created in 1992, is composed of public health experts who are under the Ministry of Health's direct supervision. In 1996, the CNS, and the Regional Health Conferences (Conférences Régionales de Santé (CRS)) were created. The CNS is composed of representatives from health professions, administrative authorities, medical insurance and the CRS. The CRS are held in the 26 administrative regions in France and bring together representatives from health professions, administrative authorities, medical insurance and health care users. The CRS forum identifies public health priorities specific to regional health needs. CRS reports are passed on to the CNS office, where a synthesis of all CRS reports is supposed to be made.

In France, public health policy follows the priority setting process set by recent legislation. In this chapter, we try to identify the positive aspects and the difficulties encountered in applying the new paradigm to the French health care system.

Methodology

The process of setting public health priorities in France and their linkage to health care resources allocation is described based on the literature review, which included technical reports on the operations of national and regional health care systems.

The analysis of the priority setting process is based on interviews of physicians who participated in the CRS in Brittany (Pascal, 1998). The French process is also compared to experiences carried out in Anglo-Saxon countries, as described in the literature. The analysis focuses on the following: 1) the type of priorities set – explicit or implicit priorities, health needs based or health care needs based; 2) the link between the priority setting process and resources allocation; and 3) the process unfolding: technocratic or political, and the place of public debate in the process using a typology of public debates (Lascoumes, 1998).

The French Health Care System

Decision-making Levels and Structures

Reinforcing the health care system's regulation at the regional level is not new in France (Chaperon, 1993), but the process accelerated during the 1990s. It was felt that an alternative model to the centralised management of health care was needed and public authorities initiated a series of reforms:

- in 1991, the SROS was created and the second edition is now published. The development and implementation of the SROS is under the responsibility of the regional health and sanitation administrative authority: the Direction Régionale des Affaires Sanitaires et Sociales (DRASS);
- in 1993, regional associations of independent physicians, Union Régionale des Médecins Libéraux (URML), were formed to familiarise these practitioners with public health issues through studies, seminars and training sessions. At the national level, a convention was signed between the independent physicians' unions and medical insurance funds. The convention sets the annual target level of expenditures for outpatient care: the fees and prescriptions of general practitioners (GP) and specialists, which are financed through the French social security system. The target level of expenditures is implemented at the regional level, and repayments have to be made by the practitioners when spending exceeds the set target;
- in 1996, the regional level was further reinforced by the creation of regional structures and conferences: 1) the regional agencies for hospital regulation, Agence Régionale de l'Hospitalisation (ARH) (with ARH directors being appointed by the government); 2) the regional associations for medical insurance systems, Union Régionale des Caisses d'Assurance Maladie (URCAM); and 3) the CRS.

Setting Health Priorities in France

Since 1996, three authorities – the HCSP, the CNS and the CRS – have been the key to setting public health priorities.

In 1992, in the report *Stratégie pour une Politique de Santé*, the HCSP laid down the methodological basis for priority setting by proposing a set of objectives to achieve, and interventions to be carried out (Haut Comité de Santé Publique, 1993). Following this first report, the HCSP consulted several hundred public health professionals through a DELPHI survey (Demeulemeester and

Baubeau, 1996). These professionals were asked to identify major health problems and determinants and to specify the selection criteria they used for the identification process. Fourteen health priorities and four health determinants were identified on the basis of the survey results and national mortality data. Five criteria were most commonly reported by the professionals: severity (defined in terms of morbidity and mortality); frequency; socio-economical impact; feasibility (cost and acceptability of solutions); and social perception (perception of the importance of the problem). These results are compiled in the report *La Santé en France* (Haut Comité de Santé Publique, 1994).

The CRS has several purposes: 1) to assess population health needs and to examine regional medical and social data; 2) to identify regional public health priorities that can be addressed through regional programmes; and 3) to develop proposals for improving the health of the population while taking into account regional resources in health, sanitation and social domains.

The *Préfet* is the government representative in the region. The *Préfet* coordinates the development and the implementation of the regional health programmes. Each year, the *Préfet* initiates the one-day CRS and selects participants. The 200 to 300 CRS participants are divided into four colleges, with representatives from government services, health institutions, health professionals, and associations. The CRS panel is composed of two representatives from each of the four colleges and, if necessary, one or two public health professionals. The *Préfet* appoints the president of the panel. Conclusions and recommendations drawn at the CRS are compiled into the CRS report, which is passed on to the *Préfet*, the CNS office, the ARH, URCAM, and URML.

In Brittany, the first CRS was held *after* the CNS. The legislative requirements were thus not met due to time constraints and the delayed involvement of the DRASS in organising the CRS. Prior to holding the CRS, and following a Ministry of Health recommendation, the DRASS, carried out a survey of 160 public health professionals selected from Brittany's four administrative subdivisions (*Départements*). These professionals were provided with relevant documents including the HCSP's 1994 report, and epidemiological and demographic data issued by the regional health monitoring institute, Observatoire Régional de la Santé de Bretagne (ORSB). The professionals were requested to select health priorities in their *Département* by:

- selecting two health problems and one health determinant from the national

list of priorities, and justifying their choice;
- identifying one major health problem and one major health determinant, which were not included in the national list.

CRS members and panel were provided with the DRASS survey results, the HCSP report, and the ORSB data to identify priorities. A public debate was held during the CRS, but discussions were limited in time and the minutes of the meeting were not recorded. As a result, the CRS panel drew up its report based on a compilation of materials previously written: the HCSP's report, the ORSB data, and the DRASS survey results.

The CNS is composed of 72 members divided into three groups: 36 representatives of independent health professionals and public and private institutions; 26 CRS members (each region is represented); and 10 leading public health figures. The panel is composed of and elected by CNS members. Each CNS group elects its representatives at the panel: four representatives from health professionals and health institutions; three CRS members; and one leading public health figure.

CNS's conclusions and recommendations ought to be based on the HCSP's report and a synthesis of CRS reports. However, because of limited human and financial resources to closely examine the recommendations issued by the CRS in the regions where conferences could be held, CRS reports were seldom taken into account at the CNS. Again, debates were limited and only part of the information intended for participants was used, leaving aside many of the specific regional priorities. In the end, for lack of preparation time, the first CNS adopted the priorities set by the HCSP (Moatti, 1996).

Resources Allocation

Parliament has voted the ONDAM target amounts for the following year since 1996. In 1998, the ONDAM accounted approximately for 75 per cent of health care expenditures, the rest being financed by patients directly or through mutual or private health insurance. The ONDAM funds are divided up among five sectors and allocated by the Ministry of Health, sector by sector, to the regions (Haut Comité de Santé Publique, 1998). The five sectors are:

- the public hospital sector (which includes private non-profit hospitals);
- the private hospital sector;
- the medico-social sector;
- the general practitioners (GP) outpatient sector (GP's fees and prescriptions);

- the specialists outpatient sector (specialists' fees and prescriptions).
- Funds allocated to the public hospital sector are adjusted per region. Four criteria are used to set the regional allocation: the level of hospital expenditure per inhabitant (weighted for age), the mortality comparative index, hospital productivity, and patients' flow between regions.

  At the sub-regional level, funds are allocated to public hospitals according to their productivity, which is derived from hospitals' information system data. However, since 1998, when allocating resources to health institutions, the ARH must also take into account the public health policy objectives and government priorities. These priorities are included in the second edition of the SROS.
- Funds allocated to the private hospital sector are not adequately adjusted per region. Only 1 or 2 per cent of the total allocation is somewhat adjusted: small funds allocated for interventions aimed at improving the collaboration among institutions.
- Funds are allocated to the medico-social sector on a historical basis without adjustment per region. The amounts allocated are based on preceding years' allocations.
- The funds allocated to the two outpatients sectors (GP and specialists) are supposed to be based on the estimated use rate of practitioners' services by the regional population (weighted for age). However, no real adjustment per region is made for allocations made to these two sectors.

A Quality Fund (approximately FF500 million) was created in 1999 by the national medical insurance system for the two outpatients sectors. The fund is managed primarily at the regional level by the URCAM. The Quality Fund is intended to finance activities such as studies and training sessions aimed at improving professional practices and their evaluation, and improving the coordination among health care services.

Lastly, regional health programmes, Programmes Régionaux de Santé (PRS) – devised according to health priorities identified at the CRS – were developed and implemented in each region. The Ministry of Health is the major fund provider for these programmes. Other sources of funding are:

1) regional and sub-regional state services for health promotion;
2) the national fund for prevention, education and information in health, Fond National de Prévention, Education et Information pour la Santé (FNPEIS)

(managed by the national wage earners' health insurance, Caisse Nationale d'Assurance Maladie des Travailleurs Salariés (CNAMTS));
3) the ONDAM regional funds for the public hospital sector, managed by the ARH.

In some rare cases, PRS can be financed through agreements between the state and the region.

Discussion

Criteria for Priority Identification

In France, priorities are defined according to health problems or health determinants as opposed to medical fields or services. Priorities are defined based on available data (Haut Comité de Santé Publique, 1994). This process is founded on methods developed in Quebec for programming community health interventions (Ministère de la Santé et des Services Sociaux du Québec, 1998).

Government health priorities have evolved since 1996. Today, the HCSP's highest priority is the reduction of inequalities in health within regions and between regions.

In Scandinavian countries, New Zealand and Great Britain, priority setting takes into account the capacity for the population to benefit from a given health service. Accordingly, clinical guidelines, developed by health professionals, reinforce public authority's decision-making in allocating resources. The guidelines are considered the reference for decision-making on rationing (Feek, 1998). The public must have access to these guidelines and the process for developing guidelines must be open and explicit (Norheim, 1999). In New Zealand, a debate on criteria selection was held, but the debate focused on criteria used to identify priorities within medical fields. The criteria used to lay down the general orientations for priorities identification are not as clearly stated.

In Oregon State, in the United States of America, a range of precise and transparent criteria was initially developed. The list of priorities selected on the basis of these criteria turned out to be politically unacceptable; therefore, a second list was developed. The development of the second list still rested largely, but less absolutely, on explicit criteria.

In contrast, in France, criteria selection for priority setting was not transparent. At the national level priorities selection was founded on HCSP's preliminary work (Haut Comité de Santé Publique, 1993) using criteria explicitly defined during consultation with experts (Demeulemeester and Baubeau, 1996). Criteria selection in preparation for the Brittany CRS was far less explicit.

In both cases no open public debate was held to decide which type of criteria to use. But the ability to use explicit criteria seems primarily related to the political acceptability of heath care rationing. The way of experts' intervention is secondary.

The criteria taken into account by the French *HCSP* are primarily epidemiological, thus relating to the frequency and severity of health problems. In contrast, New Zealand emphasises the complementarity of epidemiological, economical and social criteria and focuses on effectiveness, social usefulness, equity and cost. The criteria are defined through experts surveys (DELPHI surveys) and public forums (Hadorn, 1997b). In Great Britain, health funds are allocated to medical fields by the district health authorities. Three criteria are used to integrate new services into the national health system: effectiveness, equity and patient choice. (Klein, 1998). In Norway, working groups were formed within each medical field to define the degree of severity of a pathology and to determine the social usefulness and cost effectiveness of the related case management (Haut Comité de Santé Publique, 1998b). The results are submitted to the government for its final selection of priorities.

Taking into Account Health Priorities while Allocating Resources

By changing paradigms the French government displays its will to expand its health policy beyond improving access to services and reducing health care expenditures. The goal of the new policy is to improve public health indicators in France. Unlike the previous curative model, the new approach aims at identifying health priorities and implementing rationally programmed interventions. To achieve this, the government has to reallocate some of the resources currently used to merely 'repair damages caused by diseases' (Setbon, 1993, p. 115). This objective seems ambitious when considering the power of curative medicine professionals in the French health care system. This calls into question what ought to be the relative importance of prioritisation in resources allocating. This issue was raised by the CNS president (Dupuis, 1999).

Under the new process, resources are allocated taking into account the health priorities identified by the three key authorities: the HCSP, the CNS and the CRS. However, the major benefit of the priority setting process for the community remains the involvement of members of parliament in thinking through health care policy and its financing. Politicians' involvement is a first step toward using public debate to determine how many resources should be allocated to the health sector.

Indeed, setting a national objective for public expenditure and basing it on health priorities is a radical change in France. At the time of writing, the implementation of the process in its totality is incomplete, though: in 1999 only a fraction of regional allocations was based on health priorities set by the CRS to finance regional health programmes.

In Oregon State, authorities have tried to take local health priorities into account while allocating resources. The priority setting process was entirely carried out at the state level, as opposed to the federal level. In 1987, the state administration sought to rank health problems and corresponding health interventions and to establish a threshold beyond which Medicaid would not cover patients' care (Coast et al., 1996). All medical fields were concerned with the ranking.

Rationing of health care resources and improving access to and quality of health care services are difficult objectives to combine. This problem is common to other fields in public policy (Weale, 1998). During the 1990s, French public authorities initiated reforms after finding significant disparities between regions in several health domains: mortality rates (Garros and Bouvier-Colle, 1990; Jougal et al., 1997); availability of health care services (Coca, 1995; Simon, 1996); and the level of health care expenditures (de Roquefeuil, 1996; Jourdain, 1991). However, these reforms tend to put emphasis on the control of expenditures and the link between public health policy and health care costs containment policy remained weak in France (Tonnelier and Lucas, 1998).

In its 1998 report, the HCSP discussed health resources allocation in relation to the reduction of inequalities in health (Haut Comité de Santé Publique, 1998). Even though reducing inequalities is publicly declared as a chief objective of the new reforms, the authors note that the new process has little impact on reducing inequalities in health care delivery and in resources allocation among regions. They also state that 'there is no direct association between increasing resources to an area disadvantaged as regards to health, and the subsequent improvement in the population's health' (ibid., p. 9), since health care accounts for only 10 to 20 per cent of all health determinants. The process should thus seek to reduce inequalities in resource allocation between areas with similar health care needs. Achieving this will be difficult with current resource allocation methods:

- health care consumption norms are calculated based on the effective recourse to health services instead of actual health care needs;
- health care consumption norms are defined for each sector and funds are not interchangeable between sectors. Taking into account the population needs and setting up priorities is difficult when resources allocation varies according to the type of health care provider;
- too many players are involved in establishing regional funds allocations (URCAM, ARH and health care providers), and, as seen above, regional adjustment methods vary from sector to sector.

Several scenarios are suggested in the HCSP report to improve the regional resources allocation. All aim at strengthening the link between the two processes: resources allocation and health priorities setting (Haut Comité de Santé Publique, 1998). In one scenario, the HCSP goes as far as considering special funds for interventions targeted at health priorities as defined by the CRS and the CNS.

The government's public display of well-defined priorities and their link to resources allocation has positive consequences, since it demonstrates its commitment to 'health', a widely valued field. Indeed, by defining health priorities and subsequently establishing rational public health policies the government is able to achieve two objectives: to show its will to regulate with rigorous methods a sector (health) which consumes an increasing amount of resources and to limit the power of the real decision-makers in health spending – the clinicians (Setbon, 1997).

According to Holm, no health priority setting process is ideal, but the process must include a public debate to ensure transparency and responsibility (Holm, 1998). It has been shown in other countries that patients and health professionals will understand and accept constrained resources allocation if they are grounded on explicit criteria and dialogue (Sabin, 1998).

The Unfolding of the Health Priority Setting Process

The French approach shows the government's commitment to take into account views from both the regional and the national levels. Thus one would expect that the two levels agree on a common definition of health priorities. In reality, regional priorities are merely seen as a complement to the national priorities.

Northern European countries such as Sweden and Norway, having a largely decentralised global political organisation, chose to decentralise the priority setting process (Haut Comité de Santé Publique, 1998b). In New Zealand a national consultative committee established a list of general orientations for health priorities while more specific priorities were defined at local levels such as medical services.

In most Anglo-Saxon countries, priority setting is a political process, not a technical one (Klein, 1998). Key actors such as clinicians and politicians must first adopt the process. Thus, this process is dependent on clinicians' support and strong political leadership. Clinicians' support is in turn dependent on their adherence to public health ethics. Unless the administration, politicians and health professionals agree on the priority setting process, the public will neither understand nor accept it (Sabin, 1998).

Priority setting experiences in New Zealand, Great Britain, the USA, Sweden or Norway are grounded in experts' recommendations and public opinion. The methods used for consulting with experts and the public, and the relative importance given to their respective opinions, vary from country to country. For example:

- in Oregon State, experts' recommendations were given greater importance than public preferences (Coast et al., 1996). No real consultation with the public was held. Public views were only used to build a matrix of preferences;
- in Great Britain, the debate on priority setting took place at the district level. Participants included outpatient and inpatient health care professionals, heads of health institutions, health administrative authorities and politicians. Politicians were intended to serve as advisors (Hope, 1998). The public was not represented.

In France, consulting with the public is carried out through conferences such as the CRS. When talking about the new methods for consulting with the public, the sociologist P. Lascoumes refers to a deliberative model for public action. This model was previously used in sectors other than health. Lascoumes emphasises the need to distinguish between debates used as 'communication tools' which are intended to legitimise decisions made, and debates intended to 'produce a decision' or to 'contribute to its development'. Lascoumes proposes four criteria to differentiate between these two extreme models of debate (Lascoumes, 1998). These are:

1) 'representation': the representatives are designated by the administration, or the representatives are selected according to specific criteria;

2) 'interaction': the information is simply presented or is 'worked on' to produce new data;
3) 'integration': a consensus is sought out at all costs, or each one's position is clarified and adjustments are proposed;
4) 'productivity': participating in the debate is the chief element, or participants can appropriate the tool and reformulate questions.

According to Lascoumes's criteria, the priority setting process delineated by the French Ministry of Health is closer to a 'communication tool intended to legitimise decisions', than a process 'producing a decision' or 'contributing to its development' (Lascoumes, 1998, p. 27). Indeed, in France, public opinion appears to be relatively unimportant and secondary to the views expressed by experts. The public representatives are designated by the government administration. Typically, experts and non-experts are grouped together in public debates with experts being the majority as conference members and in the panel. Participants do not work on the information that is available; a consensus is arrived at based on priorities definition without any possibility of adjustment. The Oregon experience also fits Lascoumes's 'communication' model since experts' views prevail over public preferences. In New Zealand the public was consulted on multiple occasions and on diverse subjects. Without specifications about the course of consultations with the public, though, it is difficult to discern the significance of the democratic debate and to what degree participants 'appropriated the tool' (Hadorn, 1997a, p. 134).

In France health conferences promoters seemed more concerned about the views of key actors in the health care system: clinicians and institutions having supervisory and management responsibilities. Public authorities did not seem to consider raising population awareness a priority, at least in this first phase of the process.

As reported by a HCSP member, however, defining the process remains largely unfinished (Sailly, 1999). Adjustments must be made to ensure adequate 'representation' at health conferences and to define the respective roles of the public, health professionals, and experts. The gap between the intentions displayed by the government to hold an open debate and the actual organisation of the health conferences is primarily due to the underestimation, from the part of public authorities, of the time and means required to hold such meetings. This reflects the structural weaknesses and the lack of public health expertise of the French Health Administration (Morelle, 1996).

The Ministry of Heath has since tried to increase the participation of the population in priorities setting debates. In 1999, the government held the Etats

Généaux de la Santé, a countrywide consultation with the public organised by government administrative services at the regional and subregional levels. A large population was mobilised through the media to discuss various health subjects such as cancer, pain-relieving care and ageing.

Conclusion

Health priority setting is carried out at a different pace in each country. In the USA, Oregon State chose to enforce the process by law. New Zealand raised awareness of local actors, a more lengthy process. In the European Union, public health priority setting processes are being initiated (Weil et al., 1999).

France seems to have adopted a softer approach to setting health priorities. The process initiated in 1996 with the creation of the CRS remains at an early stage of development: major orientations and strategic programming are being developed. The implementation of interventions is slow to start. Most regions experience difficulties in defining their operational objectives and implementing their regional programmes for lack of funding, since a small part of global health funds is allocated to regional specific priorities. Nevertheless, meetings regrouping the various actors and debates on defining priorities are perceived as a positive result in France. The question is, does raising awareness do enough to induce real changes in the system?

Adopting the 'public health process' is a quasi-cultural revolution for the actors involved in the French health system. For the reform to succeed, substantial structural and organisational changes will have to be made both in the health system and to the balance of power of key actors. These changes include the provision of strong incentives to encourage prescribers to participate actively in non-curative activities, amendments to physicians' fee-for-service payment system, decentralisation of the health system's regulation and allocation of significant budgetary margins to the regions.

Indeed, much remains to be done in France before the new paradigm is operational.

References

Chaperon, J. (1993), 'L'empire éclaté', *Revue des Affaires Sanitaires et Sociales*, 3, pp. 215–27.

Coast, J. et al. (1996), *Priority Setting : The health care debate*, John Wiley, Chichester.

Coca, E. (1995), *Les iInégalités entre Hôpitaux. Obstacles à l'efficacité et à l'équité de la maîtrise des dépenses hospitalières*, Berget-Levrault, Paris.
Demeulemeester, R. and Baubeau, D. (1996), *Les Priorités Nationales de Santé Publique – Étude Delphi : janvier – mai 1994*, Direction Générale de la Santé, February.
Dupuis, C. (1999), 'Les Nouvelles Ambitions de la Conférence Nationale de Santé', *Quotidien du Médecin*, 6592, 19 November, p. 3.
Feek, C.M. (1998), 'Experience with Rationing Health Care in New Zealand', *British Medical Journal*, 318, pp. 1346–8.
Garros, B. and Bouvier-Colle, M.H. (1990), 'Variations Géographiques de Mortalité', in M.H. Bouvier-Colle, J. Vallin and F. Hatton (eds), *Mortalité et Causes de Décès en France* Editions INSERM Doin, Paris.
Hadorn, D.C. and Holmes, A.C. (1997a), 'The New Zealand Priority Criteria Project: Part 1 – Overview', *British Medical Journal*, 314(11), pp. 131–4.
Hadorn, D.C. (1997b), 'The New Zealand Priority Criteria Project: Part 2 – Coronary Artery Bypass Graft Surgery', *British Medical Journal*, 314(11), pp. 135–8.
Haut Comité de Santé Publique (1993), *Stratégie pour une Politique de Santé*, La Documentation Française, Paris.
Haut Comité de la Santé Publique (1994), *La Santé en France en 1994*, La Documentation Française, Paris.
Haut Comité de la Santé Publique (1996), *La Santé en France en 1996*, La Documentation Française, Paris.
Haut Comité de Santé Publique (1998), *Allocation Régionale des Ressources et Réduction des Inégalités de Santé. Rapport à la Conférence de Santé*, La Documentation Française, Paris.
Holm, S. (1998), 'Goodbye to the Simple Solutions: The second phase of priority setting in health care', *British Medical Journal*, 317, pp. 1000–2.
Hope, T. (1998), 'Rationing and the Health Authority', *British Medical Journal*, 317, pp. 1067–9.
Jobert, B. (1981), *Le Social en Plan*, Editions Economie et Humanisme, Paris.
Jougla, E., Millereau, E. and Le Toullec, A. (1997). 'La Santé Observée: Un bilan contrasté', *Actualité et Dossier en Santé Publique*, 19, pp. ii–ix.
Jourdain, A. (1991), 'Peut-on Rawper les Inégalités de Santé en France?', *Cahiers de Sociologie et de Démographie Médicale*, 31, pp. 309–44.
Klein, R. (1998), 'Puzzling out Priorities', *British Medical Journal*, 317, pp. 959–60.
Lascoumes, P. (1998), 'L'information, Arcane Politique Paradoxale', in *L'information, Consultation, Expérimentation: Les activités et les formes d'organisation au sein des forums hybrides*, papers given at the seminar on collective risks and crisis situations at l'Ecole Nationale Supérieures des mines de Paris, pp. 15–34.
Ministère de la Santé et des Services Sociaux du Québec (1998), *Priorités Nationales de Santé Publique – 1997–2002*, Montréal, Editions Excell.
Moatti, J.P. (1996), 'Priorités de Santé Publique: Les dangers d'une dérive utilitariste', *Actualité et Dossier en Santé Publique*, 17, pp. 38–40.
Morelle, A. (1996), 'Les Faiblesses de l'Etat Sanitaire Français', *Esprit*, 1–2(218), pp. 6–27.
Norheim, O.F. (1999), 'Healthcare Rationing: Are additional criteria needed for assessing evidence based clinical practice guidelines ?', *British Medical Journal*, 319, pp. 1426–9.
Pascal, J. (1998), *Les Conférences Régionales de Santé: l'Appropriation de la démarche par des médecins bretons*, unpublished thesis, Université de Rennes.
de Roquefeuil, L. (1996), 'Les Disparités Géographiques des Dépenses de Santé: Deux modèles explicatifs pour le secteur libéral', *Solidarité Santé*, 4, pp. 57–73.

Sabin, J.E. (1998), 'Fairness as a Problem of Love and Heart: A clinician perspective on priority setting', *British Medical Journal*, 317, pp. 1003–6.
Sailly, J.C. (1999), 'Nécessité et Difficultés de la Détermination des Priorités en Matière de Santé Publique: l'Expérience française', *Journal d'Economie Médicale*, 17(6), pp. 405–21.
Setbon, M. (1993), 'Des Politiques de Santé à Leur Management: un sujet sans objet ou une nécessité sans capacités?', *Politiques et Management Public*, 11(1), pp. 111–27.
Setbon, M. (1997), 'Le Risque Comme Problème Politique', *Revue Française des Affaires Sociales*, 4–6(2), pp. 11–28.
Simon, M. (1996), 'L'Inégale Répartition Géographique des Professionnels de Santé', *Solidarité Santé*, 4, pp. 101–7.
Tonnelier, F. and Lucas, V. (1998), 'Health Care Reforms in France: Between centralism and local authorities', *CREDES*, 1152, pp. 1–19.
Weale, A. (1998), 'Rationing Health cCare', *British Medical Journal*, 316, p. 410.
Weil, O., McKee, M., Brodin, M. and Oberlé, D. (1999), 'A Framework for Identifying Public Health Priorities', *Priorities for Public Health Action in the European Union*, SFSP, Nancy, pp. 9–13.

Chapter Seventeen

Turkish Healthcare Reforms and Reasons for Failure

Mehtap Tatar and Gülsün Erigüç

Introduction

The Turkish health sector has been undergoing a radical reform process since the beginning of the 1990s. Although the expectations were initially high, developments since the publication of the *National Health Policy* (Ministry of Health, 1993) have not met the requirements of this reform process. The enthusiasm and allegiance attached to the reforms has left in its place disappointment and frustration. After 10 years of debates, revisions, consultations and discussions over the proposals, no substantial improvement has yet been achieved. Why did an initiative that started with widest support from related parties fail to achieve its objectives? How can the policy making and implementation gap be explained? What is the role of the policy making environment in this process? This chapter attempts to answer the above questions with special reference to the Turkish policy making environment. First of all, a brief overview of the Turkish health sector will be presented to make readers familiar with the system and its specific problems. Second, Turkish health policies and policy making environment will be analysed. The three critical phases of Turkish health policies will be explored in order to elucidate the policy making process at the macro level. Later, the reform proposals and progress since their introduction will be presented. Last, but by no means least, the future awaiting the Turkish health sector will be analysed.

Health Policy and Economics: Strategic Issues in Health Care Management, M. Tavakoli, H.T.O. Davies and M. Malek (eds), Ashgate Publishing Ltd, 2001.

An Overview of the Turkish Health Status and Health Sector

Health Status

Turkey, as a developing country, reflects the main characteristics of other countries in her development level. Diseases of underdevelopment and development prevail together, creating a formidable challenge to meet. Basic indicators such as infant mortality rate (42.7 in 1998), and child death rate (52.1 in 1998) are still very high in Turkey. Infectious diseases, mainly responsible for the high death toll among youngsters, are high priority areas. Diseases of underdevelopment, such as pneumonia, diarrhoea, measles, tuberculosis, malaria and polio need special consideration. The figures above are exacerbated when the regional inequalities are also taken into account (Table 17.1). It can safely be claimed that the current health care system, with its problems in terms of accessibility, availability, quality, finance and organisation perpetuate the existing problems in the health status of the population.

Table 17.1 Infant mortality rate and under-5 mortality rate by urban/rural residence and region (1998)

Residence	IMR	Under-5 mortality
Urban	35.2	42.4
Rural	55.0	68.0
Region		
West	32.8	38.3
South	22.7	43.0
Central	41.3	49.6
North	42.0	50.5
East	61.5	75.9
Total	42.7	52.1

Source: Hacettepe University Institute of Population Studies and Macro International Inc., 1999

Health Care System

The Turkish health care system is characterised by its fragmented structure both in terms of finance and provision. So far as the provision side is concerned, multiple providers, responsible for the health of certain sections of the population, provide health services with differing quality and accessibility.

The Ministry of Health (MoH) is the major provider of health services, both curative and preventive, and delivers its constitutional role of improving the health status of the population through a referral chain composed of health houses, health centres, and hospitals. The second organisation on the provision side is the Social Insurance Organisation (SIO). SIO, financed primarily by the premiums collected from the employers and employees, provides health services to the manual workers and their dependants through its dispensaries and hospitals. In 1998, 16 per cent of all hospital beds were owned by the SIO (Sağlık Bakanlığı, 1999).

In addition to the above-mentioned organisations, some other ministries such as the Ministries of Defence and Education, etc., some state economic enterprises and some municipalities also provide health services to different segments of the population. University hospitals, supposed to provide tertiary care, own 14 per cent of total hospital beds (Sağlık Bakanlığı, 1999). The private sector, especially in recent years, has expanded its role in the provision of health services. Although its share in terms of total hospital beds is low (8 per cent in 1998 [Sağlık Bakanlığı, 1999]), outpatient visits to private practitioners, working on a part-time basis (i.e. working both in the private and public sector) have an important share on the provision side. As stated elsewhere (Roemer, 1991), it is widely believed that over half of the time of Turkish doctors is devoted to private medical practice.

So far as the financing of the sector is concerned, the picture becomes more sophisticated. Turkey allocates 3.8 per cent of her GNP to the health sector of which 2.7 per cent comes from public and 1.1 per cent from private sources (Sağlık Bakanlığı, 1999). Insufficient resources allocated for health, coupled with the inefficient use of existing resources exacerbate the problems on the financing side.

The population can be divided into two main groups in terms of their financing status for health services. The first group without any coverage for health expenditures constitutes approximately the quarter of the population. The majority of this population comprises of the rural population and the urban poor. These people are issued with a Green Card, which is supposed to cover their expenses in public facilities, upon the proof that they are below a poverty line. However, this scheme has been fiercely criticised both for the issuing process and problems in utilisation. The health insurance scheme proposed by the reforms is for covering this uninsured segment of the population. It has been estimated that only 10 per cent of this population could not afford to pay premiums for the scheme (The World Bank, 1990). As will be discussed later, under the reformed health services the premiums of those unable to pay will be subsidised from the budgetary resources.

The second group, where the majority of the population falls, is divided into a further five groups according to the scheme by which they are covered. In the first group, there are civil servants and their dependants enjoying free health services from the MoH and university hospitals and facilities. Their expenses are met from the budgetary allowances for their department. The second group comprises of the SIO beneficiaries using their own facilities whose expenses are met by the premiums paid by their employers and themselves. In recent years, due to problems in meeting the demand and long waiting lists, particularly for coronary heart diseases and kidney failure, the Organisation has started to contract out these services to the private sector. In the third group, there are retired civil servants and their dependants covered by the Government Employees Retirement Fund (GERF). This organisation, financed by the contributions of active civil servants and the State, contracts out services to the MoH facilities, universities and private sector. The Social Insurance Agency of Merchants, Artisans and Self-Employed (Bağ-Kur) is the fourth funding scheme for the people who are not covered by the aforementioned schemes. As in GERF, the organisation contracts out its services to other organisations but there are serious problems both in terms of availability and accessibility. The last group comprises of a small group of people mainly working for banks and insurance companies and their expenditures are covered by private funds.

Problems of the Turkish Health Sector

In this section, the main problems that were also the driving force for health sector reforms will be addressed.

Multiple Providers and Financiers

As seen above, a variety of schemes and organisations provide and finance health services to different segments of the population. There is no standardisation among these organisations in terms of coverage, quality, accessibility and availability. The gap amongst the services could range from the best (for instance services of the military) to the worst (for instance services of the Bağ-Kur (Sağlık Bakanlığı, 1990; State Planning Organisation, 1990).

A Highly Centralised Health System

Turkey has a highly centralised public management structure. This is inevitably reflected in the health system as well. Strict bureaucratic rules and dependence on the centre for even minor decisions are the most frequently cited problems.

Lack of an Efficient, Functional Referral System

Although a referral system was established with the socialisation of health services in the 1960s, the failure of this system has led to inefficient use of scarce resources. As there is no motivation for patients to follow this route, and as there are not any bypass charges or penalties in the case of waiving the system, people prefer to use the outpatient departments of hospitals as their first level of care. The main reason for bypassing the referral system could be stated as the lower quality of services provided by these facilities. In particular, those in rural areas and small cities suffer from serious personnel and equipment shortages. In addition to this, there is a widely held public opinion that health services provided by big hospitals in cities are better than those in their counterparts in small and remote cities. As revealed by the utilisation survey, 57.6 per cent of users prefer hospitals as a first contact of care (Ministry of Health, 1995a). This inevitably leads to overcrowded hospital facilities and lower quality health services.

Problems in the Secondary and Tertiary Level of Care

There are severe problems in the services provided by hospitals. Neither the patients nor the providers are satisfied with the current situation. Occupation rate in hospitals is quite low (57.3 per cent in 1998) (Sağlık Bakanlığı, 1999), indicating inefficient use of resources. Accessibility problems, coupled with the problems in the quality of the services provided and managerial issues have urged the need for change (Roemer, 1991; State Planning Organisation, 1990; Tatar et al., 1998; The World Bank, 1986).

Problems in Equity

As stated above, there are enormous inequalities in terms of finance, provision, quality of health services and health status indicators. Existence of a variety of schemes covering certain segments of the population and a group of people without any coverage reflect a serious concern for inequity in the financing of health services. In addition to this, there are also inequalities within the schemes in provision of health services. For instance, civil servants, both active and retired, are the most favoured group when compared to others. However, members of Bağ-Kur for instance, have to pay for their health services upon utilisation, are reimbursed this money after a long period of time and the amount given does not usually cover the whole cost. As stated earlier in Table 14.1, urban/rural difference and differences among geographical regions in terms of health status indicators reveal that the discrepancies among different sections of the population need to be seriously considered.

The Turkish Health Policies and Policy Making Environment

Health Policies

Turkish health policies can be analysed in three different phases. The first phase between 1923–60 witnessed the introduction of new Acts aimed at shaping the health sector as a whole. The statist character of economic and social policies during the first decades of the Republic required an overwhelming state involvement in every sphere of life including the health sector. Building hospitals and vertical programmes for malaria and tuberculosis characterised health policies during this period.

In this phase, health in general did not occupy a high priority on governments' agenda. The main reason for this can be given as the heavy involvement in other sectors, especially economic sectors. Social sectors regarded as a 'bottomless pit' of those times did not generate much attention not only in Turkey but also in other countries as well (Gish, 1979).

The year 1960 epitomised the second phase with the introduction of Socialisation Act regarded as a watershed in the health sector. This Act was the product of the military rulers of the time. The Constitution of 1960, mainly aimed at establishing a liberal and democratic country, covered social sectors such as health for the first time. In the Constitution, the state was held responsible for the physical and psychological well being of the people and for the provision of medical care. This Constitutional article formed the basis of the Socialisation Act of 1961. The Act was born out of an ambition to create an egalitarian health system financed mainly out of general taxation with some user-charges. The proposed system would enable the entire population to benefit from health services along a hierarchical referral chain almost free of charge at the point of contact. The referral chain was supposed to start from the health houses and/or centres in rural areas to hospitals in urban areas. As a major health policy, socialisation has officially never been scrapped. However, even after four decades, neither the aims and principles nor the health care delivery system envisaged by the model have been achieved. One of the underlying reasons for this could be the special feature of the policy making environment that will be discussed below.

The late 1980s denote the third phase in Turkish health policy. During the 1980s, Turkey, as in other parts of the world, witnessed a move towards liberal policies and privatisation. After the 24 January 1980 (liberalisation decisions) Turkey embarked upon an attempt to stabilise her economy in close cooperation with international organisations such as the World Bank and International Monetary Fund. The World Bank's involvement in the Turkish health sector is crucial. This is because the range of health policies adopted after the 1990s were shaped by the conditions imposed on the Turkish government by the Bank. The Bank's involvement in the sector started in the mid-1985s after a visit to Turkey to report on the Turkish health sector. The report (World Bank, 1986) contained elements of a vision that the Bank envisaged for the country such as limiting the role of the state in preventive care and environmental issues and leaving the provision and finance of the sector mainly to the private sources. The World Bank's involvement in the Turkish health sector continued with another report in 1990 (The World Bank, 1990).

Health Policy Making Environment

Policy as a concept has attracted a wide range of attention and debates about its meaning, policy making and implementation still provoke the social scientists. However the scope of this chapter does not allow us to address these issues. Here, policy is defined as 'authoritative statements of intent, probably adopted by governments on behalf of the public, with the aim of altering for the better the health and welfare of the population' (Lee and Mills, 1982, p. 4). Within this context, the analysis of the health policy environment is restricted to 'high politics' issues defined as 'policies that are usually the domain of government, formulated by government and passed as law through the legislature' (Walt, 1994, p. 42).

The Turkish health policy making environment is not distinct from the health sector itself with its fragmented structure. The MoH listed the problems in policy development as follows:

- no long-term, consistent and stable health policies;

- involvement of a variety of institutions in health policy;
- no scientific support in the policy development process;
- lack of qualified personnel for policy development (Ministry of Health, 1995b).

The Ministry of Health, the State Planning Organisation, the Parliament, the State Insurance Organisation and professional organisations are the main actors in the Turkish health policy making arena. The MoH is the major authority to formulate health policies and monitor their implementation. However, because of the existence of other financier and provider organisations, with their own distinct status in terms of health policy making and implementation, the MoH has for a long time produced and implemented policies on an ad hoc basis (Ministry of Health, 1993; State Planning Organisation, 1990; Tatar and Tatar, 1997; The World Bank, 1986).

In the first phase of Turkish health policies discussed above, because of the distinctive characteristics of the time, health policies were formed just to meet the emerging needs of the population. Health did not have a high priority on the governments' agenda. This situation prevailed until the introduction of the Act of Socialisation.

The Socialisation Act was the outcome of the military coup of 1960 and the ministerial staff and bureaucrats did not play a significant role in its preparation process. The Act was a product of extraordinary conditions and was introduced very quickly without evaluating its feasibility in depth, with minimum participation of related parties and without considering the realities of the country. It was enacted without the approval of the Ministry of Finance connoting the disapproval of the Ministry. The main theme of this disapproval centred on the scepticism of the Ministry about meeting the financial burden of the Act. After taking the power from the military rulers the civil authority has never provided enough support during the implementation process. The health centres, backbones of the system, were deprived continuously of personnel, materials and equipment. The resources of the country were not sufficient enough to construct and maintain these facilities at the time when the system was introduced. In addition to this, the implementation of the system began in the most deprived areas of the country with an insufficient infrastructure. Unappealing conditions of these areas to professionals already scarce in the country plus lack of measures to motivate these people to work in these areas contributed to the deprivation of the system. Although at the beginning, there were incentives for doctors working in the socialised areas, these incentives were abolished after the continuous opposition of other professionals such as lawyers and soldiers already working compulsorily. Its other fundamental proposals, such as full-time working hours for physicians, were also scrapped over time leading to the inevitable failure of the system. One of the reasons for its failure can be stated as the association of the model with leftist parties providing strong support. However, since the beginning of the implementation process, generally rightist governments have been in office apart from a short-lived governance by the Republican Populist Party. The term socialisation was used synonymously with 'socialism', an unpalatable concept of those years in Turkey. These governments could not stand against socialisation directly because of the wide support from especially professional organisations and the military. That is why, instead of taking a clear stance and proposing their own policies they preferred to show their disapproval by depriving the model of financial and other resources.

In terms of countrywide health policy making, the MoH's existence was quite negligible until the 1990s, i.e. introduction of the reforms. The reform proposals, outlined in detail below, were the outcome of both international and national developments. In the international arena, liberalisation policies of Reagan and Thatcher, conditions of international organisations such as the World Bank and International Monetary Fund and trends in reforming the health sector in other countries have also influenced the Turkish health sector. As will be seen below, the similarities of the proposals with the proposals in the England's National Health Service and attempts to create an internal market reflect the influence of an international ideology. At the national level, the dissatisfaction with the current health care system, deteriorating health status indicators, inequalities among certain groups but most importantly the changing ideologies of the governments that took office after 1982 were the driving forces for proposals.

The second partner in health policy making environment is the State Planning Organisation (SPO). The Organisation, responsible for preparing five-year development plans and annual programmes was also the outcome of the 1960 military coup. Eight development plans have been produced thus far and after 40 years of existence, there is a fierce debate about the compatibility of development plans with an environment where liberal economic policies prevail. These plans, involving health along with other sectors were the main policy documents until the MoH's National Health Policy Document. The plans so far have attempted to shape the health sector but in line with the decreasing status of the SPO, they did not go beyond wishful statements.

So far as the health policy making environment is concerned, parliament stands as the ultimate authority where the policies formulated by the MoH,

SPO or other organisations are enacted. The Health Sector Sub-Commission, comprised of the members of parliament usually from medical background evaluates and discusses all legislative proposals. The influence of medical profession on health policies is quite strong and this, as stated elsewhere (Tatar, 1996; Tatar and Tatar, 1997), means equating health with medical care. The proposals are transferred to Parliament for ratification after their acceptance by this commission.

Other groups in the policy making environment are organisations such as the SIO or professional organisations such as the Turkish Medical Association. As stated earlier, the SIO has a distinct status with its own facilities and large group of dependants. The MoH's control over these institutions is almost nonexistent and their collaboration status is quite weak. The influence of the SIO has been crucial during the first stages of the preparation of the National Health Policy Document. The organisation is fiercely opposed to the proposal that recommended the unification of all programmes under one social security scheme. Their opposition was so strong and influential that the MoH had to change its original proposals and instead established a new scheme for the uninsured.

The Turkish Medical Association plays a formidable role in health policy making arena as a consequence of the strong domination of the medical profession. The Association has fiercely opposed the reform proposals on two grounds. First, they perceived the proposals as a major threat to the socialisation of health services to which they adhere persistently. The terminology used in the reforms, such as privatisation, autonomous status, liberalism etc. alarmed the Association with it's leftist stance. Secondly, with the influence of consultants the Association rejected the family practitioner scheme.

Reforming the Health Sector

As stated above, the reform process was the product of the liberal wave of the late 1980s. In 1990 the English firm Price Waterhouse was invited by the SPO to prepare a sectoral master plan. Taken from four options proposed by Price Waterhouse, the SPO opted out of the intermediate option based on the separation of provision and financing roles (State Planning Organisation, 1990).

The Master Plan Study coincided with the MoH's attempts to prepare a National Health Policy Paper (hereafter, the document). During the preparation of this document the Turkish health sector witnessed a participative, consensus building and enabling environment for the first time in the health policy making arena. In 1992, the First National Health Congress was assembled with representatives from all related sectors, institutions, universities, professional organisations and media. At the end of this exercise, the framework of the Turkish health sector reforms was determined and the first National Health Policy Document was prepared (Ministry of Health, 1993).

The aims of the reforms were declared as; equity, physical and financial accessibility, quality, efficiency and effectiveness of health services (Ministry of Health, 1993; Sağlık Bakanlığı, 1992 and 1997). The strategies to achieve these aims are listed below. However, as the proposals have not materialised since their introduction, virtually none of these strategies were implemented. Only some steps were taken to improve the managerial capacity of the system with very limited success and attempts have been made to establish an information system.

- More emphasis on health promotive and preventive activities, strengthening the primary level of care and allocating resources in accordance with this strategy.
- Purchaser–provider split in order to inject a competitive character into the system.
- Creating a competitive environment on the provision side based on the principles of internal market.
- Appropriate use of technology.
- Strengthening intersectoral action.
- Improving the managerial capacity of the system.
- Establishing an information system to provide timely and accurate information for effective decision-making.
- Supplying an appropriate number and mix of human resources of the right skill, at the right time and in the right place.
- Decentralisation of decision-making to the smallest service units.

On the provision and financing sides, major strategies were introduced in line with the developments in other countries that embarked on a similar reform process. Among these, reforms in Europe, in countries such as England, The Netherlands and reforms in the independent states of the former Soviet Union could be stated. The English NHS reforms were particularly important as the Turkish proposals were heavily inspired from the concepts of internal market, purchaser–provider split and self-governing trusts. The heavy involvement of British consultants during this process has also contributed to this inspiration. Two initiatives on the provision side constitute the backbone of reforms: a family practitioner scheme and self-governing hospitals. The family practitioner scheme is unequivocally the most important component of the proposals because of the strong emphasis made on strengthening the primary level of care. Initially, health houses and centres in rural areas will be retained as the first level of contact but their status and physical environment will be improved. Public Health Centres in each district will be established with the responsibilities of planning and coordinating health services in their catchment areas, providing public health services to the population and logistic support to health centres and family practitioners. Family practitioners will mainly serve urban populations under their list and have contracts with provincial health directors. These practitioners will be paid on a per capita basis and their rates will vary according to the geographical and socioeconomic status of the area and special needs of the people registered on their list. Health centres and houses in rural areas and family practitioners in urban areas will act as gatekeepers to the more complex secondary and tertiary care.

The second initiative on the provision side is concerned with transferring hospitals into a self-governing status, with the aim of improving efficiency, effectiveness and quality of their services. It has been stated that this status change is the first step on the road to privatisation of hospitals in the future (Sağlık Bakanlığı, 1992). The autonomous status or decentralisation of hospitals means that hospitals will be free to allocate their resources in relation to their needs and to select and recruit their personnel and determine their level of payment. Their main source of finance will be the revenues generated from the block contracts made with provincial health directors. Private, self-governed and state hospitals can negotiate with the provincial health directorate and the competition among these institutions is regarded as a prerequisite for efficient, effective and high quality health services. The service provision model is outlined in Figure 17.1.

So far as reforming the financial side is concerned, introduction of an insurance scheme for those who are not covered by any arrangement was the most important challenge. At the earlier stages of reforms, gathering all social security institutions mentioned earlier under a new framework and also extending their coverage to the uninsured were proposed but this was later abandoned (Sağlık Bakanlığı, 1990). Unification of all social security organisations under one umbrella is a long-standing dream of Turkish politics. However, this is easier said than done because of the strong opposition from existing organisations. This was clear in the health reforms as the SIO was

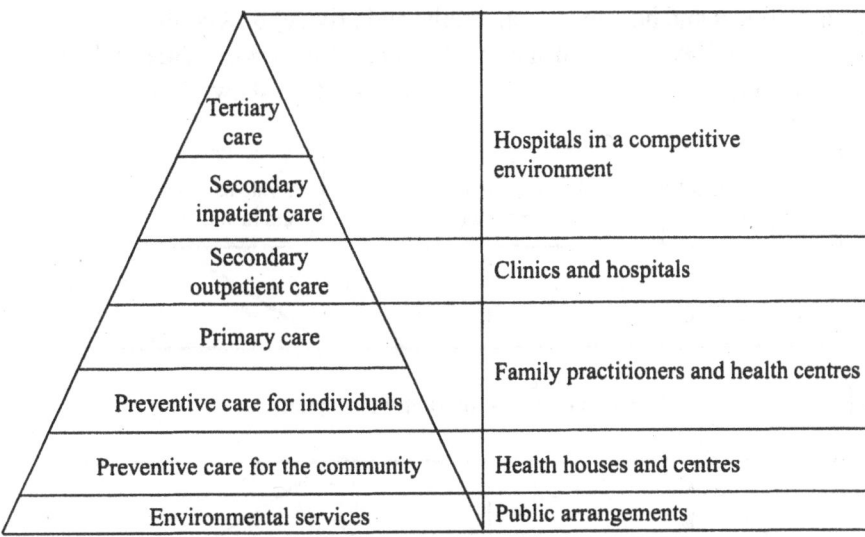

Figure 17.1 Healthcare reforms: provision model

Source: Sağlık Bakanlığı, 1992

fiercely opposed to merging with other schemes. The underlying reason for this opposition was the hesitance to share their facilities with others. They also argued that the quality of the services provided by these facilities (which is already under an acceptable level) would decline with this unification. This strong opposition resulted in abandoning the initial arrangements, leaving the existing schemes as they are, and establishing a brand new one for the uninsured. During the last decade, the changing governments have frequently altered this section of the proposals. The Health Financing Organisation proposed at the beginning was changed to a General Health Insurance Scheme first and then altered again to Personal Health Insurance. Today, there are initiatives to change its name yet again. The main reason for these alterations is completely political as these are generally minor and unnoticeable amendments. According to the proposals, registration to the scheme would be compulsory and with its introduction all the population will obtain health coverage. Premiums will be determined on an actuarial basis and for those who are under the poverty line, the state will subsidise either the full or changing proportions of the premiums.

The provincial health director will have a key role in the proposed system. The resources from the new insurance scheme and already existent ones will be transferred to these directorates. They will purchase services from the family practitioners and hospitals (both public and private) on a contractual basis. In this way, the main aim of the reforms i.e. purchaser–provider split will be achieved and an internal market will be created, as shown in Figure 17.2.

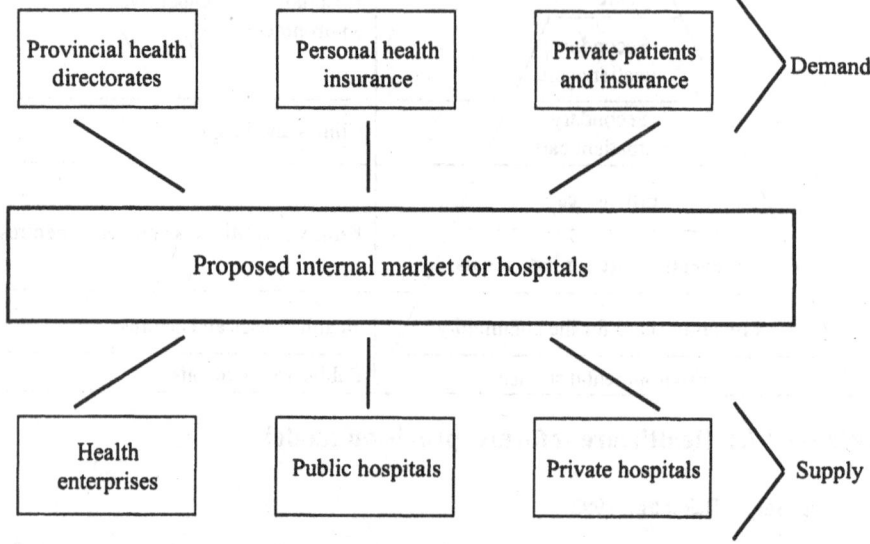

Figure 17.2 The Turkish internal market

The reforms in the provision and financing side inevitably require reforms in other areas such as management and organisation, human resources, information system and also legislation . New proposals in these areas, in accordance with the requirements of the system are also prepared.

The Future

The proposals outlined above have been debated, revised and altered several times since their formulation. Although countries that embarked on similar restructuring processes have already implemented them and started to evaluate their results, Turkey has not moved a step forward yet. The main reason for this, inter alia, could be found in the policy making environment.

As discussed above, major policy changes in the Turkish history generally occurred after military coups. The policies have changed or were easily introduced by the oppressive character of the time but problems have arisen after handing the power over to civil authorities. This case has been epitomised by the socialisation of health services.

Reforms, on the other hand, were the product of a civil administration with considerable support. However, a stable political environment is a prerequisite for introduction and implementation of such radical reforms. Unfortunately, Turkey, apart from short periods, has always suffered from a hostile political environment and stable, strong, determined governments have rarely taken the office in the last decades. Frequent changes in the government and weak hung parliaments mean terminating the developments so far and starting from scratch. With each changing minister, the majority of the bureaucrats and civil servants responsible for reforms also change, as do the ideas and framework. For instance in the last 10 years 12 ministers were assigned to the Ministry. The changing name of the health insurance scheme can be given as an example for this situation. As stated earlier, the name of the scheme has changed with each governmental move with a drive to identify the scheme with their political parties. Currently a three party coalition government is in office and has strong determination to change the economical outlook of the country. However, its stance in terms of the proposals is yet to be seen.

What is the future of reforms? The trends so far indicate that the chaotic picture presented above would prevail for the foreseeable future. Nonetheless, Turkey, as a country on the verge of entering the European Community, has to meet some predetermined criteria in all sectors including health. Increasing the quality of living standards of the Turkish people is among the prerequisites of this process. That is why these reforms, either after some alterations or as they stand would be implemented in the future. A radical change is inevitable but the timing of this change could not be foreseen now. A major drawback in the Turkish context is the indifference of social scientists to policy making and environment. It is to our belief that an in depth analysis of the policy making process would reveal the main reason for problems in policy making and implementation not only for health reforms but also for other changes within the system.

References

Gish, O. (1979), 'The Political Economy of Primary Care and "Health by the People": An historical explanation', *Social Science and Medicine*, 13C, pp. 203–11.
Lee, M. and Mills, A. (1982), *Policy-Making and Planning in the Health Sector*, Croom Helm, London.
Ministry of Health (1993), *National Health Policy*, Ministry of Health, Ankara.
Ministry of Health (1995a), *Health Services Utilisation Survey*, Ministry of Health, Ankara.

Ministry of Health (1995b), *Reforming the Health Care System in Turkey*, Ministry of Health, Ankara.
Roemer, M. (1991), *National Health Systems of the World. Volume 1*, Oxford University Press, Oxford.
Sağlık Bakanlığı (1990), *2000 Yılında Herkese Sağlık. Türk Milli Sağlık Politikası*, Sağlık Bakanlığı, Ankara.
Sağlık Bakanlığı (1992), *Türkiye Sağlık Reformu. Sağlıkta Mega Proje*, Sağlık Bakanlığı, Ankara.
Sağlık Bakanlığı (1997), *Hastane ve Sağlık İşletmeleri Temel Kanunu Tasarı Taslağı*, Sağlık Bakanlığı, Ankara.
Sağlık Bakanlığı (1999), *Yatakli Tedavi Kurumları İstatistik Yıllığı 1998*, Sağlık Bakanlığı, Ankara.
State Planning Organisation (1990), *Health Sector Master Plan Study*, State Planning Organisation, Ankara.
Tatar, M. (1996), 'Community Participation in Health Care: The Turkish case', *Social Science and Medicine*, 42(11), pp. 1493–500.
Tatar, M. and Tatar, F. (1997), 'Primary Health Care in Turkey: A passing fashion?', *Health Policy and Planning*, 12(3), pp. 224–33.
Tatar, F. et al. (1998), 'Turkish Hospital Management at a Crossroads : Prospects for the year 2000', *The Journal of Health Administration Education*, 16(3), pp. 283–96.
Walt, G. (1994), *Health Policy*, Zed Books, London.
The World Bank (1986), *Turkey. Health Sector Review*, The World Bank, Washington.
The World Bank (1990), *Issues and Options in Health Financing in Turkey*, The World Bank, Washington.

List of Contributors

Massimo Arcà	Agency for Public Health, Lazio, Italy
Giovanni Baglio	Agency for Public Health, Lazio, Italy
Lee Berney	LSE Health, London School of Economics and Political Science
Astrid Brousselle	Groupe de Recherche Interdisciplinaire en Santé (GRIS), University of Montreal
Allan Bruce	Lecturer in Public Administration, Glasgow Caledonian University
Laura Cacciani	Agency for Public Health, Lazio, Italy
Giulia Cesaroni	Agency for Public Health, Lazio, Italy
François Champagne	Groupe de Recherche Interdisciplinaire en Santé (GRIS), University of Montreal
Jacques Chaperon	Public health physician, PROTIMES, University of Rennes
Damien Contandriopoulos	University of Montreal
Bruce Crawford	MAPI Values, Boston
Marina Davoli	Agency for Public Health, Lazio, Italy
Diane Dawson	Senior Research Fellow, Centre for Health Economics, University of York

---

Health Policy and Economics: Strategic Issues in Health Care Management, M. Tavakoli, H.T.O. Davies and M. Malek (eds), Ashgate Publishing Ltd, 2001.

Jean-Louis Denis	Professor, Health Administration and GRIS Associate, University of Montreal
Marsha A. Dowell	Associate Professor and Associate Dean, University of Alabama in Huntsville, College of Nursing
Matthew Dowell	Metrocall, Alexandria, Virginia
Richard Elliott	Professor of Marketing and Consumer Research in the School of Business and Economics, University of Exeter
Gülsün Erigüç	Assistant Professor, Hacettepe University School of Health Administration, Turkey
Christopher Evans	MAPI Values, Boston
Mark Exworthy	LSE Health, London School of Economics and Political Science
Marc-André Fournier	Groupe de Recherche Interdisciplinaire en Santé (GRIS), University of Montreal
Maria Goddard	Assistant Director, Centre for Health Economics, University of York
Miriam Greenstein	Health Policy Research Unit, JDC–Brookdale Institute of Gerontology
Pascal Jarno	Public health physician, PROTIMES, University of Rennes
Lisa Kennedy	Planet Medica, London
Ann Langley	Professor, Management School, University of Quebec in Montreal

List of Contributors

Pierre Le Beux	Public health physician, PROTIMES, University of Rennes
Christophe Lerat	Sociologist, National School of Public Health, University of Rennes
Anne Ludbrook	Health Economics Research Unit, University of Aberdeen
Mo Malek	Department of Management, University of St Andrews
Annabelle Mark	Reader in Organisational Behaviour and Health Management, Middlesex University Business School and Research Associate of Templeton College Oxford
Enrico Materia	Agency for Public Health, Lazio, Italy
Nurit Nirel	Health Policy Research Unit, JDC–Brookdale Institute of Gerontology
Jean Pascal	Public health physician, PROTIMES, University of Rennes
David Pencheon	Consultant in Public Health Medicine Institute of Public Health Cambridge, and Regional Training Co-ordinator for the Postgraduate Programme in Public Health
Carlo A. Perucci	Agency for Public Health, Lazio, Italy
Dina Pilpel	Faculty of Health Sciences, Ben-Gurion University of the Negev
Martin Powell	Department of Social and Policy Sciences, University of Bath

Christine Quelier	Sociologist, National School of Public Health, University of Rennes
Françoise Riou	Public health physician, PROTIMES, University of Rennes
Bruce Rosen	Health Policy Research Unit, JDC–Brookdale Institute of Gerontology
Billie R. Rozell	Associate Professor (Emeritus), University of Alabama in Huntsville, College of Nursing
Brian Salter	Professor of Health Services Research, School of Nursing and Midwifery, University of East Anglia
Richard D. Smith	Senior Lecturer in Health Economics, School of Health Policy and Practice, University of East Anglia
Andrew Street	Medical Research Council Fellow, Centre for Health Economics, University of York
Mehtap Tatar	School of Health Administration, Hacettepe University, Turkey
Manouche Tavakoli	Department of Management, University of St Andrews
Luke Vale	Health Economics Research Unit, University of Aberdeen
John O.S. Wilson	Department of Management, University of St Andrews
Yavuz Yıldırım	Gata Yayın Kurulu Bakanlığı
Sima Zalcberg	Health Policy Research Unit, JDC–Brookdale Institute of Gerontology

Irit Zmora   Faculty of Health Sciences, Ben-Gurion
                    University of the Negev